BORDER POLITICS

Border Politics

Social Movements, Collective Identities, and Globalization

Edited by Nancy A. Naples and Jennifer Bickham Mendez

NEW YORK UNIVERSITY PRESS

New York and London

NEW YORK UNIVERSITY PRESS
New York and London
www.nyupress.org

© 2015 by New York University
All rights reserved

References to Internet websites (URLs) were accurate at the time of writing.
Neither the author nor New York University Press is responsible for URLs that
may have expired or changed since the manuscript was prepared.

ISBN: 978-1-4798-9899-2 (hardback)
ISBN: 978-1-4798-4776-1 (paperback)

For Library of Congress Cataloging-in-Publicaton data, please
contact the Library of Congress.

New York University Press books are printed on acid-free paper,
and their binding materials are chosen for strength and durability.
We strive to use environmentally responsible suppliers and materials
to the greatest extent possible in publishing our books.

Manufactured in the United States of America
10 9 8 7 6 5 4 3 2 1
Also available as an ebook

To our children,

William and Sofia Mendez Bickham

and

Alexandra and Samantha Bernstein-Naples

May they be inspired to make a better world possible.

CONTENTS

ACKNOWLEDGMENTS

This book project took flight at a session organized by Jennifer for the session on "Cross-Border Organizing and Transnational Activism" held during the Political Economy of the World System's (PEWS) Mini-Conference in San Francisco in 2009. Jennifer invited Nancy to be the discussant on this panel. We have been in dialogue since that time, thinking through the significance of linking the insights from border studies and social movements scholarship to generate an intersectional approach to what we came to call border politics. Our thanks to the presenters and participants in this session and to the organizers of the PEWS miniconference, "The Social and Natural Limits of Globalization and the Current Conjuncture," for facilitating our collaboration.

The College of William & Mary provided generous funding and support for the completion of this book. Jennifer also acknowledges the Virginia Foundation for the Humanities for offering a supportive and stimulating intellectual environment during her residency there, which helped enormously in moving this project through its final stages. Special thanks go out to Mary Bernstein and Amy Quark for their close reading and inspired comments on earlier versions of our introductory chapter. Nancy is especially grateful for Mary's ongoing support and lively conversations that continue to inspire in countless ways.

Our appreciation to the anonymous reviewers for their deep engagement with the vision for the book and their extremely valuable suggestions that helped us better achieve our goals.

We are also grateful to Rebecca Nelson Jacobs, Malaena Jo Taylor, and Becca Gallahue for their research and editorial assistance. Assistant editor Caelyn Cobb has also provided invaluable editorial assistance. Our editor, Ilene Kalish, has been steadfast in her enthusiasm for this project, and we are extremely grateful to her support.

Finally, we thank all the authors for their willingness to contribute their chapters to the book and grateful for their patience throughout the long process of putting this volume together.

Introduction

1

Border Politics

Contests over Territory, Nation, Identity, and Belonging

JENNIFER BICKHAM MENDEZ AND NANCY A. NAPLES

In 2007 a group of protesters gathered outside the Office of the High Representative of the European Union in Sarajevo, Bosnia. Ethnic Bosnian "erased" workers whose citizenship had been revoked following Slovenia's independence were joined by their allies from the newly formed country—the Invisible Workers of the World—to protest the unjust enforcement of EU borders, which had rendered these workers illegal immigrants in their own homeland. That same year, activists from across Europe and beyond camped on the border between the Ukraine and neighboring new Eastern European member states of the EU to protest the increased militarization of the border and an unjust visa regime. Across the Atlantic at another border, grandmothers dressed in pink camouflage T-shirts posed for a picture as part of a publicity stunt to recruit for the Minutemen, a self-proclaimed civil defense corps of mostly white men who undertake patrols and surveillance operations along the US-Mexican border to prevent migrants from Mexico from reaching the United States. Half way around the world in Pakistan, veiled Muslim women mobilized in armed defense of the Lal Masjid (Red Mosque), proclaiming their willingness to give their lives to protect the border between what they saw as foreign immorality and religious purity.

Despite the contrasting motivations and political orientations that underlie mobilizations such as these, they share important characteristics. They emerged in a historical moment characterized by global political, economic, and cultural interconnections, and they have developed in contexts of struggle marked by the effects of reinforced borders that delineate systems of difference and belonging. Finally, intersecting dynamics of race, ethnicity, gender, sexuality, class, and other vectors of power and privilege are woven through such border politics at local, national, and transnational scales of action.

The central aim of this volume is to further understandings of the contestations that erupt in today's globally interconnected world by exploring the implications of borders—defined broadly to include territorial dividing lines as well as sociocultural boundaries—for the politics, identities, and meaning-making of contemporary social movements. As illustrated in the cases presented here, social movements may "target the state, other institutions, or cultural meanings" (Armstrong and Bernstein 2008, 84).[1] Struggles around literal and figurative borders of inclusion and exclusion—what we call *border politics*—coalesce around diverse goals and political orientations. As such they may challenge, reconfigure, or exacerbate preexisting structures of inequality. An intersectional approach to border politics focuses attention on how social movements inevitably draw upon as well as reshape cultural meanings and collective identities through these contestations.

The case studies in *Border Politics: Social Movements, Collective Identities, and Globalization* capture the complex ways in which geographic, cultural, and symbolic dividing lines are blurred and transcended, but also fortified and redrawn. Critical analysis of border politics attends to the ways in which contestations over identity and social belonging that contour sites of struggle are shaped by globalization's twin processes of "deterritorialization" and "reterritorialization" (Deleuze and Guattari 1972).[2] By analyzing these struggles over social inclusion and exclusion both within and across national boundaries, we are also able to see how border politics destabilize constructions of agency and belonging as linked to formal legal categories of political membership.

Border Studies and Border Politics

Our approach to border politics is informed by the insights from the interdisciplinary field of border studies, especially the work of Chicana feminists. An early, influential stream of border studies developed in the 1970s when scholars hailing from diverse conceptual, methodological, and disciplinary backgrounds focused their attention on the complex political, economic, and cultural processes at play in the borderlands between the United States and Mexico (see Alvarez 1995). Researchers working on immigration, state politics, labor practices, and cultural tensions along this iconic border shared a commitment to empirical investigations and addressing the challenging social problems on the border (Vila 2003).

After some abeyance during the years of the Cold War, the study of borders underwent a renaissance, as scholarly attention was captured by the multiplication and redrawing of borders in Europe, the Palestinian and Israeli conflict, and the creation of new nation-states, like Eritrea and Namibia (see Newman 2011).[3] Border studies scholars in a variety of fields have advanced the analytical construct of the border, extending its meaning beyond literal and territorial definitions, and in so doing they have begun to theorize the close ties between the physical borders of nation-states and the social and cultural boundaries of membership and identity (Aleinikoff 2001; Anderson 1996).

Foundational to border studies has been scholarship in Chicano/ Latino studies, cultural anthropology, and cultural studies, which has interrogated the ways in which national, racial-ethnic, gender, and other identities intersect and are organized and reorganized in the social and cultural space of "borderlands" (Gómez-Peña 1996; Behar 1993; Rosaldo 1989; Anzaldúa 1987). In her highly influential work, Chicana feminist Gloria Anzaldúa's conceptualizes borderlands as paradoxical, contested spaces of everyday life characterized by in-betweenness and instability where "the lifeblood of two worlds" merge "to form a third—a border culture" (1987, 3). Her analysis of *nepantla* (the in-between space) brings together the experiences of the physical space of borderlands with emerging political consciousness and multiple, intersecting identities that straddle sociocultural boundaries (Naples 2009b). Those who find their home in such spaces negotiate and inhabit multiple contradictions and forms of difference (Anzaldúa 1987). Her conceptualization of borderlands thereby offers a critical approach to the categories that define us, calling attention to how they exclude (see Alvarez 1995, 451). Borderlands are sites of boundary-making, conflict, and fragmentation, but also of resistance and continual reconstruction where new identities are formed and "radical political subjectivities" are forged (Nayak and Suchland 2006, 480; see also Lugo 1997). Feminist scholars have expanded on this work to use "the border" as a theoretical device to interrogate how multiple systems of exploitation and oppression intersect and also are resisted, and this body of work informs our approach to border politics (Segura and Zavella 2008; Alarcón et al., 1999).

Building on these theoretical insights, we conceptualize border politics as struggles that challenge, transcend, or reinforce territorial borders and their effects, or that contest borders *within* nationally defined territories, including social and symbolic boundaries of inclusion and exclusion. In *Border Politics* we also unsettle a binary of right-wing versus left-wing movements. As a mutually exclusive categorization of progressive and conservative mobilizations, the binary is far too limited to capture the complexities at play in the cases of border politics presented here. Placing right-wing and social justice initiatives in the same analytical frame allows for the identification of patterns in the activities and meaning-making of struggles that span the political spectrum. Our intent is not to develop a typology of social movements. Rather, we forward border politics as a conceptual lens through which to understand the connections between geopolitical borders and other kinds of social and symbolic boundaries as they become both objects and sites of struggle (Newman 2011, 56; Lamont and Molnár 2002, 168). The analyses of border politics presented in this collection clearly break from traditional approaches that locate movements within "container" nation-states.

As the meeting place between state and people, geopolitical borders symbolize and structure the security and sovereignty of the nation-state. Since borders function to draw the distinction between citizen and alien (Donnan and Wilson 1999, 13; see also Bosniak 2006), border politics include struggles over the processes of economic and political integration (for example, in the formation of the EU) that contour shifts in constructions and practices of citizenship (see, for example, Leontidou et al. 2005; Momen 2005). The authors in *Border Politics* chronicle efforts to carve out and define (as well as challenge) the parameters of social membership in nations, racial-ethnic groups, and communities. In this manner, border politics brings together both the external and internal dimensions of borders—social processes that occur between divided groups, social categories, and nation-states as well as those that play out within borders and boundaries.

By highlighting the contradictory spaces in which social formations, identities, and resistance strategies are constituted and reimagined, the cases in this collection call into question a dichotomous construction of local and global, and the spatial hierarchy implicit within this binary (Gupta 1998, 24; Naples 2009a). Brought into sharp relief are the "global assemblages" (Ong and Collier 2005) through which many contemporary social movements are constituted and which shape the terrain of struggle. We borrow this concept from Steven Collier and Aihwa Ong to capture the way in which decontextualized global phenomena "land" in particular territorialized contexts or assemblages to produce social domains of interaction that "define new material, collective and discursive relationships" (Ong and Collier 2005, 4). The relevance of global assemblages for the study of border politics reveals the need for analyses at various scales—geopolitical, national, regional, and local.

We argue that a conceptualization of power as multisited, context-specific, and intersectional is essential for fully recognizing the complexities of struggles around borders and boundaries as they take shape within and across complex social and political terrains.[4] Such a view enables us to see power not only as external to movements, but imbricated within the internal dynamics of these struggles. In line with feminist conceptualizations, we argue for a critical and intersectional approach toward territorial and social boundaries (Eschle 2001). Thus, we seek to dissect and analyze the politics surrounding these divisions without reifying borders and their attendant social dynamics.

Globalization, Border Struggles, and Social Protest

Tensions associated with global political, economic, and cultural integration have galvanized border struggles. In the 1990s scholars, activists, policymakers, and analysts heralded worldwide cultural, political, and economic interconnections as "globalization," truly the buzzword of the times. The revolutionary transformation of information and communication technologies as well as substantial changes in transportation increasingly fueled global interconnectivities and heightened the permeability of physical and political boundaries (Harvey 1990). With accelerated transnational flows of capital, people, and information, the world was said to be getting smaller.

The idea of globalization conjures up an image of socioeconomic, cultural, and political processes that occur without reference to place or territorial boundaries. However, far from giving rise to a borderless world, the promotion of the free flow of capital across national borders that is so central to neoliberal globalization has been accompanied by the systematic and oppressive social control of populations through the militarization of national, territorial borders and increasingly restrictive migration regimes. Thus, while globalization's open markets facilitate the exchange of goods and information and stimulate the movement of people to new places, its closed borders restrict human mobility through intensified policing of reinforced geopolitical boundaries. Meanwhile, contemporary societies increasingly seem to resemble bastions with borders and controls (Walters 2006) and erected walls and gates (Low 2003; Nevins 2002; see also Blumberg and Rechitsky, chapter 11 in this volume).

Another defining element of the era of globalization is the heightened mobility of increasing numbers of populations. International migration flows increased dramatically in the last half of the twentieth century and into the twenty-first. In 1965, the number of international migrants was estimated at 75 million people, increasing to 120 million by 1990 and 160 million in 2000. By 2010 the United Nations (2011) reported that approximately 214 million people resided outside their country of birth. Global migration patterns have changed to incorporate new nation-states, cities, and localities as sites of immigrant origin and destination, generating new points of social and political tension. In an increasingly globalized labor market some developing countries, like the Philippines, have taken advantage of colonial ties to wealthier nations, becoming brokers of labor as a principal export (Rodríguez 2010). Countries that receive immigrants contend with a set of irreconcilable issues stemming from the growing demand for inexpensive labor combined with the perceived threat that new immigrants pose to the social and cultural cohesion of nations, fueling contests over political identities and social membership (Lewis and Neal 2005; see also Johnson, chapter 2 in this volume).

Migrants' border crossings take them from one economic, social, and political space to another, implicating "twin narratives of inclusion and incorporation on one hand and exclusion and dispossession on the other" (Donnan and Wilson 1999, 107). The border becomes a material and symbolic site, signifying daily realities shaped by economic and political inequalities and marginalization. The in-between spaces of the borderlands produce ambiguous identities among undocumented, migrant populations who defy the state's power to control their mobility and also their identities as criminal "others" (Kearney 1991). Social protest by undocumented workers and those displaced by economic hardship and political conflict challenge liberal constructions of politics that privilege citizenship as a basis for political agency (Zimmerman 2011; see also Blumberg and Rechitsky, chapter 11, and Téllez and Sanidad, chapter 12, in this volume).

Such conflicts have arisen in a context of the many contradictions of social life in the borderlands. They foreground the heightened material and symbolic significance of borders in defining who we are, contouring our sense of the world, and shaping the social and political landscape. By dividing those who belong from those who do not, borders demarcate and define "us" and "them," deepening structures of exclusion that fracture local communities. Thus, borders and the symbolism that surrounds them are highly implicated in the intense struggles over national boundaries, social identities, and belonging that shape how people view each other as members of diverse communities (DeChaine 2012; see also Maddison, chapter 6, and Rohlinger et al., chapter 7, this volume). Given the gendered and sexualized constructions of nation, images of womanhood and motherhood as well as women's bodies are mobilized in border struggles and intersected with constructions of sexuality, race, ethnicity, and class in ways that both reinforce and challenge gendered expectations (see McDuie-Ra, chapter 4, and Charania, chapter 5, in this volume).

Globalization has involved integration and interconnection, but also fragmentation and particularization, evidenced in the coalescing of struggles around subnational, ethnic identities. Along with ethnic conflict, the current era has witnessed heightened activities on the part of conservative, extreme nationalists and religious fundamentalist groups (Wimmer 2002, 20013). Islamic fundamentalism in the Middle East, as well as the US Christian conservative Right, perhaps represent the epitome of this phenomenon, but numerous other examples abound (see, for example, Blee 2008; Payne 2000; Sarkar and Butalia 1996). In the United States, Australia, and Europe a backlash against multiculturalism and the perceived cultural, economic, and social threat posed by international migration has been fueled by nativist and antiterrorist discourses promulgated by the conservative media (Perea 1996). In Western Europe the far Right has witnessed a resurgence in opposition to an integrated Europe, and right-wing, nationalist parties have put forward anti-Islam and closed-border platforms, as they seek to harness the discontent brought on by soaring unemployment rates (*Washington Post* 2012).

The events of 9/11 and other terrorist attacks in different parts of the world ushered in the US-sponsored War on Terror, elevating the urgency with which nation-states police citizenries, displaced populations, and border zones, as safety and security became increasingly conceived as tenuous. Thus, the "debordering" of economies coexists with "rebordering" in the form of the reenforcement of racial-ethnic boundaries and the reterritorialization of nation-states through newly configured forms of governmentality, national security initiatives, and intensified surveillance of populations (Gusterson and Besteman 2009; Spener and Staudt 1998).

In the United States and other immigrant-receiving countries the War on Terror conflated national security with the control of borders, in many cases galvanizing a moral panic around immigration. In this context anti-immigrant sentiments have resonated globally (Kretsedemas and Brotherton 2008; Fassin 2011), reinforcing boundaries between "legitimate" members of societies and "others," to produce climates of fear and insecurity among immigrant communities. Such hostile climates provide a backdrop for the deportability that accompanies unauthorized immigration status and which compounds the marginalization of immigrant groups, reinforcing their vulnerabilities in the workplace and their exclusion from various spheres of social participation (De Genova and Peutz 2010).

As cultures of securitization and a politics of fear have come to permeate daily life even far beyond border regions, the effects of economic restructuring and neoliberal policies have given rise to economic insecurities confronted by increasing numbers of groups and communities (Gambetti and Godoy-Anativia 2013). Such insecurities, as well as changing demographics and increased cultural interchange associated with globalization, have thrown into question the dominance of previously privileged groups, undermining their ability "to maintain . . . advantages within established institutions" (McVeigh 2009, 43). These conditions have produced new incentives for right-wing mobilizations, as localized efforts to stem the tide of change often turn anger and frustration into violence against those deemed as responsible for the lost advantage (see, for example, Rydgren 2006; Wodak, KhosraviNik, and Mral 2012).

Despite these tensions, such experiences have also engendered new collective identities that form the basis for challenging these same systems of subjugation, as evidenced by the "dreamers" in the United States who, as undocumented youth, are challenging the limits of US citizenship as well as by the erased workers of Slovenia (Razsa and Kurnik, chapter 8 in this volume). A range of other social justice movements, including the Occupy movement, have also mobilized in response to these same conditions, focusing opposition on neoliberal globalization and blaming deepening inequalities and increased insecurities for the majority of the world's people on corporate greed.[5]

Border Struggles and Global Assemblages

Borders and associated social divisions with their attendant power dynamics crosscut the struggles presented here. Some movements have "gone transnational," transcending physical and geographic borders through the establishment of cross-border alliances and networks (Keck and Sikkink 1998; also see Paternotte and Ayoub, chapter 9 in this volume). Transnational linkages such as those cultivated between Mexican women's labor organizers in the export-oriented assembly factories along the US-Mexican border and their allies in the North (Téllez and Sanidad, chapter 12) and those between antimega-dam activists in Lesotho and international environmental organizations provide opportunities (Braun and Dreiling, chapter 10) to increase political resources and influence global political change. In this way they strengthen the global public sphere by mobilizing [a] disenfranchised public into discussions of global issues" (Smith 1998, 102; see also McAdam et al. 1996; Smith et al. 1997).

Global assemblages make possible the transnational diffusion of ideas and information, which facilitates the sharing of discursive strategies, ideologies, and social movement tactics (Smith and Johnston 2002; see also Braun and Dreiling, chapter 10), creating new possibilities for transnational cooperation and cross-border coalitions (Bandy and Smith 2005; Keck and Sikkink 1998). The development of new technologies has also hastened global interconnections in the form of increased cultural interchange and expanding communication networks that have brought about some new and exciting possibilities for activism aimed at unsettling systems of domination, including "cross-race and cross-national projects, feminist movements, anticolonial struggles and politicized cultural practices" (Lowe and Lloyd 1997, 25).

Social media and digital technologies have become new tools for mass mobilization. In the late 1990s and early 2000s, popular mobilizations like the Zapatistas of Chiapas Mexico (Khasnabish 2010; Olesen 2005), the Global Justice Movement (also known as the alter-Globalization Movement), and the World Social Forums challenged the notion that neoliberal policies would raise all boats, and global communications allowed them to spread a counterhegemonic message (Evans 2000). Likewise, new media and Internet technologies facilitated women's mobilization (sometimes as feminists) nationally and transnationally to address the gendered effects of globalization as they unfold in disparate locations around the world (Naples and Desai 2002; Hewitt and Karides 2011; Thayer 2010).

During the Arab Spring of 2011, activists harnessed Facebook and Twitter to organize massive mobilizations that resulted in the toppling of military dictatorships in Tunisia and Egypt. Months later the Occupy movement put to use viral flows of images and information made possible by social and mass media to spark local movements around the globe (Juris and Razsa 2012; see also Razsa and Kurnik, chapter 8 this volume). The No Border Network, described by Renata Blumberg and Raphi Rechitsky in chapter 11, utilized digital media and communications to convene activists from across Europe and beyond to protest and raise awareness about injustices associated with a visa regime that controls and polices migration into what activists term "Fortress Europe."

Rebordering processes crystallize in regions where military techniques and detection strategies, and technologies of surveillance engineered for war have been put to the service of border enforcement. In this context military logics for resolving conflict and solving social problems have been applied to border enforcement, extending it beyond the purview of the state to include nonstate actors. For example, in Israel's Modi'in area, Border Police train youth to assist them in enforcing security measures and apprehending "illegal aliens" (Nevins 2012), while in the United States the Explorers program, a subsidiary of the Boy Scouts of America, partners with Border Patrol to train young people "in skills used to confront terrorism, illegal immigration and escalating border violence" (Steinhauer 2009). From nativist groups like the Minutemen in the United States (see, for example, Johnson, chapter 2 in this volume), to white supremacy groups in Australia and extreme nationalists in Europe, such extraofficial, border-enforcement initiatives aim to strengthen and reinforce the boundaries and lines that purportedly safeguard a nation, people, or way of life, as well as a set of corresponding moral codes.

Analysis of border politics must be situated within intersecting power relations across global, local, and national sites of mobilization and struggle. Power differentials at these various levels shape the strategies by which movement participants engage to achieve their goals. But they also structure the interactions and relationships among social movement participants, and, thereby, the possibilities for establishing cross-border alliances. For example, the achievement of certain objectives on the part of the No Border Camp held in the borderlands of Ukraine were hampered by "borders of difference" among activists that emerged despite an imagined, shared political culture of solidarity. Such social divisions highlighted differences of language and nationality and corresponding degrees of privilege and disadvantage. Activists' varied relationships to the Transcarpathia area where the camp was held meant that actions carried differing meanings and risks for camp participants. Those hailing from EU member-states did not face the same repercussions for confrontational activities, while camp organizers with ties to the region would be held more accountable (see also Braun and Dreiling, chapter 10). Likewise, when faced with the outside threat of a physical attack by fascist opponents, unity and shared orientations in the camp broke down and participants were unable to agree on a course of action (Blumberg and Rechitsky, chapter 11). This case illustrates the fleeting, contestable nature of solidarities across differences of nation, region, class, religion, and ethnicity. Contradictions associated with deterritorialization and reterritorialization that shape localized contestations, and their gendered, racialized, ethnic, and sexualized dynamics are central to what we term "border politics." These complex, intersecting dynamics underscore the need to unpack the shifting meanings of social membership, constructions of citizenship, and relations to nation-states.

Several cases presented in this volume (chapters 2–5, 11, 12) take place within contexts marked by the militarization of contested borderlands. Such frontiers are imagined as wild, lawless, and marginal (Earle 1999). State agents as well as ethnic militants and paramilitary groups justify human rights abuses committed against workers, migrants, and residents of ethnic communities as necessary in order to maintain law and order in these "out-of-control" areas in efforts to protect the "homeland."

Several of the authors illustrate how the powerful nationalist trope of women as the cultural bearers of the nation and the political deployment of motherhood are important components of militarization. The dichotomy of men as protectors of the nation and women as in need of protection is mobilized to support and rationalize militarized, ethnonationalist projects and exclusionary racial politics. Analysis of the contradictions evident in border politics reveal the complexity of the contests over territory, nation, identity, and belonging that are being fought across, within, and along diverse territorial dividing lines as well as sociocultural boundaries.

Organization of the Volume

This volume presents eleven case studies of social movements that feature diverse political orientations, movement tactics, and goals. Bringing together these varied cases as illustrative of border politics allows us to delineate the various relationships that social movements have with geopolitical and territorial divisions, sociocultural and symbolic boundaries, and the intersecting and often "in-between" identities associated with them (Anzaldúa 1987). In the cases of border politics

presented here, borders and boundaries operate as sources of grievances, targets of action, and sites of struggle. Symbolic boundaries and
other internal borders also permeate the internal dynamics among
social movement participants as well as processes of identity formation
and meaning-making. The cases are organized around three themes:
Gendered, Ethno-Nationalist Struggles and Militarization (part I);
Politicized Identities and Belonging (part II); and Contested Solidarities and Emerging Sites of Struggle (part III).

In the first section, the cases highlight the diversity of ways that
militarization operates within border politics. Militarization refers to
a process through which a worldview that promotes militaristic values—discipline, hierarchy, and obedience—achieves ascendancy and
predominance across arenas of social life. Military solutions to problems come to be seen as commonsensical, inevitable, and effective in a
context of impending threat, heightened insecurity, and danger (Enloe
2007). At the same time, the militarization and policing of borders is
interwoven with and reinforces hierarchies of gender, sexuality, class,
ethnicity, and race (Mains 2002, 204; see also Light and Chaloupka
2000). For example, movements organized in conflict-ridden geographic borderlands marshal traditional constructions of gender identities to justify militarized actions (Enloe 2007). In this way, women's
bodies become a battleground for ethnic conflicts implicated in border
policing. Women are also empowered as militarized agents who unsettle gendered expectations at the same time as they reinforce gendered
and sexualized constructions of womanhood and motherhood.

The second section foregrounds questions of collective identity and
belonging that are also sites of contestation within border politics.
Building on the first section, the authors attend to the ways in which
constructions of identities and belonging are further contoured by race,
ethnicity, religion, class, nation, gender, sexuality, and geographical origin. Cases in this section examine the activism of indigenous peoples
in North America and Australia, the US Tea Party, the Occupy movement, "erased workers" in Slovenia, and LGBT movement activists in
an integrated Europe. Questions addressed by the authors include who
gets to define and represent collective identities, who gets left out, and
what compromises are made in order to achieve social recognition and
movement goals.

The third section focuses on the limits and possibilities for cross-border solidarities. Global assemblages are sites of contradictions where power imbalances and access to resources pose ongoing challenges to collective action, even in the context of shared political goals. Differing interpretations or "border distortions" of movements' goals and strategies inevitably emerge in such coalitions (Braun and Dreiling, chapter 10). However, as illustrated in the last chapter, despite contradictions of power, the fabric of transnational connections and relationships among women's movement participants and feminists can produce hybrid social arenas or "counterpublics" (Fraser 1992) where oppositional perspectives can be articulated, debated, constructed, and shared (see also Naples 2013b.)

Gendered Ethno-Nationalist Struggles and Militarization

The first section of the volume features cases that highlight the intricacies of gender, sexuality, race, ethnicity, and nationalism as they intersect with border enforcement and militarization. The four chapters in this section feature struggles situated on the borders between nations as well as boundaries among ethnic, racial, and religious groups. The varied goals range from peace keeping to affirming ethnic divisions and bolstering exclusionary racial politics. The authors discuss the implications of movements' deployment of gender, ethnic, religious, and national identities for dominant, gendered social arrangements and women's agency.

In the first chapter in this section, Jennifer Johnson examines the contradictory role that grandmothers assume in the civilian patrols along the US-Mexican border to prevent unauthorized immigration into the United States. The routinized, structural gender violence in cities along the dividing line between the United States and Mexico and the high incidence of rape of migrant women while in transit is well documented (Morales and Bejarano 2009). Johnson shows how the fear of rape is used to justify militarized border enforcement and also to constrain the participation of women who participate in the Minutemen, confining much of their involvement to reproductive and symbolic activities. Indeed, her own fieldwork was hampered by the invocation of this threat and its alignment with the construction of men as protectors of the nation and women in need of protection as vessels of cultural reproduction. Johnson's analysis demonstrates how the Minutemen's project to police the geopolitical, legal, and cultural boundaries of the nation incorporates aging white women in ways that reproduce gendered and racial hierarchies of power. Her ethnography shows how the contributions of "border grannies" to efforts to keep immigrants of color *outside* the boundaries of nation is inextricably bound up in women's gendered subordination *within* national borders.

The traditional gendered identity of grandmother is based on moral strength and presumed powerlessness and fragility. The Minutemen employs this identity as a mobilizing frame, invoking the symbol of the granny to protect "the family" and indeed, the nation, against the threat of a racial "other." Ironically, the strategic deployment of the gendered and aged identity of "granny" occurs alongside the invocation of the threat of rape and women's need of male protectors. Thus, women's integration into militarized, ethno-national projects like the Minutemen simultaneously constructs them as vulnerable, potential victims in need of protection, and protectors of the nation. The Minutemen wield these interrelated, patriarchal narratives as a weapon of defense against a foreign invader, justifying militarized action. Simultaneously, the gendered subordination of the grannies bolsters the ethno-nationalist, exclusionary politics of the Minutemen, reinscribing hierarchies of masculinity, femininity, and racialized sexuality to reinforce the militarization of borders and the marginalization of nonwhite, racial, and ethnic "others."

In chapter 3, Meera Sehgal describes paramilitary camps in India in which middle-class, urban Hindu women's gender identities are deployed to support interethnic violence and militarization. She shows how the Hindu nationalist movement mobilizes the threat of sexual violence to produce a "feminine siege mentality" at the paramilitary camp that she studied. However, women active in this movement challenge patriarchal, ethno-nationalist expectations as they participate in paramilitary training that conflates "women's self-defense with national self-defense," thus transforming women into "symbolic border guards" who "deepen and regulate boundaries between Hindu and Muslim communities in the name of women's empowerment." The instruction and trainings that young women receive at the camps socialize them into a particular Hindu nationalist worldview through the cultivation of a siege mentality that is built on the fear of a sexually violent male,

Muslim "other." Sehgal shows how, through these camps, anti-Muslim hatred is used as an antidote to the fragmentation of ethno-nationalist allegiances in order "to patch the fractured Hindu polity together." Hindu nationalist women's elevation to the symbolically powerful position of citizen warriors is nonetheless tempered and circumscribed by an emphasis on feminine duty and sacrifice. Thus, despite the potential for empowerment of women, the dichotomy of women as in need of protection and men as natural protectors remains intact within the militarized, nationalist ideologies promoted at the camps.

The next chapter, by Duncan McDuie-Ra, analyzes the gendered, ethnic tensions within Northeast India along the border with Myanmar. In the ethnic conflict in the Naga region, women mobilize around identities of mothers and caretakers both to end violence and to resist peace efforts. This chapter illustrates the contradictory, gendered constructions employed by competing mobilizations. Ethnic Naga women's organizations who were organizing for peace throughout years of conflict over ethnic territories came head-to-head with ethnic Meitei women's organizations who were protesting *against* the peace agreement. Women's organizations associated with both ethnic groups took on multiple roles within demonstrations surrounding a blockade that sealed the region off from the rest of the country in protest efforts directed at both supporting and disrupting peace agreements in the adjoining territories of Nagaland and Manipur. McDuie-Ra shows how women's organization in the India-Myanmar borderlands deploy motherhood and its accompanying moral authority both to oppose and legitimate conflict and argues that as a political frame, motherhood is not effective in transcending hardening ethnic boundaries. He deftly attends to the contradictions these women face as they negotiate conflicting demands of peace keeping and ethnic solidarity.

In the last chapter in this section, Moon Charania offers a reading of antisecular, anti-Western militarization in Pakistan and the complex ways in which Muslim women's bodies have been used to mark borders. Pakistani women's militant defense of the Lal Masjid (Red Mosque) defies simplistic characterizations of covered Muslim women as either indoctrinated political actors (and victims of gender oppression) or anti-imperialist freedom fighters. Her analysis of Western media narrations and imagery elucidates dominant imaginings of the veiled female subject that undergird the War on Terror, and explains how such representations operate as mechanisms of power that discipline subjects by resolidifying notions of dangerous nations. The border politics that Charania analyzes foregounds the role of Western media representations in constructing the violent incidents at the Lal Masjid (Red Mosque) in Pakistan, in which a group of young, covered Muslim women defended the mosque to their death against Pakistani military forces and what the activists perceived as foreign impositions of secularism and immorality. During the course of the protests the women abducted Pakistani and Chinese women whom they accused of running a brothel and selling their labor as sex workers. The abductions brought into view the contested identities of femininity and womanhood for Muslim women and the struggle over who gets to define them.

The Pakistani women's political activities are framed by the Western media using hegemonic liberal conceptualizations of agency as rooted in Western individualism. Charania offers a multilayered reading of this example of resistance. She points out that the activists' violent rejection of Western imperialism and secularism defies the traditional gender order, even as it seeks to reinstate and protect it. And perhaps more ironically, it does so through the very subject-positioning made available to these women through the global circulation of dominant, feminist constructions of the Western, liberated woman. In other words, these women's efforts to protect the border between religious purity and "foreign" immorality are framed by globalized, gendered subjectivities (oppressed, victimized, veiled Muslim women versus liberated, empowered Western women) which their political activities heighten and reinforce (through Western readings of them) even as they are mobilized for anti-imperialist ends. These chapters all raise the specter of the politics of representation—namely, who gets to define the nation and how race, class, ethnicity, sexuality, and gender figure into these constructions. Chapters in the next section take up these questions again by foregrounding contestations over identities and belonging.

Politicized Identities and Belonging

The chapters in this section highlight the politics of belonging and identity that emerge from globalization's challenges to territorially defined state sovereignty and notions of "imagined community" (Anderson 1991). The four cases reveal how the binary of "citizen" and "noncitizen" fails to capture the multitude of social categories and forms of membership that exist in a context of global integration. The authors call attention to the ways in which diverse forms of membership are further structured along the lines of race, class, ethnicity, sexuality, and geographical origin.

The chapters demonstrate how marginalized groups seek to challenge, contract, and redraw boundaries of democratic inclusion established within nation-states as well as within an integrating Europe. Their efforts both invoke and challenge Western, liberal notions of citizenship and rights. While liberal discourse, such as that of human rights, offers marginalized groups powerful tools that lend international legitimacy to political demands, tensions arise from the use of this universalized discourse to address social inequalities due in part to the normative constructions of race, ethnicity, gender, sexuality, and family embedded within them (Naples 2002). Liberal conceptualizations of citizenship and human rights are founded on a concept of universal personhood equated with an autonomous, property-owning individual who acts within a masculinized public sphere and is assumed to be both male and heterosexual. The challenge facing such groups is to construct new political imaginaries of inclusive, participatory democracy based on an expanded definition of social and political membership.

The reinforcement of racial and ethnic boundaries that has accompanied globalization has deepened animosities over who can lay legitimate historic and cultural claims to particular lands, fueling contestations over what appear as natural links "between a people, their culture, and the geographical space" (Cerwonka 2004, 23). As Sarah Maddison points out in chapter 6, state projects in colonial settlements were premised on the erasure of indigenous people, and colonial borders "crossed" their cultures and societies.

Individualist conceptions of rights and definitions of citizens are at the core of nation-state–building projects, which strive for territorially defined cultural unity. In a context in which nation-states dominate as the sovereign entities that guarantee the enforcement of rights, the struggles of indigenous peoples for self-determination and autonomy challenge national boundaries as sole arbiters of claims-making (Donnelly 1993). Making claims to sovereignty based on rights discourse poses several dilemmas for indigenous peoples and ethnic minorities. Perhaps foremost among these is the tension between individual and collective rights (Jelin 1997). Indigenous peoples and other displaced and oppressed groups have called for collective and cultural rights, rejecting Western precepts of rights discourse as well as individualist notions of rights reflected within it (Stavenhagen 1996; Zubaida 1993).

Sarah Maddison's chapter highlights how indigenous peoples' relationship to land and notions of belonging contrast with the beliefs held by European invaders and contemporary neoliberal states. Maddison attends to the production of a pan-Indigenous political identity that challenges imposed colonial and postcolonial borders. Indigenous peoples face the strategic dilemma of having to gain political voice and recognition within neocolonial states while claiming a pan-Indigenous identity that transcends precolonial national borders.

While Maddison discusses efforts to create politicized identities that transcend borders of the nation-state, in the next chapter Deana Rohlinger and her coauthors describe a social movement's efforts to contract the boundaries of a collective "we" and in so doing define "American" in increasingly narrow ways. Initially, the Tea Party movement (TPM) in Florida articulated a collective identity based on broadly shared values (individual rights and love of country), which enabled it to mobilize citizens from across the political spectrum. However, after the 2010 electoral success, the TPM began to draw more narrow boundaries of membership. While avoiding the open racialization of these dividing lines, the TPM began to base its collective identity on opposition to illegal immigrants and their allies and a government perceived to have a socialist agenda. Finally, the TPM drew a sharp boundary to differentiate participants from the Occupy Wall Street (OWS) movement, which emerged in response to the global banking crisis. Instead, the TPM carves out an ideology that blends support for tightening the enforcement of racial boundaries and national border with extolling the benefits of free market capitalism.

The Balkan states of former Yugoslavia serve as the setting for chapter 8, in which authors Maple Razsa and Andrej Kurnik analyze the social marginalization associated with the redrawing of borders and the integration of labor markets and economies. They argue that the experiences and struggles of the "erased," ethnic minority workers, whose citizenship was revoked in 1992 following Slovenia's independence, demonstrates how border regimes function not only to physically exclude marginalized groups but also "to socially include them under imposed conditions of enforced and protracted vulnerability" as a subordinated labor force (De Genova 2002, 429). Indeed, these workers' struggle for dignity, social inclusion, and labor rights as "foreigners" in the very place that they knew as home illustrates the articulation between redrawn territorial borders, social exclusion, and precarious labor regimes that undergird neoliberal globalization. The analysis highlights the social boundaries that emerge when different sociocultural groups come into contact in borderlands where the dividing lines between collectivities are drawn, maintained, and allowed to endure (Fassin 2011; Barth 1969).

Razsa and Kurnik explore the political alternatives developed among the erased in their struggle against exclusionary politics in the borderlands between Bosnia and Slovenia. Migrants' transnational organizing in the region called for the opening of borders and the outright abolition of border controls. Their protests, some of which targeted the Office of High Representative (OHR) headquarters in Sarajevo, also raised provocative questions about the relationship between the former Yugoslavia and the European Union. The political practices of democracy of direct action enacted by erased workers in Occupy Slovenia highlight the crisis of representative democracy in the liberal nation-state. The workshops organized by Occupy Slovenia created meaningful spaces for creating collective subjectivities that challenged the fragmentation stimulated by globalization. For the authors, the struggles of the poor and marginalized Bosnian workers in Slovenia and their allies and their experimentation with new practices of direct democracy suggest the emancipatory potential of new forms of citizenship. Razsa and Kurnik also counter the dominant narrative that the Yugoslav experience represents an anomalous case in an otherwise smoothly integrating and globalizing Europe. They argue instead that the multiplicity of borders and the displacement of populations contribute to institutionalized hierarchies of nations and labor within an integrated Europe. Razsa and Kurnik's analysis raises the question of who can make claims to European membership and who are marginalized within "the idea of Europe" even when formal membership is granted to states.

In the next chapter, Phillip Ayoub and David Paternotte present a contrasting picture of the construction of Europe. They analyze how activists created a normative framework of Europe that links LGBT rights with European values. Lesbian, gay, bisexual, and transgender activists have imagined a new sociopolitical European community, challenging the frontiers of exclusion and the modes of belonging of the liberal nation-state. These activists are not simply extending a liberal notion of rights to an unrecognized group. By imagining Europe as, in part, defined by the inclusion of LGBT people, they are redefining "rights" and forms of citizenship that transcend the bounded nation-state. LGBT activism in Central and Eastern Europe, then, contributes to rebuilding the meaning of Europe from the ground up. Yet, borders remain when these efforts created new hierarchies among activists and paradoxically reinforced a distinction between the "modern West" and the "homophobic East." Again, we see the importance of bringing together the analysis of internal and external dynamics of border construction and resistance to develop more comprehensive understandings of material and symbolic border politics.

Contested Solidarities and Emerging Sites of Struggle

The last three chapters examine the shifting spaces of social movement activity that have accompanied globalization as well as the opportunities for and challenges to cross-border solidarities. Global connectivities have fueled transnational social movements, allowing for the diffusion and exchange of information, resources, discourses, and strategies of contention (Guidry, Kennedy, and Zald 2000). Organizers mobilize, establish, and maintain transnational networks often with the goal of pressuring governments to make reforms that address the demands of marginalized groups. Although many such initiatives have emerged to challenge the effects of neoliberal globalization, their formation is made possible by the very advancement of information technologies and the time-space compression that are hallmarks of the global age.

Such initiatives illustrate the potential for transnational cultures of solidarity that can create a space for dialogue and exchange across differences of national origin, race, ethnicity, religion, gender, sexuality, and class (Bandy and Bickham Mendez 2003). But they also reveal how gender and sexuality, along with power relations of race, ethnicity, class, and nation, "fracture the space of transnational civil society and constrain opposition to neoliberalism" (Bandy and Bickham Mendez 2003, 174). Tensions that emerge from power disparities within transnational networks remain a challenge to local activists whose vision and goals may be overridden by more powerful transnational allies (see also Thayer 2010; Bickham Mendez 2005; Naples and Desai 2002a).

In chapter 10, Yvonne Braun and Michael Dreiling explore the limits, tensions, and possibilities of cross-border organizing in opposition to mega-dam projects in Lesotho. They uncover often-overlooked internal dynamics of the boomerang effect, a political strategy in which organizations form transnational advocacy networks to leverage pressure against targeted institutions to implement reforms or enforce laws or policies (Keck and Sikkink 1998).

Transnational oppositional initiatives to mega-dam projects constitute global assemblages (Ong and Collier 2005), bringing together a vast network of local and international movement organizations and advocates to fight the corporate takeover of land and corresponding environmental destruction. Braun and Dreiling find that the cross-border alliances, which local activists in Lesotho forged with transnational environmental groups in order to further their local efforts, were structured by power differentials that privileged the identities and interpretations of transnational allies in resource-rich organizations in the Global North. In the process of formulating frames for transnational advocacy efforts, key concerns and understandings emanating from the local level were either ignored or went unheard. While local activists were concerned with corruption, the plight of displaced persons, and environmental justice, transnational activists focused on environmental preservation.

Braun and Dreiling forward the concept of "border distortions" to advance understandings of the contradictions and tensions that emerge within transborder coalitions. The effects of intersecting power disparities on the internal processes of cross-border "frame alignment" (Snow 1986) within the transnational coalitions can diminish the range of forms of resistance available as well as the potential for the construction of shared identities. The authors delineate the disjunctures and disconnects between local activists' concerns and those of more privileged allies. Given the Lesotho-based activists' more limited mobility and rootedness in place, they faced real risks as a result of the adverse local consequences of transnational advocacy work. Both chapter 10 by Braun and Dreiling and the next chapter by Renata Blumberg and Raphi Rechitsky raise questions about divergent transformative visions within transnational mobilizations and the ways in which power disparities in transnational coalitions can limit the range and effectiveness of oppositional strategies and actions. Power disparities influence which interpretations become dominant and what strategies are enacted.

Blumberg and Rechitsky shift our attention to border politics on the redrawn border of the Ukraine and the EU to interrogate how transnational social movements that seek to challenge territorial borders can also actively construct internal social borders. They analyze the case of No Border Camp, a convergence of over three hundred activists from countries around Europe and the world, to protest unjust immigration enforcement and the militarization of European borders. Activists involved in these transnational initiatives confronted tensions that emerged around "borders of difference" and power disparities, which limited the impact of the movement's antiauthoritarian practices. While differences of language and region were pronounced and impacted network-building within the camp, collaborative efforts to advocate for more just border enforcement were also hindered by varied understandings of appropriate antiauthoritarian organizing strategies. Although the mobilization was successful in achieving some goals, the authors document how global economic inequalities as well as activists' divergent relationships to and imaginaries of place inhibited the implementation of anticapitalist, antinationalist politics. In this case organizing across borders of identity or nationality affirmed differences, rather than blurring or transcending them. Despite activists' rejection of liberal rights discourses that are foundational to nation-states, they confronted tensions emerging from national origin as well as the geopolitical power relations among countries.

In chapter 12, Michelle Téllez and Cristina Sanidad offer a more hopeful perspective in approaching the dilemmas associated with transnational organizing. They build on the work of feminist sociologist Millie Thayer to explore the cases of women's organizations in the border region of Tijuana and San Diego. Thayer (2010) offers the concept of "transnational feminist counterpublics," which she defines as political spaces where oppositional perspectives can be articulated, debated, constructed, and shared. In these transitional arenas, social networks, organizations, and individuals may engage with each other collaboratively or conflict with one another. For Thayer such counterpublics hold the potential to be spaces of solidarity and democratic participation across power differentials and differences of class, nationality, race, and ethnicity. Téllez and Sanidad see this potential come alive in the efforts of women's organizations that seek to empower and make improvements in the daily lives of women workers in the *maquila* factories of export-processing zones. These women workers understand globalization as part of their lived experience that is shaped by forces far from the places they inhabit.

Conclusion

Borders embody differing implications and meaning for those who confront them, depending on context and social actors' location within intersecting structures of power. On the one hand, borders can be experienced as protection against violation and violence against self, community, and nation. On the other hand, the divisions that borders and boundaries sustain also "carry cruelty and violence" (Connolly 1995, xiii). We build on critical constructivist and feminist approaches, which characterize neither movements nor the identities that they mobilize and produce as fixed, monolithic entities, but as always in flux.

Some cases of the border politics examined here are situated within historically politicized borderlands, others occur within relatively newly constituted sites of struggle. The first and last chapters of the collection highlight the Mexican-US borderlands and present analyses of organizations positioned on the antipodes of the political spectrum—struggles for social justice in the *maquila* factories (Téllez and Sanidad, chapter 12) and the Minutemen's mobilization of "grannies" to help patrol the US-Mexico border to prevent unauthorized immigration (Johnson, chapter 2). These cases as well as that of the Naga conflict on the frontier between Myanmar and India (McDuie-Ra, chapter 4) and the No Border Camp, which mobilized in the Transcarpathia region that serves as a gateway into "Fortress Europe" (Blumberg and Rechitsky, chapter 11) take place within contexts shaped by militarized and contested borderlands.

The engagement of social movements in border politics may be organized around opposition to border enforcement and its effects, such as those that seek to change unjust immigration policies and challenge visa regimes that create hardships for immigrants seeking economic opportunities across borders (Razsa and Kurnik, chapter 8) or workers' treatment within borders (Téllez and Sanidad, chapter 12). Other cases illustrate contestations that arise as reactions to porous borders and the perceived or actual threats they pose to state sovereignty (Johnson, chapter 2), the rights and cultural integrity of indigenous peoples (Maddison, chapter 6), religious identities and value systems (Charania, chapter 5), citizenship and belonging (Rohlinger et al., chapter 7), and the preservation of ethnic homelands (McDuie-Ra, chapter 4). In such cases we see border politics aimed at fortifying borders or protecting historical social or political identities. These mobilizations are often responses to the forces of Empire and neocolonialism or the challenges that globalization poses to a territorially defined notion of "imagined community" based on cultural and ethnic homogeneity (Anderson 1991). As well, illustrated throughout the collection, struggles over gendered and sexualized identities are also at play within movements and across levels of organizing from the local to transnational (see, for example, Sehgal, chapter 3; Ayoub and Paternotte, chapter 9).

Border Politics raises a series of questions and issues for further study. In the concluding chapter we demonstrate how the collection's analytical focus on border politics allows for the disentangling of theoretical tensions and sheds explanatory light on the complexities of these movements' dynamics as well as offers analytic power for future research. This collection brings forward the contradictions of this historical moment for reconfiguring national and symbolic boundaries and other internal borders that shape international and local mobilizations as well as internal tensions among social movement participants. Attention to these shifts and tensions further reveals contestations over nation, race, ethnicity, gender, and sexuality.

NOTES

1. We follow David Snow (2004), who defines social movements as "collectivities acting with some degree of organization and continuity outside of institutional or organizational channels for the purpose of challenging or defending extant authority, whether it is institutionally or culturally based, in the group, organization, society, culture, or world order of which they are a part." In the conclusion we explore further the implications of theoretical attention to borders and boundaries for conceptualizing social movement practices and identities.

2. Gilles Deleuze and Félix Guattari (1972) conceptualize these interrelated processes as separating or detaching local meaning, experience, or specificity of social relations, including labor relations, and reconstituting them in distant and abstracted formulations.

3. Given their spatial and territorial dimensions, it is not surprising that the study of international borders and boundaries has a long history in the fields of social (see Jones 1959; Kolossov 2005) and political geography (Prescott 1965; Kapperson and Minghi 1969).

4. The call for intersectional analyses were first heard from feminists of color, who critiqued approaches that constructed women's experiences without attention to the ways that race, class, and sexuality shaped their experiences. Subsequent work emphasized the structural dimensions of what Dorothy Smith (1987) calls the "relations of ruling" and Patricia Hill Collins (1990) terms "the matrix of domination" that contour different women's experiences (Naples 2012, 2013b; see also Anzaldúa 1987; Crenshaw 1993; Hancock 2007; Sandoval 2000).We take a multidimensional approach to intersectionality in conceptualizing border politics that goes beyond identity to examine the "interrelationship or intersections between the 'actualities of everyday life' [drawing on Dorothy Smith's (1987) conceptualization], the local context, as well as the social structures or relations of ruling that are far from view" (Naples 2013).

5. Fueled in part by the Arab Spring, Occupy Wall Street activists called attention to the many ways that money has a corrupting effect on politics. Occupy Wall Street framed their 2011 protest as "We are the 99%" to call attention to the concentration of wealth in the top 1 percent of the income distribution in the US. National implementation of austerity measures might explain the urgency with which people in other countries took up the Occupy movement. Occupy protests include calls to Occupy Homes to challenge banks' predatory loan practices and their subsequent treatment of homeowners, end fuel subsidies in Nigeria, resist tuition increases in Colombia, and counter economic inequality and the role of the European Central Bank and International Monetary Fund in government in Italy. Australia, Canada, Germany, Malaysia, Mexico, South Africa, South Korea, the UK, and other countries have held Occupy-inspired protests (Naples 2013a).

REFERENCES

Alarcón, Norma, Caren Kaplan, and Minoo Moallem. 1999. Introduction: Between Woman and Nation. In *Between Woman and Nation: Nationalisms, Transnational Feminisms, and the State* edited by Caren Kaplan, Norma Alarcón, Minoo Moallem, 1–24. Durham, NC: Duke University.

Aleinikoff, T. Alexander. 2001. Policing Boundaries: Migration, Citizenship, and the State. In *E Pluribus Unum? Contemporary and Historical Perspectives on Immigrant Political Incorporation*, edited by Gary Gerstle and John Mollenkpf, 267–291. New York: Russell Sage Foundation.

Alexander, M. Jacqui, and Chandra Talpade Mohanty, eds. 1997. *Feminist Genealogies, Colonial Legacies, Democratic Futures.* New York: Routledge.

Alvarez, Robert R., Jr. 1995. The Mexican-U.S. Border: The Making of an Anthropology of Borderlands. *Annual Review of Anthropology* 24: 447–470.

Anderson, Benedict. 1991. *Imagined Communities: Reflections on the Origin and Spread of Nationalism.* 2nd ed. Brooklyn, NY: Verso Books.

Anderson, Malcolm. 1996. *Frontiers: Territory and State Formation in the Modern World.* Oxford: Polity Press.

Anzaldúa, Gloria. 1987. *Borderlands/La Frontera.* San Francisco: Aunt Lute Books.

Armstrong, Elizabeth, and Mary Bernstein. 2008. Culture, Power, and Institutions: A Multi-Institutional Politics Approach to Social Movements. *Sociological Theory* 26(1): 74–99.

Bandy, Joe, and Jennifer Bickham Mendez. 2003. A Place of their Own? Women Organizers in the Maquilas of Nicaragua and Mexico. *Mobilization: An International Journal* 8 (2): 173–188.

Bandy, Joe, and Jackie Smith. 2005. Factors Affecting Conflict and Cooperation in Transnational Movement Networks. In *Coalitions Across Borders: Transnational Protest and the Neoliberal Order*, edited by Joe Bandy and Jackie Smith, 231–252. Lanham, MD: Rowman & Littlefield.

Barth, Fredrik. 1969. *Ethnic Groups and Boundaries: The Social Organization of Culture Difference.* New York: Little, Brown and Company.

Behar, Ruth. 1993. *Translated Woman: Crossing the Border with Esperanza's Story.* Boston: Beacon Press.

Bickham Mendez, Jennifer. 2005. *From the Revolution to the Maquiladoras: Gender, Labor and Globalization in Nicaragua.* Durham, NC: Duke University Press.

Blee, Kathleen M. 2008. *Women of the Klan: Racism and Gender in the 1920s.* Berkeley: University of California Press.

Bosniak, Linda. 2006. *The Citizen and the Alien: Dilemmas of Contemporary Membership.* Princeton, NJ: Princeton University Press.

Burawoy, Michael, Joseph A. Blum, Sheba George, Millie Thayer, Zsuzsa Gille, Teresa Gowan, Lynne Haney, Maren Klawiter, Steve H. Lopez, and Sean Riain. 2000. *Global Ethnography: Forces, Connections, and Imaginations in a Postmodern World.* Berkeley: University of California Press.

Cantú, Lionel. 2009. *The Sexuality of Migration: Border Crossings and Mexican Immigrant Men*, edited by Nancy A. Naples, Salvador Vidal-Ortiz. New York: New York University Press.

Cerwonka, Allaine, 2004. *Native to the Nation: Disciplining Landscapes and Bodies in Australia*. Minneapolis: University of Minnesota Press.

Collins, Patricia Hill. 1990. *Black Feminist Thought: Knowledge, Consciousness and the Politics of Empowerment*. New York: Routledge.

Connolly, William. 1995. *The Ethos of Pluralization*. Minneapolis: University of Minnesota Press.

Crenshaw, Kimberly 1993. Mapping the Margins: Intersectionality, Identity Politics, and Violence Against Women of Color. *Stanford Law Review* 43: 124–199.

De Genova, Nicholas. 2002. Migrant "Illegality" and Deportability in Everyday Life. *Annual Review of Anthropology* 31: 419–447.

De Genova, Nicholas and Nathalie Peutz. eds. 2010. *The Deportation Regime: Sovereignty, Space, and the Freedom of Movement*, Durham, NC: Duke University Press

DeChaine, Robert. 2012. *Border Rhetorics: Citizenship and Identity on the U.S. Mexico Frontier*. Tuscaloosa: University of Alabama Press.

Deleuze, Gilles, and Félix Guattari. 1972. *AntiOedipus*. Trans. Robert Hurley, Mark Seem, and Helen R. Lane. London: Continuum. 2004. Vol. 1 of *Capitalism and Schizophrenia* 2 vols. 1972–1980. Trans. of *L'AntiOedipe*. Paris: Les Éditions de Minuit.

Donnan, Hastings, and Thomas M. Wilson. 1999. *Borders: Frontiers of Identity, Nation and State*. Oxford: Berg Publishers.

Donnelly, Jack. 1993. *International Human Rights*. San Franscisco, CA: Westview Press.

Earle, Duncan. 1999. The Borderless Borderlands: Texas' Colonias as Displaced Settlements. In *Identities on the Move: Transnational Processes in North America and the Caribbean Basin*, edited by Liliana Goldin. Vol. 7, 169–183. Albany, NY: Institute for Mesaoamerian Studies, University at Albany.

Enloe, Cynthia. 2007. *Globalization and Militarism: Feminists Make the Link*. Lanham, MD: Rowman & Littlefield.

Eschle, Catherine. 2001. *Global Democracy, Social Movements, and Feminism*. Boulder, CO: Westview Press.

Evans, Peter. 2000. Fighting Marginalization with Transnational Networks: Counter-Hegemonic Globalization. *Contemporary Sociology*. 29(1): 230-241.

Fassin, Didier. 2011. Policing Borders, Producing Boundaries. The Governmentality of Immigration in Dark Times. *Annual Review of Anthropology* 40: 213–226.

Fernandez Kelly, Maria. 1983. *For We Are Sold, I and My People: Women and Industry in Mexico's Frontier*. Albany: SUNY Press.

Gambetti, Zeynep and Marcial Godoy-Anativia, eds. 2010. *Rhetorics of Insecurity : Belonging And Violence In The Neoliberal Era*. New York: New York University Press.

Gómez-Peña, Guillermo. 1996. *The New World Border: Prophecies, Poems and Loqueras for the End of the Century*. San Francisco: City Lights Books.

Grewal, Inderpal, and Caren Kaplan. 1994. *Scattered Hegemonies: Postmodernity and Transnational Feminist Practices*. Minneapolis: University of Minnesota Press.

Guidry, John A., Michael D. Kennedy, and Mayer N. Zald, eds. 2000. *Globalizations and Social Movements*. Ann Arbor: University of Michigan Press.

Gupta, Akhil. 1998. *Postcolonial Developments: Agriculture in the Making of Modern India*. Durham, NC: Duke University Press.

Gusterson, Hugh, and Caroline Besteman. 2009. *The Insecure American: How We Got Here and What We Should Do About It*. Berkeley: University of California Press.

Harvey, David.1990. *The Condition of Postmodernity: An Enquiry into the Origins of Cultural Change* . Malden, MA: Blackwell Publishers.

Hewitt, Lyndi, and Marina Karides 2011. More Than a Shadow of a Difference? Feminist Participation on the World Social Forum. In *Handbook for World Social Forum Activism*, edited by Jackie Smith, Ellen Reese, Scott Byrd, and Elizabeth Smyth, 85–104. Boulder, CO: Paradigm Publishers.

Jelin, Elizabeth. 1997. Engendering Human Rights. In *Gender Politics in Latin America: Debates in Theory and Practice*, edited by Elizabeth Dore, 65–83. New York: Monthly Review Press.

Jones, Stephen. 1959. Boundary Concepts in Setting Time and Space. *Annals of the American Association of Geographers* 49 (3): 241–255.

Juris, Jeffrey, and Maple Razsa. 2012. Introduction: Occupy, Anthropology, and the 2011 Global Uprisings. *Cultural Anthropology*. www.culanth.org/?q=node/641.

Kaplan, Caren, Norma Alarcón, and Minoo Moallem, eds. 1999. *Between Women and Nation: Transnational Feminisms and the State*. Durham, NC: Duke University Press.

Kapperson, Roger E., and Julian V. Minghi, eds. 1969. *The Structure of Political Geography*. Chicago, IL: Aldine Publishing Company.

Kearney, Michael. 1991. Borders and Boundaries of State and Self at the End of Empire. *Journal of Historical Sociology* 4 (1): 52–74.

Keck, Margaret E., and Kathryn A. Sikkink. 1998. *Activists Beyond Borders: Advocacy Networks in International Politics*. Ithaca, NY: Cornell University Press.

Khasnabish, Alex. 2010. *Zapatistas*. New York: Zed Books.

Kolossov, Vladimir. 2005. Border Studies: Changing Perspectives and Theoretical Approaches. *Geopolitics* 10: 606–632.

Kretsedemas, Philip, and David Brotherton, eds. 2008. *Keeping Out the Other: A Critical Introduction to Immigration Enforcement Today*. New York: Columbia University Press.

Lamont, Michèle, and Virag Molnár. 2002. The Study of Boundaries in the Social Sciences. *Annual Review of Sociology* 28: 167–195.

Leontidou, Lila, Hastings Donnan, and Alex Afouxenidis. 2005. Exclusion and Difference Along the EU Border: Social and Cultural Markers, Spatialities and Mappings. *International Journal of Urban and Regional Research* 29 (2): 289–407.

Lewis, Gail, and Sarah Neal. 2005. Introduction: Contemporary Political Contexts, Changing Terrains, and Revisited Discourses. *Ethnic and Racial Studies* 28 (3): 423–444.

Light, Andrew, and William Chaloupka. 2000. Angry White Men: Right Exclusionary Nationalism and Left Identity Politics. In *Gender Ironies of Nationalism: Sexing the Nation*, edited by Tamar Mayer, 329–350. New York: Routledge.

Low, Setha. 2003. *Behind the Gates. Life, Security, and the Pursuit of Happiness in Fortress America*. New York: Routledge.

Lowe, Lisa, and David Lloyd, eds. 1997. *The Politics of Culture in the Shadow of Capital*. Durham, NC: Duke University Press.

Lugo, Alejandro. 1997. Reflections on Border Theory, Culture, and the Nation. In *Border Theory: The Limits of Cultural Politics*, edited by Scott Michaelson and David Johnson, 43–67. Minneapolis: University of Minnesota Press.

Mains, Susan P. 2002. Maintaining National Identity at the Border: Scale, Masculinity, and the Policing of Immigration in Southern California. In *Geographies of Power: Placing Scale*, edited by Andrew Herod and Melissa Wright, 192–214. Oxford: Blackwell Publishers.

McAdam, Doug, John D. McCarthy, and Mayer N. Zald, eds. 1996. *Comparative Perspectives On Social Movements: Political Opportunities, Mobilizing Structures, and Cultural Framings*. New York: Cambridge University Press.

McVeigh, Rory. 2009. *The Rise of the Ku Klux Klan: RightWing Movements and National Politics*. Minneapolis: University of Minnesota Press.

Moghadam, Valentine M. 2011. *Making Globalization Work for Women*. Albany: SUNY Press.

Mohanty, Chandra Talpade. 1991. Under Western Eyes: Feminist Scholarship and Colonial Discourses. In *Third World Women and the Politics of Feminism*, edited by Chandra Talpade Mohanty, Ann Russo and Lourdes Torres, 51–80. Bloomington: Indiana University Press.

Mohanty, Chandra Talpade. 2003. *Feminism without Borders: Decolonizing Theory, Practicing Solidarity*. Durham, NC: Duke University Press.

Momen, Mehnaaz. 2005. Are You a Citizen? Insights from Borderlands. *Citizenship Studies* 3 (3): 323–334.

Moraga, Cherríe, and Gloria Anzaldúa, eds. 1983. *This Bridge Called My Back: Writings by Radical Women of Color*. Latham, NY: Kitchen Table/Women of Color Press.

Morales, Maria Cristina and Cynthia Bejarano. 2009. Transnational Sexual And Gendered Violence: An Application of Border Sexual Conquest At A Mexico—US Border. *Global Networks* 9(3): 420-39.

Nagel, Joanne. 1994. Constructing Ethnicity: Creating and Recreating Ethnic Identity and Culture. *Social Problems* 41 (1): 152–176.

Naples, Nancy A. 2002. The Challenges and Possibilities of Transnational Feminist Praxis. In *Women's Activism and Globalization: Linking Local Struggles and Transnational Politics*, edited by Nancy A. Naples and Manisha Desai, 276–281. New York: Routledge.

Naples, Nancy A. 2009a. Crossing Borders: Community Activism, Globalization, and Social Justice. *Social Problems* 56 (1): 2–20.

Naples, Nancy A. 2009b. Teaching Intersectionality Intersectionally. *International Feminist Journal of Politics* 11(4): 566–577.

Naples, Nancy A. 2010. Borderlands Studies and Border Theory: Linking Activism and Scholarship for Social Justice. *Sociology Compass* 4(7): 505–518.

Naples, Nancy A. 2013a. "It's Not Fair!": Discursive Politics, Social Justice, and Feminist Praxis. *Gender & Society* 27(2): 133–157.

Naples, Nancy A. 2013b. Sustaining Democracy: Localization, Globalization, and Feminist Praxis. *Sociological Forum* 28(4): 657–681.

Naples, Nancy A., and Manisha Desai. 2002. *Women's Activism and Globalization: Linking Local Struggles with Transnational Politics*. New York: Routledge.

Nayak, Mechana, and Jennifer Suchland. 2006. Gender Violence and Hegemonic Projects. *International Feminist Journal of Politics* 8 (4): 467–485.

Nevins, Joseph, ed. 2002. *Operation Gatekeeper: The Rise of the "Illegal Alien" and the Remaking of the U.S.-Mexico Boundary*. New York: Routledge.

Nevins, Joseph. 2012. Border Wars. *North American Congress on Latin America* (blog), Jan 18. https://nacla.org/blog/2012/1/17/border-patrol-youth.

Newman, David. 2011. Contemporary Research Agendas in Borders Studies: An Overview. In *The Ashgate Companion to Border Studies*, edited by Doris Wastl-Walter, 33–48. Farnham, UK: Ashgate Publishing.

Olesen, Thomas. 2005. *International Zapatismo: The Construction Of Solidarity In The Age Of Globalization*. New York: Palgrave.

Ong, Aihwa, and Stephen J. Collier, eds. 2005. *Global Assemblages: Technology, Politics, and Ethics as Anthropological Problems*. Oxford: Wiley-Blackwell.

Payne, Leigh A. 2000. *Uncivil Movements: The Armed Right Wing and Democracy in Latin America*. Baltimore, MD: Johns Hopkins University Press.

Perea, Juan, ed. 1996. *Immigrants Out!: The New Nativism and the Anti-Immigrant Impulse in the United States*. New York: New York University Press.

Prescott, John Robert Victor. 1965. *The Geography of Frontiers and Boundaries*. Hawthorne, NY: Aldine Publishing Company.

Rodriguez, Robyn Magalit. 2010. *Migrants for Export: How the Philippine State Brokers Labor to the World*. Minneapolis: University of Minnesota Press.

Rosaldo, Renato. 1989. *Culture & Truth: The Remaking of Social Analysis*. Boston: Beacon Press.

Rydgren, Jens. 2006. From Tax Populism to Ethnic Nationalism: Radical Right-wing Populism in Sweden. New York: Berghahn Books.

Sandoval, Chela. 1991. U.S. Third World Feminism: The Theory and Method of Oppositional Consciousness in the Postmodern World. *Genders* 10 (Spring): 1–24.

Sandoval, Chela. 2000. *Methodology of the Oppressed*. Minneapolis: University of Minnesota Press.

Sarkar, Tanika, and Urvashi Butalia, eds.1996. *Women and Right-Wing Movements: Indian Experiences*. Boston, MA: Zed Books.

Sassen, Saskia. 2006. Global Cities and Survival Circuits. In *Global Dimensions of Gender and Carework*, edited by Mary K. Zimmerman, Jacqueline S. Litt and Christine E. Bose, 30–38. Stanford, CA: Stanford University Press.

Segura, Denise and Patricia Zavella. 2009. Introduction: The Gendered Borderlands. *Gender and Society* 22(5): 537–544.

Smith, Jackie. 1998. Global Civil Society? Transnational Social Movement Organizations and Social Capital. *American Behavioral Scientist* 42(1): 93–107.

Smith, Jackie, Charles Chatfield, and Ron Pagnucco. eds. 1997. *Transnational Social Movements and Global Politics*. Syracuse, NY: Syracuse University Press.

Smith, Jackie, and Hank Johnston, eds. 2002. *Globalization and Resistance: Transna-tionl Dimensions of Social Movements*. Lanham, MD: Rowman & Littlefield.

Snow, David A. 1986. Frame Alignment Processes, Micromobilization, and Movement Participation. *American Sociological Review* 51(1): 464–481.

Snow, David A. 2004. Social Movements as Challenges to Authority: Resistance to an Emerging Conceptual Hegemony. In *Authority and Contention: Research in Social Movements, Conflicts and Change*, vol 25. edited by Daniel J. Myers and Daniel M. Cress, 3–25. Bingley: Emerald Group Publishing Ltd.

Spener, David, and Kathleen Staudt. 1998. A View from the Frontier: Theoretical Perspectives Undisciplined. In *The U.S.-Mexico Border: Transcending Divisions, Contesting Identities*, edited by David Spener and Kathleen Staudt, 197–218. Boulder, CO: Lynne Rienner Publishers.

Stavenhagen, Rodolfo. 1996. Indigenous Rights: Some Conceptual Problems. In *Constructing Democracy: Human Rights, Citizenship, and Society in Latin America*, edited by Elizabeth Jelin and Eric Hershberg, 141–159. Boulder, CO: Westview Press.

Steinhauer, Jennifer. 2009. Scouts Train to Fight Terrorists, and More. *New York Times*, March 13.

Thayer, Mille. 2010. *Making Transnational Feminism: Rural Women, NGO Activists, and Northern Donors in Brazil*. New York: Routledge.

United Nations Department of Economic and Social Affairs, Population Division. 2011. Trends in International Migrant Stock: Migrants by Age and Sex. United Nations database, POP/DB/MIG/Stock/Rev.2010.

Vaughan-Williams, Nick. 2009. *Border Politics: The Limits of Sovereign Power*. Edin-burgh: Edinburgh University Press.

Vila, Pablo. 2003. The Limits of American Border Theory. In *Ethnography at the Bor-der*, edited by Pablo Vila, 306–341. Minneapolis: University of Minnesota Press.

Walters, William. 2006. Border/Control. *European Journal of Social Theory* 9 (2): 187–203.

Washington Post. 2012. Geert Wilders of the Netherlands Reveals a Resurgent Far Right in Europe. April 30. www.washingtonpost.com/world/geertwildersofthenetherland-srevealsaresurgentfarrightineurope/2012/04/30/gIQAA9zsrTstory.html.

Wimmer, Andreas. 2002. *Nationalist Exclusion and Ethnic Conflict: Shadows of Moder-nity*. Cambridge: Cambridge University Press.

Wimmer, Andreas. 2013. *Ethnic Boundary Making: Institutions, Power, Networks*. Oxford: Oxford University Press.

Wodak, Ruth, Majid KhosraviNik, and Brigitte Mral, eds. 2012. *Right-Wing Populism in Europe: Politics* and Discourse. New York: Bloomsbury Academic.

Zimmerman, Arely M. 2011. A Dream Detained: Undocumented Latino Youth and the DREAM Movement. NACLA Report on the Americas. 44(6): 1417.

Zubaida, Sami. 1993. Human Rights and Cultural Difference. Strategie II: Peuples Mediterraneens (6465): 277–285.

PART I

Gendered, Ethno-Nationalist Struggles and Militarization

2

"Border Granny Wants You!"

Grandmothers Policing Nation at the US-Mexico Border

JENNIFER L. JOHNSON

Introduction

On a bright October day in the desert, a dozen ladies array themselves to be photographed along the skeleton of a fence that demarcates the sovereign territory of the United States of Mexico and that of the United States of America.[1] Dressed uniformly in pink camouflage T-shirts and tennis shoes, they call themselves the Granny Brigade and have come to this place at the behest of Minuteman organizers. In a moment they will link their arms, twist their hips, and raise their legs to strike a classic chorus-line pose for the photographer.

This chapter examines how grandmotherhood is performed at the US-Mexico border in service of the new nativist movement in the contemporary United States and the broader ethno-nationalist project to which it contributes.[2] Like the photograph described above, it makes visible what remains largely invisible to both scholars and activists concerned with the US-Mexico border, namely, how the work of women, especially older women, sustains this project to police the geopolitical, legal, and cultural boundaries of the nation. Through a case study of one active Minuteman chapter and its articulation with national efforts to reach out to women, it elucidates how this collective impulse to protect the border incorporates women in seemingly contradictory ways that nonetheless work together to reproduce hierarchies of power grounded in both race and gender. Indeed, women's work to keep new immigrants of color *outside* the boundaries of this imagined community we call nation appears inextricably tied to those women's own gendered subordination *within*.

For the purposes of this chapter, I conceptualize the nationalist project underway in the United States as an effort to more tightly control or police membership in our national community that is evident especially, but not exclusively, in societal angst over the place of immigrants of color in America today. Scholars of globalization have theorized that as state boundaries in many parts of the world have become extraordinarily permeable to capital, goods, and information flow, governing elites have crafted new forms of control and sovereignty over national territories and populations (Ong 2006; Sassen 1996). In the United States, immigration policy that criminalizes unauthorized border crossers but not the employers and consumers that benefit from the cheap labor they supply constitutes one way that these projects sustain economic globalization even as they intensify control over and selectively exclude certain populations. I posit that the metaphoric and literal policing of nation described in this chapter exemplifies how private citizens participate in these exclusionary projects by helping to discursively delineate the line between those newcomers who merit permanent inclusion in our national community and those who do not.

Scholars of the US-Mexico border and Latino immigration to the United States have made similar arguments that point to the heightened salience of national borders in the context of economic globalization. Joseph Nevins, for one, has elucidated what he calls "the growing 'gate-keeping' role played by states [that] entails simultaneously maximizing what dominant classes represent as the benefits of globalization, while protecting against what they frame as the detriments of increasing transnational flows—especially unauthorized migrants" (2010, 10). Today, this gate-keeping project is spearheaded by the state and manifest most directly in policies that tighten security at the US-Mexico border and criminalize undocumented immigration, but it has deep historical roots that date back at least to the acquisition by force of large swathes of Mexico in the nineteenth century and subsequent attempts to "Americanize" this territory.

As other chapters in this volume highlight, the complex and frequently violent history of nation-building at geographical peripheries shapes the nature of contemporary border politics and the variable significance of race and ethnicity in these politics. In the case of the United States' southern periphery, this history spans the nearly two hundred years since Anglo settlers, motivated by a belief in their Manifest Destiny and in some instances the intent to perpetuate slave-holding, began colonizing the Mexican territory that would become the states of Texas, California, New Mexico, Arizona, Colorado, Utah, Wyoming, and Kansas (Perea 2003). As data on the lynching of Mexicans and violence perpetrated by self-appointed agents of justice like the Texas Rangers indicate, these settlers policed the racial boundaries of an incipient national community well before and after the stroke of a pen marked the official boundary separating the United States from Mexico on the map (Acuña 2000; Carrigan 2004; Gordon 1999; Yoxall 2006). By the 1920s, however, the dominant expression of anxiety surrounding the place of Mexicans in the body politic had shifted from vigilante violence diffused throughout the Western states to a fixation with immigration focused geographically on the border and borderlands. In part, this concern responded to an uptick in border crossings from the south prompted by the turmoil of the 1910 Mexican Revolution and the earlier Chinese Exclusion Act that had rerouted Chinese immigration from Ellis Island to surreptitious entry by land. It also reflected, however, profoundly racist ideas fostered by the turn-of-the-century eugenics movement that associated Mexicans (and other immigrants of color) with dirt, disease and genetic degeneration (Stern 2005, 2004).

The link between these ideas and the imagining of Mexicans as outsiders to the nation strengthened with the passage of laws that at once legitimated national origins construed in racial terms as the legal basis for determining immigration and citizenship eligibility *and* assigned those who violated these statutes to the category of "illegal alien" (Chavez 2008a; Nevins 2010; Ngai 2004). The creation of the Border Patrol in 1924 and the unprecedented policing of Mexican border-crossers through Draconian measures such as quarantines and mass deportation reinforced this association between alleged racial inferiority, illegality, and Mexican national origin, even though Mexicans were technically exempt from the national origins quotas of the day. This history paved the way for the conflation of "Mexican" and "illegal" so central to immigration politics in the United States today and which lends plausibility to nativist claims that opposition to Mexican immigration is race-blind, motivated solely by a desire to uphold the law.

Moreover, these early developments established the physical space of the borderlands as a privileged site for the production and reproduction of meaning surrounding the place of Mexicans in the body politic. This is evident today in the way that social movements on both sides of the contemporary immigration debate embrace this space as a stage on which to enact competing visions of who belongs (or should belong) to the national community and on what basis. Pierrette Hondagneu-Sotelo has documented, for instance, how religiously-inspired immigrant rights activists mobilize annual vigils at the border fence that dramatize family separation caused by restrictive immigration policies to challenge notions of national inclusion and exclusion pinned to arbitrary distinctions such as country of birth (2008). Similarly, but for distinct ideological purposes, the Minutemen rally at the border fence to enact rituals drawing on historically-fraught images of an embattled frontier that frame Mexicans as intruders and perpetual outsiders, and private citizens—largely white, working-class, and male—as the legitimate gate-keepers of nation. Circulated widely by mass media, these rituals and images contribute to what Chavez calls a "spectacle of surveillance" that has very real consequences for how we as a nation construct the boundaries of belonging (2008a, b).

Existing studies of the Minuteman movement highlight how these performances are inflected by race, class and gender by focusing primarily on the actions, bodies, and sensibilities of *men* engaged in the quasi-militaristic activities associated with patrolling the border (Castro 2007/2008; Chavez 2008b; Doty 2009; Shapira 2013). Although the precise line of argument varies, these studies share the assumption—sometimes explicit, sometimes implicit—that the Minuteman movement responds to twin imperatives that have gained urgency in post-9/11 America: to bolster national security against a foreign enemy and to shore up white, working-, and middle-class masculinities threatened by economic globalization, multiculturalism, and the advances of feminism in the late twentieth century. Fewer studies have analyzed the actions, bodies, and sensibilities of women. Oliviero, however, has begun the task of interrogating how femininity factors into the Minutemen's show of militarized masculinity by examining the role of guns in

the construction of what she calls "armed femininity." Citing recruitment materials posted to the Minuteman Project's website that portray
women wielding firearms, she argues that "the gun becomes the symbol
through which these women can access normatively masculine spheres
of power, allowing them to transgress gendered boundaries enough to
participate in militarized imaginings of nation" (2011, 696).

This chapter explores how a different symbol and the identity it
connotes—grandmotherhood—enables women to participate in the
nationalist project promoted by the Minutemen, and how the gendered
nature of this project intersects with its racial/ethnic dimensions. Other
social movements have united women around the experience of grandmotherhood to protest the disappearance of family members by repressive authoritarian regimes (Arditti 1999) or to wage antiwar campaigns
(Kutz-Flamenbaum 2007; Narushima 2004; Roy 2007; Wile 2008). In
these cases, grandmotherhood as a frame that inspires collective action
and imbues it with the potential to effect change draws on the moral
authority that women claim as mothers, but also on assumptions about
the complacency and apolitical nature of old age. The politicized enactment of grandmotherhood, situated at this particular intersection of age
and gender, introduces an element of surprise into collective action that
differentiates it from movements that mobilize around motherhood.
Kutz-Flamenbaum describes this dynamic in the following terms: "Age-
ism and dominant gender norms construct the grandmother as a nice
old lady content with the domesticity of baking cookies and spoiling her
grandchildren dismissing the knowledge, wisdom, and skills that come
with many years of living. We do not expect grannies to be out protesting" (2007, 97). Nor, I would add, to be policing the US-Mexico border.

The intersectionality of grandmotherhood, however, extends beyond
its age and gender dimensions to include race and class, though the latter remain largely unmarked in the predominantly white, middle-class
movements cited above and in the Minutemen's deployment of grandmotherhood analyzed below.[3] To the extent that the image put into play
by these movements relies on connotations of full-time, stay-at-home
grandmotherhood dedicated to the superfluous tasks of baking cookies
and spoiling children, it ignores the experiences of working class grandmothers and grandmothers of color burdened with providing for the
essential material needs of family well into old age and often through

sustained employment outside the home. Mary Romero has shown how the nativist movement in the United States, through organizations like the Arizona-based Mothers Against Illegal Aliens, capitalizes on these unmarked differences by framing opposition to immigration as a native-born mother's duty to protect her family from the myriad threats posed by dark-skinned immigrants, especially the dangers presented by unfit mothers. The rhetorical move she identifies hinges on impugning immigrant women by measuring them against impossible standards of "ideal" motherhood grounded in the privileged experience of white, middle-class women (2008).

Romero's findings on the uses of motherhood to mobilize women for racially and ethnically exclusionary agendas resonate strongly with broader insights gleaned from feminist scholars of nationalism attentive to intersectionality. These scholars note that women have long been marginalized but not absent from racially and ethnically exclusive projects, even though mainstream theorists of nationalism have typically not taken them into account (Hogan 2009; Yuval-Davis and Anthias 1989; Wilford and Miller 1998). They have also observed, however, that notwithstanding some cross-national and historical variation, nationalist discourses have proven remarkably and consistently patriarchal, subordinating women to men as a means of achieving exclusion on the basis of race-ethnicity. In practice, this has manifested as an emphasis on wives and mothers who accomplish the work of the nation as biological reproducers who uphold ethnic and racial homogeneity as well as transmit cultural markers that define the dominant in-group (Albanese 2006; Brennan 2008; Koven and Michel 1993; Yuval-Davis and Anthias 1989).

Although motherhood—and by extension, grandmotherhood—as a mobilizing frame clearly has the potential to unite women across ethnic and racial lines, chapters in this volume on border politics raise the question of whether and how the dynamics of territorially-grounded social movements and struggles attenuate this possibility. As McDuie-Ra (chapter 4) brings to light in his case study of ethnic minorities in the India-Burma borderlands, motherhood may be a powerful means of enabling women to act collectively and to do so across ethnic boundaries by drawing on gendered commonalities and subsuming ethnic differences. In the context of competing territorial claims that unfold in borderlands, however, motherhood may lose its ability to bridge ethnic divides even among women who have overcome these differences under other circumstances. Applied to the polarized politics of immigration in the contemporary United States, McDuie-Ra's insights beg the question of how the long history of conflict surrounding the US-Mexico border weights the uses of motherhood and grandmotherhood toward collectively underscoring rather than undercutting racial and ethnic divides as criteria for inclusion in the nation.

To shed light on these issues, this chapter analyzes two moments of Minuteman activism in which women are integrally involved. The first is the mobilization of Operation Granny Brigade 2007, a recruitment campaign-cum-publicity stunt orchestrated from the Arizona headquarters of the Minuteman Civil Defense Corps (MCDC). The MCDC is one of two organizations that planned and executed the debut of the Minuteman movement in 2005, though it disbanded officially in 2010 in the wake of several high-profile controversies.[4] Through Operation Granny Brigade, the MCDC attempted to publicly construct grandmothers as uniquely patriotic subjects and to marshal grandmotherhood as a resource to enhance the movement's stock of political capital. It did so by staging grandmotherhood in defense of nation at the US-Mexico border.

The second moment of activism I describe is the enactment of grandmotherhood at the border nearly three years after Operation Granny Brigade in 2007. Drawing on ethnographic fieldwork with a Minuteman chapter that had participated in Operation Granny Brigade 2007, I contrast the glorification of "border grannies" during public spectacle with the ordinary and understated work that border grannies do during the chapter's monthly border gatherings. During these "musters," volunteers physically patrol border areas and report unauthorized crossings to the Border Patrol. Although Minutemen engage in a variety of activities ranging from protests at day labor recruitment centers to fundraising campaigns to build or repair border fencing, these musters constitute the symbolic core of Minuteman activism. Examining the gendered division of labor that unfolds during these musters is, therefore, crucial to understanding women's position and power within the movement.

Methods

This chapter is grounded in archival data downloaded from the Internet and ethnographic data gathered during the early stages of an ongoing study of women's participation in anti-immigration activism. The Internet research for this project began in 2008 when a keyword search ("Minuteman Civil Defense Corps") of a newspaper database returned a *Washington Times* piece entitled "Grannies on Patrol: Women Help Lead Minuteman Border Vigil" (Seper 2005). A Google search for "grannies," "borders," and "Minutemen" subsequently generated dozens of Internet newspaper articles, blog posts, and discussion board comments referencing Operation Granny Brigade 2007. Most of this commentary was posted to the main MCDC website under announcements of upcoming border operations or as threads comprising the Border Granny discussion board. I also came across a photo gallery documenting the event under a separate URL.[5]

Intrigued by possibilities these materials raised about women's participation in the Minutemen, in July 2010 I initiated an ethnographic study of one local chapter in a border state that continues to spearhead regular border patrols years after the formal dissolution of the MCDC. At the time of writing this chapter, this fieldwork consisted of participant observation at five of the border gatherings or musters that took place over long weekends once each month between July 2010 and December 2011. For each muster I attended, I spent anywhere from three to five days and nights in constant interaction with members who also travel—sometimes long distances from other parts of the state—to attend these events at their base camp located just miles from the international border. During this time I spent upward of 300 hours conducting ride-alongs with Minutemen gathering "intel" by day and executing surveillance "operations" by night, combing trails on foot for evidence of recent smuggling activity, target shooting at a makeshift range, shopping for and preparing camp meals, or accompanying members for dinner out and some gambling at the nearest Indian casino. Though I am not registered as a member, I currently receive electronic newsletters from this chapter and a few members have included me on e-mail distribution lists to which they forward political and sometimes personal items of interest with some regularity.

On average, eighteen card-carrying Minutemen attended each muster, and no more than a quarter of these were ever women. Two of these women were regular attendees and, as I learned, had donned pink camouflage for Operation Granny Brigade in 2007. Others attended musters more sporadically to take advantage of a specific training course (e.g., an NRA basic pistol skills certification), guest speaker, or commemorative event. Typically, these women were younger than the stable membership, and their demeanor and routines contrasted sharply with those of other Minutewomen. Though ostensibly welcome within the ranks of this chapter, their presence occasionally served as a breach experiment of sorts, generating rich data on the supposedly normative behaviors of "proper" Minutemen and women. Together, these ethnographic data trace the gendered contours of everyday and out-of-sight Minuteman activism. It is only against the backdrop of these relatively invisible routines that the hypervisibility of the "granny brigades" described below can be fully understood.

"Border Granny Wants You!": The Spectacle of Operation Granny Brigade

"If you want to do something about the illegal alien crisis, diseases that affect our children and grandchildren, food that is unsafe and on and on and on," ran the post that caught my eye, "volunteer to come to the border in October. We will be running a line just for grannies on a yet to be determined Saturday afternoon. We will train you and give you a free T-shirt to boot."[6] I had been combing the "Border Granny—On the Border" discussion board on the Minuteman Civil Defense Corps (MCDC) website when a thread entitled "Border Granny Wants You!" initiated by none other than Border Granny herself scrolled across my screen. I knew that appeals for volunteers to put in time at the border appeared frequently on the MCDC site. I also knew that the image of Uncle Sam beckoning "I WANT YOU as a MINUTEMAN VOLUNTEER to SECURE the US BORDER" was readily employed by the MCDC website, so Border Granny's use of this trope was not unusual. Still, I wondered, why grandmothers? And why "grannies" at that?

My Internet archive of running commentary posted to this discussion board before, during and after Operation Granny Brigade 2007 helped me answer this question. MCDC organizers officially announced Operation Granny Brigade on the main website where they confirmed that the outfit would indeed run "lines just for grannies" in multiple border states on the weekend of October 6. In addition to providing practical advice for first-timers (bring "sunblock, snacks, and good sturdy shoes") and disclaimers about firearms ("many of the ladies have concealed weapons permits [but] not all volunteers carry firearms"), this announcement promised "a day you will remember for the rest of your life." It was, after all, "your opportunity to let our government and the American people who are sitting on the sidelines know you will secure our country if they will not." From the perspective of the planners at MCDC headquarters, at least, Operation Granny Brigade would be the opportunity of a lifetime to perform patriotism not only for an apathetic American citizenry, but for Uncle Sam himself.

This intention became even clearer when it was challenged in the course of preparations leading up to the big day. As plans for Operation Granny Brigade progressed, some objections bubbled to the surface in discussion board exchanges. One participant questioned the use of the label granny and pink camouflage T-shirts. Border Granny, the mastermind of Operation Granny Brigade and most authoritative voice in these exchanges, clarified: "The object is to get women to the border and to promote the issue of securing the border with women when the government refuses to do it." To the Minuteman who had conveyed his wife's concerns to the discussion board on her behalf, Border Granny went on to explain: "I am an old hard-core feminist also and appreciate your wife's opinions but I am also proudly a grandmother and feel it is my duty to protect my family." She ended her rebuttal with a rhetorical question that in the original post tellingly lacked a question mark: "The family issue overrides the feminist issue, doesn't it?" Other discussion board participants, like one who self-identified as a "patriotic army mom," weighed in on the debate: "I agree with you, Border Granny! If I didn't have an 11- and 12-year-old, this old lady would be there all the time." Ultimately, the lone voice of dissent was deleted from the Internet record by its author with a simple note marking its place: "Removed by poster, missed the point."

From the perspective of Border Granny, one point that this poster had missed was that women who are proudly grandmothers must put family first. Family, after all, trumps feminism. This is so even or perhaps especially when protecting one's family requires acts that violate women's claims to equality or provoke a loss of dignity. Plausibly, parading along the border fence in pink camouflage for the media might constitute one such humiliating, thus sacrificial, act. Another point that merited repetition, however, was the value of this performance of grandmothers putting family first as a rhetorical weapon in the political battle for stricter immigration controls.

This second point was hammered home in the virtual trail of photographs and congratulatory remarks that materialized in the wake of the event. The same Minuteman who had voiced his wife's reservations during the planning stages trumpeted the success of Operation Granny Brigade. "Here are some pictures from our outing to Anderson Valley," he wrote in a post uploaded the day after the festivities had wound down. "We shut down the entire valley . . . from illegal traffic . . . !" he continued. "And who did it? This bunch of wild women!" He ended his post in bigger and bolder font: "Hey Mr. Bush, even our grannies can do it, why can't you?"

The photographs uploaded included a portrait of border grannies in pink posed against a larger than life American flag. Another discussion board participant quipped that they had "'dressed' up the neighborhood quite a bit" (though none of the women in the photos I glimpsed wore dresses). Even skeptics lauded the grannies for being at the border. "I may disagree with some people at MCDC," Hell-on-Wheels from New Mexico commented, "but the Granny Brigade is just too cool . . . I can just imagine some macho type or better yet a Muslim male getting busted by ladies in pink camo."

Why grandmothers, then? This commentary suggests that Minutemen positioned grandmothers—nay, "grannies"—on the border because flaunting their presumed powerlessness made a spectacle of the cowardliness of their enemies—"macho types" conspiring to subvert the sovereignty of the United States by violating its territorial borders, "Muslim males," and even, if not especially, "Mr. Bush." Predicated on hypervisibility rather than on stealth, these grannies policed nation symbolically, not tactically. In stark contrast to the covert nightly border patrols that I would observe during fieldwork, the latter donned pink camo in broad daylight for a single afternoon to perform the moral strength but physical frailty of grandmothers. This exception to what policing the border constituted for Minutemen under ordinary circumstances worked to manufacture a symbolic exception that proves the rule that those who could and should protect America's border—government officials—were derelict in their duty. Indeed, the granny brigades arguably extended the Minutemen's broader strategy of illustrating how ordinary citizens can and will do the job the government won't do to its logical extreme by demonstrating that even the weakest of the weak could and would do the job: "Hey Mr. Bush, even our grannies can do it, why can't you?"

Of the several women cast in the role of border granny in 2007, I would meet two nearly three years later—Liz and Millie—during fieldwork with a Minuteman outfit on the border. At first blush, neither fit the stereotypical image that the term "granny" conjures up. Indeed, neither were even grandmothers in the strictest sense of the word, having borne no biological children of their own. Liz, a widow and retiree who appeared to be in her seventies, explained that she had adopted children early in life so that she could be a grandmother, and now had eight grandchildren, though she rarely referred to them in our informal conversations at camp. Millie, a divorcée and clerical worker for a municipal water treatment facility, had no children of her own but—in contrast to Liz—spoke often and at length of her nieces and nephews and their children, and proudly considered herself to be "the favorite aunt."

The ethnography below explores how women like Liz and Millie negotiate the highly gendered terrain of Minuteman activism at the border. It begins by detailing how Minutemen—especially male Minutemen—mark the borderlands as distinctly masculine, then describes how Minutewomen create activist spaces of their own within this environment. Ultimately, I argue, the gendered division of labor that operates renders women's work both invisible and indispensable in an exact mirror image of the hypervisible and seemingly frivolous granny brigades.

Performing the Perils of the Border

"Welcome to BFE." When I arrived at camp for the first time, I found Jim lounging on the back patio of the low-lying building that serves as the camp's common area with a cigarette dangling between his fingers. As the contact who had vetted my request to visit on this occasion, Jim would be in charge of initiating me into the ways of Minuteman musters. Already, he had laid down some of the rules during the phone calls and e-mail exchanges that preceded this visit: tan, olive, and beige clothes only; no colors that attracted attention. No camouflage, long guns, or Confederate flags. Beware of rattlesnakes. Now, as I approached Jim in person, he greeted me with a handshake, a few pleasantries, and "welcome to BFE." Smiling wryly, he added, "Butt-fucking Egypt."

Although not every Minuteman I came to know during this visit and future ones employed such colorful language, most welcomed me into their world by warning me in so many words that I had ventured far beyond the bounds of civilization into a desolate and dangerous no-man's land that they were fighting to reclaim. "Hostile territory" is the term Tony preferred and invoked repeatedly as he and Pete introduced me to the contours of this desert wasteland later that afternoon from the safety of Pete's air-conditioned, four-wheel drive jeep. The jeep wound up a rutted dirt road that would have been inaccessible to a less intrepid driver until we reached a lookout point that revealed a great expanse of the border. Miles of new and formidable-looking border fencing snaked across the landscape below for as far as the eye could see. We disembarked at the summit and Pete beckoned for me to follow as he started up then down a steeply inclined trail that veered away from the paved road. I concentrated on staying upright as the gravelly path gave way under me feet, but Pete—an aging Vietnam veteran with a heart condition—scaled the slope effortlessly. As he did, he lectured me on the dangers of traversing this terrain. There were the very real risks of dehydration and heat exhaustion, of course, not to mention rattlesnakes. And then there were the coyotes—"the two-legged kind," he clarified.

As if to illustrate the power of this uniquely human predator, when we returned to the jeep, Pete headed straight to a place in the valley below where the border fence ended abruptly. Makeshift fencing— barbed wire, boulders, and a low-lying auto barrier of railroad ties and metal tubing to obstruct vehicular traffic—took its place. Here, the sandy road running along the modern fence turned to rocks and scrub, so we were free to roam this area on foot without concern for disturbing Border Patrol efforts to "cut sign" of unauthorized border crossers in the sand. Lest the hostility of the borderlands be lost on me, Pete led me to a stick planted in front of the auto barrier. On this stick, he claimed, Minutemen had found a pair of bloodied underwear belonging to a coyote's rape victim. Coyotes—slang for guides paid large sums to lead unauthorized individuals across the border—collected and displayed these "trophies" on "rape trees" all along the border, Pete alleged. He added that Minutemen had even found backpacks full of these trophies. Pete ended this cautionary tale by pointing to the hills in front of us and recounting how one Minuteman patrol had listened on at night as a woman on the other side of the border was being raped. They had wanted to intervene, but Border Patrol forbade them. My blood ran cold at the thought.

While Pete and Tony escorted me through this borderlands house of horrors, other Minutemen that afternoon teamed up to conduct reconnaissance missions for signs of recent smuggling activity. When we returned to camp, we learned that in addition to the usual fresh footprints, broken-down brush, and trash of obviously recent vintage, one such recon team had come across a shrine to Jesús Malverde, the patron saint of drug dealers, replete with candles and offerings of water that had not yet evaporated. The camp buzzed with excitement and a few volunteers planned to return to the site to take photographs even though it was located across the US border a short distance into Mexico. When I asked to go along, Jim vehemently vetoed the idea, growing red-faced and visibly agitated. "No woman is going to be raped on my watch," he exclaimed.

At the end of the day, both literally and figuratively, I began to wonder about the meaning of these interactions with Jim, Pete, and Tony. It occurred to me that these men had not simply given me a tour of the US-Mexico border during my first field experience with the Minutemen. They had also schooled me—visually, verbally, and emotionally—in the dangers that they confronted as Minutemen, the extraordinary vulnerability of women's bodies to these dangers, and the burdens they shouldered protecting women—their own and ostensibly others'—from these threats. Interrogating my response of apprehension and submission to Jim's emotionally charged prohibition to return to the border, it also struck me that I had experienced in a small but visceral way how this performance of the perils at the border might discipline even relatively privileged women like myself by circumscribing their movement in both physical space and the social space of anti-immigration activism.

I returned home to the Midwest still speculating about the rhetoric and reality of rape trees. Genuinely disturbed about the possibility that they actually existed but also intellectually curious about the power of this discourse to structure Minuteman activism in highly gendered ways, I searched for more information. My search turned up a pair of scholarly articles on the rape of women border crossers at the hands of US Border Patrol agents and "racist vigilantes" (Falcón 2006, 119; 2001), but I could not locate a single academic reference to "rape trees." An essay circulating in the conservative blogosphere, however, shed further light on the rape tree discourse and its articulation with the broader nationalist project in which the Minutemen are implicated. In "The Botany of Illegal Immigration," Mike Vanderboegh writes:

> There is a new kind of tree growing out west . . . In an era of free trade agreements . . . they represent a new Mexican export to the United States. They are called "rape trees" and they bear a strange kind of fruit. Panties. Yes, panties . . . After the coyotes get the women across the border, safely on US soil, they gang rape them to show they have total control over them. They hang their panties in the trees as signs of conquest . . . George W. Bush, an otherwise decent man, has done nothing about these evil arboretums because he would have to offend . . . all the fat-cat American businessmen who kick in to the GOP party coffers a portion of the profits they glean from an eminently exploitable illegal workforce. Watered by the blood of innocents, fertilized with crazed machismo and Yanqui political indifference, the rape trees continue to blossom along our border . . . For any decent, law-abiding American, to see a rape tree is to gaze upon the face of the enemy of civilization. (2005, n.p.)

It was precisely because of rape trees, Vanderboegh claimed, that he would be participating in the next big Minuteman vigil.

Thus, rape tree discourse marked violence in the borderlands as distinctly male and Mexican, the product of economic globalization left unchecked by corrupted political leaders—the very same leaders that ostensibly delegated border security to grandmothers. It also framed all women—even unauthorized Mexican migrant women—as innocents in need of protection and elevated Minutemen to the status of the guardians of civilization. My thoughts turned to Liz and Millie. What place might these women have on the frontlines of this epic battle?

A Camp of Her Own

It wasn't until she had turned off the headlights of her vehicle, locked the doors, and carefully covered the dashboard lights with the stuffed monkey that usually hung from the rearview mirror that Liz loaded her weapon. Staked out at the edge of the private campground the Minutemen rented from a local entrepreneur, Liz and I were preparing to do "site security." Music from an adjacent campsite wafted in through my rolled down window and the porch lights from a home perched just above the main highway that ran parallel to the Minuteman site turned on as dusk fell. Located in a relatively populated area miles from the border proper, the spot we would be watching lay well off the beaten paths that coyotes used to smuggle their cargo—human and otherwise—into the United States from Mexico. Border-crossers who had been separated from their coyotes, however, had been known to wander into the Minuteman camp in search of aid (which Minutemen claim they gladly provide in the form of water, granola bars, and a call to the Border Patrol). Other stragglers traversed the campsite at night as they made their way to the Indian casino rumored to be a pick-up point on their journey inland and whose lights shone like a beacon on a hill in the distance. Liz and I—and Millie and Gretchen parked in another vehicle just a few hundred feet away—were to secure the perimeter of the Minuteman campground from these unwanted guests.

The four of us—the only women present at this month's muster—had been assigned to camp security during the strategy meeting held after dinner where Pete and Tony divvied up tasks for this evening's patrols. During the weeks leading up to this field visit, I had worried about how I would cope with walking the border at night in the company of Minutemen—How would I keep up? What would I do if we encountered border-crossers? Would I speak up if I objected to their treatment of defenseless migrants?—but this turned out to be a moot point because "border ops" was not the domain of women. Liz did not even attend the meeting where volunteers were slotted into teams to take four-hour shifts patrolling clandestine spots at the border and to man the two-way radio system back at base. Before the meeting, though, she had offered to take me to do site security if I wished to get out in the field before my visit was over.

We now found ourselves taking turns peering through Liz's night vision scope in search of movement in the surrounding brush. To pass the time, Liz recounted how she had spent her entire career as an expert tracker for mountain search and rescue missions, including a stint in Antarctica. Most recently she had been employed by the sheriff's office of a large metropolitan county. Unhappily married for most of her life to a man whom she described as mean and miserly, Liz was now happily widowed with eight grandchildren from two adopted children she had raised. She currently shared her home in the northern part of the state with a sister and a disabled nephew, but spent two weeks every month at her home away from home with the Minutemen.

I had begun to get to know Liz earlier that day as she cooked breakfast (then dinner) for the eighteen Minutemen and two guests who had turned up for this month's muster. When I volunteered to help, she set me to work opening cans, washing produce, and stirring scrambled eggs as she fretted over the quality and quantity of the food she was preparing. Would the eggs be overcooked? Should she add more milk? Would there be enough? Too much? In the evening as she made dinner, she carried on a running commentary about grocery shopping that afternoon—where she had gone, what was on sale, what she couldn't find that she needed and what she would substitute in its stead. Singlehandedly responsible for grocery shopping, cooking, and cleaning up after meals, Liz clearly had a lot on her mind.

Now, in the front seat of her sea green SUV that blended perfectly into the desertscape at dusk, the irony began to sink in. With her extensive background in law enforcement, Liz struck me as one of the best trained yet least utilized volunteers that this group of Minutemen could mobilize for border ops. However, as ostensibly less qualified men—an air purification systems salesman, a retired magazine editor, an enfeebled World War II veteran—took up their positions on the frontlines of the Minutemen's battle at the border, Liz found herself playing hostess to me. I recalled now how she had met me at the door to the Minuteman lodge upon my arrival, directed me to sign in, and collected fees for room and board. She had then planted herself in front of a laptop to continue working on the organization's monthly newsletter that needed to be sent out "pronto," but not before offering me hot coffee and snacks. Tomorrow, she noted, she would need to update the organization's volunteer database to include me and the girlfriend who had accompanied me.

With her mental and physical energies channeled continually into keeping campers well-fed, guests feeling welcomed, and the organizational apparatus humming along, it was no wonder that Liz was ready to turn in well before our 8:00 p.m. to 1:00 a.m. shift was over. My head ached from the unaccustomed strain of using the night vision scope, so I was happy to oblige. We returned to base by 10:30 having spotted nothing more out of the ordinary than jackrabbits foraging in the brush.

Of the eighteen card-carrying Minutemen who turned up for that monthly muster, Liz and Millie were the only women and they were not the wives of Minutemen. Most of the male Minutemen men I spoke with were married but had left their wives at home for the weekend, and they seemed surprised that I would find this unusual. Mitch stated bluntly that "the wife" had stayed home to shampoo the carpets and another explained that his wife no longer came due to health concerns. For the rest, the question didn't quite seem to register. Liz and Millie had their own ideas about why Minutemen wives avoided the border. With a lifetime of service in law enforcement, Liz was used to being the only woman among many men, but she surmised that most women were not. Millie was less charitable. Though she personally liked many of the wives of the Minutemen she volunteered with, she disdained the fact that they permitted their men to "play soldier" by themselves at camp on the weekends. Distinctive in many respects, Liz and Millie nonetheless shared a certain attenuated relationship to immediate family that may have contributed to their willingness and ability to serve as Minuteman volunteers at the border for extended periods of time.

And Operation Granny Brigade 2007? Try as I might to prod Liz and Millie into reminiscing about this momentous occasion and opportunity of a lifetime to prove a political point, neither recalled more than a good time with family and friends. Liz, perhaps predictably, wondered what had happened to the rest of those pink camouflage T-shirts and vowed to look for them when she could find a free moment, in case I wanted one as a souvenir. Framed photographs of the event that hung on the walls of the lodge testified to the fact that a good time had indeed been had by all, including the men. Next to the photo of the Minutewomen in pink camouflage described at the beginning of this chapter, I gazed upon a photo of the men—minus the pink camoflauge, of course—posed in a chorus line against the border fences as well. Apparently, these Minutemen had more of a sense of humor than the event planners at MCDC headquarters had anticipated.

Discussion: Grandmothers and Nationhood

> As long as the family is intact in structure and function, grandparents live on the fringes of group activity. They stand ready to intervene as first and last aid as soon as the framework of the group is flagging or breaking up. Grandparents, and especially the grandmother, reassume a sociological function the moment a gap has to be filled.
> —Hans von Hentig, "The Sociological Function of the Grandmother"

The empirical analysis developed in this chapter suggests that women like Liz and Millie together with their male counterparts enact womanhood and, indeed, grandmotherhood in seemingly contradictory ways. Participants in highly scripted public events orchestrated for the media, these women become complicit in an ideological battle designed to leverage political support for closed geopolitical borders. They serve, in this capacity, as symbolic capital in a war of words and images that indicts elected leaders, policymakers, and the American public for ostensibly turning a blind eye to the perils of undocumented immigration. In this regard, they contribute to the Minutemen's overarching goal of fueling a moral panic about immigration in our nation today and pressing for restrictive immigration controls. Beyond deploying grandmotherhood for these immediate strategic ends, spectacles like Operation Granny Brigade may also help define and redefine the boundaries of the nation. As Chavez writes, "media spectacles are productive acts that construct knowledge about subjects in our world. This is particularly the case for how we internalize who we are as a people" (2008a, 5).

Apart from these moments of high drama, however, the Minute-women described in this chapter carved out more pragmatic spaces of their own at the Minuteman camp and in the movement as a whole. As cooks, clerical workers, hostesses, and friends, they assumed the mundane tasks that ensured the material and psychological reproduction of this movement. By willingly confining their activism to these quasi-private spaces on an everyday basis, they also contributed to the ideological reproduction of Minutemen and men more generally as guardians of female innocents and the properly masculine protectors of nation.

What do these enactments of grandmotherhood—one very much front-stage and the other largely backstage—reveal about gender, power, and the policing of national identity? For one, they point to a relatively understudied way in which women participate in nationalist projects that is not tied directly to their sexuality or reproductive capacity, but that may gain traction in contemporary times. Although grounded in a single case study, the research presented here raises the possibility that in aging and affluent nations with a downwardly mobile middle class and high levels of immigration from the global South, grandmotherhood may gain saliency as a mobilizing frame that unites native-born women in opposition to newcomers and elevates them to the status of symbolic gate-keepers of nation. In the contemporary United States, an unusually large and disproportionately white baby boomer generation is on the cusp of entering the realm of potential grandparenthood and the younger generations replenishing it consist increasingly of immigrants of color. These conditions coupled with the weight of US-Mexico border history help explain the apparent anomaly of grandmothers policing nation at the US-Mexico border.

The quote that opens this discussion suggests another possible explanation. Feminist theorists of nationalism have observed that the making of nations is almost always intimately intertwined with the achievement of masculinity (Nagel 1998) and that nations are frequently conceived of metaphorically as a traditional patriarchal family (McClintock 1993). Within this schema, men are the architects in the construction of nation and the heads of the national family, and women "occupy an important symbolic place as the mothers of the nation" (Nagel 1998, 254). Written in

1946, in the wake of a world war that had eviscerated male-headed households through the prolonged absence, disability, and death of a generation of fathers, von Hentig's analysis of the sociological function of grandmotherhood posits that in times of crisis, grandmothers "stand ready to intervene as first and last aid as soon as the framework of the group is flagging or breaking up" (1946, 389). Extended to the metaphorical national family, this observation yields a curious proposition that merits further investigation. Could it be that be that border grannies lend first and last aid to the racially and ethnically exclusive national family that they perceive to be flagging or breaking up under the forces of globalization?

Although scholars have documented the rise, media savvy, and political import of the Minuteman branch of the new nativist movement, few have yet to place women, much less grandmothers, at the center of analysis. This tendency to downplay the work of women in the Minuteman movement characterizes scholarship on the new nativist movement more broadly. If knowledge is power, then scholars who seek to combat the prejudices perpetuated by the anti-illegal immigration movement do ourselves a disservice by neglecting the systematic study of women active in these campaigns. This chapter begins to address that gap by demonstrating how the performance of grandmotherhood is an integral component of the Minuteman's border policing movement.

NOTES

1. I would like to thank Jennifer Bickham Méndez and anonymous reviewers for their comments on earlier drafts of this chapter.

2. As I have noted elsewhere (Johnson 2011), the phenomenon referred to as the new nativist movement (Burghart, Ward and Zeskind 2007; Jacobson 2008; Jaret 1999; Perea 1997) took root in the late 1970s and 1980s as a response to the changing demographics of immigration spurred by the 1965 Immigration and Naturalization Act that opened legal avenues for greater numbers of Asian and Latin American newcomers. Initially, the movement operated as a highly professionalized political lobby aimed at legislative reform but a series of significant defeats in the 1990s fractured this coalition. The most salient of these failures was the Save Our State campaign that put Proposition 187 before Californians in 1994. Although Proposition 187 mobilized unprecedented popular support for restrictivist measures such as eliminating access to public education for undocumented immigrants, it was ultimately declared unconstitutional by California's Supreme Court. The nativist vitriol and disillusionment with politics that this Pyrrhic victory generated became the impetus for more militant expressions of anti-immigration sentiment (Jacobson

2008; Ono and Sloop 2002). The Minutemen's debut in 2005 captured this outpouring of grassroots dissent and did so in an extremely mediagenic fashion. A number of ad hoc civilian border patrol organizations had existed prior to 2005, and some of these—like Glenn Spencer's American Patrol—had openly peddled racist anti-immigrant rhetoric (Vina et. al. 2007). The Minutemen, however, brought national attention to these efforts, expanded their ranks to include more and more diverse elements, and succeeded in framing their actions as those of ordinary, law-abiding Americans fed up with ineffectual government and willing to step in to do a job the government had been unable to do (Doty 2009; Juffer 2006).

3. I would like to thank an anonymous reviewer for bringing this observation to my attention.

4. These included accusations of financial impropriety, the emotional instability and flamboyancy of MCDC leader Chris Simcox, and a home invasion and homicide prosecution (and subsequent capital conviction) of former MCDC member Shawna Forde.

5. All of these data were accessed on July 8, 2008 with the exception of the photo gallery accessed on November 25, 2009.

6. Unless otherwise noted, all place names, individual names, and Internet user-names or avatars that I employ in this chapter are pseudonyms. Although discussions posted to the MCDC board were accessible to anyone with Internet access and legally form part of the public domain, the tone and content of theses posts suggest that not all users understood this space as public. I generally use pseudonyms, therefore, to honor this expectation of privacy and to afford deniability to individuals identified in this research.

REFERENCES

Acuña, Rodolfo. 2000. *Occupied America: A History of Chicanos*, 4th Edition. New York: Longman.

Albanese, Patrizia. 2006. *Mothers of the Nation: Women, Families and Nationalism in Twentieth Century Europe*. Toronto: University of Toronto Press.

Arditti, Rita. 1999. *Searching for Life: The Grandmothers of the Plaza de Mayo and the Disappeared Children of Argentina*. Berkeley: University of California Press.

Brennan, Mary C. 2008. *Wives, Mothers and the Red Menace: Conservative Women and the Crusade Against Communism*. Boulder: University Press of Colorado.

Burghart, Devin, E. Ward, and Leonard Zeskind. 2007. *Nativism in the House*. Chicago: Center for New Community.

Carrigan, William D. 2004. *The Making of a Lynching Culture: Violence and Vigilantism in Central Texas, 1836–1916*. Urbana: University of Illinois Press.

Castro, Robert F. 2007/2008. Busting the Bandito Boyz: Militarism, Masculinity, and the Hunting of Undocumented Persons in the U.S.-Mexico Borderlands. *Journal of Hate Studies* 6(7): 7–30.

Chavez, Leo R. 2008a. *The Latino Threat: Constructing Immigrants, Citizens, and the Nation*. Stanford: Stanford University Press.

———. 2008b. Spectacle in the Desert: The Minuteman Project of the U.S.-Mexico Border. In *Global Vigilantes*, edited by David Pratten and Atreyee Sen, 25–46. New York: Columbia University Press.

———. 2001. *Covering Immigration: Popular Images and the Politics of the Nation*. Berkeley: University of California Press.

Doty, Roxanne Lynn. 2009. *The Law Into Their Own Hands: Immigration and the Politics of Exceptionalism*. Tucson: University of Arizona Press.

Dove, April Lee. 2010. Framing Illegal Immigration at the U.S.-Mexico Border: Anti-Illegal Immigration Groups and the Importance of Place in Framing. In *Research in Social Movements, Conflict and Change* Vol. 30, edited by Patrick Coy, 199–235. Bingley, UK: Emerald Books.

Falcón, Sylvanna. 2006. "National Security" and the Violation of Women: Militarized Border Rape at the U.S.-Mexico Border. In *Color of Violence: The INCITE! Anthology*, edited by INCITE! Women of Color against Violence, 119–29. Cambridge: South End Press.

———. 2001. Rape as a Weapon of War: Advancing Human Rights for Women at the U.S.-Mexico Border. *Social Justice* 28(2): 31–50.

Gordon, Linda. 1999. *The Great Arizona Orphan Abduction*. Cambridge, MA: Harvard University Press.

Hogan, Jackie. 2009. *Gender, Race and National Identity: Nations of Flesh and Blood*. New York: Routledge.

Hondagneu-Sotelo, Pierrette. 2008. *God's Heart Has No Borders: How Religious Activists Are Working for Immigrant Rights*. Berkeley: University of California Press.

Jacobson, Robin Dale. 2008. *The New Nativism: Proposition 187 and the Debate over Immigration*. Minneapolis: University of Minnesota Press.

Jaret, Charles. 1999. Troubled by Newcomers: Anti-Immigrant Attitudes and Action during Two Eras of Mass Immigration to the United States. *Journal of American Ethnic History* Spring 1999: 9–39.

Johnson, Jennifer L. 2011. Mobilizing Minutewomen: Gender, Cyberpower, and the New Nativist Movement. In *Critical Aspects of Gender in Conflict Resolution, Peacebuilding, and Social Movements (Research in Social Movements, Conflicts and Change 32)*, edited by Anna Snyder and Stephanie Stobbe, 137–61. Bingley, UK: Emerald Books.

Juffer, Jane. 2006. Introduction. *South Atlantic Quarterly* 105(4): 663–80.

Koven, Seth, and Sonya Michel, eds. 1993. *Mothers of a New World: Maternalist Politics and the Origins of the Welfare State*. New York: Routledge.

Kutz-Flamenbaum, Rachel V. 2007. Code Pink, Raging Grannies, and the Missile Dick Chicks: Feminist Performance Activism in the Contemporary Anti-War Movement. *NSWA Journal* 19(1): 89–105.

Larsen, Solana. 2007. The Anti-Immigration Movement: From Shovels to Suits. *NACLA Report of the Americas*, May/June 2007: 14–8.

Levario, Miguel Antonio. 2012. *Militarizing the Border: When Mexicans Became the Enemy*. College Station: Texas A&M University Press.

McClintock, Anne. 1993. Family Feuds: Gender, Nationalism and the Family. *Feminist Review* 44 (Summer 1993): 61–80.

Nagel, Joane. 1998. Masculinity and Nationalism: Gender and Sexuality in the Making of Nations. *Ethnic and Racial Studies* 21(2): 242–69.

Narushima, Miya. 2004. A Gaggle of Raging Grannies: The Empowerment of Older Canadian Women through Social Activism. *International Journal of Lifelong Education* 23(1): 23–42.

Nevins, Joseph. 2010. *Operation Gatekeeper and Beyond: The War on "Illegals" and the Remaking of the U.S.-Mexico Boundary*. New York: Routledge.

Newton, Lina. 2008. *Illegal, Alien, or Immigrant: The Politics of Immigration Reform*. New York: New York University Press.

Ngai, Mae M. 2004. *Impossible Subjects: Illegal Aliens and the Making of Modern America*. Princeton, NJ: Princeton University Press.

Oliviero, Katie E. 2011. Sensational Nation and the Minutemen: Gendered Citizenship and Moral Vulnerabilities. *Signs: Journal of Women in Culture and Society* 36(3): 679–706.

Ong, Aihwa. 2006. *Neoliberalism as Exception: Mutations in Citizenship and Sovereignty*. Durham, NC: Duke University Press.

Ono, Kent A., and J. M. Sloop. 2002. *Shifting Borders: Rhetoric, Immigration and California's Proposition 187*. Philadelphia: Temple University Press.

Perea, Juan F. 2003. A Brief History of Race and the U.S.-Mexican Border: Tracing the Trajectories of Conquest. *UCLA Law Review* 51 (October): 283–312.

———, ed. 1997. *Immigrants Out! The New Nativism and the Anti-Immigrant Impulse in the United States*. New York: New York University Press.

Romero, Mary. 2008. "Go After the Women": Mothers Against Illegal Aliens' Campaign Against Mexican Immigrant Women and Their Children. *Indiana Law Journal* 83 (4): 1355–89.

Roy, Carole. 2007. When Wisdom Speaks Sparks Fly: Raging Grannies Perform Humor as Protest. *Women's Studies Quarterly* 35 (3/4): 150–64.

Sassen, Saskia. 1996. *Losing Control? Sovereignty in an Age of Globalization*. New York: Columbia University Press.

Seper, Jerry. 2005. Grannies on Patrol: Women Help Lead Minuteman Border Vigil. *Washington Times*, November 8, A01.

Shapira, Harel. 2013. *Waiting for José: The Minutemen's Pursuit of America*. Princeton, NJ: Princeton University Press.

Stern, Alexandra Minna. 2005. *Eugenic Nation: Faults and Frontiers of Better Breeding in Modern America*. Berkeley: University of California Press.

———. 2004. Nationalism on the Line: Masculinity, Race, and the Creation of the U.S. Border Patrol, 1910–1940. In *Continental Crossroads: Remapping U.S.-Mexico Borderlands History*, edited by Samuel Truett and Elliott Young, 299–323. Durham, NC: Duke University Press.

Vanderboegh, Mike. 2005. The Botany of Illegal Immigration. *Free Republic*. www. freerepublic.com/focus/f-news/1471676/posts.

Vina, Stephen R., Blas Nunez-Neto, and Alyssa Bartlett Weir. 2007. Civilian Patrols Along the Border: Legal and Polity Issues. Washington, DC: Congressional Research Service.

Von Hentig, Hans. 1946. The Sociological Function of the Grandmother. *Social Forces* 24(4): 389–92.

Walsh, James. 2008. Community, Surveillance and Border Control: The Case of the Minuteman Project. In *Sociology of Crime, Law and Deviance*, Vol. 10, edited by Matthieu Deflem, 11–34. Bingley, UK: Emerald Books.

Wile, Joan. 2008. *Grandmothers Against the War: Getting Off our Fannies and Standing Up for Peace*. New York: Citadel Press.

Wilford, Rick, and Robert L. Miller, eds. 1998. *Women, Ethnicity and Nationalism: The Politics of Transition*. New York: Routledge.

Yoxall, Peter. 2006. The Minuteman Project, Gone in a Minute or Here to Stay? The Origin, History and Future of Citizen Activism on the United States–Mexico Border. *The University of Miami Inter-American Law Review* 37 (Spring/Summer): 517–66.

Yuval-Davis, Nira, and Floya Anthias, eds. 1989. *Woman-Nation-State*. New York: St. Martin's Press.

3

Defending the Nation

Militarism, Women's Empowerment, and the Hindu Right

MEERA SEHGAL

Introduction

This chapter examines how women in the right-wing Hindu nationalist movement in India conflate women's personal self-defense with national self-defense in ways that transform these women into symbolic "border guards," who deepen and regulate boundaries between Hindu and Muslim communities. Hindu nationalist women are taught to see themselves as embodiments of symbolic boundaries in the national iconography, as "symbols of the fecundity of the nation . . . vessels for its reproduction . . . and territorial markers" (Mostov 1995, 515). Skillfully appropriating elements from feminist discourses about violence against women, and under the guise of empowering Hindu women, the movement uses training programs to foster a "feminized siege mentality" and socialize its female activists into a militarized Hindu nationalist worldview (Sehgal 2007).

A feminized siege mentality is a learned disposition in which female members of a community perceive themselves as potential prey to male members of a community of "outsiders" (in this case, Muslim men). Cognitively, it involves learning who the Other is and why the Other is classified as the enemy. Emotionally, it involves learning to feel fear, shame, anger, and hate toward the Other. In order to be enduring, the cognitive and emotional elements must be translated from a macro impersonal discursive level to a micro personal level. By mobilizing fear and hate, such a militarized worldview legitimizes acts of violence against the Other, serving as both a precursor to and justification for violence.

In this chapter, I focus on the discursive and embodied practices used to construct this militarized worldview.[1] Specifically, I examine the mechanisms through which the Hindu nationalist discourse of an endangered Mother India (the imagined Hindu nation) is translated and transformed into personally embodied and emotionally charged worldviews internalized by activists in a women's wing of the Hindu nationalist movement. This translation relies upon entwined discourses that frame Hindu women's empowerment by the Hindu nationalist movement as necessary to counteract their historic victimization by Muslim men and Islam. The embodied practices include a physical training program that militarizes women's self-defense by heightening these women's fears of sexual attacks by Muslim men in the public sphere and deflecting their attention away from sources of violence in the private sphere (i.e., from upper-caste, Hindu patriarchal families).

Within the Hindu nationalist movement, stories of abduction and sexual violation of Hindu women (and by extension of the Hindu nation/mother India) by "sexually predatory" Muslim men is a hegemonic trope which symbolizes the victimization and humiliation of the entire Hindu community (Basu 1995; Bacchetta 2004), and justifies the vigilance of border guards by emphasizing the vulnerability of women and/or porousness of borders (Mostov 1995, 516). Women are used as symbols to embody differences between the imagined Hindu collectivity and its various Others (predominantly Muslims, but also Christians, feminists, communists, socialists, and secular Hindus). The feminine Hindu nationalist worldview has two central axes: politicized motherhood (an orientation to the biological and cultural reproduction of the Hindu nation) (Sehgal 2012), and femininized siege mentalities (orientations to physical and cultural threats to the nation).

In the Hindu nationalist movement, a militarized siege mentality is constructed through a highly charged injustice frame which dramatizes the illegitimacy of violence against women, but identifies Muslim men and Islam as the root cause of women's oppression in general (and of Hindu women's oppression in particular), while simultaneously rerouting these activists' attention away from Hindu patriarchal formations. Hindu nationalist activist women are socialized to fear what Muslim men have ostensibly done to Hindu women in the past and present, and what they are imagined to be capable of doing in the future.

These feelings of being personally in danger of sexual attack from male Others is common to most rightwing women's worldviews across the world (Bacchetta and Power 2002; Blee 2002), as they actively police borders between their ethnic group and the racialized Other (Blee and Deutsch 2012). This women's wing reproduces women as signifiers of group identity/difference and as border guards by rewriting the masculinist Hindu nationalist discourse of nation-as-woman (in which the territory/women are denied agency) to include women as powerful agents of the Hindu nation. This rewriting results in the deepening and entrenchment of borders of hostility between Hindu and Muslim communities in India.

My analysis is based on ethnographic research in a core women's organization called the Rashtra Sevika Samiti (hereafter, the Samiti) in the movement. This research, which extended over 21 months between 1995 and 1997, included participant observation at a Samiti paramilitary camp, approximately 30 informal conversations and 28 in-depth interviews with instructors and rank-and-file activists, and an analysis of the camp's lectures and instructor physical training manuals (Sehgal 2004). Although my fieldwork was conducted in the late 1990s, to date the Samiti, in addition to other Hindu nationalist women's wings, continue to conduct such camps in different parts of India and, as I demonstrate, played an important role in legitimizing and perpetrating violence in the 2002 anti-Muslim pogroms in the western state of Gujarat.

During my fieldwork I mistakenly assumed that as an Indian woman from a north Indian Hindu cultural background with a Hindu name, I would have few problems accessing the movement and its activists. However, the movement was profoundly suspicious of me and viewed me as an outsider (possibly as a "westernized" feminist traitor to the "Hindu nation"). I emotionally experienced what I already knew intellectually and politically—that the movement drew a sharp boundary between India's "true" citizens (i.e., Hindu nationalists striving toward the establishment of a Hindu nation) and its pseudocitizens (those who disagree with the Hindu nationalist worldview and need to be taught to accept secondhand citizenship rights).

My careful plans of locating prominent female Hindu nationalist leaders, explaining my research objectives to them, and getting their consent to conduct participant observation and interviews did not work. All of my attempts of conducting fieldwork in a direct, neutral, and consensual manner were met with stiff resistance by the movement. Thus, in response to this resistance, my fieldwork identity developed in the borderlands between disclosure and secrecy. I strategically front-staged essential aspects of my identity and veiled or back-staged other aspects of my biography, ideological alignments and political stand-points (Sehgal 2009). My front-stage identity emphasized a strategic essentialism in which I presented myself as an underinformed Hindu daughter/wife from a valued class and caste position doing fieldwork on the status on Hindu women. I used personal, familial contacts to get access to lower level activists, who provided me with referrals to other local rank and file activists. Once I had developed a rapport with them, I worked my way up to the national level leaders. They, in turn, viewed me as an activist in training that they could use to start a branch of the movement in the United States. Given the documented violent tendencies of this movement and the danger of possible retribution to myself and to my family, I decided to remain covert both for the sake of my own safety as well as the quality of my research. By remaining covert I was able to investigate areas that would have otherwise been less accessible, if not completely off-limits, such as how the official ideology of the movement was modified to appeal to different demographics within the membership and also how women were taught and encouraged to incorporate the movement's agenda into their homes and communities upon the completion of training. By presenting myself as a naïve sympathizer of the movement and framing my research as a general inquiry into the status of Hindu women, I was able to obtain a wide range of responses, including internal critiques of the camps, than I would have been able to had I revealed my true opposition to Hindu nationalism. In addition, by attending the training camp as a purported recruit I was able to analyze the nature of what was being taught and, as I will demonstrate later in this chapter, problematize movement claims that the Samiti was actually empowering its female recruits.

This chapter is divided into three parts. First I situate the Samiti within the Hindu nationalist movement; second, I describe the Samiti's paramilitary camps; and finally, I analyze the discursive and embodied practices that militarize women's self-defense and mobilize a feminized siege mentality.

The Hindu Nationalist Movement

The Hindu nationalist movement, which has existed in India in different forms since the beginning of the twentieth century, mobilizes Hindus to propagate its exclusivist, right-wing Hindu nationalist ideology called "Hindutva" (literally "Hindu-ness"). Ideologically, the movement subscribes to a notion of cultural nationalism, arguing that Hinduism should be the basis of Indian citizenship. It has three major goals. The first is to increase its hegemony by intensively transforming the minds of a Hindu collectivity. The second goal is to gain state power in order to implement various Hindu nationalist policies and relegate non-Hindus to second-class citizenship (see, e.g., Gowalker 1947, 55–56); (a crucial precondition for state power in India is the development of a Hindu vote-bank).[2] Third, the goal is to establish a Hindu nation in the territory presently occupied by the modern nation-states of Pakistan, Bangladesh, Burma, Nepal, Sri Lanka, and Afghanistan.

As a mass movement, it has diversified branches: a parliamentary party, mass sociopolitical organizations, women's wings, and a paramilitary wing. The movement refers to itself as the "Sangh Parivar" ("Sangh Family") to emphasize its joint familial structure and lineage deriving from the all-male, gender segregated Rashtriya Svayamsevak Sangh, the National Volunteers Association (hereafter RSS), the patriarch of the movement. In contemporary India, the RSS is the most influential; it is one of the largest organizations in northern Indian civil society, with several million male followers who meet daily in neighborhood units of the RSS called *shakhas* (branches). Although its geographical areas of strength are in north, central, and western India, it has spread to south India, has diasporic branches in 47 foreign countries, is "perhaps South Asia's largest international, micro-nationalist organization ever" (Bacchetta 2004, 128) and its critics view it as "the largest voluntary, private paramilitary body existing in any nation" (Bhatt 2001, 113). Over the years, the RSS has created a diversified network of affiliate organizations, reflecting the movement's expansion into party political process, civil society and institutions of local and national state governance. Although each affiliate organization has developed its own distinctive thrust, they have internally circulating members, interlocking functions, and interests that are carefully monitored by the RSS (Sarkar 1991).

The Samiti is a hierarchical, cadre-based Hindu nationalist women's organization that functions as the women's wing of the RSS. While the Samiti is subordinate to and less powerful than the RSS (as are most women's organizations in relation to the male organizations in the movement), it is also the most powerful women's organization within the Hindu nationalist movement; it is an agenda-setting and institutionally well-established organization, with clearly demarcated boundaries, codified rules, regulations, goals, functions, and office bearers. Most of the women in leadership positions in the other organizations of the movement have been trained by the Samiti before they circulate to these other organizations.

The Samiti has over a million members predominantly from urban, upper-caste, middle-class trading families or from middle-ranking government service backgrounds (Bacchetta 2004; Sarkar 1995).[3] The Samiti is organized into units at the neighborhood, city, district, statewide, and national levels. Each neighborhood unit has approximately 8 to 10 members and is further divided into four categories on the basis of age—children, adolescents, adults, and elderly—and structure their activities to appeal to these age groups. This structuring reflects how the Samiti as an organization attempts to reduce or contain the disruption that its public sphere movement activities might create in the domestic duties of women of different age groups—a crucial consideration for the recruitment and retention of traditional upper-caste Hindu women.

The Samiti's main activities include weekly neighborhood meetings, annual paramilitary camps at the regional and national level, conferences, teacher training camps, five annual festivals, demonstrations, and processions and marches supporting various Hindu nationalist campaigns. The Samiti also runs primary schools, a hostel where they educate and house girls for free, tutorial classes, discourses on selected Sanskrit texts, free library facilities, three teacher training institutes, free dispensaries, hostels for single working women from Sangh Parivar affiliated families, family counseling centers, a small bank that gives cheap loans to poor women, self-employment centers for poor women, a meeting hall for Samiti activities, hymn and worship classes, financial trusts to receive locally collected funds, and sewing classes and programs to initiate female priests. The Samiti also has a "history of intervention in the public space" (Bacchetta 2004, 134)—that is, organizing

demonstrations and hunger strikes, courting arrest, supporting controversial Hindu nationalist campaigns, and organizing boycotts of Muslim owned businesses.[4] Of all these activities and services, the Samiti
spends an extraordinary amount of time and energy on the weekly
neighborhood meetings and its annual paramilitary camps.

The Samiti owns a publishing company through which it publishes
hagiographies, training manuals, magazines, pamphlets, and books containing the life stories of ideal women, Hindu nationalist history, geography, songs, prayers, and games and pamphlets. These are intended
for an internal circulation and are sold only at the Samiti's paramilitary
camps and conferences (being unavailable at Hindu nationalist book-
stores). This internal circulation enables the Samiti—with its discourse
of Hindu women's empowerment—to address its members without
posing a challenge to the RSS's hegemonic, hypermasculine worldview
that posits men as protectors and women as *protected.*

Although a significant majority of India's population—about 78
percent—is Hindu, the Hindu population is very heterogeneous and
divided by caste, class, religious beliefs and practices, language, and
regional politics. The Hindu nationalist movement has to convince this
fractured Hindu polity to put its "Hindu" interests before other allegiances and uses the glue of anti-Muslim hatred to patch the fractured
Hindu polity together. It does this by constructing a militarized worldview in which siege mentalities predominate.

Hindu Nationalist Siege Mentalities, Gender,
and Violence against the Other

Hindu nationalist violence takes the form of large-scale anti-Muslim
riots or pogroms that are systematic, preplanned, recurrent, and highly
gendered. It usually involves large mobs of armed men targeting Muslim neighborhoods, looting, arson, the killing of Muslim men, and sexual brutalization of women (Chenoy, Nagar et. al. 2002; Chenoy, Shukla
et. al. 2002; National Human Rights Commission 2002). Women are
specifically targeted because the honor of the community is understood
to be located in and on the bodies of women, and any violation of wom-
en's bodies is symbolic of the violation of the community.[5] In February
and March of 2002, Hindu nationalists in the BJP ruled state of Gujarat

conducted gruesome anti-Muslim pogroms in which two thousand Muslims were killed and 100,000 were rendered homeless refugees (Chenoy, Nagar, et. al 2002).

Hindu nationalist women play an important role in sustaining the atmosphere of fear and hostility between Hindu and Muslim communities that gives rise to such violence (Butalia 2001; see also Basu 1996, 76). They participated in anti-Muslim violence by "breaking down houses [and] helping wash away the blood of those killed"; by preventing other women from helping the victims of violence; blocking roads to prevent army trucks, fire engines, and police from rescuing Muslim victims; and indulging in arson and looting (Butalia 2001, 106). The 2002 pogroms reached their zenith after *Sandesh*—a leading Gujarati language newspaper—ran a false story stating that "ten to fifteen Hindu women were dragged away by a fanatic mob from the railway compartment" (Hameed et. al 2002). A human rights group found that this one false story had spread like wildfire across the state of Gujarat through the channels of "overworked rumor mills" (ibid. 11). The same newspaper published a follow-up story a few days later under the following headline: "Out of the kidnapped young women on Sabarmati Express, dead bodies of two women recovered—breasts of women were cut off" (ibid. 11). Fabricated stories such as these have circulated and preceded most "Hindu-Muslim" riots in India since its independence in 1947.

During the 2002 pogroms, rumors of Muslim men raping Hindu women circulated through Hindu nationalist newspapers and pamphlets. Despite belonging to the community of perpetrators, Hindu women were reported as being "caught in a fear psychosis that the 'other' [would] attack" (People's Union for Civil Liberties 2002, 3). Cynthia Enloe argues that "the more convinced any person becomes of globalized or localized danger, the more likely he/she is to see prioritization of military needs and militaristic values over other needs and values as positive, or at least inevitable" (Enloe 2007, 161). Thus, despite the persecution of Muslims at the hands of Hindu Nationalists, the Hindu Nationalist movement discursively constructs the Hindu community as vulnerable to Muslim attack.

Hindu nationalist discourses frame Indian Muslims as treasonous, having allegiances to Mecca (Saudi Arabia) and other Muslim nations instead of India. According to the movement, the emergence of

Muslims as a geographic and political block will ultimately give rise to another partition of India (i.e., similar to the 1947 partition of India) or cause another separatist movement like the one in Kashmir. The Hindu community is also seen as under siege from Christian missionaries, who—they argue—receive large sums of money from the papacy to convert "unsuspecting" lower-caste Hindus and tribes.

According to Hindu nationalists, then, the urgent need of the hour is to "unmask conspiracies to break up Hindu society," "throw out of [the] country hundreds of thousands of foreign Muslim infiltrators," inform everyone of Pakistan's terrorist conspiracies, increase expenditures on defense and military, ensure that Kashmir remains a part of India, close down all butcheries, stop the "central government's policy of Muslim appeasement," and counteract the attacks on Hindu culture through the medium of cable television. To this end, the movement urges every Hindu to support Hindu nationalist policies, resist religious conversion, and closely monitor Muslims in their communities.[6]

Representations of gender and sexuality play a key role in the construction of a beleaguered, victimized majority in right-wing movements around the world.[7] Within Hindu nationalism, there are masculinized and feminized discourses of insecurity mobilized by gender segregated wings of the movement. Both discourses argue that the need of the hour is to become "powerful"—generally interpreted as becoming strong, disciplined, well-trained, and organized. The difference between the two discourses lies in what the male and female wings interpret these concepts to mean, in how men and women are addressed, in the kinds of power envisaged for women and men (and what that power should be used for), in the reasoning given for the necessity of becoming powerful, and in the plan of action needed in order to become powerful.

Historically, the ideologues of the all-male RSS have used a strategy of stigmatization and emulation (Jaffrelot 1996) to construct idealized notions of the kind of masculinity their members should aspire toward (Bacchetta 2004; Bhatt 2001). The RSS constructed a "cult of masculinity and strength through which" it tries to "overcome the effeminate Hindu man and to emulate the demonized enemy—the allegedly strong, aggressive, potent and masculine Muslim" (Hansen 1999, 112). Thus, the masculinized discourse of power addresses Hindu men in terms of physical strength and sexual virility, while women are addressed in terms of domesticated notions of *shakti* (or feminine power, discussed below). For men, the reason they need to be powerful is to overcome weakness and impotence, save the motherland and Hindu women from sexual violation, and to be the sexual equal to Muslim men. For women, the reason they need to be powerful is to regain Hindu women's "original" position in "Vedic" society—as powerful mothers, actors, and leaders able to defend themselves against sexual violence, rather than be dependent on "manly" Hindu men. Feminine honor is equated with the preservation of upper-caste notions of virtuousness and sexual purity. In terms of the action needed to become powerful, for women it is by going through a militarized self-defense training, while men (although also given paramilitary training) are additionally encouraged to establish their virility through violence against the Other, which often includes taking revenge through rape.

Two additional issues need to be noted. First, the cultural construction and collective psychological perception of threat differs by gender, in that what makes upper-caste, middle-class, urban Hindu women feel threatened is different from what makes men from the same background feel threatened. For instance, for Hindu nationalist men rape is perceived as revealing Hindu men's inability to protect their womenfolk and their motherland, thus violating their male honor (Bacchetta 2004; Hansen 1999). This inability is conceived by the movement as being caused by Hindu men's physical weakness, cowardice, indiscipline, and lack of virility in comparison with Muslim men. The masculinist discourse of insecurity is a provocative one of incitement addressed to masculine subjects, goading them to commit acts of violence to establish and avenge their virility (Hansen 1999, 214).

This masculinized discourse, which typically dominates large Hindu nationalist rallies and audio-visual tapes, was conspicuously absent at the Samiti's paramilitary camps. Instead, the Samiti used a discourse that highlights the necessity of protection and self-defense for women. The threat of rape and sexual violence is the core motivation mobilized in the construction and activation of a feminized siege mentality. Attendant with physical fear are intense emotions of shame and horror at being raped in an upper-caste, Hindu patriarchal culture that blames women for being raped in the first place. This fear of sexual violation shapes the experiential world (public and private) of most Indian women, particularly of upper-caste Hindu women, in a literal way from a very young age. Not only is it experienced emotionally, it is physically inscribed into upper-caste women's bodies through their socialization into a feminine upper-caste, Hindu identity. They are constantly told how to sit, stand, walk, and dress in ways that do not draw attention to their bodies—especially those parts that are considered sexual. This socialization, though presented as grooming for an appropriate feminine identity, is about disguising and hiding the upper-caste Hindu female body from all kinds of male gazes (particularly those of the lower castes and Muslim males) so as to maintain upper-caste notions of purity. The cultural implication underpinning this is the belief that any violation of the female body is the woman's fault, as she failed to guard her body (and *mutatis mutandis,* the body of the nation) adequately.

Secondly, the same discourse is usually interpreted differently by men and women of the same community. For instance, while anti-Other discourses and practices are common to right-wing movements across the world in that they serve as sites for the "production and mobilization of collective fear," these discourses and practices are gendered (Bacchetta and Power 2002; Blee and Deutsch 2012). Male and female Others are imagined and targeted differently by male and female right-wingers. Female Others are imagined simultaneously and contradictorily as aggressors and victims (who illustrate the inferiority of the Other community) and are represented as sexually overactive, predatory, and duplicitous, yet also asexual, passive victims of their men or male breeders. Male Others are the target of most right-wing movements' disgust, violence, exclusion, and annihilation. Male and female right-wingers see male Others differently from one another. Bacchetta and Power (2002) argue that although right-wing women are stronger in their discursive condemnation of the Other, the actual enactment of violence is typically monopolized by right-wing men (though, as discussed above, Hindu nationalist women's involvement in violence against Muslims has been documented in India). This gender difference is due to the following reasons: men are seen as the ultimate agents of their community, and right-wing women support this construction of upper-caste Hindu male power. This view is then projected onto the

Other community so that men are viewed as epitomizing the Other's community. Secondly, most right-wing women see Othered men in personal terms, "as sexualized threats to their and other women's physical purity and integrity" (Bacchetta and Power 2002, 9). Third, most right-wing women direct the anger they feel about misogyny in their own communities primarily toward Othered men. Using the Other male to exemplify misogyny enables right-wing women to keep peace in their own communities.

In an effort to understand how the Samiti shapes these gendered and militarized worldviews among its members, I now turn to the paramilitary camps that are sites at which the mechanisms for this construction are most visible.

The Paramilitary Camp

Every year in May and June the Samiti conducts around 50, fifteen-day long paramilitary camps throughout India. Each state branch of the Samiti is responsible for organizing its own camp, but the syllabus, teaching materials, style, and content are all centrally controlled and prepared by the upper echelons of the Samiti.

While the camp programs evolve to address the exigencies of the day, their basic structure is based upon that developed by Samiti's founding figure, Lakshmibai Kelkar (1905–1978). When Kelkar founded the Samiti in 1936, she was interested in the physical training program of the RSS and modeled the initial women's training camps and physical programs after these exclusively male training programs (Rai 1996). In these early camps (1937–1959) women received the same training as men, although subsequently this was altered when Kelkar "consulted various doctors, physical trainers and yoga experts to design a health and fitness program which would be in accordance with the physique of a woman" (Rai 1996, 49). From the 1950s through the 1980s, the Samiti established training camps along these lines and by the mid-1990s was conducting around 48 to 50 such camps in different parts of India annually.[8]

On average, 150 women and girls attended each of these camps. The camp I attended as a participant observer drew 135 participants and 13 instructors from 17 cities.[9] Three-fourths of the participants were teenage schoolgirls (between 12–19 years) and one-fourth were women between the ages of 20 to 40 years. The majority was from middle- to upper-middle-class and upper-caste, urban backgrounds.

The overall atmosphere of this camp (and the Samiti's camps in general) is rigid, authoritarian, and strict, with harsh and intense indoctrination of sanskritized Brahminical Hinduism. They are run in a militarized fashion, with a strong emphasis on discipline. The work of running the camp (with the exception of cooking and teaching) is systematically divided and shared among the participants, with daily and weekly duties being assigned to different contingents.[10]

The camp I attended was held in an isolated school located about 20 kilometers outside the main city, and was at all times completely closed off and guarded by armed RSS men. Once at the camp, no one was allowed to leave before the finishing date. If friends or family came to visit, they were allowed to meet a participant only during specific allotted hours for brief periods. No one came to the camp unaccompanied; all the girls from one city or district came together under the strict supervision of older Samiti leaders who were responsible for their safety during the camp. Each participant had to pay a nominal sum of money to defray the costs of transportation and fees for the Samiti uniform, and the host city unit of the Samiti had to raise a substantial amount of money to make the camp economically viable.[11]

The weather and living conditions at the camp were relatively harsh, with summer temperatures hovering around 110 to 120 Farenheit, frequent electricity outages, and water shortages. There were eight bathrooms for two hundred women. Everyone slept on the hot, dusty floor with whatever bedding each person brought along—usually just a small woven mat and a sheet. For many of the participants, it was the first time they were spending time away from the comforts of home and family. After talking to many girls about why they came, it became evident that many had been given the mistaken impression that they were coming to a recreational camp with other girls for activities such as sightseeing tours to historic places. Most were from Hindu nationalist families, with one or both parents involved in the movement in some capacity.

The training took place at a frenetic pace in physically trying conditions. I would surmise that the systematic deprivation of adequate rest and food was a deliberate ploy of the camp organizers to reduce the chances of dissent or ideological criticism developing, since one needs time, energy, initiative, and planning to articulate criticism and griev- ances. Thus, grievances concerning the ongoing discomfort suffered by the participants were never voiced to the Samiti leadership, though there were gripe sessions among the participants themselves.

Adolescent girls were prime targets for the Samiti's training camps, and training these girls was compared to preparing and fertilizing a field for future cultivation and harvest. In terms of movement strategies it was advantageous to have a majority of teenage participants, since they were unmarried and unencumbered by in-laws, children, and hus- bands, inexperienced and impressionable, and possessed the flexible bodies, buoyant spirits, and high levels of physical energy necessary to withstand the rigors of such camps and make them successful.

Approximately four hours a day were devoted to physical training; five hours a day to ideological indoctrination via lectures, group dis- cussions, and rote memorization; and two hours a day to indoctrina- tion through cultural programming (i.e., songs, stories, plays, jokes, and skits). This indoctrination was the Samiti's first priority and ranged in format from classroom lectures and small and large group discus- sions led by different instructors, to skits, storytelling, songs, and chants based on the lives of various mythical and historical Hindu women. The lectures and discussions covered both broad topics—such as the social history and geography of India and the country's contemporary social and political terrain—and micro-level topics such as the work of the Samiti, the kind of activists Samiti members were supposed to be, the necessity of mobilizing an organization of Hindu women in contempo- rary India, the significance and procedure of the Samiti neighborhood unit, the female role models revered by the Samiti, and what aspects of their lives the participants should emulate.

There was a strong emphasis on training the participants (par- ticularly the younger ones) to become articulate and confident public speakers. In both large and small group settings girls would be called upon to participate and speak out in public. When they did speak, they were told how to speak properly (loudly, confidently), and how to stand properly ("stand straight, straighten your *kameez* and *dupatta*, hold your head up, don't slouch"). The Samiti's leaders and instructors understood the relation between discursive and embodied practices, the significance of which I pursue more explicitly in the next section. Kelkar, the founder, was projected as the ideal role model to emulate, and she was lauded as an example of an ordinary housewife who managed to gain power and influence by becoming a great orator.

The classroom-style lecturing and the question-answer sessions did not capture the interest of the girls as much as the physical training sessions, games, band practice, storytelling, and song learning (out of a 5–6 hour long daily indoctrination period, these lectures were typically carried out for 2–3 hours, while the rest of the 2–3 hours consisted of small group discussions, storytelling, singing, and dramatic enactments of incidents from the lives of legendary Hindu women and goddesses). A large repertoire of Hindu nationalist songs and chants were systematically taught—dinned into the participant's heads so that they could be relied upon to burst into an appropriate Hindu nationalist song or chant or story on any given occasion on command. The lectures didn't interest the participants, as they were delivered in a boring, tediously didactic style and focused on the rote memorization of key points of Hindu nationalist heritage. Also, they were mainly scheduled for after lunch when most girls were lethargic rather than attentive.

The best parts of the day—mornings and evenings, when it was comparatively cooler and the participants rested, bright, and alert—were reserved for the physical training sessions. In these sessions participants learned how to organize and physically conduct a neighborhood unit of the Samiti (with its requisite paramilitary drills, marching, and flag salute), yoga, martial arts, and combat. In camps conducted in border areas like Kashmir, Punjab, and the northeastern states, rifle training is also included as an integral part of the Samiti's physical program. All these were emphasized as ancient Hindu techniques and all the commands were given in Sanskrit—from standing at attention and at ease, to counting and martial arts steps.

The late evening cultural programs were considered a nuisance by many of the girls, who were at that time exhausted by the day's activities. The cultural programs were generally organized by one of the older participants, whose responsibility it was to decide in advance a suitable theme or topic and enlist some girls to perform in a play or skit, regional folk dance, or nationalist song. If no one was willing to volunteer and rehearse in advance, they would call on girls on the spur of the moment to improvise a cultural performance based in traditional Hindu folklore. The Samiti encouraged stories based on the lives of historical queens and mythical goddesses. In this retelling, the mixing of mythological characters from Hindu legends with historical characters contributed in a significant way to the feminized siege mentality. All these camp activities took place within a discursive framework that intertwined discourses of victimization and empowerment and served as the foundation of a militarized and feminized siege mentality. In the next section, I analyze the discursive and embodied practices through which the feminized siege mentality was mobilized.

Mobilization of the Feminized Siege Mentality
Discursive Practices

The practices at the camps involved two intertwined discourses—of Hindu women's victimization and their empowerment. The discourse of victimization focused the camp participants' attention on violence against women, but divided it into public sphere violence and private sphere violence. Public sphere violence against women was framed as being caused by Muslim men, while private sphere violence was constructed as being caused by Hindu women themselves. This discourse of victimization, then, served to deflect attention away from violence by Hindu men against Hindu women in the private sphere and delegitimized Indian feminist claims that Hindu men and Hindu patriarchal formations were responsible for public and private sphere violence against Hindu and non-Hindu women. The discourse of empowerment emphasized the necessity of militarized self-defense training to prevent Muslim male violence against Hindu women.

These two discourses complement each other and represent two sides of the same coin. Empowerment for Hindu women is necessary to counteract their historic victimization by Muslim men. The discourse of Hindu women's victimization by Muslim men originates in the Hindu nationalist movement's larger narrative on Muslim male "threat" to and violation of the "honor" of Hindu women. This is a common nationalist trope in which metaphors of the "nation-as-woman" and the "woman-as-nation" reduce women to the "symbolic markers of the nation" the "carriers of tradition," and transform women (as bodies and cultural repositories) into the battleground of group struggles (Peterson 2000; Yuval-Davis 1997; Mostov 1995). Both these metaphors serve to posit victimized Hindu women as both devoid of agency and as victimized symbols of Mother India (the nation-as-woman) who the Hindu nationalist male citizen warrior needs to defend in order to affirm his virile masculinity (Chowdhry 2000).

The Samiti expands "the specter of the rape of Hindu women by lustful Muslim men" to lay the generalized charge of women's oppression at the doorstep of Islam and Muslim men (Chowdhury 2000, 105). The Samiti feminizes this Hindu nationalist discourse of victimization by explicitly granting agency to Hindu women as citizen warriors and reproducers of the nation. However, although the Samiti's discourse of empowerment seems like the Samiti's way of transforming women from victims to agents, the empowerment it upholds is circumscribed and contained by the discourse of feminine duty and sacrifice for the nation; in short, one's nationalist duty becomes equated with empowerment. Through this discourse, the Samiti portrays itself as an agent of change, correcting the wrongs perpetrated by Islam and Muslim men against Hindu women (women-as-nation) and Mother India (nation-as-woman).

The Samiti's Discourse of Victimization

The Samiti carefully picks issues which are relevant to and resonate with the lived experiences of its members; it acknowledges the physical dangers faced by women in the public sphere, such as sexual harassment on the streets, women's inability to move freely and safely, and the objectification of women by the mass media. Yet the Samiti discuss this violence only in the context of Hindu nationalism. For instance, contemporary violence against women is contrasted with the absence of violence against women in the golden Vedic age,[12] with the decline in the status of Hindu women being attributed to the invasions of "barbaric Muslims" from Central Asia. Similarly, Muslim lust for Hindu women was posited as the original cause for the veiling of Hindu women, child marriage, the cloistering of Hindu women in the house, and to the end of education for Hindu women. In the contemporary period, the Samiti blames women's own provocative behavior and style of dressing for the sexual harassment of women. This allows for the existence of Hindu male harassment, and the blame, rather than falling on Hindu men, fell on Hindu women themselves.

Abduction and rape of Hindu women by Muslim men is an important theme the Samiti returns to consistently and repeatedly. A prominent Samiti pamphlet widely read and discussed by camp participants, retells the life story of one of its favorite role models, Queen Jijabai (a seventeenth-century queen in the Maratha empire in western India) in which the writer emphasizes that this queen

> had from her childhood observed the Mughals committing atrocities on Hindu temples and Hindu women used to get kidnapped in broad daylight. Jijabai's soft heart used to get tormented witnessing all this. It used to make her wonder—isn't there anyone to punish these depraved and wicked villains? (Rashtra Sevika Samiti 1990, 62).

She used the stories of such atrocities to incite her son, King Shivaji, to wage war on the Mughals by telling him:

> Your very own aunt was taken by Muslim men. All the mothers and sisters of our country are constantly suffering such atrocities, and you avoid even listening to such stories! You have to take revenge for all this—you have to liberate mothers and sisters from such atrocities. Sit down and listen up! (Rashtra Sevika Samiti 1996, 22).

In the larger Hindu nationalist discourse, the trope of an eternal Muslim lust for the Hindu woman is well entrenched and used extensively to justify violent riots against Muslims.

The Samiti's discourse of victimization presents its activists with two main alternatives: to defend one's virtue by fighting physically or, if unable to do so, to sacrifice oneself in the name of protecting one's virtue and honor. Thus, the Samiti not only upholds women warriors as role models, but also exalts women who committed suicide to protect their virtue, like Queen Padmini and the Daher princesses, who killed themselves with daggers after making false allegations about their sexual violation by Mir Qasim (Rashtra Sevika Samiti 1988, 55).[13]

Additional evidence for this eternal Muslim lust for the Hindu woman is derived in large part from the skillful manipulation of collective memories of the violent partition of British India into India and Pakistan in 1947 and the presentation of one-sided versions of Partition riots. In the Samiti's discourse, partition is also a code word for the extreme sexual violence directed against Hindu women by Muslim men.

During one camp lecture, a national-level Samiti leader warned the adolescent participants to be wary of wealthy, young Muslim men hanging around outside their schools, waiting to lure them into sexual slavery in Saudi Arabia:

I have seen such men wearing fancy clothes, driving Maruti cars and Hero-Honda motorcycles, hanging around the gates of girls' schools. They pretend to be in love with our girls. They say they don't believe in caste or in any traditional bonds and ultimately, the girls get fooled by their sweet talk and land up in Saudi Arabia.

Six years later in 2002, the same warning was reiterated in leaflets found circulating in riot-affected areas in Gujarat:

There is a separate bank run by Muslims. It finances the Muslim gangs. With an intention of deceiving and defrauding the Hindu girls studying in schools and colleges they take Hindu names . . . In Gujarat alone, there are at least 10 thousand cases of defrauding Hindu girls and as many cases of Hindu girls being raped, every year . . . Hindu boys studying in colleges could save Hindu girls from the hands of Muslim gangsters either by themselves or with the help of Hindu organizations (Chenoy, Nagar et. al 2002, 37).

The main difference between these two warnings of the danger posed by Muslim men is that while the Samiti advocated self-reliance and alertness for women through its discourse of empowerment, the *general* leaflet advocated the policing of (i.e., the extension of patriarchal control over) Hindu women by complete strangers and by nonfamilial Hindu men and Hindu nationalist organizations.

This difference is based on protector-protected dichotomies inherent in most militarized ideologies in which men are constructed as the natural protectors (being endowed with physical strength and the capacity to think more rationally and strategically) of women, who naturally need to be protected (being physically weak, sexually vulnerable, unable to think rationally and strategically) (Enloe 2007, 60–61). Furthermore, protectors claim and are granted more authority to speak for others, while the protected are more easily silenced and accept that silencing. The Samiti's discourse of empowerment subverts the gendered hierarchy of the protector-protected dichotomy by refusing to be forced into the role of the protected (with its attendant physical weakness and passivity) and by redefining femininity as physical strength and decisive action. Yet as I illustrate in the next section, it also reinforces a militarized notion of obedience and hierarchy that women need to adhere to in order to rationally and strategically secure their safety.

The Samiti's Discourse of Empowerment

The Samiti's discourse of empowerment mobilizes hope among its activists by constructing Hindu women as active and powerful agents, leaders of society, and mothers of the nation capable of choosing and transforming their own and the nation's destiny at will and through their collective struggles as movers and shakers of the universe. However, underlying this construction is a nationalist discourse of women's duty and self-sacrifice for the Hindu nation. Thus, the Samiti focused on enabling women and girls to see themselves as protectors by feeling independent, self-reliant, and at ease in the public social movement world, away from the traditional domestic environment of the protected, in which they seemingly do not have to subjugate their thoughts, needs, and desires to those of male protectors in order to secure their protection. Yet the question is *what* are they protecting, *how*, and with what consequences. Does this protection and empowerment reproduce collective insecurity and deepen borders of hostility between Hindus and Muslims?

The Samiti's discourse of empowerment reflects its response to feminist discourses on equality, women's rights, and liberation. With the decade of the 1980s being declared as the "decade of women" by the UN, the issue of empowering and liberating women has been a ubiquitous and contentious one in India, with hardly any organization or movement able to escape addressing it in one way or another (Sharma 2008). Women in social movements across the Indian political spectrum argue from divergent standpoints over the definitions of empowerment and liberation and the best way to bring it about (with debates in the mass media and people's homes on reservation for women in parliament, women's literacy, maternal health, voting rights, welfare services, violence against women, the Indian women's movement, transnational feminist movements, and the Beijing conference).

The Samiti responds to these discourses by seeming to incorporate them, while transforming the significance and form of these discourses. Thus, its discourse of empowerment focuses on women's power (deploying the principle of divine feminine Shakti) as opposed to women's liberation (*mukti*) and excludes feminist issues like the right to divorce, marital rape, rape of Dalit women by upper-caste Hindu men, wife battering, inheritance of family property, and maternal health. Women's liberation is framed as a confrontation between men and women that results in the disruption of family life and leads to the ruin of Hindu culture.

The Samiti's notion of empowerment is consonant with and contained within the Hindu nationalist view of women as iconographic identity markers and symbols of the nation. As a camp instructor lectured, "Since woman is the symbol of the identity of our nation, it is imperative that her behavior-conduct should be in conformity with her being a symbol of the nation's identity" (Camp Lecture May 30, 1996). Part of the attraction of the Samiti and its camps lies in its promise of fulfillment in the here and now—all that Hindu women needed to do was to claim it by following the path shown by the Samiti. This is a potent discourse given the restrictive conditions that many of the Samiti members live under. To this end, the Samiti presented itself as doing something positive and empowering for oppressed womanhood through its various programs, including its paramilitary camps. Camp instructors repeatedly conveyed this point—as one of them articulated during a lecture, "we are going to have all kinds of programs to make you aware of and increase your strengths."

As a solution to violence against women, the Samiti provides physical self-defense training for women. The Samiti rationalizes the physical training program as a means of increasing their confidence and self-reliance in an era of increasing violence against women. As an instructor pointed out during a lecture at the camp:

> In today's society, women are unsafe. Only if women defend themselves will they be safe. Women should be able to defend and protect themselves by using their bodies, minds and spirits. This capacity should be there and inculcated in every woman. They should believe and have faith in themselves. Only then will all the fear disappear (Camp Lecture 1996).

Sexual harassment of women by strangers was cited by another instructor as an important reason for organizing women and training them in self-defense:

> Girls cannot leave their houses because they are so fearful. A chain has been put around women's necks. When there is an organization, then one's courage increases. Four to six women can do a lot. Rather than being chased by men, they can chase away sexual harassers who trouble us on the streets. When men realize that women are organized they won't harass women anymore . . . Your fathers and brothers can't be with you all the time to protect you. Of course you can lock yourself in your house always, but even there you're not safe. Five men can force their way into your home when you're alone and then what? (Camp Group Discussion 1996).

It is significant that this instructor is conspicuously silent about the possibility of the Samiti's physical training being used for defense against domestic violence. Rather, she directs the participants' attention to a riot-like scenario in which groups of men (by implication Muslim) could force their way into these Hindu women's homes with the purpose of looting and sexually brutalizing its inhabitants. This mobilization of fear is used to support militarized Hindu nationalist solutions for situations in which women find themselves feeling unsafe and insecure.

Old Hindu legends were reinterpreted within the framework of this discourse of empowerment in order to make them more relevant and applicable in the context of contemporary Indian society and to inspire

its camps' predominantly adolescent participants. The Samiti successfully deployed the narrative tradition of the "*Viranganas*" in order to
fire the imagination of many young girls. A *Virangana* is "a valiant
fighter who distinguishes herself by prowess in warfare, an activity nor-
mally reserved for men" (Hansen 1988, 25). These narratives encourage
the girls to imagine themselves as part of an army of pure, virgin female
warriors—skilled in wielding weapons and capable of using their bodies as weapons—ready and waiting in the wings to fight in the war of
the righteous and usher in the reign of the "glorious Hindu nation."

In the following reinterpretation of a popular Hindu legend (in
which the Goddess Durga destroys the buffalo demon Mahisasur) presented in a camp lecture, the intention of the instructor was to infuse
the adolescent audience with the belief that it was possible to transform
themselves into mini incarnations of goddess Durga by participating in
the Samiti's training camps:

> You surely didn't think the demon, Mahisasur, lived only in one place!
> There were innumerable Mahisasurs throughout the country. Who
> would slay all of them? It is said, that infinite forms of Durga were to be
> seen throughout the country. What were these infinite forms of Durga?
> All of these were the young virgin daughters of India, our great nation.
> They all were heroic, majestic and powerful . . . ! And that is why, they
> were able to destroy immorality (*adharma*) and establish the rule of
> morality (*dharma*) (Camp Lecture June 1, 1996).

This reference to the existence of innumerable Mahisasurs evokes
images of invisible demons, consistent with the Samiti's imagery of
Muslim men lurking in the shadows, waiting to attack virtuous Hindu
women.

The Samiti's discourse locates the causes for the problems faced by
Hindu women outside of the Hindu community, in the public sphere,
or in the Muslim community or blames them on women themselves.
Thus, although women's gender consciousness and anger is roused by
the Samiti, the Samiti takes care that this is not directed inward toward
the upper-caste Hindu patriarchal community. This way of addressing
the issue also serves to deflect and displace the typical Samiti activist's awareness of their oppression and their potential anger at Hindu

patriarchy and refocus it on the "enemies of the Hindu nation." It constricts the possibility of internal critique and clamps down the potential of the Samiti's activists challenging Hindu patriarchy. In the vacuum created by the deflection of its activists' awareness and anger, the Samiti fills up with anger toward Muslims.

The camp lectures were also filled with warnings of the terrible consequences of women becoming angry and using their power to rebel against their own community, especially against challenging their husbands and proving to be more powerful than them. For instance, while retelling the legend of goddess Kali killing the demon Raktavir, the instructor told the story of how Kali got drunk, crazed in her lust for killing, and almost ended up killing her husband, Shiva. In this version of the legend, Goddess Kali became insane in her killing spree, destroying everything in the world after she finishes slaying all the demons. As the legend goes, Kali proved to be even stronger than Shiva and while he was trying to make her see sense, she almost killed him, but stopped just in time because she happened to look down and see that it was Shiva she was trampling. What is implied in this telling of the legend is that women's power is extremely destructive if not controlled and reined in by men and that women can lose their senses in their exercise of power. This represents a domestication of the wild, aggressive, sexual aspects of *shakti* (divine feminine power).[14]

The participants were exhorted to become like the lotus, blossoming, despite growing in "filth," while never reprimanding the filth it grows in. This particular metaphor of the lotus, a symbol of purity surrounded by filth, encapsulates the Samiti's injunction to its activists that women should not criticize their family and community for their oppression. In this interpretation of empowerment, the individualistic basis of rights is elided and seeks to be replaced by a collective notion of the Hindu community's rights that are at stake. The Samiti defines the demand for one's rights, particularly women's rights, as an act of self-centered selfishness that would ultimately be against the interest of the Hindu nation. Women's rights are framed as a western conception—which make them, from the Samiti's perspective, extremely harmful for the nation. In the Samiti's discourse the cause of women's problems does not lie within Hindu society, but in the larger non-Hindu society.

Women's rights are defined as alienable and contingent on their being dutiful members of the Hindu nationalist community. Female duty and sacrifice are reinterpreted as being "real empowerment" for women, and the constraints imposed on women are erased by this discourse. If a woman does not fulfill her duties, then she has to give up her rights. Furthermore, non-Hindu women do not any of these rights.

The Samiti's message combined with the physical training program resonated with many women and girls because the Samiti makes it easy for these girls from Hindu nationalist homes to feel strong and powerful, to have a legitimate excuse to get out of their homes, and to have a male scapegoat to target their anger at a patriarchal society. The largest group of girls at the camp I attended were the second- and third-timers, those who chose to repeatedly return to the Samiti's camp for the second or third summer. On the face of it, especially in the eyes of these girls, it would appear as though the Samiti was well aware of and sympathetic to the problems faced by these girls on a daily basis, a big one being sexual harassment in the public sphere. Furthermore, the Samiti explains the causes for their problems and suggests a way out that is recognized as legitimate and valid by their families.

Through its construction of a feminized siege mentality, the Samiti reproduced women as signifiers of group identities and differences with a feminized twist, blurring and redrawing gender-boundaries. It rewrote the masculinist Hindu nationalist rhetoric of nation-as-woman in which the territory/woman is denied agency to include women as active empowered agents, border guards of the imagined future Hindu nation. However, in this redrawing of gender-based boundaries, the Samiti also framed some boundaries as sacrosanct, nontransgressable lines (i.e., those that homogenized the Hindu community and erased the hierarchies within, and simultaneously differentiated the Hindu nationalist community from its Others).

Embodied Practices

Embodied practices at the camp served to inscribe the discourse of victimization onto the worldview of the Hindu nationalist women. The physical training program exacerbated and mobilized women's existing fears of male violence, infusing them with Hindu nationalist elements and reinscribing them on the participants' emotional landscape. These forms of training served to keep women in fear of the Other rather than enhance their feeling of safety and security. The program deflected these women's attentions away from domestic violence and instead portrayed violence against women as occurring predominantly in the public sphere and during riot-like situations in which Muslim men are the aggressors. Notably, however, these women seldom directly encountered Muslim men in their daily lives (living as they did in predominantly urban Hindu middle-class enclaves). Such redirection made these women more vulnerable and ill-prepared to defend themselves against actual harassment and violence in their homes and communities. In addition, the camp participants were made more vulnerable to assault because they thought they had been well trained in self-defense, when in fact they were not. By creating myths about Hindu nationalist female warriors, the program prepared women to blame themselves rather than the training when they fall short of mythical ideals.

In the martial arts training, the students were taught a variety of maneuvers like the balanced stance, hand strikes and hand blocks, and voice training—loud assertive yelling in Sanskrit, "Hah!," "Hut!"— to accompany the strikes. In the weapons training, the students were taught to use two kinds of weapons—daggers (large, wooden, silver-painted) and bamboo staves (*laathis*). Stave (*laathi*) fighting involved learning to handle a *laathi* (a long heavy bamboo pole, taller than some of the participants). The emphasis was on learning how to twirl it fast in front of the body from side to side. Two maneuvers were taught with the *laathi*: hitting the enemy on the head and on the legs. Again, the emphasis was on learning how to swing and twirl the stave in the required directions as swiftly and smoothly as possible, similar to how a band leader twirls the baton stick while leading the band on a march.

There are several indications that this physical training was meant to construct a militarized siege mentality rather than self-defense skills. First, techniques were structured and taught in the manner of Indian classical dance, as complex, patterned sequences of movements. The emphasis was on learning elaborate steps and coordinating hand and feet movements with elaborate sing-song Sanskrit commands, rather than learning how to stand or move effectively for self-defense. This pedagogical model of physical training as dance fit well with participants' feminized gender identity and the cultural patterns considered appropriate for Hindu women from upper-caste, middle-class, urban Indian backgrounds.

Second, the emphasis in training sessions was on learning how to attack and not on how to defend oneself when attacked. Participants were repeatedly taught how strike, stab, and hit a man using their bodies, staves or *laathi,* or daggers as weapons, but did not learn what to do if attacked first or if their weapons were used against them. This taught them to escalate the level of confrontation rather than defuse it, which would be dangerous if an attacker then responded more violently. Rather than being an effective form of self-defense, the Samiti's emphasis fit its effort to creating valorous, heroic Hindu women, regardless of whether this made real-life Hindu women more vulnerable.

Third, the Samiti's training lacked material or visual targets. Students were taught to stab, slice, punch, and strike at the air with no assessment of how far or close they needed to be to the target for the strike to be effective. Not surprisingly, students ended up seeing themselves as part of an elaborate pantomime or dance-drama. Yet the absence of physical or visual targets reinforced a mental imagery of being surrounded by an army of invisible men. As a result, most students frantically stabbed and kicked in all directions in the hope that one blow would knock out the invisible enemy.

Finally, the training was taught with male rather than female bodies in mind. All maneuvers were based on upper-body strength—like punches, hand strikes, *laathi,* and knife fighting—although upper-caste, middle-class, urban Indian women typically have underdeveloped muscles in these areas and can be easily overpowered by an attacker. The strength of these women's bodies (strong legs, hips, and pelvises) was not used at all. Furthermore, there was little practice of physical movements. Emphasis was placed on the *quantity* of movements taught rather than the *quality,* and most maneuvers were taught a maximum of two or three times before students moved on to the next.

Since students found these maneuvers hard to learn, the training— rather than increasing their self-confidence—generated feelings of inadequacy, incompetence, and discomfort with their bodies, which failed to execute the given maneuvers successfully. Such training was more effective in constructing an alarmist, besieged mentality rather than a self-confident and self-reliant one as proclaimed by the Samiti's discourse of empowerment.

Dagger training provides a good example of how the Samiti physical training program served more to remind the women of Hindu nationalism than to teach them to effectively defend themselves. The first thing taught was that the dagger had always to be kept in a scabbard tied to the left side of one's waist. In the absence of scabbards during training, the participants were taught to position their left hand at their waists as an imaginary scabbard into which the wooden, silver painted dagger had to be tucked. In the first place, a sari-clad woman would be far less likely to wear a scabbard containing an ornate, medieval dagger on a daily basis than she would be to utilize a kitchen knife or an easy to conceal switch blade. Moreover, the two main dagger maneuvers that were taught—targeting of the neck and throat area and drawing a diagonal slash from shoulder to pelvis—were impractical, if not impossible. The training was conspicuously silent about effective moves that could be executed easily, and there was no mention of the harmful psychological impact that carrying a dangerous weapon could have upon a person.

Moreover, these trainings did not create a sense that women have the right to defend themselves from any kind of abuse and assault, no matter who the perpetrators are. Indeed, the Samiti taught that this was a "western" idea, alien to the duties of good Hindu women. Instead, Samiti training programs made its participants identify Muslim men as their attackers in a mythologized past, present, and future. Hindu men did not feature as attackers. Camp participants were supposed to learn to defend not themselves (as individual women), but rather to defend the honor of the Hindu nation, embodied in themselves, against the bestiality of Muslim men and Islam. Ultimately, this made Samiti women more, instead of less, vulnerable because it taught them to overlook the violence they were more likely to encounter in their daily lives—namely, emotional and physical violence within their own communities.

The myth of the Muslim abductor/rapist and Hindu female victims, emphasized insistently as a historical fact during the intellectual training sessions, did not need to be verbally articulated during the physical training sessions. It was choreographed into the martial arts and weapon training in various ways, including the practice of dance-drama. The Samiti used bodywork to elicit women's fears of physical attacks by men and help them internalize a bodily memory of a Muslim rapist against whom Hindu women needed to defend themselves.

Conclusion

Group identities are shaped through the construction and maintenance of boundaries between "us" and "them" (Van der Veer 1996). Any collective practice integrates its participants into a community and simultaneously sets apart those who do not participate in the practice—so the self is constructed by an opposition to an Other (an "alien presence") who is conceptualized as threatening and needing to be violently subjugated or conquered: "Moreover, the 'alien' elements can be understood to be both 'within' the self and 'outside' of it, so that violence is directed simultaneously to discipline the self and conquer the 'other.'" (Van der Veer 1996, 157).

For the Samiti, a regime of disciplining the female self extends to both the public and the private spheres. In the private sphere the alien presences are defined as westernization, which is represented as culturally polluting the minds of virtuous Hindu women, causing them to resist or rebel against the authority of the patriarchal Hindu family and demand their rights as individual women. The Samiti defines the oppression suffered by Hindu women in the private sphere as being the responsibility of women themselves. According to the Samiti, any Hindu woman undisciplined enough to disturb the sanctity of the Hindu household by demanding her rights has been polluted by the westernized, anti-Indian (read anti-Hindu) women's movement. Hindu nationalist women are similar to most other right-wing women around the world who direct the anger they feel toward misogyny in their own communities primarily against Othered men (Bacchetta and Powers 2002). Using the Other male to exemplify misogyny enables right-wing women to keep peace within their own communities.

Although one might argue that the Samiti's advocacy of both the right and possibility of women defending themselves leads to some sort of individual empowerment (Naples 1998) in terms of increased self-confidence, heightened awareness of body postures, and self-reliance, this case study problematizes the notion of women's empowerment, demonstrating the need to think about which group of women are being empowered, by whom, how, and for what purpose (Sharma 2008; Cruikshank 1996). It provides evidence for how feminist discourses of violence against women and self-defense have been appropriated by the religious right-wing women and points to the slippery and permeable border between self-defense programs and militarism. It also demonstrates that the ideology of a right-wing movement is not monolithically interpreted by its activists; rather, there are gender differences in how male and female activists interpret and deploy the ideology (Blee 2002; Bacchetta 2004).

While the Samiti claims to build its activists' leadership potential and capacity to defend themselves and their communities, the end result of its discursive and embodied practices is collectively disempowering for women due to the inculcation of paranoia (in which an imaginary enemy replaces real threats) and a false sense of one's own self-defense skills. Furthermore, it systematically deepens borders between Hindu and Muslim communities in India, enabling Hindu supremacists to wage violence against minorities in order to protect a "victimized majority." The Samiti, by conducting such paramilitary camps for women, perpetuates the idea that these are not normal times. Implicit in the training is the notion and even the expectation of civil war in India (in the form of riots) between the "besieged Hindu" community and its various internal enemies, as constructed by Hindu nationalist discourse. The Samiti's training camps attempt to ensure that even in times of relative peace, its Hindu nationalist version of history and collective cultural memories of violence (in which women were specifically targeted) and extreme conflict remain preeminent and hegemonic in the subjective reality of its participants.

Bacchetta and Power argue that most right-wing women see the Othered male in personal terms "as sexualized threats to their and other women's physical purity and integrity" (2002, 9). The discourse of victimization, when combined with the physical training program (which helps embody the Samiti's vision of empowerment for women) creates and reproduces a femininized siege mentality. The camp's physical training program is a medium through which the Samiti activates heightens and embodies this fear, while discursively encoding it in ideological indoctrination sessions as being caused by Muslim men.

By the end of the camp, participants were worse off than when they first came. Most now thought they knew how to use weapons and martial arts to defend themselves, but, in fact, they did not. The Samiti was invested primarily in perpetuating the Hindu-woman-as-victim discourse rather than teaching women to fend for themselves. As a result of their physical training, women became concerned about Muslim men waiting to attack them and decided that their bodies were inadequate to defend against this enemy. These two interact with each other to form the key components of a militarized worldview. The Samiti, due to its militarization of women's empowerment and reproduction of feminized siege mentalities, is complicit in contemporary Hindu nationalist violence against the Muslim community in India, regardless of whether or not its activists engaged in literal acts of violence or simply incited and indirectly supported them. Hindu nationalist women end up situated as symbolic border guards who deepen, enforce, and reproduce the borders of distrust between Hindu and Muslim communities in South Asia in the name of women's empowerment.

NOTES

1. Militarism refers to the adoption of militarized values as one's own (e.g., beliefs in hierarchy, obedience, discipline, use of force), seeing military solutions as particularly effective and the world as a dangerous place, "best approached with militaristic attitudes" (Enloe 2007, 4; Chenoy 2002).

2. Vote banks are groups of people mobilized on the basis of their caste, class, religion, region, or language to vote for a particular political party.

3. No precise membership figures exist because the Samiti does not disclose its membership lists; Bacchetta estimated that the membership was one million in 1996; Sarkar estimated the membership as 100,000 in 1995; and the Samiti itself stated it was running 3,500 branches (yielding a self-calculated estimate of 35,000 members).

4. Interviews with Samiti activists and participant observation at meetings where they explained the importance of boycotting Muslim businesses.

5. This brutalization is not limited to individual and gang rape, but includes the videotaping of gang rapes; the insertion of metal rods and swords into girls' and women's vaginas; the branding of religious symbols on women's breasts, thighs, and foreheads; tearing out live fetuses from pregnant Muslim women's uteruses; and burning women alive after such brutalization or leaving them naked in public spaces. For more information see Hameed et. al. 2002; People's Union for Civil Liberties 2002; Advanni et. al 2002.

6. All quotes in this paragraph are drawn from an RSS Pamphlet titled "Awakening Hindus."

7. For Hindu nationalism, see Sarkar and Butalia, 1995; Bacchetta, 2004; ; Sehgal 2004, 2007, 2012; Menon, 2012; for right-wing movements and fascism in other parts of the world, see Blee, 2002; Blee and Deutsch, 2012; Powers and Bacchetta, 2002.

8. Interview with Dr. Sunita (pseudonym), state-level head of the Samiti and chief organizer of camp, July 1996.

9. In order to protect the confidentiality of the camp's participants and organizers, I have not specified the location or date of this camp.

10. Each contingent consisted of people from one city who shared a classroom for sleeping and storing their baggage.

11. All quotes are drawn from camp lectures and interviews conducted by the author at the camp in 1996, transcribed and translated from Hindi to English by the author.

12. The Vedic age is the mythical golden age of the Hindus when the Sanskrit scriptures, the *Vedas* were composed.

13. The story of Queen Padmini is well known in north India. When her husband's armies were defeated in battle by the Mughals in the seventeenth century, she led some five hundred palace women to commit *jauhar*—suicide by self-immolation—in order to preserve community honor (i.e., so as not to get raped by the enemy).

14. For more on this domestication of Shakti, see, Bacchetta 2004; Hiltebeitel and Erndl 2000; Hansen 1999, 112.

REFERENCES

Primary Sources

Advani, Poornima. 2002. Report of the committee constituted by the National Commission for Women to assess the status and situation of women and girl children in Gujarat in the wake of the communal disturbance. Delhi: National Commission for Women.

Camp Group Discussion. 1996. The power of organizing a union of Hindu women.

Camp Lecture. 1996. Introduction to the work of the Samiti.

Chenoy, Kamal Mitra, S. P. Shukla, K. S. Subramanian, and Achin Vanaik. 2002. Gujarat carnage 2002: A report to the nation. New Delhi: National Human Rights Commission.

Chenoy, Kamal Mitra, Vishnu Nagar, Prasenjit Bose, and Vijoo Krishnan. 2002. Ethnic cleansing in Ahmedabad: A preliminary report, SAHMAT Fact Finding Team to Ahmedabad, March 10–11, 2002.

Gowalkar, Madhav Sadashiv 1939. We or our nation defined. Nagpur: Bharat Publications.

Hameed, Syeda, Ruth Manorama, Malini Ghose, Sheba George, Fara Naqvi, and Mari Thekaekara. 2002. How has the Gujarat massacre affected minority women? The survivors speak, Fact-finding by a women's panel. Citizens Initiative, Ahmedabad, April 16.

National Human Rights Commission. 2002. Gujarat carnage: A report. New Dehli: Popular Education and Action Center.

People's Union for Civil Liberties and Shanti Abhiyan. 2002. Women's perspectives on the violence in Gujarat. In Gujarat: Laboratory of the Hindu Rashtra, edited by Indian Social Action Forum, n.p.: New Delhi.

Rai, Rajani. 1996. Life sketch of Vandaniya Mausiji: Founder and chief of Rashtra Sevika Samiti—Srimati Lakshmibai Kelkar's. Nagpur: Sevika Prakashan.

Rashtra Sevika Samiti. 1998. River of knowledge (Bodh sarita). Nagpur: Samiti Prakashan (personal translation from Hindi).

———. 1996. Motherhood, leadership, agency (Matritva, netritva, kartritva). Nagpur: Samiti Prakashan (personal translation from Hindi).

———. 1992. The study of physical force-physical syllabus: elementary (Bal-Saadhana—sharirik pathyakram: prarambhik), Fourth Edition. Nagpur: Rashtra Sevika Samiti Head Office (personal translation from Hindi).

———. 1990. Women to remember every morning (Prateh smarniya mahilayen). Nagpur: Sevika Prakashan (personal translation from Hindi).

Renu, Sharad, ed. 1996. Samiti editorial. In Vishambhara: A 60th anniversary commemoration, 2–3. Nagpur: Sevika Prakashan (personal translation from Hindi).

Secondary Sources

Bacchetta, Paola. 2004. *Gender in the Hindu nation: RSS women as ideologues.* New Dehli: Kali/Women Unlimited.

Bacchetta, Paola, and Margaret Power, eds. 2002. *Right-wing women: From conservative to extremists around the world*, New York: Routledge.

Basu, Amrita. 1996. Mass movement or elite conspiracy? The puzzle of Hindu nationalism. In *Contesting the nation: Religion, community and the politics of democracy in India*, edited by Ludden, David, 55–80. Philadelphia: University of Pennsylvania Press

———. 1995. Feminism inverted: The gendered imagery and real women of Hindu nationalism, in *Women and the Hindu right: A collection of essays*, edited by Tanika Sarkar and Urvashi Butalia, 158–180. New Dehli: Kali for Women.

Bhatt, Chetan. 2001. *Hindu nationalism: Origins, ideologies and modern myths.*; New York, NY: Berg.

Blee, Kathleen M. 2002. *Inside organized racism: Women in the hate movement.* Berkeley: University of California Press.

Blee, Kathleen, and Sandra McGee Deutsch. 2012. *Women of the right: Comparisons & interplay across borders.* University Park, PA: Pennsylvania State University Press.

Butalia, Urvashi. 2001. Women and communal conflicts in India: New challenges for the women's movement in India. In *Victims, perpetrators or Actors? Gender, armed conflict and political violence*, edited by Caroline Moser and Fiona Clark, 99–114. New Delhi: Kali for Women.

Chenoy, Anuradha. 2002. *Militarism and women in South Asia.* New Dehli: Kali for Women.

Chowdhry, Geeta. 2000. Communalism, nationalism, and gender: Bharatiya Janata Party (BJP) and the Hindu right in India. In *Women, states, and nationalism: At home in the nation?*, edited by Sita Ranchod-Nilsson and Mary Ann Tetreault, 1–17. London: Routledge.

Cruikshank, Barbara. 1994. "The Will to Empower: Technologies of Citizenship and the War on Poverty". *Socialist Review*, vol. 23, No. 4, 29-56.

Dutta, Pradeep, and Sumit Sarkar. 1994. Manufacturing hatred: The image of the Muslim in the Ramjanmabhumi movement. In *Communalism in India: Challenge and response*, edited by Mehdi Arslan and Janaki Rajan, 83–97. New Delhi: Manohar.

Enloe, Cynthia. 2007. *Globalization & militarism: Feminists make the link.* Lanham, MD: Rowman & Littlefield.

Hansen, Kathryn. 1988. The Virangana in North Indian history, myth and popular culture, *Economic and Political Weekly* 23 (18), Apr. 30, WS 25–23.

Hansen, Thomas Blom. 1999. *The saffron wave: Democracy and Hindu nationalism in modern India.* Princeton, NJ: Princeton University Press.

Hiltebeitel, Alf, and Kathleen M. Erndl, eds. 2000. *Is the Goddess a Feminist? The Politics of South Asian Goddesses.* New York: New York University Press.

Jaffrelot, Christoph. 1996. *The Hindu nationalist movement in Indian politics.* New York: Columbia University Press.

Menon, Kalyani. 2012. *Everyday nationalism: Women of the Hindu right in India.* Philadelphia: University of Pennsylvania Press.

Mitchell, Richard G., Jr. 1993. *Secrecy and fieldwork*, Qualitative Research Methods, Volume 29. Thousand Oaks, CA: Sage.

Mostov, Julie, "Our Women":/ "Their Women": Symbolic Boundaries, Territorial Markers, and Violence in the Balkans". 1995. *Peace and Change*, 20: 515-529. Blackwell Publishers.

Naples, Nancy A. 1998. *Grassroots warriors: Activist mothering, community work, and the war on poverty.* New York: Routledge.

Peterson, V. Spike. 2000. Sexing political identities/ nationalism as heterosexism, in *Women, states, and nationalism*, edited by Sita Ranchod-Nilsson and Mary Ann Tetreault, 55-82. New York: Routledge.

Pettman, Jan Jindy. 1996. *Worlding women: A feminist international politics* New York: Routledge.

Pfister, Gertrud, and Dagmar Reese. 1995. Gender, body culture and body politics in national socialism. *Sports Science Review* 4(1): 91–121.

Sarkar, Tanika. 1991. The woman as communal subject: Rashtrasevika Samiti and the Ram Janmabhoomi movement. *Economic and Political Weekly*, August 31, 2057–2067..

Sarkar, Tanika, and Urvashi Butalia, eds. 1995. *Women and the Hindu Right: A Collection of Essays.* New Delhi: Kali for Women.

Sehgal, Meera. 2012. Mothering the nation: Maternalist frames in the Hindu nationalist movement. In *Women of the Right: Comparisons and Exchanges across National Borders,* edited by Kathleen Blee and Sandra McGee Deutsch, 193-207. University Park, PA: Pennsylvania State University Press.

————. 2009. The veiled feminist ethnographer: Fieldwork amongst women of India's Hindu right, in *Women Fielding Danger: Negotiating Ethnographic Identities in Field Research*, edited by Martha Huggins and Marie-Louise Glebes, 325–352. Lanham, MD: Rowman & Littlefield.

————. 2007. Manufacturing a feminized siege mentality: Hindu nationalist paramilitary camps for women in India. *Journal of Contemporary Ethnography* 36(2):165–183.

————. 2004. Reproducing the feminine citizen-warrior: The case of the Rashtra Sevika Samiti, a right-wing women's organization. PhD diss., University of Wisconsin-Madison.

Sharma, Aradhana. 2008. *Logics of empowerment: Development, gender and governance in neoliberal India*. Minneapolis: University of Minnesota Press.

Van der Veer, Peter. 1996. Riots and Rituals: The construction of Violence and Public Space in Hindu Nationalism, in *Riots and Pogroms*, edited by Paul R. Brass, 154–176. New York: New York University Press.

Yuval-Davis, Nira. 1997. *Gender and nation*. Thousand Oaks, CA: Sage.

4

Borders, Territory, and Ethnicity

Women and the Naga Peace Process

DUNCAN MCDUIE-RA

Introduction

In mid-2010 the federal state of Manipur, located on India's eastern border with Myanmar, was cut off from the rest of the country. During the blockade, the leader of National Socialist Council of Nagalim (Isak-Muivah), Theungaling Muivah, attempted to enter Manipur to visit his home village for the first time in forty years. The visit was part of a peace and reconciliation tour in preparation for peace talks with the Indian government. Naga secessionists have been fighting the Indian government for over six decades. Muivah had not been to his home village for forty years after decades in exile. Yet to get to his home village Muivah had to pass through northern Manipur, an area claimed by Naga secessionists as part of a unified Nagalim: the imagined Naga homeland, a claim rejected by the majority Meitei community in Manipur. The government of Manipur banned Muivah from entering. Protests, shootings, and counterprotests followed. Manipur remained cut off for two months. One of the most striking aspects of the protests at Mao Gate was the involvement of masses of Naga women. Similarly, in Manipur's political center, the Imphal valley, women's organizations from the Meitei ethnic group were prominent in protests *against* Muivah's visit and against the peace process. Women had been instrumental in making peace, yet fourteen years later they were seemingly engaging in counterpolitics set to unravel the peace process.

In this chapter I analyze the role of women in the politics of two adjoining territories in the India-Myanmar borderland: Nagaland and

Manipur. Women's organizations and activists have been instrumental in making peace within their respective ethnic communities during decades of insurgency and counterinsurgency. As peace has slowly come to the region, competing territorial claims have been catalysts for ethnic tensions between hill-dwelling Naga communities and valley-dwelling Meitei communities. In this chapter I explore the relationship between women's agency, peace, territoriality, and ethnicity in the India-Myanmar borderlands focusing on three factors. First, women's organizations from the Naga and Metei communities deploy motherhood in their protests and counterprotests, affirming accepted gender roles within each community. Second, the political possibilities of motherhood as a discursive frame are bound by the dominance of territorial politics. Motherhood is an effective tool for mobilizing political action, but not effective enough to transcend hardening ethnic boundaries in the borderland. Third, as in other locations, women must contend with the dual expectation of working toward peace and upholding the interests of the larger community: a duality difficult to maintain in the political environment of the borderland.

The chapter is divided into five sections. The first introduces the India-Myanmar borderland and the various fissures of state and ethnonational territoriality shaping social and political life. The second section examines the 1997 peace accord between the Indian government and the National Socialist Council of Nagalim (Isak-Muivah) and its catalytic role in escalating ethnic tensions between Naga and Meitei communities. The third section analyses women's organizations and their political agency in both the Naga and Meitei communities, with a particular focus on motherhood. The fourth section describes the events of Mao Gate in 2010 and the participation of women and women's organizations in the standoff itself and in the counterprotests in the valley. The final section discusses the links between women's agency, peace, territoriality, and ethnic politics focusing on the three factors discussed above.

The India-Myanmar Borderland

The focus of this chapter is the territory on the Indian side of the India-Myanmar border known as Northeast India. The region shares over 90 percent of its borders with other countries: Bangladesh, Bhutan, Myanmar, China, and Nepal. The Northeast is barely connected by land to the rest of India and is home to a diverse population ethnically distinct from the rest of the country, even when accounting for India's ethnic and cultural diversity. There are eight federal states in the region: Assam, Arunachal Pradesh, Manipur, Meghalaya, Mizoram, Nagaland, Sikkim, and Tripura, as well as a number of autonomous territories. Nagaland and Manipur will be the focus of this chapter. The region is populated by three main categories of people: indigenous communities classified as Scheduled Tribes, which make up the majority of the population in five out of eight of the federal states in the region; other ethnic groups not classified as tribes but sharing ethnic lineage with groups in East and Southeast Asia and also considered indigenous to the region (principally the Ahom of Assam and Meiteis of Manipur); and migrant communities from other parts of India and surrounding countries.

Since Indian Independence the Northeast has been characterized by armed struggles. These struggles responded to forced integration into the Indian Union, uneven local political and economic autonomy, and the neglect of basic needs. In response, the Indian government has created new states and territorial units normalizing the notion of "ethnically exclusive homelands" (Baruah 2003). Groups without homelands sought new territorial units leading to local struggles between ethnic groups with the Indian state acting as arbitrator. Furthermore, the inability of successive Indian governments and local governments to control migration into the region has furthered grievances and violence. As a result conflicts exist between different ethnic and tribal groups (and the territorial units representing them), between particular ethnic groups and the Indian state, and between communities indigenous to the region and migrants (Baruah 2003; Bhaumik 2009).

Decades of insurgency and counterinsurgency have militarized the borderland. Militarization comes from the Indian Army and paramilitary groups (referred to as armed forces hereafter) and local militant groups primarily organized along tribal and ethnic lines. Armed personnel are encountered on the roads, in towns, in villages, and in markets. Military cantonments and bases occupy town centers, strategic hills, bridges, and border crossings. Members of the armed forces frequently stop vehicles to search passengers and cargo. Checkpoints are numerous, heavily curtailing movement. The Indian armed forces have come to symbolize an occupying force for the peoples of the region.

Sack famously defined territoriality as "the attempt to affect, influence, or control actions and interactions (of people, things, and relationships) by asserting and attempting to enforce control over a geographic area" (1983, 55). This definition is helpful in understanding the politics of the borderland wherein the desire to control different areas by the Indian government, the Indian Army and paramilitaries, federal state governments (Manipur and Nagaland), insurgent groups, and ethno-nationalist movements has engendered a highly unstable environment. In this environment ethnicity is deeply embedded in notions of territory, leading to what Van Schendel (2011) refers to as an "exclusive politics of belonging."

A useful (if somewhat limited) device for coming terms with the ethnic complexity of the area is to divide it into hill and valley areas. Members of the Naga ethnic group live in the hills in northern Manipur and into the federal state of Nagaland, while Meiteis live in the valley areas and form the majority population in Imphal, the state capital and seat of Manipur's political power. Generally speaking, the dominant religion in the hills is Christianity, and in the valleys it is Vaishnavite Hinduism mixed with other traditional Meitei faiths. Women's organizations have been instrumental in challenging militarism in both the hills and the valley respectively.

Manipur is the site of competing territorial claims born out of two separate armed struggles. The first and longest running is the struggle for an independent Nagalim. Nagalim is distinct from the federal state of Nagaland, which was created in 1963 and is an officially recognized federal state in the Indian Union. Nagaland is a much smaller territory than Nagalim, which encompasses the erstwhile Nagaland plus tracts of territory in the surrounding federal states of Assam, Arunachal Pradesh, and Manipur as well as across the international border in Myanmar. In essence Nagalim is the imagined homeland of Nagas, and Nagaland is the homeland granted by the Indian government. The struggle for Nagalim began as a struggle against the Indian state but is increasingly being contested between different communities within the Northeast—in this case Nagas and Meiteis.

In the valley areas of Manipur the situation is more complex. Meitei resentment to forced integration of the Manipur kingdom into the

Indian Union in 1949 sparked hostility toward India that manifested in armed uprisings in the 1980s, bringing the Indian Army and paramilitary in vast numbers. Three decades on they remain, and Manipur has been the site of frequent human rights abuses furthering local grievances. State police and security forces have also increased in size and power throughout Manipur, increasing the intensity of localized struggles in a fragmented polity (see Parratt 2005).

The territory at the heart of the case presented here is part of the desired Nagalim but outside the federal state of Nagaland; located in the neighboring federal state of Manipur. The "internal" border between Nagaland and Manipur is where ethnic politics are played out and where activists, especially women, converged in 2010 to support Naga unity.

The struggle for Naga independence began during the last decade of British rule in India. On of August 15, 1947 the Naga National Council (NNC) led by Angami Phizo declared independence from Britain and India, a day before India itself gained independence (Ao 2002; Das 2011; Dutt-Luithui 1985; Shimray 2005). A series of negotiations with the Indian government followed in which many Naga leaders felt they were disrespected, affirming the desire for Naga independence (Iyer 1994; Hazarika 1995, 103). The NNC agreed to what they believed was a ten-year period of guardian power, after which they would be able to vote on independence. During this same period the Indian Army began its occupation of the Naga areas.   In 1956 the NNC declared that the ten-year period of guardian power had expired and they would secede (Misra 1978). During this period the Indian Army and paramilitary engaged in counterinsurgency operations in Naga areas (Chasie and Hazarika 2009; Fernandes 2004). These included a number of violent attacks on civilians, extrajudicial killings, targeted sexual violence, and the tactic of "grouping," wherein villagers were relocated close to roads and army camps (Bhatia 2011). One of the most notorious counterinsurgency operations was Operation Bluebird in the Naga areas of Manipur in 1987 (the same territory at the heart of the present case), during which members of the Assam Rifles paramilitary murdered fifteen persons, tortured hundreds, and raped women at gunpoint in the village of Oinam. The perpetrators were protected under the Armed Forces Special Powers Act 1958 (AFSPA), an extraordinary law deployed in the Northeast that prevents members of the armed forces and paramilitary from going to trial for actions undertaken in counterinsurgency operations (McDuie-Ra 2009). The AFSPA has also been used to protect human rights violations throughout the Imphal valley and other parts of Manipur (Ningthouja 2010). Despite violating the central tents of India's democracy the AFSPA has persisted, justified as a necessary tool for security in an unruly borderland (Kikon 2009).

In 1960 an agreement was reached between a moderate group of the NNC (called the Naga People's Convention) and the Prime Minister of India, Jawaharlal Nehru, that resulted in the creation of Nagaland as a federal state in 1963. Phizo denounced the 1960 agreement and fighting between insurgents and the Indian Army continued, though the state of Nagaland was formed (Ao 2002; Hazarika 1995; Means 1971). By the late 1970s a new insurgent group had emerged called the National Socialist Council of Nagalim (NSCN), formed by Theungaling Muivah and two other senior NNC members, Isak Swu and S. S. Khaplang. In 1988 the NSCN split into two factions, one led by Muivah and Swu (NSCN-IM) and the second by Khaplang (NSCN-K). The rivalry between the groups tore Nagalim apart during the late 1980s and early 1990s (Banerjee 1992).

In the valley areas of Manipur an even more fragmented set of armed groups ranging from communists, Meitei ethno-nationalists, and monarchists escalated violence and brought heavy counterinsurgency operations from the 1980s (Parratt 2005). Coupled with the growing dysfunction of the government of Manipur, murders, disappearances, torture, corruption, and extortion came to characterize life in the valley (Ganguly 2008). This manifests in posttraumatic stress, drug use, high levels of gender-based violence, and extortion and blackmail by insurgent groups and those pretending to be (Sabhlok 2009).

In this environment gender-based violence is widespread. Murder, rape, beatings, and sexual harassment by the armed forces in the Northeast has been well documented in a number of international and national human rights reports (ACHR 2008a, 2008b; Ganguly 2008; HRW 2008), and by local women's organizations, activists, and human rights groups in the region. Furthermore, gender-based violence is not only perpetrated by the occupying armed forces, but by the local law enforcement agencies. While this also takes place in other parts of India

and the world, violence by law enforcement agencies in the unruly borderland is more possible and less extraordinary when it occurs. The
proximity to international borders means additional security personnel are constantly on the move throughout the region. Furthermore, the
rivalry between NSCN factions perpetrated gender-based violence in
the 1980s and 1990s (Manchanda 2001). As Chenoy argues, in this environment "the very sight of men in uniform is traumatizing" (2002, 133).

Women's experiences of violence go beyond incidences of violence
they are personally subject to. Goswami and co-authors identify six categories of women affected: women relatives of armed activists, women
relatives of state armed forces, women militants or combatants, women
as shelter providers, women as victims of sexual and physical abuse,
woman as peace negotiators, and women as rights activists (2005, 19). It
is also conceivable that many women fulfill multiple categories in their
varied roles inside and outside the household. Women in affected areas
have formed active organizations to contest violence, and these will be
discussed in detail in the following sections.

Peace and Territoriality

In 1997 NSCN-IM signed a ceasefire agreement with the Indian government (see Das 2011; Hussain 2008; Rajagopalan 2008). The peace
talks have been sustained through over forty rounds and three different
Indian governments. In order to understand the standoff at Mao Gate
in 2010, it is crucial to note the ways the ceasefire between the Indian
government and the NSCN-IM has become a catalyst for ethnically
defined territoriality between the hill and valley areas of Manipur. The
desire of the NSCN-IM to unite all the Naga areas of India and Myanmar means that Manipur would lose a large portion of its territory to a
united Nagalim. As such civil society actors in Manipur have opposed
the Naga peace process, with women's organizations at the vanguard.

Opposition to the peace process accelerated in the Imphal valley
in 2001 when the Indian government extended the ceasefire "without
territorial limits" (Shimray 2001), lending legitimacy to the notion of
a unified Nagalim. Protests erupted in Imphal, and Meitei women's
organizations were prominent participants in these protests. Thousands
took to the streets, burning debris and trees and blocking military

vehicles. The Manipur Legislative Assembly was burned down. Police and security forces opened fire on protestors and eighteen people were killed. Protestors directed their anger toward the Indian government and toward the NSCN-IM. This came at a time of increased anger at the Indian government in Manipur after a string of violent counterinsurgency campaigns in 2000 and 2001.

In the period between 2001 and 2010 ethnic politics began to take hold of society and state in Manipur and divided the hill and valley communities (Bhagat and Akoijam 2002; Oinam 2003). In 2005 the government of Manipur declared June 18, 2001 as State Integrity Day, and labeled those killed in the protests as martyrs, bringing a new level of symbolism to ethnic politics. At the heart of these politics is maintaining the present boundaries of Manipur at any cost. This led to the Mao Gate incident of 2010. Before Mao Gate is discussed in detail, further analysis of the role of women in these politics is necessary.

Women, Peace, and Motherhood

Women's organizations operate in an environment of limited political possibilities in the borderland. First, the AFSPA, in operation throughout Nagaland and Manipur, makes the assembly of more than five people illegal (McDuie-Ra 2009). This makes protests and demonstrations difficult, but it also makes meetings and other public activities hazardous, especially when interethnic and factional tensions are high. Meeting during church and tribal gatherings as well as festivals have enabled organizations to circumvent this through the years. However, the main point here is that assuming that the vibrant civil society existent in other parts of India naturally exists in the Northeast is inaccurate. Second, insurgent groups also constrain civil society. Mistrust has been a characteristic of social relations, even at the village level, and this has fragmented networks and associational life. Third, local government, including the government of Nagaland and government of Manipur in particular, place their own restrictions on civil society. The chief mechanism is requiring registration of civil society actors in order to make them eligible for funding from within India or abroad.

Registration can be taken away by the federal state governments, often based on accusations that a certain actor is in league with insurgents. Corruption and patronage with local authorities also distorts the position of different civil society actors, to the advantage of some and detriment of others. Lastly, the subnational and international borders make networking between different civil society actors difficult. While this may seem a minor point, movement between the different hill states in the Northeast is constrained by military checkpoints, poor roads, and poor communications infrastructure outside the main towns, isolating many civil society actors from one another. In practice this means there are distinctions between say, Naga women's organizations in Nagaland and Naga women's organizations in Manipur. They come together at times, but remain largely isolated and contained within federal state boundaries (see McDuie-Ra 2012).

In this environment it is difficult for women's organizations to transcend the constraints on political agency (Das 2008a). However, it is through the discursive framing of motherhood that women's organizations have been able to gain political agency and legitimacy within, though not necessary between, their respective ethnic communities. This applies to organizations of Naga women in the hill areas, and organizations of Meitei women in the valley. Literature on motherhood and political protest is extensive, particularly in environments of conflict.

Motherhood is utilized in a number of ways, including as maternal moral authority to oppose conflict, in seeking justice for atrocities and disappearances, to legitimize conflict by equating maternity with nationalism or ethno-nationalism, in constructing symbols and memories of conflicts, and in postconflict nation-building (Fluri 2008; Helman 1999; Koch 2011; McDowell 2008; Moser and Clark 2001; Yuval-Davis 1997). Importantly, motherhood elicits emotive responses across cultures (De Volo 2004). As Tami Jacoby argues in the case of Israel, motherhood is used by women "to legitimize their protest in ways that conform with socially accepted norms" (1999, 385). Thus while often effective, motherhood enacts traditional gender roles, whether in the pursuit of radical or conservative politics (Dowler 1998). Perhaps most compelling is Ruth Gilmore's work on the intersections of race, class, and motherhood in women's activism against the California penal system (1999; 2007). Gilmore demonstrates the ways that women's activism pushes the notion of motherhood "past the limits of household, kinship, and neighborhood, past the limits of gender and racial divisions of social space" (1999, 28) to directly challenge state power.

Motherhood is invoked in similar ways to challenge state power in the Northeast while at the same time perpetuating ethnic divisions, making the transcendence of ethnic boundaries extremely challenging. The two main women's organizations in Nagalim are the Naga Mothers Association and the Naga Women's Union of Manipur, who operate on either side of the internal border between Nagaland and Manipur. Formed in 1984, the Mothers Association has attempted to bring peace through the centrality of motherhood and draws on the respect that mothers hold in Naga society to pressure militants and politicians (Das 2008b; Haksar 1985). The moral authority of Naga mothers enables them to transcend factional politics. In this way the Mothers Association resembles other peace initiatives in locations such as Argentina, Israel, and Sri Lanka (Afshar 2003; De Alwis 2008; Helman 1999). The Mothers Association began to shift toward adopting a proactive peace-making agenda in the 1990s. The most renowned was the formation of a peace team in 1994 during some of the worst factional violence. The peace team is credited with intervening in factional violence at the local level and in publically criticizing insurgent leaders, individual cadres, and members of the Indian Army. Along with churches and some of the Hohos (traditional Naga political councils), the Mothers Association launched the Shed No More Blood campaign to try to heal the rifts within the society, which ran for over ten years. Manchanda (2004) has noted that the use of motherhood has been a very effective way for women to have a voice during times of conflict and in the peace process, but it has not necessarily translated into challenging gender relations in other aspects of Naga society. In fact, motherhood affirms gender relations, as women have few avenues through social and political institutions to affect Naga society and, thus, depend upon the recognition of traditional roles as leverage in their activism. Yet members of the Mothers Association are revered and respected and the organization has made political breakthroughs where other actors have failed.

The second key organization is the Naga Women's Union of Manipur, which operates across the internal border in northern Manipur, part of the territory claimed as Nagalim. The Union draws together smaller women's organizations in different parts of the Naga areas of Manipur.

The Union grew out of the violence between Naga and Kuki communities in Manipur in the 1990s and created space for interethnic dialogue at a time of heightened violence (Banerjee 2010). The Union has a more radical women's rights agenda than the Mothers Association and challenges social norms in Naga society, as well as engaging in peace-making. Members have confronted the Indian Army, acted as human shields, negotiated with insurgent groups in jungle camps, negotiated for hostage releases, attempted to bridge community tensions, brought factions of the NSCN together for talks, been part of the formal peace process, and pressured the leaders of NSCN-IM to bring their own cadres to trial for sexual violence (Manchanda 2004, 16–18). The Union has also been integral in pursuing greater political rights for Naga communities in Manipur.

There is also a very strong women's movement among the Meitei population in the Imphal valley, the main population center of Manipur. Most notable are the Meira Paibis (torch-bearing women). The Meira Paibis are a mass membership women's organization and every married Meitei woman is considered a member. The Meira Paibis have been profiled extensively by scholars particularly those focusing on their opposition to the Indian Army and the AFSPA (Chakravarti 2010; Parratt and Parratt 2001). Attention to the Meira Paibis has grown after members of the organization staged a naked protest outside the headquarters of the Assam Rifles paramilitary organization following the rape and murder of a local woman in 2004 (Bora 2010; Gaikwad 2009; Misri 2011). Less discussed is the role of the Meira Paibis in curbing social ills in Meitei society, in particular enforcing the ban on alcohol in Manipur, and since the Naga peace process began, protesting *against* the peace agreement and supporting the territorial integrity of Manipur. As such the Meira Paibis use motherhood to pursue a conservative social agenda utilized to preserve Manipur's territory while also opposing militarism.

It is important to note the relative acceptance of women's organizations and motherhood within the different communities. In the hills, Naga women have long been excluded from traditional decision-making bodies, the Hohos, the armed organizations pursuing an independent Nagalim, and from elected political posts in Nagaland and the northern districts of Manipur (see Kikon 2005; Zehol 1998). Thus activism by Naga women in the face of the NSCN, and later in support of the NSCN, has helped to create a space for women's agency. By contrast, in the valley, Meitei women's organizations have been active since the early twentieth century when women mobilized to resist the forced conscription of men by British officers in 1904 (Veda 2005, 15). Parratt and Parratt argue that the "women's war" of 1939–1940, initially concerned with the impact of rice shortages, escalated into a movement over control of food supply, against the overzealous responses of the military to the initial protests, and against the corrupt local regime (2001, 906). They add that this generated "popular political awareness" and was the main catalyst in overthrowing the monarchy and bringing about democratic elections in Manipur in 1948, four years before the first elections in independent India and a year before the controversial merger of Manipur into the Indian Union (2001, 918). The Meira Paibis thus operate within a social environment where women's organizations and the frame of motherhood have historical legitimacy, and contemporary activism maintains a space created in the past.

Despite the shared trope of motherhood and shared opposition to the military occupation of the borderland, there are few avenues of communication between women's groups in the Naga areas and those in the Meitei areas—though as the president of the Naga Women's Union of Manipur has discussed in personal interviews, at times of crisis they do try to come together, though as ethnic politics have escalated since 2001 these meetings have become increasingly fragmentary and even hostile.[1] This demonstrates the bind for women's movements in the Northeast. They are pursuing peace on what Gaikwad refers to as "unstable ground," where it becomes difficult to pinpoint the "wrongdoers" (2009, 300). Motherhood has been successful in giving women a voice in pursuing peace, yet it has also drawn women's organizations deeper into territorial politics.

Mao Gate 2010

Mao Gate reveals the contours of this unstable ground. Mao Gate is the entry point to Manipur on the highway from Nagaland. It is located in the Senapati District, which is a Naga-dominated area claimed as part of Nagalim. In a sense Senapati and the neighboring Ukhrul district are the frontline of competing subnational territorial claims by Nagas and Meiteis, and also sites of decades of militarization by the Indian Army and paramilitary forces. However, it was not an act of violence that precipitated the crisis; rather, it was an attempt at peacemaking.

In May 2010 Theungaling Muivah, the Ato Kilosner (leader) of the NSCN-IM, conducted a peace and reconciliation tour of all the Naga districts on the Indian side of the India-Myanmar border in preparation for peace talks with the Indian government.[2] Political and insurgent factionalism, tribal and clan affiliations, interfaith divisions, and the legacy of insurgency campaigns, arrests, and human rights violations by all sides in the Naga struggle necessitated a push for unity. The peace and reconciliation tour was a highly symbolic gesture. Muivah was received by all of the different Naga clans and tribes and spoke about unity and peace on each stop. Throughout Naga areas Hohos, local governments, and local NSCN-IM chapters organized receptions for Muivah in villages, churches, and schools. Children lined the roads into towns and villages and waved the unified Nagalim flag to welcome Muivah to their locality. Muivah's entourage included NSCN-IM members, the press, and a number of Naga civil society organizations, including many women's activists and members of the Mothers Association and the Women's Union, some of whom had been critical of the NSCN in the past. The symbolism was very clear. Divisions were no longer important in the wake of an historical agreement.

The Meitei community and the government of Manipur viewed Muivah's tour with suspicion. The tour came at a particularly sensitive time in community relations in Manipur. For many years Naga civil society groups in Manipur have pushed for an autonomous district council in the Naga areas. Such councils exist in other hill areas of the Northeast and were legislated in the Sixth Schedule of the Indian Constitution in 1947. Autonomous district councils in Manipur have fallen under a more complex and at times opaque regime. Six councils were created in 1971 and subject to direct elections (Hassan 2008; Ray 1996). After violence escalated in Manipur during the 1980s, the councils were suspended under the orders of the governor of Manipur. Under pressure from civil society groups a new act was passed in 2000, the Manipur (Hill Areas) Autonomous District Council Act, which replaced the 1971 act. This helped to ease one of the major grievances of the hill population, but the act was never brought into force and in 2006 the maligned 1971 act was reinstated. In 2008 the act was amended once again and these amendments were seen as further stripping autonomy from the hill areas (Chamroy 2008).

The government of Manipur announced elections to the hill councils in late 2009. In April 2010 a number of Naga civil society groups led by the All Naga Students Association of Manipur and the umbrella United Naga Council called for a boycott of these elections (Samon 2010, 33). The government of Manipur was undeterred and scheduled the elections for late May. In response, the boycott became a blockade of the two main highways into Manipur, the national highways 39 and 53. This cut off Manipur from the rest of India. The Imphal valley, the Meitei dominated area and home to the government of Manipur, is highly vulnerable to such blockades. With steep hills surrounding the valley to the north, south, and west and with the international border with Myanmar to the east, the heart of the state's economic and political power can be severed by blockades on the two main highways. Such was the animosity between Naga and Meitei communities in mid-2010 that the blockade lasted two months.

It is in this environment that Muivah attempted to bring the peace and reconciliation tour into northern Manipur to the areas where Nagas were boycotting the council elections. Perhaps Muivah also aimed to provoke the government of Manipur, but his visit was certainly welcomed by the bulk of the Naga community in Manipur at a time when they were feeling increasingly alienated. Muivah planned to enter Manipur at Mao Gate in Senapati and travel to all the Naga areas of Manipur before reaching his home village of Somdal. The government of Manipur announced they would bar Muivah from entering. Crisis meetings were held between members of the government of Manipur, the government of Nagaland, and the peace negotiators from the Indian government. Meanwhile, Muivah waited on the Nagaland side of the border between the two federal states while these deliberations took place. As he waited, his supporters set out for Mao Gate to welcome Muivah back home.

A number of crucial events took place in the first days of May. Civil society organizations in the Imphal valley protested *against* Muivah's visit, including the Meira Paibis, the mass Meitei women's organization discussed above. Protestors supported the decision of Chief Minister of Manipur, Ibobi Singh, to stop Muivah. They also blamed Naga groups for the blockade of the valley. As Bhattacharjee argues, for Ibobi Singh barring Muivah "seems to have been a master stroke by a politician whose effigy was being burnt and kicked around the valley's roads just a few months back" (2010, 35). By this time, the blockade by Naga civil society organizations and members of the hill communities had been in place for twenty-five days.

The announcement that Muivah would be denied entry was a fillip to the anti-election protest, and it evolved into a widespread movement of frustration by Naga communities in Manipur. Communities from all over the hills converged on Mao Gate to welcome Muivah, stationed just a few kilometers away, and protest against the government of Manipur. Those supporting Muivah attempted to stop security forces from reaching the gate to block his entry. On May 6, an enormous gathering of Naga women organized by the Mothers Association and Women's Union staged a sit-in protest on both sides of the border. The photographs of these sit-in protests are extraordinary. On both sides of the border Naga women occupied the entire highway, with state security forces stuck in between them guarding the gate. In a photograph in *Himal* magazine, a group of Naga women on the Manipur side sit and stand in the face of security forces, and one woman is holding a sign reading "Set Us Free."[3] At Mao Gate being a Naga was more important than any of the divisions of the past. Several of the women involved in these protests related their experiences during my visit to Manipur in early 2011. They came from all over the hills areas and from the valley, where many women live and work. They shared food, prayed, and sang songs.

As tensions escalated, Manipur security forces tried to stop the demonstrators from reaching the border post and fired tear gas and bullets. The protestors scattered. Footage of the shootings shows crowds of protestors, mostly women, running to the side of the road to find shelter.[4] Over seventy people were injured. The crisis escalated when security forces shot and killed two Naga youth, Neli Chakho and Dikho Loshou. Video of the shooting quickly circulated through the Internet and for a time was posted on YouTube. Naga protestors reinforced road blockades with trees, tires, stones, and trenches. The Indian Army, also present at Mao Gate, vowed to clear the road, but, as one journalist caught in the blockade reported, they "had no idea how to deal with this army of women" (Bhattacharjee 2010, 36). The uncertainty that followed meant that many protestors who had come to Mao Gate could not return home, and as many as four thousand persons were estimated to be displaced in the weeks that followed (Kikon 2010, 41).

The situation was played out thousands of kilometers away in Delhi, where large numbers of students from the borderland work and study. Student organizations in Delhi issued statements of support and condemnation, depending on whom they were representing. A group of Naga students marched to the Manipur Bhawan (Manipur House, the residence of the government of Manipur in India's capital) and damaged the building (E-pao 2010). A large public protest took place on May 10 outside the prime minister's residence. Led by the Naga Student Union Delhi, the protestors held signs criticizing the Chief Minister of Manipur, Iboi Singh, condemning the Manipur security forces, and calling for justice. Nagalim flags were also featured, and roses were laid next to photographs of the two deceased. The two youths had become martyrs. Indeed, a year after their death a memorial was unveiled at the site (Kangla Online, 2011).

After the shootings the blockade of Manipur held for six more weeks. During this time life in the Imphal valley came to a standstill. The blockade exacerbated the difficulties of urban life by adding fuel shortages, soaring prices, and feeding the thriving black-market. Hospitals, schools, and public transport virtually shut down. In the meantime, the controversial elections for the District Councils went ahead. In some Naga constituencies' *bandhs* (enforced strikes) were held, ensuring very low voter turnout, and in several constituencies incumbents had no opponents.[5] Meitei civil society actors held protests in Imphal demanding that the government of Manipur take action to end the blockade. The blockade not only affected the Meitei community, but also the large groups of Nagas and Kukis living in the capital. Interethnic tensions in the city were very high. Visiting the city a few months later these tensions were still discernible, and the various communities stayed in their respective neighborhoods as much as possible. Imphal shuts down after dark, and during fieldwork residents would hurry back to their respective ethnic neighborhoods as soon as dusk set in.

After the blockade was finally lifted, the situation for Nagas and Meiteis altered little. As the local journalist Anjulika Samom notes, "the blockade and Muivah's proposed visit have left a deep mark on the psyche of the people as well as the political equations of this tiny state" (2010, 33). Mao Gate shows the incompatibility of the imaginations of neighboring communities as seen through what the Manipuri historian Yengjkhom Jilangamba calls the "simplistic, homogenous and unilinear view of the past" promoted and reproduced throughout the Northeast (2010, 39). Jilangamba sees this view as offering "threatening and one-dimensional choices (that) not only encourage ethnic tensions, but also limit political expression only to ethnic-based articulations" (2010, 39). If Mao Gate could be viewed as the limit of the peace process, and even the failure of peace to overcome ethnic politics, where does this leave the women's organizations so involved in the protests for and against Muivah's visit?

Reading Mao Gate

How are we to account for the prominence of women and women's organizations at Mao Gate? In turn, what does Mao Gate tell us about intersecting structures of gender, ethnicity, and territory and the ways these structures affect the political possibilities, decisions, and strategies of women's organizations? First, in both the hills and the valley, motherhood is the central trope in women's agency. In their role as mothers, women's organizations have contested human rights violations by the Indian Army and state security forces. Their activism has come to symbolize resistance to militarism. Women's organizations have also contested the actions of militant groups from their own community, a much less visible politics than opposing the occupying Indian Army, and one fraught with obstacles and risks. Women's organizations have been instrumental in shaming militant leaders and individual cadres, and in bringing factions together. In the last decade and a half, the focus of women's organizations has broadened to include supporting the opposing territorial claims of their respective ethnic groups—claims that converge on the internal border between Manipur and Nagaland and are embodied in the Mao Gate incident.

Importantly, women's organizations in Meitei areas of the valley operate in a local environment where their agency is embedded in historical episodes seen as central to nation-building and resistance to domination by outside forces, whether British, Burmese, or Indian. Women's organizations have a long-standing space in Meitei society and an accepted degree of legitimacy to contest social, political, and economic conditions. In the hills, women's organizations have had to create a space for contesting violence in recent decades, particularly after the fissures of violence shifted from Nagas against the Indian army to violence between Naga factions after the split of the NSCN in 1988.

Legitimacy is drawn from their position as mothers of those affected by conflict and, by extension, mothers of the entire ethnic group. In this way women's organizations have moral authority and act as a collective consciousness to stop the violence, regardless of where it emanates. Yet the same actors are able to direct their agency toward supporting opposed positions on territoriality in the borderland. As Mao Gate demonstrates, motherhood can be just as readily deployed by women's organizations to frame opposition to the Naga peace process on the one hand, and support for Muivah's visit on the other—despite the fact that these positions have produced more violence.

Second, the political possibilities of motherhood as a discursive frame for women's agency are bound by the dominance of territorial politics and attendant ethno-nationalism. Motherhood is an effective tool for mobilizing political action, but this is contained within increasingly polarized ethnic communities. Motherhood is not effective enough to transcend hardening ethnic boundaries in the borderland. Naga women are mothers of Naga people and Naga causes, and vice-versa for Meiteis. In a contentious political environment motherhood is not imbibed with a universal quality, but is drawn into the dominant ethno-nationalist discourse. Yet women's organizations are still very effective at mobilizing action within their own communities, as demonstrated by the Mao Gate incident. Naga women's organizations were involved in the peace and reconciliation tour bringing the fractured Naga polity together, yet they were also instrumental in the blockade of Manipur and in trying to prevent the security forces from stopping Muivah. They publically mourned the shooting of two Naga youths, performing deeply symbolic public mourning vilifying the excesses of the security forces acting on behalf of the valley as the seat of Manipur's political power. While in the Imphal valley the Meira Paibis actively protested against Muivah's visit, the NSCN-IM, the blockade and the peace accord. As mothers of the Meitei nation, preservation of the social order was tied to preservation of territorial boundaries.

As in other contexts, women's organizations and their members are not by nature neutral or unaffected by divisive politics, in this case ethno-nationalist territoriality. Women's organizations have a voice, they have legitimacy, and they have agency because they are embedded in the local context and its social fabric. They shape and are shaped by the politics of that context. Individual women engaged with serving their community in difficult and dangerous circumstances usually believe in the larger cause. They are themselves involved in the struggle. They have relatives, family members, and kin and clan members involved in some way. This does not mean that such struggles don't have their own internal dimensions. There are different political positions to take within a particular movement, but throughout a long-running struggle there is a necessary solidarity. Mao Gate called upon this solidarity and women's organizations performed it, but it was solidarity with their ethnic communities as mothers, not between women's organizations.

Women's organizations, like other civil society actors, take sides in contentious struggles. This does not necessarily compromise their agency or indicate that they are coopted. It can also mean that they make strategic decisions as the context changes. For instance, many members of the Mothers Association and the Women's Union who may have been critical of the NSCN-IM over the years still want to see Muivah come home; they will still want peace and reconciliation within the Naga movement, and they will still protest the shooting of protestors at Mao Gate. This does not make them less authentic or less legitimate. It merely reflects the realities of being genuinely community-based. The same argument can be made about Meitei women's organizations. They may agitate for the removal of their chief minister for failing to control the security forces, but they will support the chief minister when perceived threats to Manipur's territory are felt.

Third, as in other locations, women must contend with the dual expectation of working toward peace and upholding the interests of the larger community: a duality difficult to maintain in the borderland since the start of the peace process in 1997. In the hills and valleys of the borderland, the pressure of peacemaking has been firmly placed upon women and women's organizations. Atrocities by members of the Indian armed forces demand a response from the Meira Paibis through vigils, protest, or direct intervention with authorities. In the hills, women's organizations arrange local reconciliation events, work with churches and Hohos to rehabilitate combatants, and attend peace talks. Women's organizations have been effective in creating and carrying out these roles, having a major impact on their communities. However, in the valley and the hills, peace is gendered. It has become women's work, women's responsibility.

Peace means different things, even within the same borderland. Interestingly, peace no longer simply means the end of conflict with the Indian state, as it did in decades past. The case of the Naga peace process is compelling because the conflicts that emerged in 2001 and 2010 were not between the original parties fighting in the first place. The Naga movement fought against the Indian state, not Meiteis in Manipur. However, the prospect of peace for Nagas exacerbates Meitei insecurity. For Naga women's organizations and activists, peace means the unification of all Naga areas. This will put an end to the factional fighting among different militant groups; it will mean that the peace process will be concluded, and it will mean that life will get back to normal. Family members will be safe. Mobility will be easier. Violence in the society will likely diminish. Yet this depends on supporting the territorial politics of Nagalim. Nagalim involves a territorial reconfiguration of the borderlands. This matters, because without a territorial 7settlement large numbers of Naga women and men will continue to live in difficult circumstances in the northern part of Manipur—circumstances that are worsening. The territorial politics of Nagalim are condoned in so far as they are seen as the best way of achieving peace.

Similarly, in the Imphal valley Meitei women's organizations and activists have staunchly resisted territorial reconfiguration, as Manipur will lose much of its land. Meitei society is itself ravaged by insurgencies opposed to Manipur's integration into India and as armed opposition to the state government. In an environment of extreme insecurity, martial law, and state dysfunction, territoriality gives politics a central narrative and focus that draws people in the valley together. In the incredibly fractured Meitei polity it is perhaps the only common ground and thus the only prospect for peace.

Simultaneously the same organizations—the same women—are also expected to uphold ethnic traditions. This entails preserving the social order and protecting and, in this case, advancing the interests of the ethnic community. Yet women's organizations have little influence on determining what these interests are. Following the peace process, ethno-nationalist territoriality has narrowed the political possibilities for members of both communities. The interests of Nagas is unity, the interests of Meiteis is territorial integrity. As currently proposed, these interests clash. Women's organizations have little prospect, and perhaps little interest, in proposing alternatives.

Conclusion

Since 2001 tensions between Naga and Meitei communities over territory in northern Manipur have destroyed interethnic relations and empowered political leaders pushing narrow ethnic agendas. The internal border between Nagaland and Manipur has become the key site of contestation, and the Mao Gate incident of 2010 demonstrated this in spectacular fashion. What remains fascinating about the last decade of tensions between Naga and Meitei communities is that they have evolved out of peacemaking endeavors: the ongoing ceasefire process between the NSCN-IM and the Indian government and Muivah's reconciliation tour to ease rifts within the Naga population. Yet new fissures of conflict have emerged as others have been resolved.

Women's organizations and activists are embedded in these politics. Women's organizations have been instrumental in pursuing and creating peace. They have challenged members of their own communities, rival militant factions, and the Indian Army and paramilitary. Yet when peace measures have inflamed ethnic tensions, women have engaged in territorial politics on both sides. Reifying women's agency outside the messiness of local contexts overlooks the deep relationships between women, ethnicity, and territory. In the borderlands this constructs the social and political fields within which women exercise their agency and reproduce their gendered and ethnic identities.

NOTES

1. President of the Naga Women's Union of Manipur. Personal interview, Imphal, February 18, 2011.

2. The tour has been documented in NSCN/GPRN 2010.

3. This photograph appears in Bhattacharjee 2010, 32.

4. This footage can be viewed at www.youtube.com/watch?v=BurxJol152U.

5. In the Kuki hills in the southern part of Manipur voter turnout was much higher, reflecting the other divisive cleavage in Manipur between the two main hill populations (Samon 2010, 33).

REFERENCES

Asian Center for Human Rights (ACHR). 2008a. *India Human Rights Report 2008.* New Delhi: Asian Centre for Human Rights.

ACHR. 2008b. *Torture in India 2008: A State of Denial.* New Delhi: Asian Centre for Human Rights.

Afshar, Haleh. 2003. Women and Wars: Some Trajectories Towards a Feminist Peace. *Development in Practice* 13 (2/3): 178–88.

Ao, A. L Lanunungsang. 2002. *From Phizo to Muivah: The Naga National Question in North-East India.* Delhi: Mittal Publications.

Banerjee, Paula. 2000. The Naga Women's Interventions for Peace. *Canadian Woman Studies* 19 (4): 137–42

———. 2010. *Borders, Histories, Existences: Gender and Beyond.* New Delhi: Sage.

Banerjee, Sumanta. 1992. Dangerous Game in Nagaland. *Economic and Political Weekly* 27 (29): 1525–7.

Baruah, Sanjib. 2003. Confronting Constructionism: Ending India's Naga War. *Journal of Peace Research* 40 (3): 321–38.

Bhagat, Oinam, and A. Bimol Akoijam. 2002. Assembly Election: Trends and Issues. *Economic and Political Weekly* 36 (6): 519–24.

Bhatia, Bela. 2011. Awaiting Nachiso. *Himal SouthAsian* 24 (8): 61–64.

Bhattacharjee, Kishalay. 2010. After 69 Days. *Himal SouthAsian* 23 (7): 32–37.

Bhaumik, Subhir. 2005. The Accord That Never Was: Shillong Accord 1975. In *Peace Processes and Peace Accords.* Edited by S. K. Das, 120–141. New Delhi: Sage.

———. 2009. *Troubled Periphery: Crisis of India's Northeast.* New Delhi: Sage.

Bora, Papori. 2010. Between the Human, the Citizen and the Tribal. *International Feminist Journal of Politics* 3 (4): 341–60.

Chakravarti, Paromita. 2010. Reading Women's Protest in Manipur: A Different Voice? *Journal of Peacebuilding and Development* 5 (3): 47–60.

Chamroy, Ngachonmi. 2008. On Autonomous Hill Districts in Manipur. *Thangkhul. com.* www.tangkhul.com/modules.php?name=News&file=article&sid=1201.

Chasie, Charles and Sanjoy Hazarika. 2009. *The State Strikes Back: India and the Naga Insurgency.* Washington, DC: East-West Center Washington.

Chenoy, Anuradha M. 2002. *Militarism and Women in South Asia*. New Delhi: Kali For Women.

Das, Nava Kishor. 2011. Naga Peace Parleys: Sociological Reflections and a Plea for Pragmatism. *Economic & Political Weekly* 46 (25): 71–7.

Das, Samir Kumar. 2008a. *Conflict and Peace in India's Northeast: The Role of Civil Society*. Washington, DC: East-West Center Washington.

———. 2008b. Ethnicity and Democracy Meet When Mothers Protest. In *Women in Peace Politics*. Edited by P. Banerjee, 54–77. New Delhi: Sage.

De Alwis, Malathi. 2008. Motherhood as a Space of Protest: Women's Political Participation in Contemporary Sri Lanka. In *Women in Peace Politics*. Edited by P. Banerjee, 152–174. New Delhi: Sage.

De Volo, Lorraine Bayard. 2004. Mobilizing Mothers for War: Cross-National Framing Strategies in Nicaragua's Contra War. *Gender & Society* 18 (6): 715–734.

Dowler, Lorraine. 1998. "And They Think I'm Just a Nice Old Lady": Women and War in Belfast, Northern Ireland. *Gender, Place & Culture: A Journal of Feminist Geography* 5 (2): 159–176.

Dutt-Luithui, Ela. 1985. Violence in India: The Case of the Naga National Movement. *Comparative Studies of South Asia, Africa and the Middle East* 5 (2): 39–42.

E-Pao. 2010. Students Storm Manipur Bhawan. E-Pao May 7. http://e-pao.net/GP.asp?src=17..080510.may10.

Fernandes, Walter. 2004. Limits of Law and Order Approach to the North-East. *Economic and Political Weekly* 39 (42): 4609–11.

Fluri, Jennifer. 2008. Feminist-Nation Building in Afghanistan: An Examination of the Revolutionary Association of the Women of Afghanistan (RAWA). *Feminist Review* 89(1): 34–54.

Gaikwad, Namrata. 2009. Revolting Bodies, Hysterical State: Women Protesting the Armed Forces Special Powers Act (1958). *Contemporary South Asia* 17 (3): 299–311.

Ganguly, Meenakshi. 2008. *"These Fellows Must be Eliminated": Relentless Violence and Impunity in Manipur*. New York: Human Rights Watch.

Gilmore, RuthWilson. 1999. You Have Dislodged a Boulder: Mothers and Prisoners in the Post Keynesian California Landscape. *Transforming Anthropology* 8(1–2): 12–38.

———. 2007. *Golden Gulag: Prisons, Surplus, Crisis, and Opposition in Globalizing California*. Berkeley: University of California Press.

Goswami, Roshmi, M. Sreekala, and Meghna Goswami. 2005. *Women in Armed Conflict Situations*. Guwahati: North East Network.

Haksar, Nandita. 1985. Naga People's Movement for Human Rights: A Report. *Economic and Political Weekly* 20 (50): 2201–3.

Hassan, M. Sajjad. 2008. The Breakdown in North-East India. *Journal of South Asian Development* 3 (1): 53–86.

Hazarika, Sanjoy. 1995. *Strangers of the Mist: Tales of War and Peace from India's Northeast*. New Delhi: Penguin.

Helman, Sara. 1999. From Soldiering and Motherhood to Citizenship: A Study of Four Israeli Peace Protest Movements. *Social Politics: International Studies in Gender, State & Society* 6 (3): 292–313.

Human Rights Watch (HRW). 2008. *Getting Away with Murder: 50 Years of the Armed Forces Special Powers Act.* New York: Human Rights Watch.

Hussain, Wasbir. 2008. The Naga Dream and the Politics of Peace. *Asia Europe Journal* 6 (3): 547–60.

Iyer, V. R. Krishna. 1994. Saga of the Nagas. *Economic and Political Weekly*: 674–8.

Jacoby, T. A. 1999. Gendered Nation: A History of the Interface of Women's Protest and Jewish Nationalism in Israel. *International Feminist Journal of Politics* 1 (3): 382–402.

Jilangamba, Yengkhom. 2010. Ethnicity and Territoriality. *Himal South Asian* 23 (7): 38–40.

Kangla Online. 2011. Mao Gate Incident Anniversary Observed, NPC Declaration Reaffirmed. *Kangla Online*, 6 May 2011. http://kanglaonline.com/2011/05/mao-gate-incident-anniversary-observed-npc-declaration-reaffirmed/.

Kikon, Dolly . 2005. Engaging Naga Nationalism: Can Democracy Function in Militarised Societies? *Economic and Political Weekly* 40 (26): 2833–7.

———. 2009. The Predicament of Justice: Fifty Years of Armed Forces Special Powers Act in India. *Contemporary South Asia* 17 (3): 271–28.

———. 2010. Valley Versus Hill. *Himal SouthAsian* 23 (7): 41–44.

Koch, Natalie. 2011. Security and Gendered National Identity in Uzbekistan, *Gender, Place & Culture: A Journal of Feminist Geography* 18 (4): 499–518.

Manchanda, Rita. 2001. Redefining and Feminizing Security. *Economic and Political Weekly* 36 (22): 1956–63.

———. 2004. *We Do More Because We Can: Naga Women in the Peace Process.* New Delhi: South Asia Forum for Human Rights.

McDowell, Sara. 2008. Commemorating Dead "Men": Gendering the Past and Present in Post-Conflict Northern Ireland. *Gender, Place & Culture* 15 (4): 335–354.

McDuie-Ra, Duncan. 2009. 50 Year Disturbance: The Armed Forces Special Powers Act and Exceptionalism in a South Asian Periphery. *Contemporary South Asia* 17 (3): 255–270.

———. 2012. Violence Against Women in the Militarized Indian Frontier: Beyond "Indian Culture" in the Experiences of Ethnic Minority Women. *Violence Against Women* 18 (3): 322—345.

Means, Gordon P. 1971. Cease-Fire Politics in Nagaland. *Asian Survey* 11 (10): 1005–28.

Misra, Udayon. 1978. The Naga National Question. *Economic and Political Weekly* 13 (14): 618–24.

Misri, Deepti. 2011. "Are You a Man?": Performing Naked Protest in India. *Signs* 36 (3): 603–25.

Moser, Caroline, and Fiona Clark, eds. 2001. *Victims, Perpetrators, or Actors? Gender, Armed Conflict, and Political Violence.* London: Zed Books.

NSCN/GPRN. 2010. *Strengthening the Peace Process: Journey for Peace and Reconciliation 5 May 2010 to 15 July 2010.* Kohima: National Socialist Council Nagalim/ Government of People's Republic of Nagalim.

Oinam, Bhagat. 2003. Patterns of Ethnic Conflict in the North-East: A Study on Manipur. *Economic and Political Weekly* 38 (21): 2031–7.

Ningthouja, Malem. 2010. Violence as AFSPA 1958 and People's Movement Against It. *Eastern Quarterly* 6 (IV): 145–155.

Parratt, John. 2005. *Wounded Land: Politics and Identity in Modern Manipur*. New Delhi: Mittal Publications.

Parratt, Saroj Nalini Arambam, and John Parratt. 2001. The Second "Women's War" and the Emergence of Democratic Government in Manipur. *Modern Asian Studies* 35 (4): 905–19.

Rajagopalan, Swarna. 2008. *Peace Accords in Northeast India: Journey Over Milestones*. Washington, DC: East-West Center in Washington.

Ray, Ashok Kumar. 1996. Territorial Issues and Manipur. In *Reorganization of North East India Since 1947*. Edited by B. Datta Ray, S. P. Agrawal, 251–259. New Delhi: Concept Publishing Company.

Sabhlok, Smita G. 2009. Civil Society and Development: Between Peace and Insurgency in the Northeast. *South Asia: Journal of South Asian Studies* 32 (3): 501–17.

Sack, Robert D. 1983. Human Territoriality: A Theory. *Annals of the Association of American Geographers* 73 (1): 55–74.

Samon, Thingjam Anjulika 2010. Timeline of a Shutdown. *Himal Southasian* 23 (7): 32–33.

Shimray, A. S. Atai. 2005. *Let Freedom Ring? Story of Naga Nationalism*. New Delhi: Bibliophile South Asia.

Shimray, Ungshungmi A. 2001. Ethnicity and Socio-Political Assertion. *Economic and Political Weekly* 36 (39): 3674–7.

———. 2004. Socio-Political Unrest in the Region Called North-East India. *Economic and Political Weekly* 39 (42): 4637–43.

Van Schendel, Willem. 2011. The Dangers of Belonging. In *The Politics of Belonging in India: Becoming Adivasi*. Edited by D. Rycroft, S. Dasgupta, 19–43. London: Routledge.

Veda, Gunjan. 2005. *Tailoring Peace: The Citizen's Roundtable on Manipur and Beyond*. Guwahati: North East Network.

Yuval-Davis, Nira. 1997. *Gender and Nation*. Thousand Oaks, CA: Sage.

Zehol, Lucy, ed. 1998. *Women in Naga Society*. New Delhi: Regency Publications.

5

Imperial Gazes and Queer Politics

Re/Reading Female Political Subjectivity in Pakistan

MOON M. CHARANIA

In July of 2007, a year marked as one of the most violent in Pakistan,[1] the infamous events of the Lal Masjid (Red Mosque) in Islamabad unfolded, and the country took center stage in the global political theatre. The Lal Masjid became the site of a violent weeklong siege between the mosque's seminary students and the Pakistani military when the students of Jamia Hafza Madrasa, the enjoining religious school for women, rose in a violent resistance against what they perceived as foreign impositions of secularism and immorality. The women embarked on vigilante raids throughout the capital to stop what they called "un-Islamic activities," such as DVD vendors, barbershops, and a Chinese-run massage parlor. This uprising began when female students abducted three Pakistani women accused of running a brothel and six Chinese masseuses who were employed there, claiming initially that they were only attacking Chinese girls who were prostitutes and CD shops who sold pornography. They released them the next day,[2] but this action paved the way for the final confrontation, the siege of the Mosque and Madrasa by Pakistani military, which the Islamic activists violently resisted.

While the standoff between the Lal Masjid and then-Musharraf's administration involved thousands of Islamic activists, at the frontlines were more than a hundred veiled women.[3] The BBC (Khan 2007) tells us, "the security personnel were met by baton-wielding women, who refused to let them enter the mosque or seminary compound." In the

New York Times, Somini Sengupta (2007) reported that "shortly before the siege began, female students had come out of the school, draped in black burqas, waving bamboo sticks and taunting troops stationed nearby. A number of media outlets dubbed them 'chicks with sticks.'" The veiled female students demanded the resignation of the then-current Pakistani administration and advocated an Islamic regime.

Despite the visibility and activity of the female students, when the events came to an end with the death of over 70 male students and the recovery of six women's bodies (veiled and burned), the press released a statement that these women were held against their will and their bodies burned. These women were described by both their Islamic counterparts and the varying journalist parties as martyrs and militants. The final note as the events faded into Pakistan's now infamous, militant, Islamic history was uncertainty as to whether these women, those dead and those who surrendered, were freedom fighters or victims.

As a globally publicized event, the Lal Masjid incidents brought to front and center a fantastic fear of today's times: veiled Muslim women who engage in abrasive, anti-American, pro-Pakistan political action to their death. I analyze the media coverage of the Lal Masjid event to elucidate how media narrations and visualities function as mechanisms of power that discipline subjects across national borders, resolidifying notions of dangerous nations and paranoid citizenship. I identify representation as a key mechanism for protecting borders, albeit one that is neither always consistent nor neat. I argue that the United States, as a hetero-normative nation, relies on, benefits from and eroticizes (repressed) female terrorists. Conceptualizing the Lal Masjid women as *erotic nationals,* I demonstrate that these women both transgress and reaffirm geopolitical borders and gender/sexual borders. I analyze the possible ways we can read these women as agentic and resistant even as they engage in the perpetual reenactment of the very roles that construct their gender domination.

Mapping Methods/Queering Gazes

My point of departure is that both discourse and visuality function as mechanisms of power for disciplining subjects across and within national borders (Barthes 1981). I examine the media narrations and photographs appearing in the *New York Times*, the *BBC, Dawn*, the *Pakistani Times, GeoTV*, and *All Things Pakistan*, all well-respected American and international outlets that covered the Lal Masjid event. Although I look at media from the US, the UK, India, and Pakistan— each of which are governed by different professional demands, political configurations, markets, and audiences—I do not seek to flatten these differences but rather to demonstrate how, despite these differences, a certain epistemology around the Lal Masjid women is taken as axiomatic by all of them.

Drawing from the theoretical work of visual scholars such as Mirzoeff (1998), Mulvey (1989), and Rose (2007), I analyze the public discourse and corresponding photographic imagery published in these global media outlets as subject to the dominant global gaze conditioned by powerful forces such as neoliberalism, hetero-patriarchy, US American hegemony, Islam-o-phobia, and the War on Terror. The photographs that I analyze were politically hailed as visual evidence of Pakistani and Islamic pathologies. However, I will elucidate how these photographs have disciplinary function, in that they corroborate paranoid, imperial borders just as they perform a tacit decolonial and queer function, consciously and unconsciously confronting gender and imperial borders (Tagg 1988).

The Lal Masjid women martyrs, I argue, demand a nuanced analysis that neither dismisses them as naively indoctrinated actors nor hails them as anticolonial heroines. My goal in this analysis is twofold. In the first part of my analysis, I work to reveal the erotic underbelly of seeing and narrating these martyrs, keeping taut the tension between the visual and the paranoid. I move from a deconstruction of this dominant gaze to a queer reading to show that the veiled martyrs of the Lal Masjid proffer a continuity between the revolutionary women (we have always seen but dismissed in colonial battles from British India to French Algeria) and the contemporary feminine, racialized Other who transforms herself from oppressed Other to border protector/crosser.

Gayatri Gopinath (2005, 176) states that "queerness names a mode of reading, of rendering intelligible that which is unintelligible and indeed impossible within the dominant nationalist or imperial logic." In considering the possibilities of queerness in the actions of the Lal Masjid women martyrs, I work to trouble and denaturalize the close relationship between hetero-eroticism, nationalism and empire. Queer-ness can be understood not as pertaining to sexual identity and prac-tice, which perhaps may also be possible, but as speaking to a mode of resistant feminist cultural practice that opposes the reconstitution of patriarchal, neoliberal masculinity. In this manner, queerness disturbs borders and homelands as well as Western notions of freedom and female empowerment, and instead addresses questions of affect, desire, and power over the Othered Muslim body.

Visualizing the Other: Muslim Women as Victims or Fighters

A number of postcolonial thinkers, such as Frantz Fanon (1963) Edward Said (1979), Gayatri Spivak (1988), and Alberto Memmi (1965), have articulated a sense of the Other at the very heart of history, culture, and politics. In recent years, with the events of 9/11,[4] the War on Ter-ror, and the Arab uprising, we've seen the revitalization of the imperial impulse to make visible the danger or deprivation of the Muslim Other, an Other imagined through sexual, gender, racial, and national borders (Puar 2007; McClintock 2009). Visual culture provides the logical step from imagined sensibility to the actual production of the Other, allow-ing the hegemonic gaze to both visualize and secure racial, national, and gender difference (Mulvey 1989). Post-9/11 visual culture points to submerged histories of racist and colonialists violence that continue to resonate in the ways the Muslim Other is imagined, desired, and destroyed (Jarmakani 2008; Williams, 2010). Significantly, this violence is justified through a narrative discourse of paranoia revolving around particular bodies and subjects, aesthetics, and freedoms (Foucault 1978; Williams 2010).

My analysis draws on the groundbreaking work of Jasbir Puar (2007) and historical insights of Ann McClintock (2009), both of whom elu-cidate the ways in which (Muslim) bodies become sites through which imperial borders are both protected and transgressed through visual culture. McClintock argues that the US state has entered the domain of paranoia,[5] "for it is only in paranoia that one finds simultaneously both deliriums of pleasure for the *other* and forebodings of the perpetual threatening *other*" (2009, 53, emphasis added). McClintock conceptu-alizes paranoia as "a way of seeing and being attentive to contradictions within power, a way of making visible the contradictory flashpoints of violence that the state tries to conceal" (2009, 53). Rather than identifying paranoia as a primary structure or identity of US imperialism, McClintock frames paranoia as an unstable tension that shapes the ways in which the United States imagines and articulates nativized and racialized Others in the context of the War on Terror, making it productive while aggrandizing its violence. This, of course, is notably exemplified by the Abu Ghraib tortures, where political torture manifested as erotic via *seen* acts of S&M, hooding, forced sodomy, and public sex. As McClintock notes, the power to *see* the Other (in this case, naked and sexed) became equated with the power to know and to dominate.

In *Terrorists Assemblages*, Jasbir Puar (2007) names the United States a hetero-normative state, provocatively arguing that emerging discourses on US exceptionalism since 9/11 have deeply sexual and paranoid dimensions. Puar shows that while heteronormativity has always been central to empire building, the recent US interest in gay rights and gay identity in countries such as Iran demonstrate that homonationalism (i.e., the model American gay citizen—white, able bodied, monied, and so on) is also deeply central to US hegemony. She argues that both US hetero-normativity and homonationalism merge to render desirable specific multicultural identities (i.e., white, middle-class, gay men) while maintaining the pathology of racial Others that don't fit this emerging consumer/legislative model (i.e., dangerous, Muslim men). In Puar's polemic, the Muslim Other is constructed as a productive foil to the liberated US citizen and to liberatory US borders, where citizenship and borders work as reflective surfaces that allow empire to avoid seeing itself.

Within the formalism of nation-state construction, borders encompass the territories between nations and create distinctions as powerful material realities. I have come to understand borders, however, as not only physical sites but as analytic constructs that nationally and transnationally create social, political, and symbolic distinctions between groups and provoke forms of resistance that seek to disrupt, transcend, and transform these various, often intersecting, lines. Borders, border work, and border identities are political and politicized in ways that that map out through visuality and representation. As Paul Landau and Deborah Kaspin (2002) argue, images have long played a critical, if largely unexamined, role—mediating relationships between the colonizer and the colonized, the state, and the individual, and the global and the local. What makes the Lal Masjid battle so analytically intriguing, in part, is the ways borders, broadly defined, were invoked through varying symbolic and material practices such as gender, sexuality, nation, empire, and visual culture. By placing visual culture alongside border politics and paranoia, I, too, point to the ways representations can be understood as signifying and silencing imperial authority, punctuating and purchasing national complacency. Visual culture, like borders, I argue, operates as a terrain, a space where struggle for representations play out.

This backdrop of gender, race, and border politics as central but sublimated dimensions of the War on Terror constitute Pakistan and the Lal Masjid events as a particularly brutal case to explore the representations and possibilities of female martyrdom. The global media has portrayed Pakistan as a center of intense terrorist activity, a pivotal locus for the War on Terror. In 2008, Pakistan was named "the most dangerous place on earth," by both *Newsweek* (November 2008) and the *Economist* (January 2008). The following *Newsweek* (Moreau 2007) excerpt elaborates the political concerns that dip images and narrations of Pakistan in US paranoia.

> Today no other country on earth is arguably more dangerous than Pakistan. It has everything Osama bin Laden could ask for: political instability, a trusted network of radical Islamists, an abundance of angry young anti-Western recruits, secluded training areas, access to state-of-the-heart electronic technology, regular air service to the West and security services that don't always do what they're supposed to do. (Unlike in Iraq or Afghanistan, there also aren't thousands of American troops hunting down would-be terrorists.)

As the *Newsweek* clip points out, Pakistan is rhetorically framed as an angry, armed, and radically Islamic country either without democracy or with a false sense of it. Unlike Afghanistan and Iraq, Pakistan's war is seen as internally implosive with real possibilities of being externally explosive (to the West).[6] Indeed, Pakistan is a complicated site, both internally and with respect to its place in the world. Pakistan has and continues to experience both a reterritorialization of the homeland as well as a simultaneous deterritorialization of the nation, through tumultuous acts of terror, US social intervention, and political instability (Khan 2007; Weiss 2003; Jamal 2005), all of which have become spectacle for the dominant global gaze. Pakistan's understated complexity in the War on Terror and how the Muslim visual subject is continually invoked as both *real* evidence of Pakistan as an unstable nation-state and the United States as a stable and free nation are important functions in my reading of the Lal Masjid event.

Not surprisingly, then, in order to tap into US paranoia and depict Pakistani danger, the 2008 *Newsweek* cover utilized a provocative photograph that displayed a mass of angry, brown men in an unnamed protest, their arms raised and mouths open with smoke in the foreground. Such depictions of racialized Muslim masculinity have become the mainstay of a post-9/11 collective imagination, underscoring how constructions of the US nation depend on particular understandings of both white domination (i.e., other nations as dangerous and barbaric) and hetero-normativity (i.e., Muslim masculinities as perverse and terrorizing). The language used by Moreau (2007) in the *Newsweek* article combined with the image appearing in the later issue of *Newsweek* (2008) coconstruct an imaginative geography that dovetails with two claims of Pakistan's exceptionalism—its unique ability to support US counterterrorist and counter-Islamic efforts and its radical potential to sleep with the enemy. Both Pakistan's exceptional position in the War on Terror and America's exceptional interest in Muslim wo/men became the twin sites paranoia during the eight-day Lal Masjid battle.[7]

Within such an ideological field, Muslim women's bodies are framed within a context of patriarchal, nationalist, racialized and de-eroticized spectacle (Khan 2007). The master narrative of the oppressed Muslim woman (and its many variants in France, Britain, and the United States) is constructed with a certain internal logic and presupposed relationship between visibility, representation and the female subject. This logic expands the paranoid gaze directed at the Other (Spivak 1988; Jarmakani 2008). To the extent that the veil is an index of social oppression and political exclusion, Muslim women who practice covering in various ways become spectacle for Western states, as both a grotesque parody of antiquated gendered oppression but also eroticized symbols of the possibilities of western freedom, where the unveiling of their bodies becomes a vested act of political interest. Shahnaz Khan (2001) argues that the "archetypal image of the veiled woman, even when accompanied by a speaking subject remains limited to the immediate sensory experience of what it is like to be confined." The hysteria around the veil and its supposed associated with oppression has risen to political commonsense in the West, from France, to Germany, to the United States, crafting a strategically and globally visible space for Muslim women.

Neoliberal globalization has transformed the politics of visibility and naming, where the symbolics of being a *seen* subject, have cleared the ground for discursive systems (from empire to the nation-state) that seek heightened opportunity for surveillance.[8] In part the incessant dependence on visualizing the Muslim female Other as powerless supports the neoliberal imagination that locates notions of self and freedom in an agentic, autonomous, and rational (unveiled) subject, with access to market freedoms, where human and market freedoms merge (Appadurai 1996; Grewal and Kaplan 1994; Jarmakani 2008). Within this paradigm, free subjectivity emerges from the dual axes of being seen (i.e., unveiled) and being named (i.e., identified). As Joan Scott (2007) argues in *The Politics of the Veil*, the culture wars over the veil provide fodder for neoliberal rationalities, servicing the dissolution of borders (where the veil functioned as Muslim border protection) as well as the expansion of forms of surveillance and identification (where the veil kept women from being *seen* and *sexualized* subjects by and for the state). The continued furor around Muslim veiling practices in the secular West demonstrates that veiled women complicate the relationship between visibility and freedom. Increasing visibility leads to power located on increasingly individualized and corporeal levels, a major strategy of surveillance we have seen since 9/11 and throughout the War on Terror (Foucault 1978). The potential of Muslim women to undo the state merely by their physical veiled presence speaks to a ferocious paranoia embedded in neoliberal state formations. Hence, the seductive binary of the oppressed Muslim woman (a subject of liberal and feminist debate) and the dangerous Muslim man (a subject to fear) is foundational to this rationality and becomes a mechanism for policing subjects that transgress symbolic borders or protect undesirable borders.

Of course, such neoliberal formulations of freedom jettison actual political realities and elide the dynamic, political subjectivities that complicate the gendered and sexualized terrain of empire and political violence (Mernissi 2005; Mahmoud 2005). Treating political martyrs or even suicide bombers as delusional, brainwashed figures dismisses the political realities that create the conditions of such forms of violence. Ghassen Hage (2003) demonstrates that Western approaches to suicide bombings versus the violence of colonial domination reveals a form of symbolic violence that shapes our understanding of what constitutes as ethical and legitimate violence. Hage's point highlight that what can be said about Muslim violence against the United States (as well as Muslim-on-Muslim violence) maintains the internal cohesiveness of the Master narrative regarding Muslim women, despite historical evidence that runs counter.

Because state power has historically always been imagined through hegemonic masculinity (Sjoberg and Gentry 2007), veiled Muslim women as political actors have either been completely ignored or are used to prop up narratives that define their actions as irrational. For example, Frantz Fanon's (1963) analysis of Algerian women's role in the revolution against France lays bare the radical role Algerian women played. Fanon moves Muslim female subjects from their perceived domestic and sexual passivity to public and revolutionary activity. Naming her as "woman-arsenal," Fanon (1963, 58) tells us the veil functioned as anticolonial camouflage to carry various essentials (such as arms, food, communications, etc.) for the revolution.

In their analysis of Palestinian women's role in war, Sjoberg and Gentry (2007) argue that Palestinian groups often characterize women's participation in martyrdom attacks as a sign that women are equal in their society. The counternarrative in Western responses is that gender emancipation through political violence is simply a continuation of their traditional, subordinated role in society. A number of feminist scholars argue that female martyrs do not unsettle gender lines because their actions take place within the framework of masculinist organizations. Likewise, during the Lal Masjid battle, Muslim women's involvement served to underscore the desperation of Pakistani society and the impossibility of diplomatic settlements with Pakistan. Involving women made Pakistan more uncivilized, legitimizing the continued and insidious use of force in the region. But it also fundamentally marked, and continues to mark, the region as a threat to America (Bhatthercharyya 2008). But to say that gender or nation is not at all recoded through these actions is mistaken. This cultural conflict over whether martyrdom liberates or oppresses women trumps any real discourse regarding these subjects and elides alternative imaginaries of freedom or subjectivity.

Because liberal humanism defines the figure of the veiled woman as the quintessential oppressed figure, the radical disruption offered by these women is foreclosed on, rendering them unthinkable as political subjects. Within the nostalgic imperial imaginary, the image of the Lal women as acting (rather than docile) and politicized (rather than privatized) sustains a logic that produces brown women as simultaneously savable and politically impossible. Hence, a parallel narrative to Muslim women as faux political subjects is the increasingly intertwined description of their political actions and indeed, themselves, as sexualized (see, e.g., Sjoberg and Gentry 2007). Jacqueline Zita (1998) argues that the gendering of stories of violent women is a representation of male dread of women or more specifically, male anxiety over female control. I suggest that the media's labeling the Lal Masjid martyrs "chicks with sticks" as well as the political actions that the women themselves performed with regard to the sexual regulation of other females simultaneously evokes and effaces imperial erotics, raising questions over the politics of agency and political subjectivity.

As a number of scholars have shown, the very fabric of the War on Terror has simultaneously revealed the deep narcissism of the west and contradictorily opened up possibilities for the emergence of distinct unruly, fragmented subjectivities (Puar 2007 Mahmoud 2005). Veena Das and Deborah Poole (2004) characterize unruly subjects as those who are insufficiently socialized into laws of gender or nation, and hence, possibly undo the state even as they simultaneously utilize the state. Frantz Fanon (1963) points out that subaltern resistance and revolution is shaped by the simultaneous and contradictory coexistence of both anticolonial conservatism and anticolonial radicalism. Saba Mahmoud, in her ethnographic study of pious Egyptian women who actively construct and participate in an Islamic movement, demonstrates how politicized Muslim women's agency cannot be seen as fixed in advance but rather as emerging through specific modes of being, responsibility, and effectiveness (Mahmoud 2005).[9] Agency should be understood as framed within discourses of domination and subordination that create the conditions for women's political enactment (Mahmoud 2005). Such a characterization of resistance is external to Western romanticizations which frame resistance as a product of individual agency.[10] In this next section, I will move through three Lal Masjid photographs to interrogate the ways power, as Landau and Kaspin (2002, 12) write, "is hidden in ways of seeing."

Visual Subjects and Violent Gazes: The Lal Masjid Women in Photographs

> We must all be of one and the same mind when we look upon the photographic evidence. It is in these photographs that Americans can meet on the common ground of their beloved traditions. Here we are all united at the shrine.
> —Francis Trevelyan Miller, *1911*

As the Lal Masjid event came to a close, every press pondered on the role of these women. The BBC's (Bano 2009) query captures this concern: "But why are more and more families sending their girls to religious schools? Are they linked to Islamic fundamentalism or was the Lal Masjid a one off?" This question, of course, fits with broader media strategies that tend to render unexplained phenomena less dangerous through the narrative of romanticized exceptionalism. It also, however, fits the odd political subjectivity that the Lal Masjid brought forward. The strikingly insistent presence of both the female body and the woman subject in this event and the political discourse that followed, begs the following questions. What is *seen* in these photographs and what effect, visually and epistemologically, did they have on the imperial gaze? What kinds of subjectivities are incited and denied?

In the first two images of the Lal Masjid (see Figures 5.1–5.2), we see masses of women, shrouded in full black *niqab,* carrying bamboo sticks raised in the air as they pound the dirt floor with them. The women's faces are not visible. The viewer only sees their eyes, which the Western media tend to describe as dark, angry, or emotionless (Sengupta 2007).

Figure 5.1.

Figure 5.2.

Figure 5.3.

The image is either taken from a distance, encompassing the masses of female bodies "draped in black burqa," or through honing closely in on one face to see, as Somini Sengupta of the *New York Times* describes, "lively eyes sparkling out of a black burqa" (see Figure 5.2). The camera is positioned so that the masses feel endless and overwhelming. In Figure 5.1, we see rows of women standing around one another forming a protest, their bodies uniformly covered, their arms raised holding bamboo sticks, the dirt floor under their feet, the gates of a mosque (denoted by the Arabic lettering over their heads) behind them, a megaphone pressed against one woman's mouth. In, Figure 5.2, we see masses of veiled women as they peel forward in protest.

These photographs invariably mobilize the colonial trope of looking at the veiled female, where the power of the gaze is aligned with (unveiled) whiteness. For example, in Figure 5.2, at the center of the photograph, the camera hones in on a close-up of a *niqab*-clad woman, her eyes staring into the camera. This shot is the prototypical "object-to-be-looked-at," inviting a fetishizing, voyeuristic gaze that is simultaneously racialized and sexualized. The image lends itself to an eerie quality of the Othered woman subject, one that is simultaneously curious and suspect. This photograph, specifically, figures into media-driven iconography rooted in fetishism, a fetish repeatedly displayed through the landscape of Muslim women's bodies. Every element of the photograph strategically elicits a fetishistic response from the viewer, naturalizing the hetero-erotic and the imperial gaze. By honing in on the eyes, the dominant gaze lays claim to the undeniable pleasures afforded to those who can *look* at iconic, Muslim femininity. Indeed the journalists' description, "lively eyes sparkling out of the black burqa," juxtaposed to the black burqa, reveals the tortured relation between the imperial gaze, which eroticizes the Other and imperial initiatives, such as the War on Terror, which demonizes the Other. This brief but evocative description by the *New York Times* foregrounds my central argument that these martyrs, despite their political action, were folded into a narrative that is at once hetero-erotic and racist. The Muslim woman in this photograph, once again, emerges as the quintessential veiled woman and the exotic whore (Naber 2006).

In Figures 5.1 and 5.3, the playful focus on the dark eyes is replaced by a fear-encoded shot of the veiled women. In Figure 5.3, we see three women wearing the burqa, two making the peace sign with their hands and the third holding a bamboo stick. We see only their hands and eyes, which are sober, serious, stern. This image was taken after the events came to an end, when the Lal Masjid women were demanding the reopening of the mosque. In Figure 5.1 we see the veiled female masses, conglomerating and protesting. Recall the *Newsweek* image that displayed masses of angry Muslim men and the precise ideological and material effects of such photographic representation. Similarly, the highly specific and deeply strategic visual signs in these photograph, such as the suspended bamboo sticks, the Arabic lettering in the background, the unpaved, dirt floors, *niqabs* blending into one another, the facelessness of the women, the megaphones, then endless masses, operate within a discursive field of power deployed to achieve certain ends—feminine irrationality, Muslim barbarism, the dangerous Muslim nation. They reiterate. They simplify. They agitate. They create an illusion of consensus. By looking, we experience all we need to know.

Described by American, British, Indian, and Pakistani media with phrases such as "burqa brigade," "baton-wielding," and "fearsome, stick-wielding, burka-clad young women . . . pouring out of the mosque," these photographs and accompanying text secures the discursive tension of the dangerous Muslim nation even as it complicates dominates readings that vilify Muslim men as only dangerous and Muslim women as only oppressed. All three figures render visible the orientalist's ambivalence in gazing at the other, seesawing from (erotic) pleasure to (political) fear (Said 1979). This split between pleasure and fear encodes Muslim female bodies as desirable only if readable as oppressed, mobilizing a political fantasy first articulated by Laura Bush in 2001 when she stated that Muslim women needed saving. Bush's nostalgically evoked notion of "the oppressed Muslim woman" gives rise to the acuity of the camera's gaze, constructing each image as signifiers of Islamic oppression, backwardness, and irrationality. In other words, the viewer is confident that "free" actors are not being represented.

The visual technologies of the veil, then, produce the subjective impossibilities of freedom. The Lal Masjid women, as unintelligible subjects (or intelligible only as oppressed), become the perfect foil through which to imagine the western liberal rational, unveiled, woman.

"Chicks with Sticks": The Erotics of the Lal Masjid Discourse

The Lal Masjid women complicate the story of women's oppression within Muslim societies, inducing an exceptional (though inv ariably ephemeral) opportunity to break with the status quo.[11] But what's most obvious here is that despite their political activity, they are not dealt with as political subjects. Even the state machines that had to contend with these women through violent means, referred to the martyrs through the conventional language of femininity. The *Prospect UK* (Hoodbhoy 2007) tells us, "Even as the writ of the state was being openly defied, the chief negotiator appointed by Musharraf described the 'burqa brigade' militants as 'our daughters' against whom 'no operation could be contemplated.'" The state's unwillingness to recognize these women's political subjectivity and the fetishistic reduction to ideological caricatures such "daughter" and "burqa-brigade," downplays the possibility of them as *really* threatening.

But an even more convoluted visual and discursive formation can be excavated here. The appropriation of these women as daughters by the state is troubled by the recurring motif produced by the media: "chicks with sticks." Both the BBC and a number of Pakistani media outlets such as the *Daily Times*, *All Things Pakistan*, and the *Daily Star* labeled the women protestors in this way. According to the *New Yorker* (Dalwymple 2007), these English-language jokes were quickly abandoned when the women kidnapped prostitutes, threatened video-store owners, and made bonfires of books, videocassettes, and DVDs that they regarded as un-Islamic. The media, as we know, carry their own agenda—to sell newspapers and find readers—thus making sensationalized language part of the competitive game to increase readership (Tagg 1988). But the media's persistence in naming these women "chicks with sticks," and then later denying responsibility for this phrase, must be more deeply interrogated, not just for effect, but for intent.[12]

As I've discussed, in these photographs every visual trope enacted to capture the events of the Lal Masjid relied upon (Muslim) femininity as dominantly understood – erotic, repressed, protected, and shrouded. But to say that the Lal Masjid events were marked by a sexual discourse is at once to say too much and not enough. Following Foucault (1978), technologies of sex create and regulate, rather than reflect, the sexual bodies that they name. As both a technology of representation and a technology of power, the phrase "chicks with sticks" demonstrates an interplay of eroticism and political dismemberment, simultaneously disidentifying these women as terrorists and reifying them (through jest) as women.

The discursive formations that render these women visible do so not to destabilize the dimension of political life that seeks to make the body irrelevant, but with a *joussance* associated with constituting female bodies as operational national texts, where both international media and state machines gender the conflict and its participants, obscure the political reality, and aestheticize political action as a ménage à trois of the nation, woman and God. As such, these subjects come to represent erotic nationals, subjects produced through the hetero-patriarchal gaze, which frames their political action as an eroticized, sensationalized, fantasized spectacle. The erotic subjectivity afforded these women is the simultaneous effect of neocolonial politics and hetero-patriarchal national discourses, overdetermining the use/utility of these feminine subjects/bodies as futile but *fuckable*. As daughters, these women can be folded into a normative structure of gender and sexuality, but as chicks with sticks, they emerge as erotic subjects pronounced by fetishized markers of embodied femininity. The phrase "chicks with sticks" cleverly interprets these women as libidinal, where sexual unavailability is replaced with sexual deviance, the mundane with fetish, and the Pakistani state with an hetero-erotic empire.

Landau and Kaspin (2002, 26) argue that "every unit of meaning, and not just every image, is a public crossroads of histories of interpretations." The visual and decontextualized photographic narrative of the Lal Masjid reveals this with immediate clarity. In the semantic shift from "veiled women of the Lal Masjid protested" to "chicks with sticks," the veil as a symbol of sexual modesty is deemphasized, if not completely bastardized. The phrase simultaneously genders and eroticizes the representations of these women, while also rendering them vulnerable, hence less threatening. As chicks, these women don't possess a political subjectivity and are reduced to gendered metaphors that feminize them. The lingual fantasy of these women as chicks demonstrates that the female body is incapable of being viewed through a neutral lens. It is always and completely sexed by the dominant gaze (Bordo 1993; Grosz 1994).

Second, the use of this phrase reduces these women to the specularity of their sexual bodies. Here, the fantasy of these women as chicks illustrates the need to produce and secure a nondangerous subject positioning through the most familiar trope of all—reducing women to sex objects. The phrase functions to make them impotent as political actors; as chicks they cease to be dangerous, except in their licentious potential for seduction. The specific visual strategies of distancing the camera from its subjects—the subjects blending into one another, the masses of black burqas, the pounding sticks, the open mouths against the language of the media, "chicks with sticks"—bespeaks the possibility of Muslim barbarism even as it caricaturizes it. Even here then, the barbarism of the Muslim society is both incited and mocked, as the media demonstrates through its jocular phrase that beneath the veiled, angry woman is a body to be fucked.

Third, the figurative imagery embedded in this phrase tactically serves the masculinist and imperial fantasy of disciplining the colonial subject and, in reverse, being (sexually) disciplined by that same subject (Pierce and Rao 2006). The women must lose political power in order to gain sexual prowess, becoming the subject Orientalist tropes have long relied upon—subjects of sexual arousal while being subjected to sexual discipline. The phrase "chicks with sticks" also seems a play on "chicks with dicks," linking them with lesbians and transgendered people, and more broadly, some abject notion of queerness and aggressive female sexuality. Here, the erotic is both enshrined in the language used to describe the women and inadvertently denied as the women are increasingly read as politically dangerous.

The language employed by the media makes it apparent that the female body in political space is confined to patriarchal and heteronormative narratives, even when it attempts to transcend these borders. As chicks with sticks, images of the Lal Masjid women become sites of social and psychic satisfaction for the dominant viewer, affording the global gaze the voyeuristic illusion of penetrating the enigma of Muslim women, but in ways that do not compromise visual control over these subjects. The construction of these women as chicks with sticks, while undoubtedly rooted in colonial longings directed at the colonized Other, ironically resonates with a familiar subject performance in Western politics—political women in the United States have long been reduced to their sexual bodies.

That their womanhood (in contrast to that of the prostitutes) operates within the realm of state-sanctioned heterosexuality does little to secure the grounds for their political insubordination. Instead, their political insubordination (to the imperial state of affairs) is imagined as beyond the boundaries of heterosexuality, slipping into deviant, alternative sexualities that both dominant nationalisms and the US heteronormative state seek to control. As Khalid Khan (2007), writing for Pakistani newspaper *Dawn*, states, in the Lal Masjid, we "see madressah girls stealing the limelight from their male counterparts in Pakistan. They do not speak softly, and they carry big sticks. . . . This time around womenfolk are the harbinger of Islamic sharia or a metropolitan jihad without charismatic leaders." Similarly, Tahira Abdulla (2009) of *Himal*, a South Asian magazine, states that "the scenes of hordes of stick-wielding, shouting, black-garbed young women on the seminary's ramparts, provoking the law-enforcement machinery, will long be etched in the region's collective memory." Such sentiments reveal a form of gendered agency that disrupts the representation of the normative Pakistani female subject. But in describing the Lal Masjid insurgency through feminine reductions, such as speaking softly, lacking charismatic leadership—a trait long associated with (white) masculinity, and chicks with sticks—these statements repeatedly enact a refusal to see the diversity and complexity of women's violent political action.

Significantly, the media and state's attempt to cast these female political actors as erotic abruptly forecloses on the queer possibilities opened up by the space of politicized female homosociality and corporeality. Subjugating these women to the erotic, then, functions as a crucial mode of discipline and production of these subjects as intelligible only as a form of ribaldry. The gender transgression of these women as political actors is successfully reinscribed as oppression rather than politically intentional, erotic rather than transformative. The queer potential of the Lal Masjid women is replaced by the primacy of the female body, keeping in tact all the ways nation, politics and gender are all "weighed down," in de Beauvoir's (1952/1989, xxiii) words, by the female body.

Transgressive Subjects: Rereading the Lal Masjid Women

> When it comes to the concomitant question of the consciousness of the subaltern, the notion of what the work cannot say becomes important. In the semiosis of the social text, elaborations of the insurgency stand in place of "utterance."
> —Gayatri Spivak (1988, 91)

> They came into the private women's quarters of Mosque, with grenades and tears gas, twenty-odd commandos. We had been threatened, our children had been threatened, our mosque had been invaded by the military . . . were we supposed to greet them with flowers?
> —Jamia Hafza woman's response when asked why the women needed to resort to arming themselves with sticks (*GeoTV* interview in Shahid 2007)

In an interview with *GeoTV* in 2007, the Mawlana of the Lal Masjid, Abdul Rashid Ghazi, said that "these women were faced with military weapons and highly-trained commandos, but they are nothing less than commandos themselves." In Ghazi's words, we hear a possible articulation of an anticolonial project that centers on a complex model of female Islamic subjectivity (Interview with *GeoTV, geotv.org, Mere Mutabik,* translated—In My Opinion). Likewise, the woman's above statement and Spivak's (1988) point compel us to engage these women's insurgencies as a point of subaltern agency that defy liberal conventions of resistance. How do the Lal Masjid women *queer* empire's contest over subjectivity and freedom?

In the events of the Lal Masjid, the women on the frontlines utilized the liminal status of the veiled women, an embodiment of oppression and tradition rendered abject by liberal-humanist codes, in order to comment on the colonized status of Pakistan and Islam. These women rework the ambivalent figure of the veiled women into a feminist predecessor of contemporary anticolonial subjectivity. Their use of the hyperbolic femininity that is presumed with the donning of the *niqab* unharnesses the pleasures of dominant representations from its disciplinary and regulatory role. Indeed, these women enact a queer appropriation of Muslim women in public space—where they are agents of, rather than subject to, violence.

Returning to Figures 5.1 and 5.2 we see endless numbers of veiled women—they appear menacing, intimidating. The images of the women martyrs are arguably a realistic representation of women's corporeal force in political space. Politicized religious nationalism is presented here as an insistent, powerful force with a life of its own. These photographs reflects the psychological reality of neocolonialism, rage turned protest—a state these women are unwilling to distinguish from death itself (Fanon 1963). In the words of Fanon (1963, 16), these women may be dominated, but they are not domesticated. They deliver a message whose poignancy is conveyed by the female body.

To be sure, I am not speaking of corporeality in the abstract. Rather, I am directly concerned with the ways in which these bodies are materialized and the political consequences of that materialization. This is a notoriously difficult ground—this taking up of the politico-analytical force of the female martyrs' bodies, and perhaps largely, the bodies of women who don't seamlessly mold into the neoliberal/neocolonial fantasy of empowerment. These women proffer a self who makes the materiality of her body highly relevant to the political schema and to her political knowledge. In so doing, they rupture the codification of Cartesian empowered subjectivity—an empowerment that rests on the excision of the corpus from the ideal subject. In other words, these female martyrs, veiled women occupying the public space to make a political statement, are saying that we are not separate from our bodies; we *are* our bodies.

The BBC (2007) quoted a young Lal Masjid student, saying that "the 18-year-old told the BBC Urdu Service that she was not held hostage by militants but had willingly remained behind during the weeklong siege. The woman, who asked not to be named, said she was prepared to carry out a suicide attack to defend the mosque." Like the Jamia Hafsa women quoted in the section opening, this woman shifts the image of the pure, unsullied, and oppressed Muslim woman to an emblem of female resistance. The mere fact that these women met the military armed with sticks (and prepared to die) in an effort to protect both the physical parameters of the Mosque and the religio-political borders of their work and families denaturalizes the image of the Muslim male as the quintessential anti-Western rebel and replaces terrorists iconography with ambivalent and gender queer figures. The opening statement by the Jamia Hafsa woman—"Were we supposed to greet them with flowers?"—empties feminine symbolism even as it uses it, as these women chose to meet violence with violence. In this event of intense decolonial dramatization, like Fanon's (1963, 50) Algerian woman, the Lal Masjid woman "rises directly to the level of tragedy."

Alongside the politicization of the Muslim feminine corporeality, these martyrs challenge hegemonic, neoliberal constructions of subjectivity. If subjectivity is defined epistemologically as knowable through observation and confession; ethically, as moderate, autonomous, civilized; and technically, as the regimens and practices we do to improve and become autonomous, free and fulfilled—then these martyrs confront all dimensions of western subjectivity. The female martyrs in the Lal Masjid events were nameless, often spoken about or referred to as a group, a mass, or a collective. This is most apparent in language of the *New York Times*, where the press lump these women together as "fearsome, stick-wielding, burka-clad young women . . . pouring out of the mosque" (Dalwymple 2007).

Within the changing modes of visibility and surveillance that emerge under globalization, being a *seen* subject enables securitizing technologies, such as in the French debate around the veil or the Abu Ghraib scandal, even as it taps into a liberal ethos of individual empowerment. In this regard, the Lal Masjid martyrs maintain a complicated in/visibility—they are both *seen* as a (dangerous) collective but remain *unseen* as named individuals. In their refusal to be named, insofar as they operated as a collective and asked not to be named, and in the media's refusal to present them as named individuals, these martyrs incite Cold War paranoia now translated to fit within the global security regime and neoliberal world order of today. Their quasi-public in/visibility demonstrates the empire's inability to govern their private selves, their intimate subjectivities, their interior lives (Rose 1989). Their techniques of self, collectivity over individuality, interrelationalism over autonomy, radicalism over moderation, endanger Western individualism and therefore, Western formulas around freedom. Their collective visibility, over named individual subjectivity, as a site of power and freedom for colonized Muslim women incorporates a radical resistance to the hegemonic, neoliberal subject as the free and fulfilled self.

The feminist organization Shirkat Gah released a report on the Lal Masjid events that spoke to complex reasons Pakistani women were drawn to the Jamia Hafsa. Kamila Hyat (2007) writes:

> The Jamia Hafsa appears to have served primarily to meet a key economic need in society. Families of young women, and in some cases young women themselves, including domestic workers, appear to have turned to it because it offered what was not always available to them in the world outside: food, shelter, clothing, respectability and learning. The realities the Jamia Hafsa exposed about society were restricted not only to the matter of "liberals" versus "extremists." Rather, a bright spotlight was directed towards the factors that have led to madrassahs mushrooming in Pakistan. These institutions serve to reduce the socio-economic burden on families. The poor condition of public sector schools, which have declined markedly over the last two decades, means that a "madrassah" is a truly tempting option for many. This of course is all the more true in the case of girls, with the Jamia Hafsa—and other madrassahs like

it—offering a convenient, socially acceptable place at which to depose of them, and thus lessen the strain on family finances.

However, well-known Pakistani feminist writer and blogger Afiya Zia explains the activities of the Jamia Hafza were largely mocked, dismissed, or reduced to patriarchal victimization by civil society members, most of whom are the liberal elite. Zia (2008) writes:

> Most civil society members were disturbed by the threat to liberal lifestyles, rather than looking at this occupation as a politics of protest that challenged the state. The Jamia Hafsa women, who wore complete black veils and carried bamboo sticks in their occupation of the mosque library, were mocked by the liberal, English-language media as the "veiled brigade" or "chicks with sticks." . . . This tendency tends to elide over and ignore the serious political spaces they have come to occupy. Progressive women's groups, as expected, made more salient statements on this incident, bringing out a historical perspective and linking extremist violence to the past thirty years of state policies.

We can see a clear distinction in feminist thinkers who are trying to situate the Lal Masjid women actors within a discourse of resistance to both neoliberal and neocolonial practices in Pakistan. Zia's (2008) point and the Shirkat Gah report introduce a more compelling critique of both transnational economic processes, which further disenfranchise women, and the nuanced political practices these women offer to transnational formations of gendered politics.

The martyrs role in the Lal Masjid battles intervenes in dominant nationalists discourses of gender, subjectivity, and empire. When the Lal Masjid women kidnapped Chinese prostitutes as a gesture of resistance to "foreign imposition of immorality," they catalogue a tacit critique of the racist amnesia that created Asian patterns of migration to Pakistan. Immigration practices and politics in South Asia have direct roots in the global economic labor trade, which often divest immigrants of citizenship status, allocate them to short-term labor contract, often sexual in nature, and render them perpetual outsiders in Pakistan (Appadurai 1996). The displaced, deterritorialized, and transient populations that constitute Pakistan after 9/11 drive the complex, hierarchical organizations of the modern Pakistani nation-state even as its sexualized and racialized realities render the nation's borders fragile and unpredictable. Indeed, the erasure of the Chinese sex workers' voice from the Lal Masjid media discourses and the fact that the Chinese women were the most accessible markers of penetrative foreign policy to the Lal Masjid women is emblematic of these globalizing border practices that displace and demarcate citizenship along gender and sexual lines. The racialized feminization of labor under global capitalism bleeds into the martyrs' advocacy of a Pakistan that wants to disassociate with such effects of globalization, even as they utilize heteronationalisms to articulate their critique (Asad 2003; Appadurai 1996). As such, these women can be understood as protecting the borders of a nation from the threat of sexualized immigration, a reflection of neoliberal globalization that cannot be dismissed.

But recognizing the antiglobalization practices that possibly undergird the kidnapping does not attend to the question of the martyrs' responsibility for Othering women even as they themselves may be victimized by global politics. Here, I turn to the question of the actual violence that the veiled women enact on the Chinese immigrants in Pakistan. The coercive kidnapping of the Chinese prostitutes was, by varying media accounts, described as lasting from twenty-four hours to three days and resulted in either the anticlimactic release of the Chinese women or a dramatic public confession after which they were released. Mostly, though, there is a general lack of knowledge of what took place in the Madrassa around the sex workers—we don't know how they were treated, we don't know how long they were held, we don't know anything. Media accounts are vague and, frankly, not focused on the kidnapping of the prostitutes.

This discursive invisibility of the Chinese prostitutes by the national and international media as well as the martyrs' kidnapping of these sex workers elucidates how the sexual/erotic operate as a particularly efficient and dangerous conduit for exercising power. But they are not parallel or analogous stories. They organized different forms of violence and exclusion and ordered different arenas of social and political action. The kidnapping of the Chinese prostitutes catalyzed military intervention into the Lal Masjid, even as this catalyzing event subsided into the margins of the public and global discourse. This narrative omission reveals both national and international discomfort with humanizing sex workers as well as the ideological refusal to provide them with liberal (celebrated) forms of visibility: Where now is the fanatic desire to render invisible subjects visible?

Visibility, as I've argued, is a complex system of permission and prohibition, of presence and absence. It is not a matter of accepting or rejecting the invisibility of the Chinese prostitutes. The political and affective modalities at play here, both in terms of the invisibility of the sex workers and the social violence inflicted on them by other women, are neither accidental nor wholly explainable. To contend with the fact the Lal Masjid women exercised, perhaps the most familiar form of patriarchal violence toward the Chinese prostitutes, is to recognize that the dogmatic positions of secularism and antisecularism have always been concerned with women's bodies and sexuality in ways that expand from violence to liberation. The martyrs violence toward the Chinese sex workers occurred on a terrain situated between patriarchy, secular-liberalism, capitalism, state terror, and the global war and the various and contradictory ambiguities, experiences, and logics that accompany such events. On the other hand, the kidnapping of the Chinese prostitutes was deemed nonviolent or less important (by both the media and the state; it was reduced to a diplomatic issue), in part through the paradigmatic phrase "chicks with sticks," which established the martyrs as less credible, dangerous, political subjects. In the end, both the Chinese sex workers and the Pakistani women martyrs were subject to familiar forms of patriarchal and imperial violence—their agency neutralized, dismissed, eroticized.

Conclusion

Gender both informed and transformed the visual terrain of the Lal Masjid. The erotic, as both a site of sexual exploitation (the martyrs as chicks with sticks/sex workers as immoral) and of agency (the body as a political and economic force) became the fertile ground of possibility and penalty. What was perceived as the spectacular gendered terrorism of the Lal Masjid was undergirded by powerful uses of the erotic. However, within the dominant western grid, this relationship between the erotic and the political—the body and the subject—is one framed by brutal separatisms, where the latter cannibalizes the former.

The contradictory relation between anticolonial violence and international mis/recognition necessitates a critical dialogue that does not reduce colonized subjects to spectacle or history to violent acts. By tracing the gendered and sexualized exploitations and possibilities of the photographic representations of the Lal Masjid, I work to highlight the voyeuristic fantasy of politicized Muslim woman subjects and the ways in which both their violence against other women (i.e., the Chinese prostitutes) and their own eventual death (i.e., martyrdom or murder) is fetishized, eroticized, and rendered unintelligible, indeed irrelevant. In the gendered and sexual power of empire, these martyrs enable a queer reworking of the very space of freedom itself. They simultaneously protect and trespass borders, just as they queer and normalize the category of woman and feminist. But enclosed within an imperial geography and colonized by the imperial camera, they have become exhibits in a contemporary museum of the War on Terror.

NOTES

1. In a report by the United Nations, 2007 was described as "an exceptionally violent year in Pakistan, which saw sharp increases in violence carried out by Islamist extremists and by the state" (Report of the United Nations Commission of Inquiry into the facts and circumstances of the assassination of former Pakistani Prime Minister Mohtarma Benazir Bhutto, April 16, 2010), culminating in the assassination of Benazir Bhutto, on December 27, 2007.

2. By some accounts, the Chinese women were held for three days within the women quarters of the mosque (*GeoTV—Mere Mutabik*; translated, *In my opinion*). But most American and British media accounts state the women were released the next day.

3. The *niqab* is the proper term to describe these women's attire. It refers to the full body and face covering, incorrectly referred to as the veil both colloquially and within Western political realms, such as during the recent French controversial debates and throughout the media narrations of the Lal Masjd women. I, however, use the term veil for this chapter to invoke its more politicized ideological contours and its dominant perception in the US and Western visual and political culture. For the intellectual usefulness of this term, see Joan Wallach Scott (2007), *The Politics of the Veil*.

4. While 9/11 is a key descriptive hinge used to frame contemporary events of the war and its consequential burgeoning images, I work against any American

exceptionalism in my reference to the events. Instead, in referring to 9/11, I allude more largely to a moment marked by the rise of imperial expansion, the policing, detention and deportation of immigrants, the construction of the foreign (brown) enemy, and the rise of Islamophobia, fundamentalist Christianity, the theocratic state, and heterosexism (Alexander 2006).

5. I do not mean to suggest that United States alone has entered a domain of paranoia. Clearly, traces of paranoia toward/against the other can be traced in France, Italy among other Western countries. I do, however, argue that in the United States this paranoia has distinct visual dimensions that are unique to the media-driven culture in that country. For an exemplary discussion of this, see Puar's (2007) discussion on the Abu-Ghraib tortures.

6. Let me note here that the discovery and assassination of Osama bin Laden in the outskirts of Islamabad, Pakistan in 2011 have only led to heightened surveillance and paranoia for Pakistanis by the United States.

7. I use slashes in words such as wo/man and in/visibility throughout this chapter for a number of reasons. My point of departure in this work is visuality and how visualities of Muslim women disrupt the epistemological possibilities of them as active border crossers. Hence, in line with my deconstruction of the visual culture that attempts to capture and colonize these women (as victims), I seek to disrupt the iconography of the language used to describe them. By slashing every use of in/visibility, I confirm the psychic processes that silently desire to see some Muslims while rendering others invisible. The slashing of axiomatic language allows me to convey the layers of meanings embedded in the terms, deliberately integrating that which is often regarded as disparate realities, divorced subjectivities. Moreover, just as these slashes invoke multiple meanings, they also visually disrupt the iconography of this popular term—visibility—rendering it ideologically porous and discursively fragile. Like the transgressive political actions of the women I analyze, the language used to describe them, too, necessitates a queering—a clear and noted departure from the comforts of what has been perceived as neat translation of language (i.e., these are Urdu speaking women, a language markedly more fluid and metaphorical than English), clean analysis, and clearly marked subjectivity.

8. The neoliberal focus of the past few decades upon privatization, deregulation, and self-help practices are characteristic of advanced economies and are promoted globally by unelected and nondemocratic institutions such as the World Bank and International Money Fund. These institutions and their ensuing ideologies fuel the economic and cultural destabilization of nonhegemonic nations, such as Pakistan. This ideological make-up of the developed world often suggest an unabashed economic egotism; the fundamental divide is the one between those included into the sphere of (relative) economic prosperity and those excluded from it (Sassen 2008; Appadurai 1996). Chomsky (2003) and Sudbury (2005) point out that in the much celebrated free circulation made possible by globalization, we actually see a deeper and more profound segregation and exploitation of people, both of which occur under the guise of liberal agendas of empowerment, development, and rights.

9. Mahmoud challenges the modernist project that seeks to categorize these pious and veiled Muslim women as nonpolitical subjects or antifeminist and instead repositions these women from docile bodies to active, agentic subjects.

10. The anthropological use of the notion "resistance" has been rightly criticized for underestimating the strength and diversity of power structures. See, for example, the article by Lila Abu-Lughod, "The Romance of Resistance," *American Ethnologist* 17(1), 1990.

11. Let me note here that Pakistani artist Nazia Khan (2008) created a few provocative pieces around the female body and female armory, noting that "at Lal Masjid, for the first time one saw a seemingly strong women's force."

12. While I recognize that intent can never really be known, the sexual subtext labeling these women as "chicks with sticks" can be contextualized within a range of practices and discourses that lasso sexuality in the deployment of US nationalism and empire.

REFERENCES

Abdulla, Tahira. 2007. "Islam's New Women Thekedars." *Himal South Asian.* http://old. himalmag.com/himal-feed/53/1330-islams-new-women-thekedars.html.

Abu-Lughod, Lila. 2010. "The Active Social Life of Muslim Women's Rights: A Plea For Ethnography, Not Polemic, With Cases From Egypt and Palestine." In *Journal of Middle East Women's Studies* 6 (1), Winter: 1–45.

Alexander, Jacqui. 2006. *Pedagogies of Crossing: Meditations on Feminism, Sexual Politics, Memory and the Sacred.* Durham, NC: Duke University Press.

Appadurai, Arjun. 1996. *Modernity at Large: Cultural Dimensions of Globalization.* Minnesota: University of Minnesota Press.

Asad, Talal. 2003. *Formations of the Secular: Christianity, Islam and Modernity.* Palo Alto, CA: Stanford Press.

Bano, Masooda. 2009. "Are These Religious Schools Linked to Islamic Fundamentalism?" BBC, May 27. www.bbc.co.uk/radio4/womanshour/04/2009_21_wed. shtml.

Barthes, Roland. 1981. *Camera Lucida: Reflections on Photography.* New York: Hill and Wang.

BBC. 2007. "Mosque Survivor 'Willing' to Die." July 19. http://news.bbc.co.uk/2/hi/ south_asia/6907107.stm.

Bhattercharyya, Gargi. 2008. *Dangerous Brown Men: Exploiting Sex, Violence and Feminism in the War On Terror.* London: Zed Books.

Bordo, Susan. 1993. *Unbearable Weight: Feminism, Western Culture and the Body.* Berkeley: University of California Press.

Butler, Judith. 1993. *Bodies that Matter: On the Discursive Limits of "Sex."* New York: Routledge.

Butler, Judith. 2004. *Precarious Life: The Powers of Mourning and Violence.* London: Verso.

Chakrabarty, Dipesh. 2002. *Habitations of Modernity*. Chicago: University of Chicago Press.

Chatterjee, Partha. 1993. *The Nation and Its Fragments: Colonial and Postcolonial Histories*. Princeton, NJ: Princeton University Press.

Chomsky, Noam. 2003. *Hegemony of Survival: America's Quest for Global Dominance*. New York: Metropolitan Books.

Dalwymple, William. 2007. "Letter From Pakistan." *New Yorker*, July 23. www.newyorker.com/reporting/2007/07/23/070723fa_fact_dalrymple.

Das, Veena, and Deborah Poole. 2004. *Anthropology in the Margins of the State*. Santa Fe, NM: School of Advanced Research Press.

De Beauvoir, Simone. 1952/1989. *The Second Sex*. New York: Vintage Books.

Fanon, Frantz. 1963. *Wretched of the Earth*. New York: Grove Press.

Foucault, Michel. 1978. *The History of Sexuality: Volume I*. New York: Vintage Books.

French, Howard. 2007. "Letter from China: Mosque Siege Reveals Chinese Connection." *New York Times*, July 12. www.nytimes.com/2007/07/12/world/asia/12iht-letter.1.6629789.html.

Gopinath, Gayatri. 2005. *Impossible Desires: Queer Diasporas and South Asian Public Cultures*. Durham, NC: Duke University Press.

Grosz, Elizabeth. 1994. *Volatile Bodies: Towards a Corporeal Feminism*. Bloomington: Indiana University Press.

Grewal, Inderpal, and Caren Kaplan. 1994. *Scattered Hegemonies: Postmodernity and Transnational Feminist Practice*. Minneapolis: University of Minnesota Press.

Hage, Ghassen. 2003. *Against Paranoid Nationalism: Searching for Hope in a Shrinking Society*. Sydney: Pluto Press.

Hassan, Syed. 2007. "Profile: Islamabad's Red Mosque." BBC, July 27. http://news.bbc.co.uk/2/hi/south_asia/6503477.stm.

Hoodbhoy, Pervez. 2007. "What Does the Lal Masjid Mosque Siege Tell Us About the Growth of Extremism in Pakistan?" *Prospect*, July 28. www.prospectmagazine.co.uk/magazine/afterlalmasjid.

Hyat, Kamila. 2007. *Shirkat Gah Annual Report*. Shirkat Gah. www.shirkatgah.org.

Jamal, Amina. 2005. "Transnational Feminism as Critical Practice: A Reading of Feminist Discourses in Pakistan." *Meridians: Feminism, Race, Transnationalism* 5(2): 5782.

Jarmakani, Amira. 2008. *Imagining Arab Womanhood: The Cultural Mythology of Veils, Harems and Belly Dancers in the U.S.* New York: Palgrave MacMillan.

Khan, Khalid Hasan. 2007. "Revolution or What?" *Dawn.com*. April 29. http://archives.dawn.com/weekly/dmag/archive/070429/dmag4.htm.

Khan, Nazia. 2008. "Nazia Khan." www.naizakhan.com/index.php?id=the-skin-she-wears.

Khan, Shahnaz. 2001. "Between Here and There: Feminist Solidarity and Afghan Women." *Genders* 33. http:/genders.org/33/2001.

Khan, Shahnaz. 2007. *Zina. Transnational Feminism and the Moral Regulation of Pakistani Women*. Oxford: Oxford University Press.

Landau, Paul, and Deborah Kaspin. 2002. *Images and Empires: Visuality in Colonial and Postcolonial Africa.* Berkeley: University of California Press.

Memmi, Albert. 1965. *The Colonizer and the Colonized.* Boston: Beacon Press.

Miller, Francis Trevelyan. 1911. *The Photographic History of the Civil War in Ten Volumes.* New York: New York Review of Books.

Mirzoeff, Nicholas. 1998. *The Visual Culture Reader,* 2nd edition. New York: Routledge.

Mahmoud, Saba. 2005. *Politics of Piety: The Islamic Revival and the Feminist Subject.* Princeton, NJ: Princeton University Press.

McClintock, Ann. 2009. "Paranoid Empires: Specters from Guantanamo and Abu Ghraib." *Small Axe* 13(1): 51–74.

Mernissi, Fatema. 2005. *Islam and Democracy: Fear of the Modern World.* London: Basic Books.

Moreau, Jon. 2007. "Where the Jihad Lives Now." *Newsweek,* October 20. www.thedailybeast.com/newsweek/2007/10/20/where-the-jihad-lives-now.html.

Mulvey, Laura. 1989. *Visual and Other Pleasures.* New York: Palgrave and McMillan.

Naber, Nadine. 2006. "Arab American Femininities: Beyond Arab Virgin/American(ized) Whore." Feminist Studies 32(1): 87–103.

Pierce, Steven, and Anupama Rao. 2006. *Discipline and the Other Body: Correction, Corporeality, Colonialism.* Durham, NC: Duke University Press.

Puar, Jasbir. 2007. *Terrorist Assemblages: Homonationalism in Queer Times.* Durham, NC: Duke University Press.

Rose, Gillian. 2007. *Visual Methodologies.* Thousand Oaks, CA: Sage.

Rose, Nicholas. 1989. *Governing the Soul: The Shaping of the Private Self.* New York: Free Association Books.

Said, Edward. 1979. *Orientalism.* New York: Vintage Books.

Sassen, Saskia. 2008. *Territory, Authority, Rights: From Medieval to Global Assemblages.* Princeton: Princeton University Press.

Scott, Joan Wallach. 2007. *The Politics of the Veil.* Princeton, NJ: Princeton University Press.

Sengupta, Somini. 2007. "Red Mosque Fueled Islamic Fire in Young Women." *New York Times,* July 24. www.nytimes.com/2007/07/24/world/asia/24madrasa.html?_r=1&oref=slogin.

Shahid, D. 2007. "Women of Lal Masjid." *GeoTV,* May 21. www.youtube.com/watch?v=H1TC2VC5mEg.

Shohat, Ella. 2001. *Talking Visions: Multicultural Feminism in a Transnational Age.* Cambridge, MA: MIT Press.

Sjoberg, Laura, and Caron Gentry. 2007. *Mothers, Monsters, Whores: Women's Violence in the Global Politics.* London: Zed Books.

Spivak, Gayatri. 1988. "Can the Subaltern Speak?" In *Marxism and the Interpretation of Culture,* edited by Cary Nelson and Lawrence Grossberg, 271–317. Chicago: University of Illinois Press.

Sudburg, Julia. 2005. *Global Lockdown: Race, Gender, and the Prison-Industrial Complex.* New York: Routledge.

Tagg, John. 1988. *Burden of Representation: Essays on Photographies and History.* Minneapolis: University of Minnesota Press.

Weiss, Anita M. 2003. "Interpreting Islam and Women's Rights: Implementing CEDAW in Pakistan." *International Sociology* 18:58–60.

Williams, Randall. 2010. *The Divided World: Human Rights and its Violence.* Minneapolis: University of Minnesota Press.

Zia, Afiya. 2009. National Commission on the Status of Women National Conference: "Extremism, Its Impact on Society, Its Implications for Women." www.ncsw.gov.pk/prod_images/pub/Report-%20Religiuos%20Extremism.pdf.

Zita, Jacqueline. 1998. *Body Talk: Philosophical Reflections on Sex and Gender.* New York: Columbia University Press.

PART II

Politicized Identities and Belonging

6

Indigenous Peoples and Colonial Borders

Sovereignty, Nationhood, Identity, and Activism

SARAH MADDISON

When colonial powers invaded North America and later Australia, the many hundreds of Indigenous nations that existed on these territories prior to the arrival of the Europeans were completely invisible to—or at least were ignored by—the invaders. Also invisible to the colonizers were the precolonial, national borders between diverse Indigenous nations. These borders had existed since time immemorial. In Australia, as elsewhere, the borders between nations had their origins in ancient, customary law, believed to have been laid down by creator beings and maintained by ancestors over many thousands of years.

Indigenous peoples' relationships to the land on which their nations lay was profoundly different, and seemingly incomprehensible, to the European invaders.[1] In contrast to European understandings of property rights, but sharing much in common with Canadian and American Indian and other indigenous relationships to land, Australian Aboriginal and Torres Strait Islander land "ownership" conferred obligations of custodianship and stewardship, determined by (among other things) place of conception and birth (Goodall 1996, 9). These responsibilities to land were and are held collectively as a part of the cosmology that underpins sociopolitical relationships and form the traditional basis of governance and social control within and between nations (Ivanitz 2002, 128). More wide ranging than the western conception of law, Indigenous customary law embraces all that non-Indigenous people might describe as law, religion, philosophy, art, and culture, and provides groups and individuals with precise and binding guidelines by which to manage relationships to others (including other nations), to land and resources, and related rights and obligations (Brennan 1995, 143), including guidelines about borders, land management, and trespass. The connection between country, law, and well-being is so strong that many Aboriginal people in Australia report feeling uncomfortable or unhappy when they are on someone else's country, often speaking of being homesick for their own country and taking special care to be mindful of the protocols of the nations whose country they are on to avoid causing any offence. Indigenous identity is bound up with these connections, most specifically the connection to a specific area of country. In simple terms, an Aboriginal person's country—their nation—is their fundamental source of identity (Myers 1991, 151).

With this powerful connection to country in mind, this chapter considers the contemporary implications for Indigenous peoples attempting to both recover and rebuild their nations while simultaneously asserting a political voice that often transcends precolonial national borders. Focused mainly on the Australian case, the chapter will also draw comparisons with Indigenous peoples in Canada and the United States in considering the challenges of trying to develop a pan-Indigenous political identity in a colonial/postcolonial nation that has never recognized the borders of Indigenous nations. Implicit in this analysis is an understanding of the deep and wide-ranging diversity of Indigenous life and culture, both within Australia (for more on diversity within Australian Indigenous political culture see Maddison 2009) and elsewhere in the world. Despite this diversity, however, the category of indigeneity still functions to denote a political solidarity among colonized peoples, including with regard to their precolonial borders, such as is evident at the United Nations through the development on the Declaration of the Rights of Indigenous Peoples, discussed further in the conclusion to this chapter.

Postcolonial Borders and the Struggle for Sovereignty

Because the invaders simply imposed themselves over the top of existing Indigenous nations, often with horrendous brutality, the recognition of precolonial Indigenous national borders continues to threaten the ter-ritorial integrity of colonial state sovereignty. As Austen Parrish notes, in the international legal system law and land are "tightly and integrally linked." Colonial statehood was based on European models of politi-cal and social organization, which did not correspond with the socio-political organization of many Indigenous societies, notable for their "decentralized political structures and overlapping spheres of territo-rial control" (Parrish 2007, 295, 297). It is correct, therefore, to refer to Indigenous groups as nations, even though historically, they, like most nations, were not and have never been structured in the statist mold. Rather, they are nations in the sense that they are comprised of people who share a language, cultural beliefs, and an economy, held together by an evident capacity to govern themselves over many thousands of years on territory that is understood by their own members and the members of surrounding nations as belonging to them (Churchill 1999, 18–19). According to Vine Deloria and Clifford Lytle (1984), nationhood sug-gests free and uninhibited decision-making within a community that is insulated from external factors in considering the options. As nations they are sovereign, even if this may not accord with definitions of sov-ereignty recognized in international law.

Ethicist Stephen Curry has argued that, in the colonial context,

> whatever indigenous sovereignty is, it is more than the right to auton-omy or regional self-government where this is possible. It has something to do with the whole country that once belonged to indigenous people and now contains them (2004, 147).

It is the way this "whole country" has been divided, and the implica-tions of these divisions for precolonial nations, that is most troubling for Indigenous peoples today. Contemporary Indigenous nations are no less sovereign because they have been subsumed within a colonial nation-state, with new borders and boundaries inscribed over the top of existing borders. And like any other sovereign nation, Indigenous nations continue to hold an inherent right "to be free of coerced altera-tions in these circumstances" (Churchill 1999, 20). That this right has been constantly violated over hundreds of years does not mean that the right itself has been diminished. Indeed, Churchill (1999, 20) goes so far as to assert that any country that sets out to unilaterally impose its own systems upon another acts in a way that is "not just utterly presumptuous but invalid under international custom and convention." The invalidity of settler colonial nations, and the brutality with which they have imposed their nation-building agendas on Indigenous peoples continues to be a source of great political tension between the original inhabitants and the invaders.

The Australian experience of settler colonialism illustrates this situation. As with settler colonies elsewhere in the world, Australian settler colonialism was predicated on the elimination of Indigenous peoples. Indeed, the nature of the settler colonial project requires the active and forceful domination of an invaded territory's original inhabitants through the repression of their culture, identity, history, and nationhood, the persistence of which challenges the legitimacy of the colonial mission (Rouhana 2008, 73). It is evident that settler colonies were and are premised on the elimination of Indigenous societies (Wolfe 1999, 2). There is, as the Australian anthropologist W.E.H. Stanner (2009, 119) has pointed out, more than an accidental correspondence between the destruction of Indigenous life and the construction of European life on colonized territories. The continued existence of Indigenous groups, communities, and nations challenges the unity of the territorial nation-state and fuels the colonial drive to suppress cultural difference (Parrish 2007, 300). Further, the philosophical underpinnings that supported the construction of European life on Indigenous territory allowed no room for the possibility of coexistence. Australia is an extreme case of this refusal, as, unlike native nations in Canada and the United States, Aboriginal and Torres Strait Islander peoples were never negotiated with by way of any form of treaty. Rather, the assertion of a politics of exclusion and denial on Australian soil reinforced a geographical imaginary in which spaces were constructed and bounded such that the European sensibility might feel comfortable. These spaces "provided certainty, identity and security" for the invaders who sought to avoid the "uncomfortable, messy reality of coexistence" (Howitt 2001, 237).

In creating new, tidy colonial spaces, however, the colonizers created chaos for Indigenous nations that persists in the present. In the United States, for example, more that 40 tribes live along or near the borders with Canada and Mexico, and a comparable number of Canadian First

Nations are affected on the north of that border. These borders are, of course, a colonial artifact. For the nations that lived in what are now borderlands, the idea that an imaginary line could come to transect their lands and separate them in both tangible and intangible ways was completely unimaginable (Osburn 2000, 471–72). The drawing of these lines through Indigenous nations was done without consultation or agreement and has interfered with intertribal trade and exchange, created unnecessary obstacles to the delivery of health and other services to members who live across the border, and weakened social and kinship networks.

These new borders have also presented an additional challenge to the sustenance of cultural tradition and the practice of ceremony, particularly with regard to the safe carriage of sacred objects across national borders without interference from border guards (Singleton 2009, 1). That these lines were drawn in a period when native nations were fully sovereign (further recognized through later treaties made between these nations and the colonizers) flies in the face of their rights as nations with borders of their own (Luna-Firebaugh 2002, 160). In Australia, the lines that were drawn through Indigenous nations were not the borders of the nation-state, but rather of the states and territories created when the colonies federated in 1901. These internal Australian borders also carved up nations and divided families, particularly during the protection era,[2] but until the power to make laws in relation to Indigenous people was ceded to the Commonwealth in 1967, lines on the Australian map also saw Aboriginal people in different states enjoy vastly different standards of living and protection of rights.

North American tribal nations have used a number of strategies in an effort to gain or retain border-crossing protocols, some of which are supported by historical treaties, which allow members of tribal nations to cross US national borders with only a tribal identification card. Since the events in New York on September 11 2001, however, and the increasing hegemony of the rhetoric of "border security" these protocols have come under increasing threat, with heated negotiations about what an "enhanced" tribal ID would require in order to meet new security requirements (Singleton 2009). Heightened concerns about drug trafficking and the entry of undocumented immigrants have also restricted cross-border tribal movements, particularly on stretches of the US-Mexico border. Eileen Luna-Firebaugh (2002, 160) describes these new, more restrictive border-crossing procedures as "an assault on indigenous sovereignty as well as an assault on the cultural integrity of native societies." New border security protocols also underscore the ongoing challenge to the claiming of Indigenous identity in the postcolonial era.

Blood, Borders, and Identity

In Australia, any understanding of the diversity and complexity of Indigenous peoples and their national borders has seemed to evade the colonial mind. In the Torres Strait Islands to the north of the Australian mainland, for example, even naming that group of islands was based on ignorance of interisland politics and has "effectively silenced territorial boundaries and political affiliations between and among the different tribal groups of the various islands" (Nakata 2003 [1994], 133). The Australian geographer Richie Howitt has suggested that, since colonization, the Australian landscape has become "plagued" by a multiplicity of imposed or ignored boundaries, intended to "divide and subdivide places, people and resources into manageable units." These boundaries, he suggests, are a legacy of the European romance with the idea of the "frontier," metaphors of which have profoundly affected Australians' "geographical imaginations" (Howitt 2001, 233).

Ignorance of Indigenous national boundaries reflects a deeper ignorance about Indigenous peoples themselves. Before colonization, the "natives" did not exist. Indigenenity, Aboriginality and Indianness are all colonial identities forced upon the members of the nations that existed prior to European arrival in Australia and North America. Before the colonization of the continent now known as Australia, for example, the group now described as Aboriginal people identified themselves according to their nation and language group, and within these their clans and kin groups. People were (and remain) Arrente, Wiradjuri, Yanyuwa, Goreng Goring, Jawoyn, Pitjantjatjara, Wongkadjera, Poorrermairrene, Yawaru, and all the other five hundred nations that existed on the continent before the invasion. Following the pattern established by the earlier invasion of Turtle Island (North America), and the creation of the "Indians," the idea of "Aboriginal" or "Indigenous" identity in Australia emerged as a distinctly colonial construct invented to both name and contain the "natives" of *terra australis*.

The arrival of the British in Australia also brought new systems of dividing and classifying Aboriginal people. Complex systems of classification and control were an intrinsic part of the colonial administration aimed at exterminating one type of Aboriginality and replacing it with a more acceptable version (Langton 2003 [1994], 116). One type of classification involved descent or degrees of blood, and is the familiar, overtly racist trope of half-caste, quarter-caste, octoroon, and so on. For much of the twentieth century these terms were used as a guide to an Aboriginal person's character, and were the foundation of policies such as child removal. For example, a child with less Aboriginal blood was considered more likely to assimilate and was, therefore, at greater risk of removal. The other mode of classification concerned the degree to which an Aboriginal person had become "civilized" or remained "tribal" (Goot and Rowse 2007, 31). These imposed definitions of Aboriginality and the inherent judgments about Indigenous culture that they contained were "a blatant attempt to manipulate and disempower, a way to divide and confine, a chance to restrict and deny" (Taylor 2003, 90). Many Aboriginal people in Australia today still understand these classificatory regimes as attempts to eliminate both the physical and social reality of Indigenous people and nationhood in what was being constructed as a "pure white" colonial nation (Birch 2007, 110).

Similar policies have been and remain in place in other settler colonies. Much of the complexity surrounding the political mobilization of Canada's Aboriginal peoples, for example, arises from the continued existence of the Indian Act. Through the Indian Act, the Canadian government has controlled and continues to control and regulate who can and cannot claim First Nation status. Although the Constitution Acts give the government responsibility for "Indians," it is the Indian Act—essentially a tool for assimilation—that defines who those Indians are with the apparent intention of defining First Nations people out of existence. For example, the Indian Act can mean that even if a band accepts a person as a member they are still not considered to have status at law. To further complicate issues, it is also possible with more recent changes to the legislation that people can have status and not be eligible for membership in a band. The Mohawk Nation is one that enforces a strict band membership regulation, including revoking band membership for marrying a non-First Nations person (Diebel 2008). Others, however, continue to contest the notion of status and advocate for a return to nation-based understanding of indigeneity (Alfred 2009).

Deeply implicated in these concerns about Indigenous identity are the imposed colonial assessments of what constitutes authenticity and the impact of these views on Indigenous voice and activism. Indigenous Australian scholar Marcia Langton has argued that these issues of identity and resolving who is and who is not Aboriginal are located uneasily "between the individual and the state" (Langton 2003 [1994], 116). In Australia, the so-called real blackfella lived somewhere in the north of the continent where the impacts of colonization had been later and less wholly destructive of traditional culture and ways of living. This conjoining of the north with authenticity was highly problematic for Indigenous activists in the south, particularly those based in urban areas, many of whom were instrumental in the drive to create a pan-Aboriginal movement in the 1970s. Many Aboriginal people understand governments to be complicit in these efforts to create a divide between north and south by challenging southerners' authenticity with the charge that if "you don't stand on your leg and show your spears" then "you're not a real blackfella" (Jilpia Jones quoted in Maddison 2009, 107).

These experiences have also been echoed or mirrored in Canada and the United States through the creation of, for example, the Dawes Rolls in the United States and the continued impacts of the Indian Act in Canada. Ultimately, a divided Indigenous population expending time and energy to compete with one another for authenticity is a far lesser threat to the settler state. As Luna-Firebaugh asserts, however, the creation of colonial borders has also inflamed these identity tensions. Writing of the Blackfeet, divided by the Canada-US border, she claims that the lines on the map "created division and divisiveness":

> While the Blackfeet were originally one people, this artificial division began to erode their self-identity, and they have come to see themselves as separate peoples. The colonizing nations afforded their indigenous groups different rights, which caused further erosion in the continuity of tradition and peoplehood, and also led to factionalism (2002, 162).

In Australia, these divisions between Aboriginal people have been further exacerbated by the advent of land rights and native title regimes that have in many ways created new challenges for the recognition of Aboriginal nations and identities. Under the Northern Territory Land Rights Act, for example, Aboriginal people must produce an identity that meets the requirements of the Act and that allows a white judge to decide "whether or not they are who they say they are." In what has been described as "a theatre of tragic farce," Aboriginal people must "'prove' their identity according to an alien means of determining truth and falsehood" (Bradley and Seton 2005, 35, 43). Native title claims processes have also imposed a new traditionalist framework onto Aboriginal communities, requiring that claimants must demonstrate their traditional connections to country despite the fact that these connections have in many cases been profoundly disrupted by colonization and in ways that are increasingly at odds with the "complex intercultural realities" that constitute their contemporary lives (Taylor et al. 2005, xi, xii). Fred Myers has described this process as requiring Aboriginal people to "stitch culture and tradition together into some kind of wearable garb" in order that their claims to land might be recognized as authentic (Myers 2005, 22).

When such claims fail, the pain and hurt that results is immense. No case demonstrates this more clearly than the Yorta Yorta Native Title claim, finally resolved on appeal in the High Court of Australia in 2002 when it was determined that the claimants' traditional connection to their land had been washed away by the "tides of history" (see Cutliffe 2006; Seidel 2004; Reilly 2001). Many Yorta Yorta believe that the outcome of the case effectively stripped them of their identity, and they feel the loss very keenly. The lack of logic in the native title claims process, and the lack of acknowledgment of the history of colonization and the dispossession of Aboriginal people from their lands and nations is something that continues to confound. As Yorta Yorta leader Paul Briggs has argued:

> Yorta Yorta, we're still on our land. We understand that people have built fences and are using it for other purposes but there's a belief in the spirituality of Yorta Yorta people that we're still connected and we still belong there (Briggs quoted in Maddison 2009, 120).

Today, claiming Indigeneity, that is claiming to be the first occupants of a country with rights of prior occupancy, is central to Indigenous political culture both in Australia and elsewhere (Maybury-Lewis 1997, 7). And despite heartbreaking setbacks such as that experienced by the Yorta Yorta, the transformation of the idea of Indigenous identity, from a colonial construct to a politicized identity, a "badge worn with pride," has occurred through generations of political struggle for recognition (Niezen 2003, 3,11). The underlying and intrinsic sovereignty of Indigenous nations remains inextricably linked with questions of identity and recognition and is central to political struggle and mobilization.

Community, Nation, and Political Solidarity

In each of the settler colonies under discussion in this chapter, the members of many Indigenous nations were subjected to forced relocation off their own countries and onto reserves and missions on other nations' territory. Today this means that in many places, and most notably in Australia, numerous Indigenous communities are something of a fiction, or at least a creation, comprised of a number of kinship or nation groups that prior to colonization would have occupied different territories and that, in many cases, still retain different languages and systems of law. The early government settlements and church missions onto which Aboriginal people were herded were "the antithesis of traditional living." Aboriginal people were often cajoled and at times brutally relocated to these areas, where several large, frequently unrelated groups lived under the "petty autocracy" of white staff in substandard conditions not dissimilar to refugee camps (Lippman 1981, 93). The dispersal and dispossession that resulted from colonization threw diverse nation groups together, on missions, in settlements on the fringes of rural towns, and increasingly in the urban Aboriginal diaspora. Further, as people began to be enticed off reserves and into towns and cities, important community members were separated from their families with negative effects for both a sense of community and for individual well-being (Mudrooroo 1995, 133).

The impact of the historical creation of these communities in Australia remains poorly understood among non-Indigenous people. Tension between different nations, clans, or kinship groups is endemic in many Aboriginal communities. Community organizations are often seen as representing the whole community when in reality they may only represent key families from a particular nation, and divisions between traditional owners and others who have had a long historical association with a particular area often complicate leadership and decision-making structures. In the 1970s, Kevin Gilbert wrote of the social problems these conditions had caused on what were then still known as reserves:

> Reserves are split into factions and the splits are deep and bitter. Families may have lived near each other for generations, but one lot is, say, Catholic and the other lot is Protestant. Groups may have different racial origins. Or one group may have been in the area three generations less than the other group and is never allowed to forget it . . . On reserves, whatever one group decides to do will almost certainly be automatically opposed by another group (Gilbert 2002 [1973], 155–56).

Forced relocation across precolonial boundaries has created different categories of Indigenous people and created tensions that are not conducive to political solidarity. But despite the conflict and appalling social conditions in many communities, over many decades they have nonetheless become *home* to many Aboriginal people who would not live anywhere else. As much as reserves and missions have been damaging they also, over time, have become places of genuine community solidarity. And as much as Aboriginal nations were damaged by their dispossession and displacement onto artificially created communities, so too, according to Irene Watson, community has become a call to "the gathering of broken and shattered pieces" (Watson 2007, 15). Many Aboriginal people claim communal identities that are real and meaningful, regardless of underlying conflict and heterogeneity. For Frances Peters-Little it is important to remember that:

> While Aboriginal people did not passively accommodate new and imposed, introduced and artificial colonial boundaries, it is clear that missions, reserves and pastoral stations have become Aboriginal communities which are now an integral part of Aboriginal people's heritage and are fundamental to Aboriginality (2000, 3).

It is evident that there are significant challenges in attempting to represent the diversity of Aboriginal society in the simplified language of community. "Community" as a term to describe areas with a predominantly Aboriginal population only came into common usage in the early 1970s when official government policies of self-determination saw a move away from the more assimilationist language of "missions" and "reserves" and the increasing use of "community" as a term that was assumed to be universally culturally appropriate (Peters-Little 2000, 10). The term "community" has become central to both Aboriginal and non-Aboriginal political rhetoric. As a concept, community is both vague and idealized, drawing on a desire for solidarity and social anchorage (Morgan 2006, 19). Frances Peters-Little has pointed to the ways in which the idea of the Aboriginal community is used to suggest a unity of purpose and action among groups considered to share a common culture (Peters-Little 2000, 2). The language is certainly important. Mudrooroo has suggested that sometimes "community" is used when really what is being described is an Aboriginal "nation" (Mudrooroo 1995, 78).

Although in Australia there is no formal system of status or any notion of an enrolled person, Aboriginal people still make a clear distinction between those with formal, traditional affiliations to Indigenous nations and those who are associated with a place through residence on missions or settlements, no matter how long such associations have endured. These two forms of association do not create equivalent rights and interests in land, and attempts to blur the two have been met with considerable opposition (Sutton 1999, 41; Martin 1999, 157). But although it is widely recognized that traditional owners have unique status and authority, the challenge to this idea is the reality that Australia's colonial history means many groups do not have traditional owner status. For people who are now unable to return to their traditional lands the old mission sites and ex-government settlements now called communities have taken on enormous significance as successive generations of families have lived and died there (Behrendt 1995, 26). Urban communities, too, despite generations of connection to those communities, are not traditional owners; members of these communities are not living within their traditional national borders.

Arguments for the recognition of traditional owners rather than more recent arrivals on a territory are based on entitlement, not ideas of equity (Martin 1999, 158). "Historical people," as they are known, with connections to a particular area of country that may span several generations, are not traditional owners and are not entitled to speak for country. While this is an accurate reflection of preinvasion national boundaries, in the light of all that colonization has done to traditional Aboriginal culture, particularly with regard to dispossession and relocation, the call to maintain recognition of traditional owners' entitlements over all others may seem unfair. Those who strongly defend these claims, however, argue that it is only through the restoration of the rights of traditional ownership that stability will be restored in Aboriginal communities.

The Challenges to Pan-Indigenous Mobilization

The imposition of settler colonial states on Indigenous nations and the dispossession that resulted still complicates contemporary political mobilization for Indigenous peoples. On the one hand, much Indigenous political culture is constituted at the level of the precolonial Indigenous nation. Ronald Niezen has observed that it is a characteristic of Indigenous movements internationally that they are free of "centralized dogma," coalescing instead around a multitude of "micronationalisms" oriented to small communities or regions connected by loose networks of communication (Niezen 2003, 13). One obstacle to the idea of pan-Indigenous solidarity is the widely shared cultural protocol that prohibits an individual from speaking for another group's country, even if they have lived there for many years. On the other hand, however, in the contemporary political context there is a need for a pan-Indigenous voice constituted and organized at the national level. Such efforts at pan-Indigenous mobilization, however, in turn risk obscuring the diversity of Indigenous nations and communities, leaving many feeling invisible or unrepresented. The important emphasis on precolonial nationalism can make a postcolonial national unity seem fragile or even impossible, presenting an extraordinary challenge to some of the foundations of Indigenous political culture.

In Australia, regional representation, both independent of government and through structures such as the now abolished Aboriginal
and Torres Strait Islander Commission, has been seen as one means of
attempting to bridge the local and the national. Tim Rowse has suggested that the effort to develop an effective means of articulating the
national with the local by means of regional representation "has been
the primary problem in the politics of Indigenous representation since
1973" (Rowse 2001, 133). A focus on regionalism, however, requires
Indigenous people to experiment with various means of inscribing new
borders that will determine regional boundaries, from the geographic
to the social and political, recognising both contemporary political and
economic ties as well as the historical nation-based foundations underpinning such alliances (Smith 2007, 29). At times these sorts of regional
aggregations have coalesced successfully into a strong national voice,
despite intense debates about what constitutes a region and exactly who
should be included within regional borders.

Despite this emphasis on regionalism, however, there remain compelling political reasons for also prioritizing the pursuit of a united,
national voice. The Tasmanian Aboriginal activist Michael Mansell
points out that gains in Aboriginal rights and freedoms in Australia—such as those achieved in the 1967 referendum, the recognition
of land rights, and inquiries such as those into deaths in custody and
the removal of Aboriginal children—have all been achieved by political
action with a strong national voice (Mansell 2007, 82). There is a recognized need that as tiny minorities within the broader population in
Australia and in North America, small Indigenous nations will remain
marginalized unless they are able to mobilize as a wider collective.

Australian efforts in this regard have been mixed. From the heady
days of the 1970s, which saw the emergence of a powerful grassroots
Aboriginal movement and the erection of the Aboriginal Tent Embassy
in the national capital, Indigenous political demands were to some
extent contained through a succession of national representative bodies: the National Aboriginal Consultative Committee (1973–1977), the
National Aboriginal Conference (1977–1985), and the Aboriginal and
Torres Strait Islander Commission (1990–2005). All three of these bodies were created and later abolished by government. Between 2005 and
2010, Aboriginal and Torres Strait Islander people were without any

form of national representative body until, in 2010, following extensive consultations, a new body, the National Congress of Australia's First Peoples, began the work of building new organizational structures and processes for the fourth time in the last thirty years, but independent of government for the first time. Much is riding on the success of this new body, which came together as an assembly for the first time in 2011, and its ability to create a strong national voice while also prioritizing the challenge of rebuilding Australian Indigenous nations.

The situation in Canada in terms of such representative bodies is also complex, with five recognized organizations. The Assembly of First Nations (AFN) defines itself as the organization representing all First Nations citizens in Canada regardless of age, gender or place of residence, although in reality this means *status* First Nations people, or at least those who are members of bands, since the organizational structure of the AFN is predicated on band membership. Often competing with the AFN for legitimacy is the Congress of Aboriginal Peoples (CAP), which represents status and nonstatus First Nations, Inuit, and Métis people who live off reserves in urban and rural areas, and focuses primarily on redirecting attention toward this large and expanding group of people. Alongside these two bodies there is Inuit Tapiriit Kanatami (ITK), which represents Inuit people in Canada and focuses their advocacy on ensuring that the difference between Inuit and other Indigenous peoples is recognized, and the Métis National Council (MNC), which represents Métis People and argues that the Métis have little or no access to the services and funding made available to First Nations. Separate to all these bodies is the Native Women's Association of Canada (NWAC), which was created in the 1970s to represent the interests of First Nations and Métis women both in Canadian society and within Aboriginal communities.

In the United States the situation is different yet again, with one strong national representative body working hard to deliver support to a tribally driven research and advocacy agenda. The National Congress of American Indians (NCAI) was founded in 1944 in response to the federal government's termination policies. The initial convention to establish the NCAI was attended by delegates from twenty-seven states, representing more than fifty tribal nations. Today around 250 of the 565 federally recognized Native American and Alaska Native tribes in the

United States are members of the NCAI. Cowger argues that not only was the NCAI part of an innovative and powerful resistance to Termination, it also became an "important instrument for the preservation of Indian culture and identity." Further, in providing a model for pan-Indian advocacy and representation, the NCAI gave new hope to ideals that Native American identity and culture could thrive in the twentieth century (Cowger 1999, 6). Other national Native American advocacy organizations have emerged and declined, but the nation-based model of tribal representation offered by the NCAI appears to be quite uniquely sustainable and effective. Today the NCAI operates its own Embassy of Tribal Nations in Washington, DC and continues to work toward its aim of securing for all tribes "the rights and benefits the traditional laws of our people to which we are entitled as sovereign nations" (National Congress of American Indians 2007).

Rebuilding Nations

In Australia, Canada, and the United States, Indigenous peoples are vocal in expressing their desire to rebuild their nations, meaning that they reject colonial impositions and are working to regain their capacities to be self-governing and autonomous. The emphasis is on *re*building because, as Onondaga Faithkeeper Oren Lyons argues, Indigenous nations have "always been here; we're not newly built" (Lyons 2007, viii). In the United States much of this work has been captured and documented by the Harvard Project on American Indian Economic Development and the Native Nations Institute (see Jorgensen 2007; Harvard Project on American Indian Economic Development 2008), which contends that where certain conditions are met, native nations tend to thrive when they are enabled to develop genuine and culturally appropriate systems of governance and government. Similar strategies are being pursued in Canada, with the Assembly of First Nations arguing that the "current structure of reserves and the governance on reserves that resulted from the imposition of the Indian Act does not reflect First Nation political, legal or governance traditions" and that "this must change" (Assembly of First Nations, n.d.).

The situation in Australia is somewhat different, in large part because the absence of a treaty framework or any form of constitutional recognition means there is, at present, no legal or institutional capacity for the rebuilding of Indigenous nations along the lines being pursued in North America. Nevertheless, there are ways in which small communities of Aboriginal people are pushing back against government desires to merge kin groups into large communities. In the more remote parts of Australia this is known as the homelands movement, and this strategy has seen many Aboriginal people in remote parts of Australia move out of troubled communities and back to their traditional lands, in an effort to become more autonomous and self-sufficient. The move to homelands was also explicitly an attempt to avoid conflict and violence in some of the larger Aboriginal communities (Behrendt 1995, 26).

Homeland communities are not without their problems, most notably a lack of employment and basic services, and options for economic development in these areas are scant (although see Altman 2005 for an important discussion of hybrid economies). Homeland communities' remoteness, small size, and lack of services led a former federal minister for Indigenous Affairs, Amanda Vanstone, to describe small homeland communities as "cultural museums" (Vanstone 2005). Conservative critics have also dismissed homelands as "socialist," "exceptionalist," and "separatist," ultimately describing them as "lands of shame" (Hughes 2007). Despite such criticism, however, evidence from recent research by the Menzies School of Health Research project, which demonstrates improved health and well-being in outstation communities around Utopia in the Northern Territory, suggests that greater support for these communities should be considered (see Rowley et al. 2008). Despite such evidence, however, much government policy still seems aimed at forcing homelands residents to move back to larger communities and towns. This strategy seems destined to fail as Aboriginal people are determined not to see a return to the days of missions, reserves and forced relocation. As one member of a small community told me, this will never happen: "People will get a scrap of tin and build a humpy in the bush over there rather than leave their country again" (quoted in Maddison 2009, 161). Even on this very small scale and without the support of a treaty framework, Australian Indigenous nations are attempting to redraw their boundaries and reclaim life on their country.

Conclusion

This chapter has sketched some of the aspirations of Indigenous peoples seeking to reclaim their territorial sovereignty and rebuild their nations within borders that have survived colonization, even when they have not been evident to the colonizer. The chapter has also considered some of the challenges obstructing these aspirations and noted some of the efforts to mobilize in spite of these difficulties.

Increasingly, Indigenous peoples around the world have turned to the domain of international law as a means of supporting and enhancing their claims to territorial sovereignty. As Austen Parrish points out, however, for the longest time the privilege accorded to the nation-state in the international legal system meant that international law was "historically inhospitable to the development of indigenous rights." At least until the Second World War, international law had little to say about what went on inside a state's boundaries as long as it did not cause harm outside that territory. Hitler changed that view, however, and since the 1950s new conceptions of human rights and human dignity began to "whittle away" at state-centric conceptualizations of territorial supremacy (Parrish 2007, 293, 296).

Beginning in the mid-1980s, Indigenous people working in the United Nations Permanent Forum on Indigenous Issues spent close to two decades drafting and lobbying for a Declaration of the Rights of Indigenous Peoples, which was finally adopted by the UN Human Rights Council in 2006 and by the UN General Assembly in 2007. The declaration pays specific attention to the issue of borders, with Article 20 noting that "Indigenous peoples have the right to maintain and develop their political, economic and social systems or institutions," and Article 36 stating that:

> Indigenous peoples, in particular those divided by international borders, have the right to maintain and develop contacts, relations and cooperation, including activities for spiritual, cultural, political, economic and social purposes, with their own members as well as other peoples across borders (the full text of the Declaration is at www.un.org/esa/socdev/unpfii/documents/DRIPS_en.pdf).

Interestingly, although the Declaration was adopted by 143 member states, the settler colonies of the United States, Canada, Australia, and New Zealand were the only four countries to vote against adoption, although all four states have since reversed their position. The declaration is not legally binding on states that have adopted it, however its adoption is intended to signal the state's intention to pursue the directions and measures enshrined in its provisions. Thus far there has been little or no indication that Canada, the United States, or Australia intend any significant change in policy or approach to the recognition of Indigenous sovereignty and nationhood.

This situation is not unique to the countries discussed here. Although this chapter has focused on the situation in Australia and North America, Eileen Luna-Firebaugh reminds us that the imposition of colonial borders continues to cause disruption in locations as diverse as Uganda and Rwanda, Serbia and Croatia, and Israel and Palestine. Given that these borders were also imposed with little or no regard for the interests or wishes of the original people of those territories it is not surprising that they have created and continue to create turmoil and political complications to this day (Luna-Firebaugh 2002, 161–62).

What might happen in the future to resolve these situations remains uncertain, and it seems self-evident that settler states will continue to resist what they perceive as the Indigenous threat to their territorial sovereignty. Parrish provides an overly optimistic reading of the impact of globalization and the alleged decline of the sovereignty of the nation-state as a positive development for Indigenous peoples seeking to have their own borders and sovereignty recognized, suggesting that "the historical reluctance of states to embrace the concept of multiple 'peoples'" within their borders will decline as these borders become "more permeable" and territoriality becomes "less constraining" (Parrish 2007, 306). Indeed, in a context of a perceived global terrorist threat and an increased hostility to the border-crossing activities of people seeking asylum in a range of countries, it seems more likely that nation-states will continue to reinforce their own borders and sovereignty, including at the expense of Indigenous nations. What is certain, however, is that despite the lines that have been drawn on the map by colonial powers, Indigenous peoples have "resisted this separation of peoples and have continued their struggle to remain cohesive" (Luna-Firebaugh 2002, 162). Pursuing self-government within the new borders of the colonial world has not been a substitute for the recognition of Indigenous nationhood. As Deloria and Lytle (1984, 14–15) argue, self-government "was not wrong, it was simply inadequate," because self-government will never replace the "intangible, spiritual, and emotional aspirations of American Indians." Nor indeed will such an approach ever satisfy the aspirations and desires of Indigenous peoples in Australia and Canada, whose strongest desire is to see their nations and their national boundaries fully recognized and rebuilt.

NOTES

1. A note on terminology: Broadly speaking, Indigenous people are the original inhabitants of a territory that has been conquered by ethnically or culturally differ-ent groups and who have subsequently been incorporated into states that consider them inferior "outsiders" (Maybury-Lewis 2003, 324). Despite the inadequacy of these terms for capturing the diversity of Indigenous nations and cultures, through-out this chapter the terms "Indigenous people" or "Indigenous peoples" are used to refer to all such groups, including the combined groups of Aboriginal peoples and Torres Strait Islanders, who make up Australia's Indigenous population. The terms "Indigenous" and "Aboriginal" are capitalized because they are used as proper nouns intended to signify the political sovereignty of these groups.

2. Between 1901 and 1946 all Australian states passed legislation intended to control Aboriginal people's independence of movement, marriage, employment, and association, and that authorized the removal of Aboriginal children from their families. During this period many Aboriginal people were forcibly moved off their traditional country, to be contained on reserves and missions where they were kept separate from white society, prohibited from practicing their culture or speaking their languages, and accorded no rights to the land on which they were contained. These policies, known as "protection" policies, assumed that Aboriginal people were merely an ancient remnant who would inevitably die out.

REFERENCES

Alfred, Taiaiake. 2009. First Nation Perspectives on Political Identity. Ottawa: Assem-bly of First Nations.

Altman, Jon. 2005. Development Options on Aboriginal Land: Sustainable Indigenous Hybrid Economies in the Twenty-First Century. In The Power of Knowledge, the Resonance of Tradition, edited by Luke Taylor, Graeme Ward, Graham Henderson, Richard Davis and Lynley Wallis, 34–48. Canberra: Aboriginal Studies Press.

Assembly of First Nations. n.d. Nation Building and Re-Building: Supporting First Nation Governments. Assembly of First Nations, Ottawa. www.afn.ca/index.php/en/policy-areas/nation-building-and-re-building-supporting-first-nation-governments.

Behrendt, Larissa. 1995. *Aboriginal Dispute Resolution.* Sydney: Federation Press.

Birch, Tony. 2007. The "Invisible Fire": Indigenous Sovereignty, History and Responsibility. In *Sovereign Subjects: Indigenous Sovereignty Matters,* edited by Aileen Moreton-Robinson, 105–117. Sydney: Allen & Unwin.

Bradley, John, and Kathryn Seton. 2005. Self-Determination or "Deep Colonising": Land Claims, Colonial Authority and Indigenous Representation. In *Unfinished Constitutional Business? Rethinking Indigenous Self-Determination,* edited by Barbara A. Hocking, 32–46. Canberra: Aboriginal Studies Press.

Brennan, Frank. 1995. *One Land, One Nation: Mabo—Towards 2001.* Brisbane: University of Queensland Press.

Churchill, Ward. 1999. The Tragedy and the Travesty: The Subversion of Indigenous Sovereignty in North America. In *Contemporary Native American Political Issues,* edited by Troy R. Johnson, 37–90. Walnut Creek, CA: AltaMira Press.

Cowger, T. 1999. *The National Congress of American Indians: The Founding Years.* Lincoln: University of Nebraska Press.

Curry, Stephen. 2004. *Indigenous Sovereignty and the Democratic Project.* Aldershot: Ashgate.

Cutliffe, Tony. 2006. *Left for Dead: An Analysis of Media, Corporate and Government Complicity in the Loss of Yorta Yorta Identity in Victoria, Australia.* Melbourne: The Eureka Project.

Deloria, Vine, and Clifford M. Lytle. 1984. *The Nations Within: The Past and Future of American Indian Sovereignty.* Austin: University of Texas Press.

Diebel, L. 2008. Band's Rules Cast Shadow on Love Story: Ex-Olympian Forced to Choose Between Marriage and Mohawk Status in Kahnewake. *Toronto Star,* June 1.

Gilbert, Kevin. 2002 [1973]. *Because a White Man'll Never Do It.* Sydney: Harper Collins Publishers.

Goodall, Heather. 1996. *Invasion to Embassy: Land in Aboriginal Politics in New South Wales, 1770–1972.* Sydney: Allen & Unwin.

Goot, Murray, and Tim Rowse. 2007. *Divided Nation? Indigenous Affairs and the Imagined Public.* Melbourne: Melbourne University Press.

Harvard Project on American Indian Economic Development. 2008. *The State of Native Nations: Conditions Under U.S Policies of Self-Determination.* New York: Oxford University Press.

Howitt, Richie. 2001. Frontiers, Borders, Edges: Liminal Challenges to the Hegemony of Exclusion', *Australian Geographical Studies* 39 (2): 233–245.

Hughes, Helen. 2007. *Lands of Shame: Aboriginal and Torres Strait Islander "Homelands" in Transition.* Sydney: Centre for Independent Studies.

Ivanitz, Michele. 2002. Democracy and Indigenous Self-Determination. In *Democratic Theory Today: Challenges for the 21st Century,* edited by April Carter and Geoffrey Stokes, 121–148. Cambridge: Polity Press.

Jorgensen, Miriam. 2007. *Rebuilding Native Nations: Strategies for Governance and Development.* Tucson: University of Arizona Press.

Langton, Marcia. 2003 [1994]. Aboriginal Art and Film: The Politics of Representation. In *Blacklines: Contemporary Critical Writings by Indigenous Australians,* edited by Michele Grossman, 109–126. Melbourne: Melbourne University Press.

Lippmann, Lorna. 1981. *Generations of Resistance: The Aboriginal Struggle for Justice.* Melbourne: Longman Cheshire.

Luna-Firebaugh, Eileen. 2002. The Border Crossed Us: Border Crossing Issues of the Indigenous Peoples of the Americas. *Wicazo Sa Review* 17 (1) 159–181.

Lyons, Oren. 2007. Foreword. In *Rebuilding Native Nations: Strategies for Governance and Development,* edited by Miriam Jorgenen, vii–ix. Tucson: University of Arizona Press.

Maddison, Sarah. 2009. *Black Politics: Inside the Complexity of Aboriginal Political Culture.* Sydney: Allen & Unwin.

Mansell, Michael. 2007. The Political Vulnerability of the Unrepresented. In *Coercive Reconciliation: Stabilise, Normalise, Exit Aboriginal Australia,* edited by Jon Altman and Melinda Hinkson, 73–84. Melbourne: Arena Publications.

Martin, David. 1999. The Reeves Report's Assumptions on Regionalism and Socio-economic Advancement. In *Land Rights at Risk? Evaluations of the Reeves Report,* edited by Jon Altman, Frances Morphy, and Tim Rowse, 155–166. Research Monograph no. 14, Centre for Aboriginal Economic Policy Research, Australian National University, Canberra.

Maybury-Lewis, David. 2003. From Elimination to an Uncertain Future: Changing Policies Towards Indigenous Peoples. In *At the Risk of Being Heard: Identity, Rights and Postcolonial States,* edited by Dean B. Bartholomew and M. Levi Jerome, 324–334. Ann Arbor: University of Michigan Press.

Maybury-Lewis, David. 1997. *Indigenous Peoples, Ethnic Groups and the State.* Boston: Allyn and Bacon.

Morgan, George. 2006. Aboriginal Politics, Self-Determination and the Rhetoric of Community. *Dialogue* 25(1): 19–29.

Mudrooroo 1995. *Us Mob: History, Culture, Struggle. An Introduction to Indigenous Australia.* Sydney: Harper Collins.

Myers, Fred. 1991. *Pintupi Country, Pintupi Self: Sentiment, Place and Politics Among Western Desert Aborigines.* Berkeley: University of California Press.

Myers, Fred. 2005. Unsettled Business: Acrylic Painting, Tradition and Indigenous Being. In *The Power of Knowledge, the Resonance of Tradition,* edited by Luke Taylor, Graeme Ward, Graham Henderson, Richard Davis, and Lynley Wallis, 3–33. Canberra: Aboriginal Studies Press.

Nakata, Martin. 2003 [1994]. Better. In *Blacklines: Contemporary Critical Writings by Indigenous Australians,* edited by Michele Grossman, 132–144. Melbourne: Melbourne University Press.

National Congress of American Indians. 2007. Constitution, By-Laws and Standing Rules of Order, Adopted 1944, Amended 2007. Washington, DC: National Congress of American Indians. www.ncai.org/fileadmin/ NCAIConstitutionBylawsStanding Rules2007e-version.pdf.

Niezen, Ronald. 2003. *The Origins of Indigenism: Human Rights and the Politics of Identity*. Berkeley: University of California Press.

Osburn, Richard. 2000. Problems and Solutions Regarding Indigenous Peoples Split by International Borders. *American Indian Law Review* 24 (2): 471–485.

Parrish, Austen. 2007. Changing Territoriality, Fading Sovereignty, and the Development of Indigenous Rights. *American Indian Law Review* 31 (2): 291–313.

Peters-Little, Frances. 2000. The Community Game: Aboriginal Self Definition at the Local Level. Research Discussion Paper no. 10. Canberra: Australian Institute for Aboriginal and Torres Strait Islander Studies.

Reilly, Alexander. 2001. Land Rights: From Past to Present to Absent. *Alternative Law Journal* 26 (3): 143–4.

Rouhana, Nadim N. 2008. Reconciling History and Equal Citizenship in Israel: Democracy and the Politics of Historical Denial. In *The Politics of Reconciliation in Multicultural Societies,* edited by Will Kymlicka and Bashir Bashir, 70–93. Oxford: Oxford University Press.

Rowley, Kevin, Kerin O'Dea, Ian Anderson, Robyn McDermott, Karmananda Saraswati, Ricky Tilmouth, Iris Roberts, Joseph Fitz, Zaimin Wang, Alicia Jenkins, James Best, Zhiqiang Wang, and Alex Brown. 2008. Lower That Expected Morbidity and Mortality for an Australian Aboriginal Population: 10-Year Follow-Up in a Decentralised Community. *Medical Journal of Australia* 188 (5): 283–287.

Rowse, Tim. 2001. Democratic Systems Are an Alien Thing to Aboriginal Culture. In *Speaking for the People: Representation in Australian Politics*, edited by Marian Sawer and Gianni Zappalà, 103–133. Melbourne: Melbourne University Press.

Seidel, Peter. 2004. Native Title: The Struggle for Justice for the Yorta Yorta Nation. *Alternative Law Journal* 29 (2): 70–96.

Singleton, Sara. 2009. Not Our Borders: Indigenous People and the Struggle to Maintain Shared Lives and Cultures in Post-9/11 North America. Working Paper no. 4. Bellingham: Border Policy Research Institute, Western Washington University.

Smith, Diane. 2007. Networked Governance: Issues of Process, Policy and Power in a West Arnhem Land Region Initiative. *Ngiya: Talk the Law* 1: 24–51

Stanner, W. E. H. 2009. *The Dreaming and Other Essays*. Melbourne: Black Inc.

Sutton, Peter. 1999. The Reeves Report and the Idea of the "Community." In *Land Rights at Risk? Evaluations of the Reeves Report*, edited by Jon Altman, Frances Morphy and Tim Rowse, 39–51. Research Monograph no. 14. Canberra: Centre for Aboriginal Economic Policy Research, Australian National University.

Taylor, Louise. 2003. "Who's Your Mob?" The Politics of Aboriginal Identity and the Implications for a Treaty. In *Treaty—Let's Get it Right!,* edited by Hannah McGlade, 88–99. Canberra: Aboriginal Studies Press.

Taylor, Luke, Graeme Ward, Graham Henderson, Richard Davis, and Lynley Wallis. 2005. *The Power of Knowledge, the Resonance of Tradition*. Canberra: Aboriginal Studies Press.

Vanstone, Amanda. 2005. Beyond Conspicuous Compassion: Indigenous Australians Deserve More Than Good Intentions. Speech to the Australian and New Zealand

School of Government, Australian National University, December 7. www.atsia.gov.
au/Media/former_minister/speeches/2005/07_12_2005_ANZSOG.aspx.

Watson, Irene. 2007. Settled and Unsettled Spaces: Are We Free to Roam? In *Sovereign Subjects: Indigenous Sovereignty Matters*, edited by Aileen Moreton-Robinson, 15–32. Sydney: Allen & Unwin.

Wolfe, Patrick. 1999. *Settler Colonialism and the Transformation of Anthropology: The Politics and Poetics of an Ethnographic Event*. London: Cassell.

7

Constricting Boundaries

Collective Identity in the Tea Party Movement

DEANA A. ROHLINGER, JESSE KLEIN, TARA M. STAMM,
AND KYLE ROGERS

Collective identity, or a shared sense of belonging to a group, is the scaffolding of social movements.[1] Identity connects individuals to a community and a cause larger than themselves, providing a motivation for mobilization and a rationale for continued engagement over the long haul (Friedman and McAdam 1992; Polletta and Jasper 2001; Taylor 1989). As such, creating and articulating the boundaries of a group are integral to collective identity. Boundaries, whether they are geographic or symbolic, promote an awareness of a collective's commonalities and effectively demarcate who is—and who is not—a legitimate member of a group (Taylor and Whittier 1992). Boundaries, in short, communicate the cognitive, moral, and emotional connections among individuals to both group members and external audiences (Gamson 1997; Polletta and Jasper 2001).

Boundaries, however, are not monolithic. Collective identity boundaries are negotiated and, consequently, may shift in response to group dynamics or political exigencies (Bernstein 1997; Gamson 1997; Reger 2002). For example, the identity of an emerging social movement can overlap with that of an existing movement, requiring activists to revise interpretative frameworks regarding group membership and the political obstacles the collective faces (Taylor and Whittier 1992). More importantly for our purposes, boundary construction is a strategic activity. Movement leaders draw distinctions that they believe are meaningful insofar as they minimize in-group conflict, maximize differences between the collective and its enemies, and optimize the potential for mobilization and successful political change (Bernstein 1997; Bernstein and De la Cruz 2009; Gamson 1995). The factors that affect boundary shifts, or how collectives define themselves relative to their opponents and broader society, are critical to understanding the trajectories and potential political effectiveness of a social movement.

In this chapter we draw on interviews, participant observation, and archival and newspaper sources, to examine boundary shifts in the Florida Tea Party movement (TPM). We find that the collective identity of the local TPM constricted with the cycle of contention. Specifically, we identify three "episodes of contention" (McAdam, Tarrow, and Tilly 2001) and highlight how electoral success and the emergence of the Occupy Wall Street movement, which made overlapping claims, forced the TPM to renegotiate its collective identity boundaries in ways that limited its political appeal. We conclude the chapter with a discussion of the implications for the study of social movement dynamics and collective identity.

Boundary Shifts and Episodes of Contention

Movement leaders typically try to garner broad support for their causes (Klandermans 1988) and, consequently, craft collective identities that draw on widely held, culturally resonant values in their mobilization efforts. Social movements, however, rarely operate in conditions of their own making. As such, a group's collective identity does not simply represent the political ideals of a collective, but the strategic efforts of leaders to mobilize a population at a particular historical moment. In order to better understand when (and why) boundary shifts occur, we analyze how a collective responds to the actions of other political and movement actors during a cycle of contention. As the name suggests, a cycle of contention is identifiable by "heightened conflict across the social system, with rapid diffusion of collective action from more mobilized to less mobilized sectors" (Tarrow 2011, 199), which eventually subsides and completes the cycle. A cycle of contention is comprised of "episodes," or "unique sequences of alterations in relations among connected elements" (McAdam, Tarrow, and Tilly 2001, 85). An episode of contention, just like the broader cycle, is characterized by the interactions among movement actors and the state. When these interactions change enough that the relational dynamics among the state, collective actors, and a broader public are altered, one episode of contention ends and another begins (McAdam, Tarrow, and Tilly 2001).

We outline how political incorporation and the emergence of a movement making competing claims cause one episode of contention to end, another episode to begin, and a shift in a collective's identity boundaries. An episode of contention can end (and a new one begin) when state actors incorporate movement claims or interests into their political thinking, rhetoric, and policies (Tarrow 2011). While political incorporation signifies movement success (Gamson 1975), it can lead to demobilization as satisfied supporters put down their protest signs and head back to their armchairs (Tarrow 2011). Consequently, movement leaders looking to reassert their strength apart from the politicians championing their causes may be compelled to renegotiate the boundaries of a group's collective identity in order to reengage the exhausted and mobilize stalwart supporters anew.

It is reasonable to expect leaders and supporters alike to constrict group boundaries and adopt more exclusive collective identities. Once state actors incorporate movement ideas into their own platforms, a group must renegotiate its collective identity relative to its political allies. The boundary shift will be strategic insofar as movement leaders simultaneously work to take advantage of new opportunities to affect political change and maintain an identity apart from state actors. A group's collective identity is likely to constrict during this new episode of contention because movement leaders' narrow focus on institutional opportunities and actors effectively contracts how a group (and its opposition) is defined.

A new episode of contention also may begin with the emergence of a movement representing competing claims (McAdam, Tarrow, and Tilly 2001). One group rarely corners the market on a grievance and, consequently, other collectives voicing related complaints may surface in a society. These "late risers" compete with "early risers" for support from the broader public, compelling the latter to articulate collective identities that clearly distinguish themselves from the former. How much leaders shift a collective's identity boundaries depends on the amount of overlap between the two groups. If the two collectives are very similar in their goals and orientation, the early riser will constrict its identity boundaries in an effort to clearly communicate who is—and who is not—a legitimate group member. Movement leaders will be particularly interested in constricting a collective identity if public discourse (e.g., mainstream media coverage and statements made by political actors) highlights the similarities (rather than the differences) between the two groups.

In sum, movement leaders and supporters tighten their ranks in response to external exigencies associated with different episodes of contention—and this has consequences for how a collective defines itself and envisions political change. Here, we examine "identity talk" in the Tea Party movement. Identity work is an "interactional accomplishment that is socially constructed, interpreted, and communicated via words, deeds, and images" (Hunt and Benford 1994, 491).[2] Communication, whether it is written, verbal, or symbolic, provides a foundation for the construction and maintenance of collective identity (Gamson 1997; Hunt, Benford, and Snow 1994; Snow and McAdam 2002). Identity talk, then, is an ideal way to track whether (and how) collective identity boundaries shift across episodes of contention.

Data and Methods

We employ several methods to examine the boundary shifts in a mid-size city TPM. First, we monitored organizational websites, public forums (such as the movement Facebook sites) and e-mails for the local TPM groups on a daily basis. Second, using Lexis Nexis, we collected all of the media coverage on the TPM in the state of Florida. Third, we attended more than a dozen meetings, rallies and events hosted by local TPM groups between April 2010 and May 2011. Finally, we conducted semistructured interviews with supporters of the Florida TPM. We used a variety of methods to locate respondents including e-mail, online surveys, giving presentations at local meetings, handing out flyers at events, and posting flyers in a variety of locations on- and offline.

These strategies yielded a total of 47 respondents; 33 of whom were interviewed formally and 14 of whom were interviewed informally at TPM rallies and events. The first round of formal interviews were conducted between August 2010 and May 2011. Respondents were asked about their range of political experience (petitions, canvassing, protests, and so on), membership in other organizations, when and why they joined the TPM, the kinds of activities and events (on- and offline) in which they have participated, their impressions of how the group has affected their participation, and their feelings about activism and politics in the United States more generally. The interviews ranged in length from 35 minutes to two and a half hours. We conducted follow-up interviews with 28 of the 33 respondents between May 2012 and January 2013. In these interviews, respondents were asked whether they still supported the TPM, the kinds of activities and events (on- and offline) in which they participated (through the TPM or other organizations), their impressions regarding how the movement has changed since its inception, and whether they saw similarities between the TPM and Occupy Wall Street movement. All respondents are identified with pseudonyms. Table 7.1 summarizes the demographics of the 33 respondents we interviewed formally. Overall, our respondents are diverse in terms of their age, gender, relationship, parental, and employment status but relatively homogenous in terms of their gender, race, and ethnicity. The gender, racial, and ethnic demographics are not representative of the city at large in which 52.77 percent of the population is female, 60.42 percent is white, 34.24 percent is African American, 4.19 percent is Latino, and 2.4 percent is Asian.

We analyzed the data chronologically and thematically. First, we organized the data by date (e.g., date posted to Facebook, date of the meeting or event, and date of the interview) and examined the ways in which leaders and participants defined the current political situation, constructed their motives for involvement, and the identities invoked as a rationale for collective action (for a similar strategy see Hunt and Benford 1994). We then looked to see whether (and when) shifts in the movement's collective identity occurred and, more specifically, whether these changes corresponded with changes in the larger political environment that would signal the end of one episode and the beginning of another (e.g., elections and the emergence of the Occupy Wall Street movement). Second, in order to verify the frequency and consistency of our qualitative findings, we coded the mention of each motive and identity, and assessed whether there were verifiable shifts in collective

Table 7.1. Demographic Characteristics of Tea Party Movement Respondents

	%	N		%	N
Sex			*Age*		
Male	70	23	18-35	30.5	10
Female	30	10	36-50	30.5	10
Employment Status			51+	39	13
Employed	61	20	*Relationship Status*		
Unemployed	6	2	Single	24	8
Retired	27	9	Partnered	6	2
Student	6	2	Married	48	16
Race Ethnicity			Divorced	19	6
White	82	27	Widowed	3	1
Asian	0	0	*Parental Status*		
Middle Eastern	3	1	No children	37	12
Latino	9	3	One child	21	7
Multiracial	6	2	Two or more children	42	14

identity (e.g., one collective identity disappears and another collective identity takes its place). While a new collective identity did not immediately replace an existing one, there is a clear transition in identity talk before the new boundaries take hold. Likewise, new boundaries regarding who Tea Partiers were did not emerge whole cloth. Narrow conceptions regarding who Tea Partiers were and what they stood for had been discussed and rejected early in the cycle of contention. However, as TPM claims were taken up by Republicans in Florida, leaders and supporters alike adopted increasingly exclusionary identities that used neoliberal and neoconservative principles to explain political engagement and the goals of the movement.

The local TPM has moved through two episodes of contention and is currently in its third. Each episode is characterized by a different collective identity. The first episode began with the movement's initial mobilization. As the movement emerged, leaders coordinated their efforts on- and offline to define movement membership broadly in an effort to affect meaningful political change and mobilize a wide range of participants. Collective identity during this early episode remained relatively open, allowing diverse membership and an open dialogue to develop. However, after the movement's electoral success in November 2010 (which signaled the second episode), leaders and supporters alike constricted the collective identity of the movement. During this episode, the TPM focused on America's geographic borders and specifically how the permeability of these borders enabled illegal immigrants and terrorists to undermine an American way of life. The identity boundaries contracted again during the third episode of contention, which began with the emergence of the Occupy Wall Street movement. Supporters of the TPM defined themselves and their participation in direct contrast to Occupiers and constructd their own engagement as legitimate and that of their opponents as unlawful and unfocused. We discuss each episode in turn.

Episode 1: Mobilizing "We the People" versus "They, the Career Politicians"

Leaders understand that collective identity is a resource in their mobilization efforts (Bernstein 1997). Not surprisingly, savvy leaders deploy identities that resonate with a broad swath of the population and, hopefully, mobilize them to action (Snow and Benford 1992). While the kinds of collective identities leaders can deploy are constrained by the causes they champion (Whittier 1997), in 2009 the stage was set for widespread mobilization as the American citizenry stewed over the government bailout of Wall Street bankers in a slumping economy. The city of study held its first TPM event on March 17, 2009 after Anthony, a 32-year-old conservative activist, attended a Tea Party organized by Brendan Steinhauser (the director of federal and state campaigns for FreedomWorks and Anthony's friend), John O'Hara (vice president of external relations at the Illinois Policy Institute), Peter Flaherty (writer for the *American Spectator*), and Michelle Malkin (syndicated columnist and Fox News contributor) outside of the White House. Invigorated by the rally, Anthony decided to spearhead a similar effort in Florida's capital. He began by setting up a Facebook page for the movement and inviting conservatives to become a fan of the group. Within a week, the page had over 500 fans. Anthony invited all the page fans to the first Tea Party rally. The event, which featured a keynote address by Dick Armey, attracted 300 Tea Partiers. Anthony capitalized on the event buzz and, using Facebook, grew the number of TPM supporters to nearly 1,000. He staged another rally the following month on tax day, April 15, 2009.[3]

Although this event was well attended and included short speeches from three state legislators, Anthony, who also works full time at a fiscally conservative think tank, found he could not maintain the movement alone. He decided to coordinate and spread the movement online and asked other local conservatives to organize the movement on the ground. The result was the creation of three additional local groups that supported the TPM banner, but adopted different orientations to politics.

The first group, which we call Citizens Holding Government Accountable, is a fiscally conservative, nonpartisan organization that works to "promote good conservative elected representatives to ALL levels of government." The group supports the TPM and specifically focuses on limiting government, fiscal responsibility, states' rights, and individual rights. The second organization, Christians for Responsible Government, also strongly supports the TPM platform but regards Judeo-Christian doctrine as critical to "uniting Americans" and "defending our country." The third group, Working for the American Way, integrates religious doctrine into its mission, which is to preserve "the rights and freedoms endowed by our Creator and guaranteed by our Constitution." Unlike the other groups, the primary goal of Working for the American Way is to provide a bridge between the TPM groups in order to increase the overall effectiveness of the movement's efforts in Florida.

Since Anthony spearheaded the local TPM movement, he had a great deal of control over how the collective identity boundaries were drawn. Instead of focusing on conservatives, Anthony capitalized on the citizenry's general discontent and drew on the culturally and institutionally resonant ideals of freedom, citizenship, and democracy to construct a collective identity that cast the local Tea Party collective as a movement of "the American people." As Anthony noted on the movement's Facebook group page:

> This isn't a conservative or liberal thing. This is about government forking over billions of dollars to businesses that should have failed. This is about taking money from responsible people and handing it over to CEOs who squandered their own.

This collective identity deemphasized political ideology and, instead, celebrated America's history of protest, emphasized the importance of political engagement, and cast the TPM as representative of America's diversity. The TPM's inclusive collective identity drew sharp distinctions between citizens and "elite Washington insiders," who made poor political decisions without consequence, which allowed local leaders to mobilize individuals across the political spectrum.

Other local leaders followed Anthony's lead and publicly championed the movement as nonpartisan, even as more particularistic political views (e.g., libertarian and socially conservative) were discussed during their group meetings. Local leaders, for example, expressly prohibited the display and distribution of politically partisan materials at events and were careful to distinguish the TPM from the Republican Party. At a luncheon, for instance, Terri (a socially conservative TPM leader) reminded 30 attendees that Republicans were as responsible as Democrats for America's financial woes:

> November second is not an end game. For too long in this country we've voted, and we think Election Day is it. And we go back about our lives trusting that the people we elect will do what they're supposed to do. We did that and especially those of us . . . who were active in the Republican Party trusting that a Republican in the White House, a Republican majority in the House of Representatives, and a Republican majority in the Senate would actually be fiscally responsible. Instead they abandoned the free markets; they raised taxes; they increased spending. They've done so much to influence and infringe on our lives and take our liberty away, and we cannot sit back and trust them to do the right thing any longer. We have to hold them accountable. We have to hold their feet to the fire!

In short, although the group page was the communication hub for the TPM (Rohlinger and Klein, 2014), the leaders publicly celebrated citizenship in ways that downplayed partisan differences and demonized elected officials.

This inclusive collective identity helped leaders to not only mobilize individuals across the political spectrum (Rohlinger, Bunnage, and Klein 2014; Rohlinger and Klein 2014), but also to manage the diversity of political opinion within the movement. The notion of individual freedom and rights, which are central to understandings of America identity, underscore that, while united by a love of country, America is comprised of diverse opinions and people (Schildkraut 2002). TPM leaders were quick to remind supporters that being united was different than being in agreement on every issue. Supporters were urged to embrace the diversity of the movement and focus on ridding the country of career politicians in both parties. This collective identity was indeed powerful insofar as it asked individuals to set aside their personal point of view on politically divisive issues like gay rights and abortion and work for a greater good.

The vast majority of respondents and all of the local leaders noted that it was critical for the movement to avoid issues that detracted from the movement's real purpose. Anthony explained:

> The Tea Party has not been focused on social issues or the cultural issues that divide America, but has been focused more on the issues that 70 to 80 percent of the people agree with a responsible government, accountable elected officials, and balancing the budget. Most people agree with that.

Logan, a leader of a TPM group in rural Florida, expressed personal distaste for both issues but argued that it was important for him to set these opinions aside so that the movement could grow its strength and influence over local and state politics. Likewise, Deborah, a 55-year-old conservative activist who has picketed as part of pro-life groups outside of abortion clinics, argued that controversial issues "could derail the central message . . . and take down the Tea Party movement." She added, "I don't know that strategically it would be the best. I think that we should concentrate more on the [political] process . . . I think that's more . . . it's not more important, I just think that hopefully, that would be the emphasis [of the Tea Party]." Nancy, a 49-year-old small business owner and long time Libertarian, warned that the movement would fail if these issues came to define the movement:

> I think it would be a big mistake for the Tea Party to focus on the immigration issue, on the abortion issue, on the gay rights issue. It's not something that would unite the people who would perceive themselves

associated with the Tea Party movement it's something that would be more likely to divide them . . . Gay marriage is a nonissue because the government has no business telling people whether they're married or not. Marriage is a business of a contract between two individuals or as a matter of religious practice. It's really not within the purview of government.

In sum, the local TPM initially emphasized an American identity that celebrated a history of protest, the importance of the average citizen's involvement in maintaining rights, freedoms, and political accountability, and the diversity of the American populace (even if only to avoid divisive issues). Movement supporters embraced this collective identity and, more importantly, helped maintain the boundaries separating "the American people" from "the career politicians." The boundaries, however, constricted considerably after the November 2010 election. As the movement ideas were incorporated into state politics, TPM leaders looked for ways to mobilize supporters anew. A different collective identity emerged during this time—one that focused on explicitly defining who were "real Americans" and who were "threats" to an American way of life.

Episode 2: "Real Americans" and "The Rest of Them"

The TPM was very successful during the 2010 election cycle. TPM-backed candidates swept races across Florida giving Republicans a super majority in the state legislature. Even Republicans who had not gotten elected under the TPM banner embraced the movement's agenda and joined the TPM caucus. The success of the movement was also evident locally in Leon County, Florida, which is heavily Democratic. For example, Nick Maddox, a businessman and former Florida State University football player, ousted Cliff Thaell, a liberal Democrat who had served on the county commission for 16 years. Maddox, who was discussed and promoted at TPM group meetings and events, parroted the political solutions favored by the TPM. For instance, Maddox argued that the financial success of the county would result through an investment in the private sector: "We have to work to make sure that we can help our private sector, our local small businesses. I think economic development incentives would be a good way to help those small businesses take in more employees and help our unemployment rate decrease." More importantly, state Republicans were quick to signal their willingness to work with the TPM. Virtually every Republican joined the Tea Party caucus in 2011 and several politicians, including the newly elected Governor Scott, spoke at a TPM rally during the first day of the legislative session.

It quickly became clear, however, that Republicans were not just championing fiscal conservatism and smaller government. Legislators introduced dozens of bills that reflected socially conservative ideologies. Among the most controversial were the 18 pieces of legislation designed to make legal abortion less accessible in the state, legislation giving the legislature more control over the judicial system (and the Supreme Court in particular), legislation requiring TANF recipients to undergo mandatory drug testing at their expense, and legislation tightening control over voter registration procedures and voter rights at the polls. These bills, which have been signed by the governor, enraged many Democrats, Independents, and Libertarians—and many of those who supported the Tea Party cause have abandoned the movement (Rohlinger and Klein 2014).

The disaffected were not the only ones who returned to their armchairs and remote controls. Many satisfied supporters, largely social conservatives, resumed their normal lives. As a result, attendance at group meetings fell, activity on the Facebook page plummeted, and finding ways to reengage supporters in order to keep the TPM agenda prominent in the minds of elected officials became a regular topic of conversation among the stalwart few. Political incorporation, in short, threatened to diminish the political clout of the movement unless leaders could reinvent the movement. In an effort to reengage conservatives in the cause, TPM leaders (except Anthony, who focused his energies on changing policy rather than mobilization) stoked the fears of supporters warning that reticence would lead to the destruction of America (Rohlinger and Klein 2014). This new focus forced leaders to redefine what it meant to be an American citizen and effectively constrict the boundaries of movement membership. In this envisioning of the movement, Tea Party represented "real" Americans; conservatives who were almost always born on American soil.

To be clear, Tea Partiers distinguished conservatives from Republicans—even Republicans who had sailed into office under the TPM banner. Tea Partiers expressed suspicion toward the Republican establishment and promised to hold newly elected officials' feet to the proverbial fire. Diane, a 56-year-old sales representative, explained that the movement represented conservatives, not Republicans:

> I think [the goal is] ultimately to replace many of the long-term candidates in Washington, DC with more conservatives, just like what happened in this last election, where TPM type conservative people who are truly respectful of the Constitution, are truly interested in reducing spending and overhauling the entitlement programs in this country. Not those that are just going to give it lip service, but those who actually have the backbone to do it. And I think that the TPM was hugely successful in getting that accomplished in this last election.

The message that Republicans were not safe from the TPM fury was echoed online. One visitor to a local TPM website warned, "All the pro-war, pro-rights taking, big government republicans better watch . . . their ass. We want peace, sound money, smaller government . . . AND A RESPECT AND RESTORATION OF OUR LIBERTY."

Conservative was defined with care, deliberately avoiding associations traditionally made to right-wing social movements or organizations. This was relatively easy to do because American conservatism has always been defined by its clash of ideas. Noted historian Alan Brinkley (1994, 414), explains:

> Conservatism encompasses a broad range of ideas, impulses, and constituencies, and many conservatives feel no obligation to choose among the conflicting, even incompatible impulses, that fuel their politics. Individual conservatives find it possible, and at times perhaps even necessary, to embrace several clashing ideas at once. Conservatism is not, in short, an "ideology," with a secure and consistent internal structure. It is a cluster of related (and sometimes unrelated) ideas from which those who consider themselves conservatives draw different elements at different times.

These inconsistencies in conservatism allowed the TPM to reject accusations that it was a right-wing, racist movement while simultaneously championing a collective identity that wove xenophobia in its refashioning of who constituted a legitimate American (Giugni et al. 2005; McVeigh, Myers, and Sikkink 2004; McVeigh 2009). As a result of this boundary constriction, "immigrants, liberals, working women, counterculturists, abortion providers, welfare recipients, secular humanists, feminists, and later, global jihadists and Muslim terrorists" (Blee and Creasap 2010, 274) all represented threats to the "American" way of life.

Although Tea Partiers were careful to avoid the racist or xenophobic labels associated with right-wing groups, the new collective identity involved reestablishing geographic borders, particularly between the United States and Mexico, and emphasizing the global terrorist threat targeting the United States. Not unlike the geographic borders and social boundaries patrolled by the "border grannies" (Johnston, this volume) or the symbolic border guards in Hindu nationalist paramilitary camps (Sehgal, this volume), Florida Tea Partiers recast themselves as "real" Americans who were concerned about the security of the country. Concerns over illegal immigrants and terrorist threats were not new in Florida, nor are they new to right-leaning movements. When the social, economic, or political hegemony of the "ruling race" is challenged, right-wingers are quick to outline the threats changing demographics pose to the status quo (McVeigh 2009). This is no less true of the TPM, where several groups and vocal supporters have connections to nativist organizations like the Minutemen and white nationalist communities such as Stormfront.org (Burghart and Zeskind 2010). Indeed, even if it is not always explicit, this racial challenge provides a backdrop for the TPM. Changing national demographics, which predict that whites will be a numerical minority before 2050, have fueled some supporters question whether concerns over citizenship and national security should be part of the movement's formal agenda.

The immigration issue, which was marginalized by leaders and supporters alike in the first episode of contention, emerged with a vengeance after the election. Again, this boundary shift should be understood in the larger political context. Satisfied Tea Partiers headed home as the Republican Party took up key TPM issues. Consequently, leaders had to define the TPM once more in order to jump start mobilization and distinguish itself from its new political allies. In this context, the notion that illegal immigrants were taking advantage of a bloated "nanny state" found legs. More specifically, TPM supporters were the hard-working taxpayers funding individuals who snuck into the country so that they too could suck on the teat of the state. Not surprisingly, this narrower collective identity manifested in the movement's support for the REAL ID program, which is a series of federal laws that make it more difficult to get drivers license and identification cards. Presumably, these laws weed out illegal immigrants from the citizen identification process and make it tougher for them to take advantage of local, state, and federal programs. At a TPM meeting, a member acknowledged that the primary reason for implementing REAL ID is so that "illegal aliens/Mexicans" cannot get drivers licenses. He voiced support for even stricter measures (tracking DNA of individuals from their birth), explaining that it was a safety issue because the "Mexicans are running amok" in South Florida and are "still driving and still crashing" even with REAL ID. While the other members did not support the idea of cataloging DNA as a way to track citizenship, another participant agreed that the government "needs to stop giving IDs to illegal aliens without checking documents."

Movement adherents also expressed support for states championing restrictive immigration legislation (namely Arizona and Alabama), arguing that illegal immigrants were undermining the infrastructure of America. For example, a moderator on a local TPM website, posted:

> Here in Florida we spend millions of dollars to educate, hospitalize, incarcerate, illegals who broke the law being here. Because of them we lay off teachers, law enforcement and other fine professionals. Many of these fine people have served in the military, risk their lives and their reward is layoff because Washington refuses to Deport [sic] people who got here illegally.

This message was echoed at a TPM rally, where a leader proclaimed, to great applause, "We're not California or Arizona. We want this issue addressed, we want it resolved and the best way to resolve it is to end employment opportunities for illegal aliens so they begin to self-deport."

The TPM's collective identity during this episode of contention also explicitly cast President Obama as the architect of America's demise and, therefore, an enemy of the movement. Since its emergence, pundits and scholars alike have questioned why Tea Partiers, a relatively privileged group of white retirees, suddenly had a bone to pick with the direction of the American government. A common response is the election of the nation's first "African American" President, which underscored the demographic changes in the United States (Barreto, Cooper, Gonzalez, Parker, and Towler 2011). Pundits have not had to look very hard for evidence to support their claim. The questions regarding President Obama's faith and the teachings of his pastor Reverend Wright as well as the debate over President Obama's birth certificate, which evolved into the Birther Movement, are often cited as examples that racial fears (rather than civic duty) motivate the TPM. Locally, leaders and supporters skirted the issue by avoiding discussions of race altogether. Instead, Tea Partiers cast themselves as "freedom fighters" who were dedicated to shoring up America's borders and ensuring that capitalist principles (rather than socialism) guided political decision-making. Diane explained:

> Freedom. You can't find that anywhere else; this is the last place for it. Once it's lost here, it's gone. And a lot of young people don't realize that, and they get very idealistic. They start following the people on the Left and it's almost like liberalism and socialism. It's almost like a fad. They don't realize how devastating it is. If you haven't served in the military, you don't know what it is to go out and fight for freedom. Everybody takes the freedom for granted and it's just stupid because it's the most valuable thing that there is. These brave people who go out and die for their country and it really ticks me off when people sit around and talk about, "Oh we ought to be a socialist country . . ." It makes me sick to my stomach.

The TPM's fight against illegal immigration and socialism had implications for the American legal system and national security more generally. TPM supporters routinely argued that getting the "right" politicians in office would prevent a Muslim takeover, at best, and another terrorist attack on American soil at worst. Concern over the Muslim threat, and how to control it, was a common topic of conversation. For example, at a meeting one male member noted that he had no problem with "Muslims who are here legally," but was worried about Sharia law circumventing American laws. After arguing that Muslims needed to adopt American customs and laws, he added, "You ain't in Sharia or whereever that stuff comes from."[4] Similarly, at a rally a Tea Partier warned that Obama's socialist agenda was weakening America from the inside out; a fact that the general public would not realize until it was too late:

> Friends, this administration is quickly doing what Osama Bin Laden and Al Qaida were not able to do. And, that is to bring this country to her knees! And speaking of Al Qaida, do not believe for a second that our enemy is not aware of what is going on. While our nation is drowning in debt, radical Islamic groups quietly build their massive infrastructure within the USA, secretly awaiting our demise. Let's not give them hope. If we care anything for this nation, we must not let that occur!

He then linked this back to the need for Tea Partiers to protect the American way of life for future generations:

> Soon my wife Emily and I will be trying to get pregnant. I do not want to leave my son or daughter with a country that is saddled with a debt that cannot be repaid. With a country that cannot be fixed. With a nation that is being built by our enemies from within. I don't want my future grandchildren to have to ask why Americans stood by and did nothing while they watched their country disintegrate. The United States was an experiment that went right. Let's not see it go up in flames. Our children's future is at stake. Let's fight keep our country the bastion of freedom that we have been used to.

In sum, the TPM's collective identity constricted during the second episode of contention as leaders scrambled to respond to its electoral success. Tea Partiers distinguished themselves from the Republican establishment and cast the collective as a group of "real" Americans, who recognized that the country's core principles were under attack from immigrants at the borders and a socialist president in the White

House. The TPM's new collective identity explicitly drew on conservative (and right-wing) ideas and, for the first time, excluded Democrats (see Rohlinger and Klein 2014 for a more detailed discussion). Thus, while TPM leaders and supporters still regarded their engagement as an expression of love for their country, they restricted definitions of who was a legitimate American and focused intently on what lax borders and a "socialist" President meant for the country's future. The TPM's reentrenchment into partisan positions became more pronounced after progressives around the world mobilized under the Occupy banner.

Episode 3: "Patriots" versus "Progressives"

The Occupy Wall Street protests, which swept across the country in fall 2011, posed a new threat to the TPM. Like Tea Partiers, Occupy supporters were responding to an economic climate characterized by bailouts for corporations and layoffs for Middle America. While the Occupy movement shared the TPM's passion to remake the political system, they also insinuated corporate power and the accumulation of wealth by the 1 percent into the equation. Occupiers, in short, did not simply demand a more responsive political system, but one that addressed economic and social inequality. The general similarities between these two movements did not escape journalists or commentators. President Obama made the comparison himself stating, "I understand the frustrations being expressed in those protests . . . In some ways, they're not that different from some of the protests that we saw coming from the Tea Party. Both on the Left and the Right, I think people feel separated from their government. They feel that their institutions aren't looking out for them."[5] News outlets, including the *Huffington Post*, *USA Today*, online magazines like *Slate*, and commentators on MSNBC, CNN, and Fox News all participated in the comparative dialogue.

The TPM responded by constricting their identity boundaries further in an effort to clearly distinguish the movement from "Occupy anarchists." The movements differ a great deal in terms of how each conceptualizes political citizenship and engagement. While Occupiers value market liberalism and constitutional democracy, Tea Partiers emphasize the importance of individual opportunity, "free" markets, and the utility of state power to enforce a singular moral vision in

America (specifically one that abhors legal abortion and gay marriage). The only purpose of the state apparatus is to simultaneously further opportunities for individual profiteering while imposing a particularistic moral-religious vision on the country. Equality has no place, nor is it desirable (Brown 2006).

Individuals that extol the benefits of free markets champion a "rhetoric of perversity," which argues that "policies intended to alleviate poverty create perverse incentives toward welfare dependency and exploitation, and thus inexorably exacerbate the very social ills that they were meant to cure. The logic behind the rhetoric is impeccable—if assistance is actually hurting the poor by creating dependence, then denying it is not cruel but compassionate" (Somers and Block 2005, 265). The result is an "undemocratic" citizen who cares a great deal about national borders and moral authority but very little about equality and a robust democracy (Brown 2006). Arguably, this understanding of politics, economics, and citizenship has taken a firm hold in the United States. Progressives, who advocate on behalf of traditional notions of market liberalism and constitutional democracy, find themselves on the defensive and cast as another threat to the American dream.

The embracement of these ideas was evident in the identity talk of Tea Partiers. TPM supporters defined themselves almost entirely in terms of their support for free markets and capitalism, and, of course, opposition to government programs and socialism. In follow-up interviews with respondents, ranging from 6 to 12 months after the emergence of Occupy, we asked whether or not there were comparisons to be made between the two movements. Supporters clearly outlined the ideological differences and the implications for political participation. For example, Connor, a 50-year-old retired law enforcement officer, noted that while the TPM and Occupy movement both mobilized people, there were fundamental differences in worldview and their expectations of government:

> The Occupy movement, as I understand it, is opposed to capitalism whether it be profit or excessive profit, however you define that, whereas the Tea Party is all about free market. We want people to have the opportunity to succeed or to fail. And I think the difference between the two trains of thought is what happens when you fail. The Tea Party

movement, whenever you fail, dust yourself off, get up and try again. The Occupy movement, well, whenever you fail, we need to have the government come in and bail you out, or prop you up, or help you out, and I think that's pretty much day-and-night type of difference.

Anthony agreed, attributing Occupy's embracement of misguided ideas to the youth of its supporters:

They seemed to be very young, not really serious. I think there were a handful of serious people there. The rest of the people were shouting and chanting things that seemed a little ridiculous to me like wanting to get their student loans paid off, things like that. I didn't see a lot of people that were taking personal responsibility themselves.

Other respondents noted that these young progressives did not "have a grasp of reality" and thought they were "owed something," when, as Beth put it, "the Tea Party feels like something is going to be taken from them."

Even respondents who regarded Occupiers as misguided, regarded their activism as dangerous to (neoliberal) American ideals, George, a 60-year-old attorney, felt strongly that the Occupiers were dangerous anarchists, who opposed free markets:

So, the comparisons and similarities between the Occupy Wall Street and the Tea Party, there aren't any. Except they both involve a number of human beings engaging in some premotivated activity. That's about the only comparison. The Occupy Wall Street, the 99 percenter concept is the same moron crowd of anarchists that has been going on. You know, the same May Day people who bash bank windows and cop cars and stuff. It's that same group except the idea of Occupy caught on. The same Leftist financiers have their fingerprints all over it. The number of people doing it [participating in the Occupy movement] pales in comparison to the Tea Party movement. The Tea Party movement is widespread and has gotten a lot of decent folks off their couches doing things political. The Occupy movement is the same violent, anarchist, communist thugs that have been smashing the Starbucks around the world for a decade or two.

George added that the Occupy Wall Street movement has been success-
ful at "exposing" the deceptive and violent tactics of progressives: "[The
Occupy Wall Street movement] is good at turning people against the
Left—reminding people of the flubbery and the deception and the vio-
lent tendencies of the Left. I think it's done much more harm for the
Left than good."

Almost all of our respondents echoed these characterizations of
Occupiers and were quick to point out the violence (they reference all
the "rapes and murders" in particular) and "filthy" conditions at the
camps. Matthew compares the two movements and makes clear that
Tea Partiers are upstanding citizens, while Occupy is comprised of
criminals and the unemployed:

> Well, of course, the Occupy Wall Street people are nothing but a bunch
> of Leftist bums. They're unemployed, maybe some of them really wanted
> job, maybe some of them really are idealist and they want good things.
> They're not quite sure about the economics of how to bring it about. But
> I guaran-damn-tee [sic] the vast majority of them are simply apolitical
> hacks. And when these poor ladies got themselves raped by all these guys
> that are wandering around! Again, you look at the Tea Party, you go, how
> many people have been murdered? How many people have been raped at
> a Tea Party? How many people have been cut, knifed, shot? Well, it didn't
> happen. It does not happen. Again, the rule is, the mantra is—Tea Parties
> are racist, Tea Parties are sexist, oh, that they've got the worst people of
> the country. Occupy Wall Street, oh, they're just poor misguided souls,
> they want the best for people, their ideals are great, we need to listen to
> them. Meanwhile, there's this poor lady screaming in her tent because
> she's getting raped! I mean, come on—the king [emperor] has no clothes.

If anything, these characterizations of the Occupy movement, and
Obama supporters more generally, gained steam leading up to the 2012
presidential election. One Tea Party supporter, who also is a relatively
well-known conservative blogger, posted:

> Obama supporters are a special breed of people. The more I learn about
> them, the more I dislike them and everything they represent in the
> form of a threat to my country. They usually fit in one of two catagories

[sic]: educated yet clueless or mindless, useful idiots. Today, I want to talk about the mindless, useful idiots with voting rights who are tweeting threats. They profess to be the tolerant and compassionate Americans, yet many of them are the most intolerant and violent citizens in this country. They want something for nothing. They come from a background of entitlement mentality. They feel we OWE them something, that somehow, somewhere along the way, they have been oppressed, mistreated, or neglected. After last week's debate, they suddenly realize their source of entitlements may be at risk of losing his job to a man who believes in putting Americans back to work instead of a welfare existence. I am relatively certain most of those Obama-lovers are not mentally capable of comprehending much of the conversation that took place in the debate, but they are bright enough to sense fear among the ranking democrats who are in the know. They are smart enough to know the difference between winning and losing. They are sore losers and now are resorting to threats in order to keep their food-stamp President in office. Their threats do not frighten those of us on the Right. The threats only confirm what most of us already know about the kind of people who support Obama. They represent the worst of America, all that is wrong with this fine country, and why someone like Barack Obama ever made it to a position of power in the first place.

In short, TPM leaders and supporters alike characterize their collective challenge as a civic and patriotic duty and progressive activism as uninformed, threatening, and, often, violent.

These characterizations of progressives were not completely new. While these points of view were marginalized in the first episode of contention at the group level, some respondents were quick to distinguish their involvement from that of progressive activists in their initial interviews. Deborah, for instance, noted that:

[Progressives are] more negative. It's people against something. And I kind of associate protests more with the way Democrats and Liberals function at their rallies. They're more negative. At times they've been more violent. Um, it's not like that at a Tea Party rally. Rallies are because we're standing up for something. Because we're trying preserve something.

In fact, TPM supporters categorized their engagement with politics as "not activism." Early in the cycle of contention, TPM supporters did not embrace the activist label because they regarded it as "risky," or having potentially negative consequences for their work or personal lives (Rohlinger and Brown 2009). For example, Jacob, a 26-year-old small business owner, argued that the riskiness of adopting a conservative activist label is function of the broader political climate, which supports progressive but not conservative causes:

> I would say that being part of the Tea Party, or being conservative, or being Republican is a little more risky than saying "I'm a Democrat" or "I'm a liberal" or "I'm a progressive" or "I'm a socialist" . . . saying [you're] a Democrat . . . I don't think [that] sounds [as] risky as if you were going to say, "Yeah, I'm a Tea Party activist." The way it has been projected by the media that the Tea Party itself has been put into a pretty negative light by . . . the president. And people listen to the president. So if he says, "Watch out for these Tea Party people," you're going to be looked at in a negative way. So I think you're more at risk being a Tea Party or Republican, than you are being a liberal, progressive, or a Democrat.

Nancy agreed noting that, "When I think of an activist, I don't think of a conservative. I think of a liberal. The word activist to me, describes someone who is involved with the political left."

The TPM, in short, constricted its collective identity again; this time in response to the emergence of the Occupy Wall Street movement. Tea Partiers embraced neoliberal and neoconservative ideologies and distanced their political engagement from the activism of the Left. In their view, "Americans" extol the value of personal responsibility, the freedom inherent in individual entrepreneurialism, and construct "civic duty" as actively defending these principles before they are taken away by progressives. This political engagement is contrasted to the misguided and unprincipled activism of progressives, who challenge the inequality at the crux of national and global politics.

Given this particularized collective identity opportunities for the TPM to reincorporate Democrats (and Libertarians) seem dim. Tea Partiers have effectively shut down avenues for identity negotiation with much of the broader public. While this may limit the TPM's mobilization efforts, it by no means signals that the movement will disappear. There continues to be a cadre of dedicated TPM supporters, who believe that they can redefine (and reinvigorate) the Republican Party and take back the White House in 2016.

Conclusions

This chapter illustrates the importance of boundary work as it relates to collective identity. We show that identity boundaries shift across episodes of contention. In the case of the midsize city TPM, we find that identity boundaries constrict in each subsequent episode of contention. These contracting boundaries were primarily in response to two political exigencies—the incorporation of movement ideas into the political apparatus and the emergence of the Occupy Wall Street movement. As the movement emerged, leaders coordinated their efforts on- and offline to define movement membership broadly in an effort to mobilize across party lines. The TPM collective identity during the first episode of contention was inclusive, which encouraged widespread mobilization. However, after the movement's electoral success in November 2010 (which signaled the second episode), leaders and supporters alike constricted the collective identity of the movement. During this episode, the TPM distinguished itself from the Republican Party by narrowing how it understood what it meant to be an "American." Here, Tea Partiers focused on America's geographic borders and specifically how the permeability of these borders enabled illegal immigrants and terrorists to undermine the American way of life. The TPM's collective identity constricted again during the third episode of contention, which began with the emergence of the Occupy Wall Street movement. TPM supporters defined themselves, what they stood for, and their participation in direct contrast to Occupiers.

In addition to highlighting how state and movement actors shape the redefinition of collective identity, this research has implications for understanding how collective identity changes across a cycle of contention. First, this research suggests that the timing of a movement's emergence has long-term consequences for collective identity. Early risers in a cycle of contention are well positioned to define themselves and their goals broadly. That said, early risers are unlikely to be able to maintain an inclusive identity throughout various episodes of contention. As other political actors respond to movement claims and the movement itself achieves some measure of success, leaders and core constituents will need to define themselves (and other political actors) anew.

Second, while leaders deploy collective identity strategically (Bernstein 1997; Gamson 1997), this is not just for the benefit of political actors. Savvy leaders can champion more inclusive collective identities online than they do in the real world, which can benefit movements in the short term. Part of the TPM success in 2010, particularly at the local level, was a result of the movement's ability to mobilize citizens across party lines. This is not to suggest that there is a complete disconnect between online and offline displays of collective identity. In the first episode of contention, local leaders tempered antiprogressive sentiment in meetings and prohibited public displays of partisanship at TPM events—a practice that disappeared in the second episode of contention (see Rohlinger and Klein 2014). The point here is that there are new opportunities for leaders to craft identities in ways that allow widespread mobilization.

Third, while collective identity boundaries shift from one episode of contention to the next, the new identity does not emerge whole cloth. Instead, the ideas that inform participation and what a movement stands for (and against) are circulated among supporters long before they come to define a movement and a cause. Antiprogressive views, for instance, were there from the beginning but kept in check by leaders. This highlights the importance of boundary-work and leadership continuity across episodes of contention. If leaders want to maintain inclusive identities, then they must work hard to do so over time. Anthony's decision to prioritize politics of movement maintenance in the wake of the TPM's electoral success was an important one insofar as the other leaders did not make an effort to maintain an inclusive identity. Perhaps, the collective identity of the movement would be different today if Anthony had remained engaged in the movement's politics. The point here, however, is that leaders and supporters take cues from one another regarding how identity boundaries should be constructed from one episode to the next, and absent a strong leader, identities can constrict at a rapid pace.

Finally, collective identity shifts often involve embracing familiar ideologies regarding the relationship between the state, economy, and society. What made the initial mobilization of the local Tea Party movement exciting was that, at least for awhile, leaders and supporters alike were challenging the lack of political accountability to the citizenry. Tea Partiers were less interested in political parties and election outcomes than they were individual rights and the role of government in the economy. The sense that government had gone too far was palpable and a new way of understanding the world was in their grasp. Once this moment passed, however, supporters reverted to identities that emphasized national borders and the virtues of market principles and logic, and that put primacy on an individual's right to succeed (or fail) personally and financially. Stated differently, ideas about the relationship between the state, economy, and society that were challenged early in a cycle of contention were embraced in later episodes. The emergence of Occupy articulated and hardened the boundaries of the TPM and the result is a predictable, and seemingly unsolvable, war of ideas.

Thinking about collective identity as a project across a cycle of protest rather than a product of a specific moment in time, however, may help activists forge new collective identities in the twenty-first century. While geographic borders are real and meaningful collective identities require constant negotiation, the ways in which activists can communicate and coordinate their collective challenges are different from those of the past. Clearly, Internet communication technology can be used to forge spaces where people holding very different political points of view can come together and find some common ground. While these projects are not without their hiccups and failures, they are important reminders that citizens, activists, and individuals can create new frameworks for understanding the world in which we live.

NOTES

1. We would like to thank Jennifer Bickham Mendez and Nancy Naples for their comments and the Department of Sociology at Florida State University for its research support.

2. The conceptualization of identity work has changed over time. For an overview of identity work and its relevance to collective identity and social movements see Snow and McAdam (2000). For examples of research that analyzes the construction of identity see Blee and Creasap (2010), Hunt and Benford (1994), and Ghaziani (2011).

3. According to Anthony, the number of fans for the local Tea Party Facebook page has fluctuated. He reports that at its height, there were nearly 1,500 fans. Since we have been monitoring the page, the number of fans has fluctuated between 920 (in April 2010) and 830 (April 2011).

4. Florida House Republicans agreed. Larry Metz, a representative from Eustis, Florida and sponsor of a bill that bans courts and other legal authorities from considering religious or foreign law in legal decisions and contracts, argued that politicians needed to "jump in front of the problem."

5. Dwyer (2011).

REFERENCES

Barreto, Matt, Betsy Cooper, Benjamin Gonzalez, Christopher Parker, and Christopher Towler. 2011. "The Tea Party in the Age of Obama: Mainstream Conservatism or Out-Group Anxiety?" *Political Power and Social Theory* 22(1): 1–29.

Bernstein, Mary. 1997. "Celebration and Suppression: The Strategic Uses of Identity by the Lesbian and Gay Movement." *American Journal of Sociology* 103(3): 531–565.

Bernstein, Mary, and Marcie De la Cruz. 2009. " "What are You?" Explaining Identity as a Goal of the Multiracial Hapa Movement." *Social Problems*,56 (4): 722–745.

Blee, Kathleen M., and Kimberly A. Creasap. 2010. "Conservative and Right-Wing Movements." *Annual Review of Sociology* 36: 269–286.

Brinkley, Alan. 1994. "The Problem of American Conservatism." *American Historical Review* 99 (2): 409–429.

Brown, Wendy. 2006. "American Nightmare: Neoliberalism, Neoconservatism, and De-Democratization." *Political Theory* 34 (6): 690–714.

Burghart, Devin, and Leonard Zeskind. 2010. "Tea Party Nationalism: A Critical Examination of the Tea Party Movement and the Size, Scope, and Focus of Its National Factions." *Institute for Research & Education on Human Rights*. www.irehr. org.

Dwyer, Devin. 2011. "Obama: Occupy Wall Street 'Not that Different' From Tea Party Protests." http://abcnews.go.com/blogs/politics/2011/10/obama-occupy-wall-street-not-that-different-from-tea-party-protests/.

Friedman, Debra, and Doug McAdam. 1992. "Collective Identity and Activism: Networks, Choices, and the Life of a Social Movement." In *Frontiers in Social Movement Theory*, edited by Aldon Morris and Carol McClurg Mueller, 156–173. New Haven, CT: Yale University Press.

Gamson, Joshua. 1997. "Messages of Exclusion: Gender, Movements, and Symbolic Boundaries." *Gender & Society* 11(2): 178–199.

———. 1995. "Must Identity Movements Self-Destruct? A Queer Dilemma." *Social Problems* 42(3):390–407.

Gamson, W. A. 1975. *The Strategy of Social Protest*, 89–109. Homewood, IL: Dorsey Press.

Ghaziani, Amin. 2011. "Post-Gay Collective Identity Construction." *Social Problems* 58(1): 99–125.

Giugni, Marco, Ruud Koopmans, Florence Passy, and Paul Statham. 2005. "Institutional and Discursive Opportunities for Extreme-Right Mobilization in Five Countries." *Mobilization: An International Quarterly* 10(1): 145–162.

Hunt, Scott A., and Robert D. Benford. 1994. "Identity Talk in the Peace and Justice Movement." *Journal of Contemporary Ethnography* 22(4): 488–517.

Hunt, Scott A., Robert D. Benford, and David A. Snow. 1994. "Identity Fields: Framing Processes and the Social Construction of Movement Identities." In *New Social Movements: From Ideology to Identity*, edited by Enrique Laraña, Hank Johnston, and Joseph Gusfield, 185–208. Philadelphia: Temple University Press.

Klandermans, Bert. 1988. "The Formation and Mobilization of Consensus." In *International Social Movement Research: A Research Annual Volume I*, edited by Bert Klandermans, Doug McAdam, Sidney Tarrow, and Charles Tilly, 173–196. 2001.

McAdam, Doug, Sidney Tarrow, and Charles Tilly. 2001. *Dynamics of Contention*. New York: Cambridge University Press.

McVeigh, Rory. 2009. *The Rise of the Ku Klux Klan: Right-Wing Movements and National Politics*. Minneapolis: University of Minnesota Press.

McVeigh, Rory, Daniel J. Myers, and David Sikkink. 2004. "Corn, Klansmen, and Coolidge: Structure and Framing in Social Movements." *Social Forces* 83(2): 653–690.

Polletta, Francesca, and James Jasper. 2001. "Collective Identity and Social Movements." *Annual Review of Sociology* 27: 283–305.

Reger, Jo. 2002. "Organizational Dynamics and Construction of Multiple Feminist Identities in the National Organization of Women." *Gender and Society* 16(5): 710–727.

Rohlinger, Deana A., and Jordan Brown. 2009. "Democracy, Action, and the Internet After 9/11." *American Behavioral Scientist* 53 (1): 133–150.

Rohlinger, Deana, Leslie Bunnage, and Jesse Klein. 2014. "Virtual Power Plays: Social Movements, ICT, and Party Politics." In *The Internet and Democracy in Global Perspective: Voters, Candidates, Parties, and Social Movements*, edited by Bernard Groffman, Alex Trechsel, and Mark Franklin, 83–110. New York: Springer.

Rohlinger, Deana, and Jesse Klein. 2014. "From Fervor to Fear: ICT and Emotions in the Tea Party Movement." In *Understanding the Tea Party*, edited by David Meyer and Nella Van Dyke, 125–148. New York: Ashgate.

Schildkraut, Deborah. 2002. "The More Things Change . . . American Identity and Mass and Elite Responses to 9/11." *Political Psychology* 23(3): 511–55.

Snow, David, and Robert Benford. 1992. "Master Frames and Cycles of Protest." In *Frontiers in Social Movement Theory*, edited by Aldon Morris and Carol McClurg Mueller, 133–155. New Haven, CT: Yale University Press.

Snow, David, and Doug McAdam. 2002. "Identity Work Processes in the Context of Social Movements: Clarifying the Identity/Movement Nexus." In *Self, Identity, and Social Movements*, edited by Sheldon Stryker, Timothy J. Owens, and Robert W. White, 41–67. Minneapolis: University of Minnesota Press.

Somers, Margaret R., and Fred Block. 2005. "From Poverty to Perversity: Ideas, Markets, and Institutions over 200 Years of Welfare Debate." *American Sociological Review* 70 (2): 260–287.

Tarrow, Sidney. 2011. *Power in Movement: Social Movements and Contentious Politics.* New York: Cambridge University Press.

Taylor, Verta. 1989. "Social Movement Continuity: The Women's Movement in Abeyance." *American Sociological Review* 54(5): 761–775.

Taylor, Verta, and Nancy Whittier. 1992. "Collective Identity and Lesbian Feminist Mobilization." In *Frontiers of Social Movement Theory*, edited by Aldon Morris and Carol Mueller, 104–130. New Haven, CT: Yale University Press.

Whittier, Nancy. 1995. *Feminist Generations: The Persistence of the Radical Women's Movement.* Philadelphia: Temple University Press.

———. 1997. "Political Generations, Micro-Cohorts, and the Transformation of Social Movements." *American Sociological Review* 62: 760–778.

8

Occupy Slovenia

How Migrant Movements Contributed to
New Forms of Direct Democracy

MAPLE RAZSA AND ANDREJ KURNIK

The fate of European identity as a whole is being played out in Yugoslavia and more generally in the Balkans. Either Europe will recognize
in the Balkan situation not a monstrosity grafted to its breast, a patho-
logical 'after effect' of underdevelopment or communism, but rather an
image and effect of its own history and will undertake to confront it and
resolve it and thus to put itself into question and transform itself . . . Or
else it will . . . continue to treat the problem as an exterior obstacle to be
treated with exterior means, including colonization.
    —Etienne Balibar (2004, 6)

Defying the blazing July sun, forty migrant laborers, local organizers,
and international activists gathered outside the concrete blast walls
surrounding the Office of the High Representative (OHR) in Sarajevo,
Bosnia in 2010. Following the bankruptcy of the Slovene construction
firm that employed them, the laborers had recently been deported back
to Bosnia from Slovenia. Now they were joined by allies from the Invisible Workers of the World (IWW), an activist collective from Slovenia. Together they demanded that the OHR—the EU agency that has
administered Bosnia since the end of armed hostilities in 1995—address
the exploitation of Bosnians employed in the EU, especially Slovenia.
Having shared a passport with Slovenes until the Yugoslav federation
unraveled two decades ago, the Bosnian workers were particularly

angry about their treatment there. When the protesters began to chant boisterously, demanding the back pay they were owed, EU Force troops escorted them further away from the OHR high-rise. "Now they are so worried about security," one laborer grumbled. "Where were they when we were under siege?"

Against the backdrop of the region's history of communal violence, the migrant-IWW action in Sarajevo stands out as a rare example of transnational organizing and interethnic cooperation. Rather than calling for the reinforcement of borders and the separation of ethnic communities, as nationalists often did, the migrant-IWW protests called for the opening of the borders, even the outright abolition of migration controls. Their public statement posed borders generally—and EU borders in particular—as integral to the abuses Bosnian laborers faced in Slovenia. The visa regime, which policed who could cross the border and under what conditions, was structured in such a way, they complained, that there was a constant danger of violating the complex rules and becoming "illegal." The protesting laborers knew this danger all too well.

In recent years migration, especially "illegal immigration," has become one of the most politically charged issues in Western Europe (Sassen 1999). Research on migration, however, even by critical scholars, has tended to view migrants generally and "illegals" in particular, from the standpoint of the migrant-receiving nation-state, representing them as an intrusion on longstanding political and cultural communities in which they have no legitimate social, political, or legal claims (De Genova 2002, 420–21). In short, most research has suffered from what Wimmer and Glick-Schiller decry as "methodological nationalism" (2002).

As seen in the Sarajevo protests, since declaring independence from socialist Yugoslavia—with the explicit goal of joining the EU—Slovenia has in many ways followed the broader European trend of adopting restrictive migration policies. Indeed, public controversies have erupted around refugees, asylum seekers, and legal as well as illegal labor migrants (Razsa and Kurnik 2012). Aspects of Slovene migration politics, however, make it an especially revealing and productive case through which to understand how migrants become illegal and challenge research methodologies that do not escape a national frame. First, whereas the nation-states of Western Europe are well established and thoroughly naturalized entities, Slovenia achieved independence for the first time only two decades ago. Second, the vast majority of contemporary labor migrants to Slovenia are from other former Yugoslav republics. In other words they were cocitizens, free to travel, live, and work in Slovenia until restrictive migration laws, modeled on West European legislation, were imposed on them overnight in 1992. For these reasons our research on migrant illegality in Slovenia—from the perspective of activist challenges to that illegality—is well positioned to contribute to the growing literature that investigates illegality not simply as a self-evident legal consequence of migrant crimes but rather as socially and legally produced (Coutin 2003; De Genova 2002; Fassin 2011). Drawing on years of collaboration with activist struggles confronting what they called the "migration regime," we argue that Slovene migration politics are not only a particularly stark example of abuse and exploitation; they also point toward potential new forms of political activism and organizing.

This chapter proceeds in three movements, each focused on a different moment of migrant organizing. First we outline the formation of Slovenia's citizenship since independence from Yugoslavia two decades ago, with a special focus on what came to be known as the erasure (*izbris*). During a period of strong nationalist sentiment across Yugoslavia, Slovenia required non-Slovene residents to apply for citizenship in the new state, while ethnic Slovenes gained citizenship automatically (Zorn 2005). More than one percent of the population—mostly unskilled laborers from other republics—was stripped of the right to reside in Slovenia, becoming illegal immigrants overnight in a territory they had long called home. In the early 2000s some of those affected formed the Association of the Erased to challenge the erasure. Their initiative elicited an extremely hostile public response, including a popular referendum against the restoration of their rights. These experiences led the Erased, along with their allies, to be skeptical of the exclusionary nature of national citizenship, even majority voting itself, which had affirmed the exclusion of the minority from the polity. The history of the erasure we offer here responds to what De Genova sees as one of the "premier challenges" of studying illegality, namely the need to "delineate the historical specificity of contemporary migrations as they have come to be located in the legal (political) economies of particular

nation-states" (2002, 423). But was the underlying meaning of the erasure better understood as a post Yugoslav particularity or in a broader
pattern of European migration politics? On the one hand, the exclusion
of the erased from Slovene citizenship seemed to be an administrative
analogue to ethnic cleansing, the violent expulsion of ethnic minorities that characterized the establishment of independent nation-states
as Yugoslavia disintegrated (Hayden 2000). On the other hand, the erasure seemed to parallel EU migration politics—which was being for-
mulated simultaneously with Yugoslavia's disintegration—and which
many critics were beginning to describe as creating a "Fortress Europe"
(Carr 2012), a bloc ever more closed to non-Europeans.

We turn next to IWW organizing among migrant laborers in Slovenia. Initiated to address miserable living conditions in workers dormitories, the IWW campaign evolved to confront the role of borders and
migration status in the exploitation of workers—including, eventually,
transnational cooperation like the Sarajevo protest. Through intensive
organizing—and what they called "militant research"—activists came
to understand that workers labored under a number of different migration arrangements. To summarize a highly complex and fragmented
system, they found that migration controls rendered migrant laborers—
in some cases the very individuals who were erased fifteen years earlier—utterly dependent on their employers for their place of residence,
visa status, and ultimately their very presence in Slovenia. To leave a job
often meant to lose the time one had accumulated toward a work permit
or permanent residence. What is more, for many workers, to quit or be
fired was to become an illegal migrant within a matter of days, with the
threat of deportation hanging over them. The restrictive migration policies that Slovenia developed after the erasure did not therefore prevent
migration—indeed, like much of Western Europe, Slovenia was highly
dependent on foreign labor during the building boom of the early to
mid 2000s. Instead of excluding migrants, as the fortress metaphor
indicates, activists came to understand that the migration regime served
to, in their words, "hierarchically integrate" migrants. As De Genova
has argued in his study of deportabilty among illegal migrants in the
United States, the constant threat of illegality served to socially *include*
migrants, but under imposed conditions of enforced and protracted
vulnerability (De Genova 2002, 429). Only with the financial crisis

beginning in 2008, which prompted the introduction of harsh austerity legislation, as in much of Southern Europe, did it become clearer that the precarity that migrants faced was becoming generalized through the liberalization and flexibilization of the labor market. Working and living conditions were transformed in ways that further stratified and segmented society. As in the migrant labor market, there was a proliferation of labor statuses, creating a spectrum of statuses between employment and unemployment and further undermining the efforts of organized labor to effectively negotiate working and living conditions.

Finally, we then turn to activist organizing against official responses to this deep economic crisis in Slovenia. Linking their struggle against austerity in Slovenia to the other global uprisings of 2011—including the Arab Spring, the Spanish *indignados*, and the North American Occupy movement—activists began a protest encampment in front of the Slovene Stock Exchange. In what we have described as a subjective turn (Razsa and Kurnik 2012), activists politicized their own living conditions as precarious students, researchers, teachers, social workers, migrant workers, and the unemployed and marginalized. They translated this political awareness of their own conditions and the heterogeneous social composition of contemporary society into an innovative project of democratic decision-making. As activists from the erased and IWW played key roles in this mobilization, Occupy Slovenia was informed by these earlier migrant struggles, developing forms of organizing that were distinct from movements elsewhere. After describing one Occupy Slovenia assembly in some ethnographic detail, we contrast the forms of decision-making and organization developed there with those of Occupy Wall Street (OWS). We argue that Occupy Slovenia's practices embody a radical break with the representative liberal democracy and national citizenship that has characterized Slovenia since independence. Activists embraced what they called the "democracy of direct action," which included both the refusal to delegate authority to representatives or to adopt the principle of majority rule (Razsa and Kurnik 2012). Instead, those who held minority positions were encouraged to take initiative on their own without seeking the approval of the majority of movement participants. For this reason Occupy Slovenia offers one experimental model of a politics that affirms rather than excludes minority positions.

2002: The Association of the Erased

The disintegration of Yugoslavia began with Slovenia's and Croatia's declaration of independence in 1991 and it extended well into the 2000s, involving a series of secessions by other republics. Each of these secessions was accompanied by proliferating borders and, in the cases of Croatia, Bosnia, Kosovo, and Macedonia, violent armed conflict. By 2012 each of the Socialist Federal Republic of Yugoslavia's six constitutive republics were independent states, several of these experienced internal secessionist movements, and one of its two autonomous provinces, Kosovo, had declared independence. Prior to the war, none other than Jeffrey Sachs—the architect of East European "shock therapy"—had predicted that Yugoslavia would be the first of the socialist states to enter the EU (Lipton et al. 1990).

Today, its successor states and territorial entities reflect the entire spectrum of possible relationships to European integration, from Slovenia's full membership in the EU and Eurozone; through Croatia's recent accession to the EU but not the Eurozone, and Serbia and Montenegro's applicant status, with no accession on the horizon; to Kosovo and Macedonia, which have yet to achieve even recognition of statehood from all member-states of the EU. Bosnia has perhaps the most contradictory relationship to the European Union. On the one hand, the ethnically divided state is an international protectorate in which the EU holds decisive power through the Office of the High Representative. On the other hand, its citizens are treated as third-country nationals—that is, as if they are from states with no relationship with the European Union—affording them no freedom to live and work within the EU itself. The territorial fragmentation of Yugoslavia, with the range of hierarchical relationships to European integration that it produced, has been accompanied by the splintering of the once unified population that held Yugoslav citizenship. These new citizenries, like the territories with which they are associated, possess varying relationships to the EU and varying degrees of mobility and access to the territory and labor market of the EU, as becomes clearer when we examine the dynamics of citizenship during the formation of Slovenia as an independent state.

With EU membership and the highest per capita income of formerly socialist states, Slovenia is often held up as a success story. The struggles of Slovenia's minorities, primarily those from other former Yugoslav republics, cast its newly gained statehood in a quite different light. As we noted above, following Yugoslavia's collapse, the formation of an independent and ethnically defined state (Hayden 2000), and accession to the European Union, citizenship and migration became the most politically charged issues in Slovenia. In the past decade, public conflicts have erupted around a series of migrant populations: preindependence migrants from elsewhere in the former Yugoslavia protesting their removal from the register of permanent residents, displaced Bosnians seeking official status as refugees, asylum seekers pushing for greater freedom of movement pending hearings, undocumented migrants denouncing their detention conditions, and workers on temporary visas objecting to labor abuses.

Slovenian popular discourse about migrants (Doupona-Horvat et al. 2001) in many ways parallels the dominant scholarly frameworks, which either treat migrants as a threat to receiving countries (for example Hirsi Ali 2006; Huntington 2004; Ye'or 2005) or as helpless victims of human rights abuses (compare Cunningham 1995; Giordano 2008). Some migrants and activist allies in Ljubljana, many of them veterans of the global justice movement of the early 2000s, insisted that a different approach was needed. Indeed, in many ways, the concept of "insurgent citizenship," a notion developed to describe the informal practices of residents in Brazilian *favelas* that "created new spheres of participation and understandings of rights" (Holston 2008, 303), describes the creative ways migrants have managed to act politically even when they have none of the legal rights afforded to citizens—as seen, for example, in the Bosnians' protest actions both before and after their deportation (compare Rosaldo 2009).

Among these migration struggles, the self-described erased were the most contentious in Slovenia and perhaps illustrate most clearly the troubling qualities of ethno-nationalist citizenship and a liberal democracy based on the rule of the majority. As such, the experience of the erased provides an important background against which the democracy of direct action was later developed. The 1992 removal (or "erasure") of more than 25,000 people—primarily those born in other Yugoslav republics—from the register of permanent residents was not controversial at the time. Indeed, though this act by the minister of internal affairs affected more than one percent of the overall population of two million, the public, even many of those affected, was unaware of the scale of erasure until the Association of the Erased was formed in 2002 to confront their dispossession. The erasure was but one facet of the exclusionary definition of Slovene nationhood, which included constitutionally defining Slovenia as the state of "Slovene people" (*slovenski narod*) and, therefore, the state of its ethnic majority (Hayden 2000). The ethnic character of Slovene citizenship was further evidenced in guaranteed citizenship for those born to ethnically Slovene emigrants abroad.

In the tradition of the Association of the Erased, who often used testimonials to dramatize the human consequences of the erasure, it is instructive to consider Asim's story. Activists first met Asim when he returned to Slovenia in 2007 and visited Social Center Rog, a central node for migrant organizing housed in a squatted former bicycle factory. Seeking legal advice about how to normalize his status in Slovenia, Asim, in his late forties, told the story of his erasure from a country he had long considered home. Like the Sarajevo protesters, he was born near Cazin, one of two Bosnian regions that provided much of the labor that fueled the rapid industrialization and modernization of Slovenia after World War II. After finishing primary school in the late 1970s, he moved to Slovenia, as did many of his peers, to attend a secondary school specializing in the building trades. After qualifying as a construction worker he worked for several major Slovene firms, living in workers' dormitories, a form of social housing for single workers coming from other parts of federal state. Later he settled in Ljubljana, moving into a studio apartment, which he registered as his permanent residence. Following Slovenia's declaration of independence in 1991 he applied for citizenship, as was required by law for non-Slovenes, but he never received an official response. In early 1992, during the severe economic crisis that gripped Slovenia following independence and the loss of access to the wider Yugoslav market, Asim's firm laid him off. He went to visit his family in Bosnia for a few weeks just as armed conflict broke out. He tried to return to safety in Slovenia but was rejected at the border. Though he did not understand why at the time, he had been erased. Forced to remain in Bosnia, he was mobilized and sent to war.

The act of erasure transformed others into illegal migrants overnight in a territory where they had lived legally for decades or, in some cases, had been born (Blitz 2006). Along with legal residence, the erased lost medical care, work permits, pensions, even the ability to obtain a driving license or to travel outside Slovenia. Because local clerks had a great deal of discretion regarding who would actually be purged from the register, ethnic Roma were targeted disproportionately in the erasure (Zorn 2005). With the exception of informal activist initiatives and a small number of formal NGOs, especially the Peace Institute, the Erased were vilified in the national media, portrayed as a dangerous fifth column disloyal to Slovenia (Zorn and Lipovec Čebron 2008). The erased, like other politically active migrant groups, worked closely with a loose-knit web of allies, the more radical of whom gathered around Social Center Rog. These activists encouraged the active participation of migrants themselves, seeking ways to valorize what they called their *protagonizem*—that is, their agency—rather than emphasize their victimhood (Kurnik 2008).

Their activism—which challenged what one erased activist called "our ethnic cleansing by bureaucratic means"—provoked a virulent response. First, the right-wing Slovenian Democratic Party (SDS) organized a popular referendum on the erased in 2004, which provided another opportunity for public attacks on Roma and "Southerners" *(južnjaki)*—those born in other former Yugoslav republics. Although participation was low, some 95 percent voted against the erased (Zorn 2005). Second, in this politically charged atmosphere, NGOs such as the Peace Institute, with its origins in the wave of activism in the late 1980s in Slovenia (Mastnak 1994), pursued a quite different approach than those associated with the Social Center Rog. They advocated on behalf of migrants, seeking to speak for them in public and legal settings and thereby mediate their relationship with the state. As one long-time radical activist critical of the Peace Institute's approach lamented, "Many of our early efforts to build new forms of power with migrants were contested by civil society organizations, which always attempted to impose themselves as mediators for the marginalized, representing them as helpless victims rather than allowing them to articulate their own politics."

In the face of both hostility and cooptation, the Erased and their more radical allies came to the conclusion that the Slovenian political context did not offer any domestic resolution; their case would have to be internationalized. Some argued for filing charges in The Hague at the International Criminal Tribunal for the former Yugoslavia (ICTY), while others advocated for pursuing a case before the European Court for Human Rights and mobilizing European public sentiment by linking the case of the erased to wider concerns about the exclusionary quality of European citizenship. Central to the discussion of legal strategy was the question of how to understand the erasure. Was the erasure best understood as an anomaly, an exceptional event characteristic of the backward former Yugoslavia? Were the erased similar, for example, to those Muslims driven from Eastern Bosnia by Serbian military forces during the war? Or was the erasure actually more closely related to the migration policies of the Global North, akin to the migration policies of the EU? Was the situation of the erased, in other words, similar to that of other migrants that are considered to be third-country nationals—neither residents of the EU country in which they are residing or citizens of another EU member state, like, Algerians in France? Some activists would later question the clear opposition of these two forms of exclusion, but in any case, with longstanding ties to European campaigns for migrant rights, and a more inclusive European citizenship, as open borders, the movement ultimately opted for Europeanization. Besides transnational links with other movements, however, there were crucial aspects of the erasure itself that led activists to understand it as related to broader EU attitudes and policies toward labor migrants.

Though this would become clearer in subsequent migrant organizing (described below), the erasure did more than institutionalize the Slovene majority's exclusion of ethnic minorities. The erasure also played a key role in the political constitution of Slovenia's labor market. While the nationalist media and populist politicians repeatedly drew attention to the tiny minority of the erased (less than 1,000 out of 25,000) who were Yugoslav Army personnel—who champions of erasure insisted were legitimate targets because they were a threat to Slovene independence—the vast majority affected were relatively unskilled industrial, manual, service, and agricultural laborers from other Yugoslav republics. Even the official estimate of 25,000 erased vastly undercounts those affected because many thousands more, such as all those living in workers' dormitories, were not eligible to apply for Slovene citizenship upon independence even if they had been living in the republic for decades.

If these workers are included, more than 100,000—or 5 percent of the population and nearly 15 percent of the workforce—were purged. Later, if they hoped to return to Slovenia, these workers from poorer Yugoslav republics were required to apply for work permits and visas, starting anew their work and residency in Slovenia. Indeed, Asim's ongoing efforts to return to Slovenia as a migrant laborer—which first led him to Social Center Rog—exemplify the consequences of the erasure for the labor market. We turn to these consequences next, but it is important to first note the lessons that the erased and their activist allies drew from the struggle against erasure.

For activists the erasure revealed fundamental fault lines within liberal democracy as it was conceived and practiced in Slovenia (and elsewhere)—that is, as the rule of the majority. First, the definition of statehood as the sovereignty of the ethnic majority and accompanying expulsion of the erased from the political community at Slovenia's founding highlighted the exclusionary nature of national citizenship. Second, this exclusion was affirmed through popular referendum—itself a form of direct democracy, though one based on the will of the majority. The majority of voters opted to negate the rights of the minority (not unlike the California referendum on marriage equality). Furthermore activists came to believe that forms of organization that sought to represent minority concerns *on behalf of* those affected by such discrimination—that is, rather than encouraging the erased to speak for themselves—further entrenched their status as victims and, therefore, denied their *protagonizem*. Finally, activists came to be skeptical of exclusively national frameworks, insisting instead on a transnational orientation in alliance with movements elsewhere. These lessons would come to inform the innovative approach to direct democracy developed later within Occupy Slovenia.

2007: The Invisible Workers of the World

Activists only became fully aware of the labor implications of Slovenia's new borders and the migration policies that governed human mobility across them when they began organizing in workers' dormitories in 2007. From their first visit to a dormitory—which nearly turned into a spontaneous resident protest—they were caught off guard by the bitter complaints of the occupants, the majority (Muslim) Bosniaks from Bosnia. They lacked hot water. Fifty shared one toilet and shower. Four to eight men were crowded into each ten-square-meter room. Infested with cockroaches and suffering from moisture damage, these dormitories nonetheless had higher rents than workers would pay on the open real estate market. These conversations also revealed just how segregated migrants were from the surrounding community; many stated that prior to these conversations with activists they had never discussed their living conditions with any Slovenes. When activists asked why they remained in the dorms, the workers replied simply: "Because we are foreigners." The causal links between being "foreigners" and enduring poor living and working conditions would soon become clearer.

Out of these initial encounters activists and migrant workers established the Invisible Workers of the World.[1] The IWW was soon present in all workers dormitories in Ljubljana and a nucleus of migrant worker activists had been formed. This made possible the first public actions. Initially the IWW's aim was to confront the terrible living conditions migrant workers faced in the dormitories (Mozetič 2009). The owners of the dormitories, however, in most cases the workers' employers, soon prohibited assemblies of workers in the dormitories and tried to prevent efforts to organize direct discussions between activists and residents. In response, the IWW developed communication tools for migrant workers that they hoped would erode their internal divisions as well as their broader segregation from Slovene social life. These included the worker-led monthly radio broadcast "Visa for the Future" (Viza za budućnost), allowing workers to study their common conditions and to foster communication among themselves and with the broader society. Indeed, those involved in the IWW understood themselves to be developing methods of militant research that made possible new collective understandings of the ways labor segmentation and precarity were enforced, and how they might be challenged. Using a variety of instruments—including, in addition to the radio broadcasts, collectively developed questionnaires, "know your rights" office hours, organized reflections on ways to improve collaboration, and fliers that were constantly revised based on the conversations they generated— the IWW developed a fine-grained portrait of workers' conditions. In the course of this research they catalogued the migrants' various legal statuses in Slovenia and how these statuses impacted them. They found that migrant laborers enter the labor market in ways that render them highly dependent on their employers.[2]

In fact most migrant laborers described complete dependence on employers. Unless they possess individual work permits—requiring two years of continuous and legally registered employment and residence in Slovenia—they are only eligible for temporary visas tied to the specific employer who hires them. In order to obtain their residence permit they must prove they have, in advance, an address of residence in Slovenia, so they agree to live in their employers' dormitories, regardless of their quality.[3] Even worse, their work permits and residence visas are tied to the employer through whom they first applied to work in Slovenia. They are therefore unable to seek another job because the moment they quit or are fired their visa and work permits expire. They have only a few days to vacate Slovenia or they become "illegal."

To further complicate matters, these workers are subdivided into an array of legal statuses—such as, to name only a few, posted workers, seasonal workers, and what activists came to call dependent workers *(odvisni delavci)*—each with their own restrictions. Posted workers are technically employed in their country of origin, although they work in Slovenia (and hence they do not accumulate months of legally registered work in Slovenia). Similarly, seasonal workers cannot accumulate the uninterrupted months of work that count toward the personal work permit. Dependent workers do accumulate months of residency and employment toward their personal work permits, which should eventually authorize them to apply for any available job or gain access to some aspects of the social security system (for example, unemployment benefits). According to migrant testimony, however, employers frequently terminated their employment just prior to the required 24 months of continuous employment, forcing them to leave the country and apply to start again with a new employer, or even the same employer, a few months later. A worker from Bosnia or Macedonia, in the best of cases, must live and work for seven years without interruption before he or she potentially obtains the full rights of a permanent resident.[4] Employers are fully aware of—and often take full advantage of—workers' need to maintain continuity of employment. Furthermore, as was the case for those protesting in Sarajevo, employers sometimes terminate employees without paying them their salaries, knowing it will be very difficult to seek legal recourse once they leave the country as required by law.

IWW organizing alongside migrant laborers shifted activist understandings of the border and the migration regime that managed movement across it. At first glance the erasure, xenophobic popular sentiment, and the restrictive visa regulations in Slovenia seemed to confirm the common leftist critique of EU policies as creating a Fortress Europe. The fine-grained understanding that the IWW developed of migrant workers' experiences with work and residency permits, however, indicates that the fortress metaphor may lead us to misapprehend the nature of the new migration laws and associated border regime (Euskirchen et al. 2007). First, it became clear that Slovenia, like much of Western Europe, was deeply dependent on migrant labor and could not, therefore, actually seal the borders without great economic disruption. The issue was not that migrants were systematically excluded, as the fortress metaphor implies, though the foundational exclusion of citizenship, like the erasure, was an essential precondition for the system that emerged. The new border regime, as embodied in the experience of the residents of the workers' dormitories, and enumerated in the categories of workers, each with its differential access to labor and social rights, was a matter of hierarchical *inclusion*, not exclusion (Beznec 2012). And it was the border that created the basic infrastructure of this hierarchy, creating the various segments of vulnerable workers who were dependent on their employers to different degrees.

Though it would leave a distinctive stamp on later organizing, this robust period of migrant activism was to be short-lived. As the financial crisis that began in 2008 deepened, the largest firms, especially in the construction sector that had expanded rapidly during the 2000s real estate bubble, suddenly found themselves saddled with debts they could not service and large real estate portfolios they could not sell. Many migrant laborers, including those who had been outspoken activists, soon found themselves ordered to leave Slovenia or face deportation. Like other Southern European states, Slovenia responded to the crisis with austerity legislation and deep cuts to public spending. Migrant laborers were often hardest hit, but depending on their employment status, other segments of workers began to feel the effects of curtailments to their social rights in ways that revealed that the precarious state of migrants was paradigmatic of broader shifts in the Slovene economy and labor market. As protests broke out first across North Africa, then in the squares of Spain and Greece before bursting across North America with the Occupy movement, activists, most with experiences in earlier campaigns, saw an opportunity for new period of mobilization and direct action. They struggled to politicize their social conditions and develop ways of bringing people together despite the increasingly segmented and plural composition of society. To put it simply, the challenge they confronted was to find common ground among precarious intellectual workers, migrants, the erased, and homeless youths, as well as those incarcerated for being "mentally ill" or "antisocial."

We turn now to this new wave of activism. Informed by the lessons learned in earlier organizing against ethnic exclusion, the electoral domination of the majority, and the subsequent hierarchical and exploitative inclusion of migrants, activists organized in ways that both protected and empowered minority and migrant participants.

2011: Occupy Slovenia

Like Occupy movement activists elsewhere (Graeber 2011; Juris 2012), Ljubljana's radicals were surprised by the public response that their call to action elicited. A crowd of thousands joined the first protests on Congress Square, leaving the small sound system utterly overwhelmed. When activists proposed a march to the Ljubljana Stock Exchange the crowd roared enthusiastically. The assembly that gathered there promptly decided to establish an indefinite encampment in front of the stock exchange. Tents sprouted like mushrooms. The situation in those first weeks of Occupy Slovenia was disorienting for many activists—who, after years of organizing alongside migrant and minority groups in Slovenia, which led to the marginalization of activism and even, at times, its public vilification—found radical activism suddenly embraced. They understood this newfound public support in relation to a political disorientation in Slovenia. In the face of this deep economic and political crisis, the goals that guided public life for two decades—economic liberalization, European integration, and democratic consolidation—had lost their self-evidence.

In light of past experiences, activists responded to their newfound popularity with an insistence on a transnational rather than national framing. An activist diary of the first days of Occupy captures this flavor: "On the way protests from abroad are heard: Madrid, Barcelona, Rome, New York, Tunis, and Argentina are echoing in our chants. *Que non nos representan! Degagez!* This is what democracy looks like! *Que se vayan todos!* And the Slovenian refrains, No one represents us! Money to people, not banks! We will not pay for your crisis!" (Večer 2011). By stressing "No one represents us," "Real democracy now," and "Que se vayan todos" (They all must go), as well as bemoaning the consequences of the "monopoly of 'democratic parties' over political life," activists positioned Occupy Slovenia as a response to a crisis of representative democracy in Slovenia.

Daily assemblies quickly became of the public forum of the movement in Ljubljana. We describe one such assembly below in some detail—one in which Andrej Kurnik, the second author of the chapter, was a direct participant. We then contrast the practices of the democracy of direct action—that is, practices which, informed by earlier struggles, empowered minority participation and initiative—with the more majoritarian and populist orientation of OWS. The description of the late November 2011 assembly *(skupščina)* below provides a sense of the dynamics of these gatherings, of the decision-making process within the democracy of direct action, as well as the forms of political action that came to define Occupy Slovenia.

Facilitating an assembly for the first time, Marko struggles to recite aloud the rules that structure the assembly, as is done at the beginning of each gathering. The crowd of fifty is pressed in a tight circle. Several voices tease him when he forgets the second of these agenda items considered at each assembly: camp logistics, workshop reports, and miscellaneous. Marko reminds everyone that the assembly does not decide the content of workshops *(delavnice)*—that is the autonomous prerogative of the workshops themselves. When Marko pauses others in the circle call out the rules:

> Raise your hand to speak, wait to be acknowledged by the moderator, respect the expression of others, and, if you have already spoken, defer to those who have not yet had a chance to express themselves. Do not

engage in dialogue with others, especially if this means criticizing the
proposals of others, but instead propose your own action—and only an
action that you yourself are willing to participate in and help organize.
Be concrete. Propose the idea for a workshop and announce
when and where it will meet.

Marko, finally catching his stride, concludes, "It's direct democracy.
Everyone present participates."

A number of workshops report back to the assembly on their activities. Emil, 51, a migrant worker from Bosnia, reports from the Workshop for the Workers Dormitory Rent Strike. He describes the difficulties former employees of Vegrad, a large construction firm that has
been in bankruptcy for nearly 11 months, are having with the management of the company-owned dormitory. The court-appointed trustee is
insisting the workers continue to pay rent to the dormitory or face evic-
tion. The workers have responded that they should be able to stay on,
subtracting the rent from the thousands of Euros of back pay they are
owed. They have declared a rent strike. If evicted, however, those without permanent residence face deportation. "Please join us for workshop
meeting next Wednesday," Emil concludes.

Other announcements? "Yes," Andrej speaks up. "The Workshop
against Precarity and for Common Welfare met on Sunday with families who have been, or are in the process of being, evicted from their
homes by Raiffeissen [Bank]." Mostly impoverished peasants, they contacted Occupy after seeing coverage of the encampment national television. Andrej describes planned direct actions, under the name Days of
Indignation Against the Banks, culminating in an action to move one
family back into their home. "We will demand the writing off of their
debts. This is a crucial turn in our struggle," he continues, "in which we
can begin to open direct conflicts with financial institutions and begin
to establish new relations of force."

"Any questions?" asks the moderator. "Yes," responds a clean-cut
man in his mid-thirties. "These people should also take some responsibility for these loans. We should be avoiding these financial institutions,
boycotting them instead of borrowing from them." "That's neither here
nor there now," retorts Andrej, "and it's impossible in today's era to get
ahead without credit." As the back and forth continues, with escalating

intensity, the moderator intervenes to remind both speakers that they should not be "dialoguing"; comments should be addressed to the assembly. "Anyway," the moderator continues, addressing the clean-cut man, "unless you have a fundamental ethical objection to what they're planning, you should just get involved in the workshop. Otherwise, propose your own damn workshop!"

The specific decision-making practices that constituted the democracy of direct action and were visible in its daily assemblies have a number of political implications. To clarify these practices, it is helpful to first contrast them with those of OWS. At first glance, the democracy of direct action, as embodied in the assembly, appears quite similar to those practices adopted by OWS, comprised of general assemblies and working groups—or assemblies and workshops, as they have come to be known in Ljubljana. However, the relationship between the workshops and the assembly is reversed, which shifts significantly how decisions are made—and therefore where power lies. Whereas at OWS all decisions need to be approved by modified consensus at the general assembly—that is, at least 90 percent approval after all objections have been heard and addressed by facilitators (#OccupyWallStreet New York City General Assembly 2011)—the assembly in Ljubljana was not Occupy Slovenia's primary decision-making unit. Workshops, although they operated under the umbrella of Occupy Slovenia and reported back to the assembly, had autonomy to organize themselves in any manner they saw fit, implementing the internal forms of decision-making they thought most appropriate. Workings groups at OWS, by contrast, were empowered only to develop proposals, which had to be approved through modified consensus at the general assembly. Participants in the general assembly sometimes numbered in the thousands, and proceedings lasted for many hours (Gessen et al. 2012). When asked about their impressions of the democracy of direct action, activists raised two themes repeatedly: that the model empowered minorities and that it unleashed energies that were otherwise dormant or even actively blocked in their daily lives.

So it was not only a matter of migrants from various backgrounds being an important constituency within Occupy Slovenia, as they clearly were in this meeting. The democracy of direct action opened a space for minority participation, not only with regard to ethnic or racial minorities *(manjšine),* but other groups as well—the homeless, LGBT, and those labeled mentally ill—in short, the heterogeneous and plural subjects that characterize Slovene society today.

Crucially, by empowering workshops and not requiring initiatives to seek majority endorsement, this model allowed minority concerns to be acted upon. Emil, for example, could propose a workshop on his specific concerns at the workers' dormitory without needing anyone's approval. Alternatively, Andrej did not have to worry if the man at the assembly fully understood his approach to addressing evictions. This strategy places emphasis on action by anyone who feels a workshop addresses issues of real concern to him or her. Similarly, proposals were grounded in a willingness to participate in them—to take action. By design there was no overarching authority, such as OWS's general assembly, that would define the direction of the movement and or determine that a minority's position did not represent Occupy Slovenia as a whole. This encouraged a variety of initiatives, not only those associated with minority positions. Indeed, activists also often discussed the democracy of direct action's capacity to unleash creative energies. As Sara, an activist who explained the matter in terms that described her own situation, "The movement here in Ljubljana is similar in composition to [that in] Tunisia and Spain—a highly educated generation whose capacities to produce, to network, to express themselves are completely blocked." In fact, activists from Ljubljana had gone to both Tunis and Barcelona in September to meet with activists and to share experiences and coordinate protests in preparation for the October 15 Global Day of Action—a day marked by protests in more than a thousand cities in 82 countries (Anonymous 2011), including the initiation of Occupy Slovenia.

With the democracy of direct action activists developed a form of decision-making and organizing that did not establish a sovereign body that might exclude minorities. They also avoided populist framings of the crisis and their response that, even if they might welcome migrants and other minorities, would do so in ways that might render them second-class participants to be hierarchically included—that is, capable of action only if the majority approved that action. The slogan of belonging to the 99 percent always had a strange ring, after all, for activists who had struggled alongside Slovenia's 1 percent for years: the erased. While the democracy of direct action was developed in response to earlier movement experiences with politics of majoritarian rule, it became more than a reaction against the dangers of sovereignty, more than hard lessons learned from struggles against discrimination. Activists insisted that it was also an affirmation of minoritarian politics as a form of organization that would be both inclusive and expansive, rather than foreclosed and exclusive as activists understood the nation-state's democratic polity to be. In other words, direct democracy based on minoritarian principles began to figure among activists not only as a proper way of organizing alongside migrants and minorities but as a universal alternative to the political representation that they believed had expressed and reinforced inequalities in societies ever more divided in the ongoing crisis.

Conclusions

In this chapter we have traced some of the complicated interactions between the processes of Yugoslav disintegration and European integration, especially around questions of borders, citizenship and illegality. Positioning our research alongside migrants and their activist allies—in the territory of Slovenia, where these two processes have intersected most directly—we find that the ethnic exclusion of Slovene citizenship, especially as seen in the erasure, which overwhelmingly affected laborers from other republics, was foundational for the subsequent hierarchical integration of noncitizens into the labor force. This exclusionary quality of national citizenship is central to contemporary practices of labor integration that intensified across the continent with the formation of European citizenship (Balibar 2004). In the Slovene case we can see vividly how illegal migrants do not so much exist a priori as they are produced by specific ethnonational framings and legal policies of citizenship—that is, at the intersection of state borders and cultural (often racialized) boundaries (Fassin 2011, 214). As Europe depends significantly on migrant labor, it cannot be understood as impenetrable, as the fortress metaphor implies. The experience of Bosnian migrant laborers, such as the Cazin workers whose protests began this chapter, can for this reason be compared to the mechanisms of hierarchical inclusion affecting, for example, Algerian migrants in France, or for that matter, undocumented migrants in the United States.

The Slovene case provides a particularly stark example of the interplay between exclusionary nationalist practices, characteristic of the historical formation of modern nation-states, and the hierarchical integration of labor from nonmember states within the European Union. In other words, our analysis indicates that "old" forms of nationalist exclusion, far from giving way to inclusive models of membership in an integrated Europe (Castles and Davidson 2000), reinforce, legitimize, and naturalize European citizenship as hierarchical, segmented, and heterogeneous (compare Rigo 2007; Ong 2006). Slovene activists' engagement with exclusionary ethnic citizenship, campaigns by the majority against minorities, and differential access to social, economic, and political rights for migrant laborers pose a fundamental challenge to the longstanding belief in the emancipatory potential of citizenship as an institution—which dates to the republican revolutions of the eighteenth century. On the contrary, citizenship has become a key institution for differentiating residents in a given territory, producing degrees of inclusion and exclusion from social, economic, and political rights and thus segmenting and stratifying societies. These realities embody a fundamental irony of globalism: the free circulation of capital and goods has been accompanied by increasing barriers to the free movement of people. The political constitution of a global market has not been matched by a global citizenship with equal rights (Walters 2006). The migrant experience is paradigmatic of these new inequalities created through unequal access to the rights of citizenship—but these inequalities are increasingly extended to other forms of labor segmentation, affecting even those with full citizenship, including temporary, part-time, and contract workers.

Citizenship has always been a contested category; however, its mechanisms of exclusion are ceaselessly called into question (Balibar 2004), especially by the insurgent citizenship of the excluded (Holston 2008). In this way, the experience of the Erased and their activist allies indicates that migrants are not only paradigmatic of the new stratification, inequality, and exploitation, but also of new forms of resistance. The democracy of direct action that activists developed as a decision-making and organizational practice for Occupy Slovenia, informed by previous migrant and minority struggles, embodies a radical break with the representative democracy and exclusionary citizenship of independent Slovenia. Activists went beyond common critiques of representative democracy that tried to address the lack of accountability and representativeness of today's governing institutions by strengthening majoritarian institutions, for example, through referendum. They have instead built alternative forms of democracy on the rejection of two of the central characteristics of representative democracy—the transfer of power, through representation and the principle of majority rule (Kurnik 2011; Hardt and Negri 2011. Valorizing grassroots forms of power built by the formally powerless and rejecting the notion that the political community is necessarily exclusive (Schnapper 1998), the struggles of the Erased, IWW, and Occupy Slovenia provide a glimpse, however tenuous, of how new forms of ever expanding and inclusive political community and an insurgent citizenship might be generated. It offers one model of how to affirm and implement alternative projects of direct democracy.

NOTES

1. Activists named the initiative the Invisible Workers of the World as an allusion to the Industrial Workers of the World of the early twentieth century. For Ljubljana activists the IWW appeared to be an important organizational model in the search for new ways of organizing labor that could overcome the crisis of the contemporary labor movement.

2. The IWW would come to compare these conditions, especially with regard to debts to employers for travel, work, and residency permits, and housing, to the historical predicament of indentured servants in North America and Australia.

3. When they do arrive in Slovenia and try to find private accommodation they find they face informal barriers because they are perceived as čefurji, the Slovenian pejorative for "Southerners" that migrants describe as the equivalent of "niggers."

4. Many of the features of this labor system mirror earlier guestworker programs see Hahamovitch 2011.

REFERENCES

Anonymous. 2011. October 15. http://15october.net/.

#OccupyWallStreet New York City General Assembly. 2011 Declaration of the Occupation of New York City, adopted September 29. www.nycga.net/resources/declaration.

Balibar, Etienne. 2004. *We, the People of Europe?: Reflections on Transnational Citizenship.*. Princeton, NJ: Princeton University Press.

Beznec, Barbara. 2012. From Ethnic Exclusivism to Creolisation: The Movements of Migration on Post-Yugoslav Territory. In *Shifting Borders: European Perspectives on Creolisation*, edited by Tommaso Sbriccoli and Stefano Jacoviello, 57–80. Newcastle-upon-Tyne: Cambridge Scholars Publishing.

Blitz, Brad. 2006. Statelessness and the Social (De)Construction of Citizenship: Political Restructuring and Ethnic Discrimination in Slovenia. *Journal of Human Rights* 5 (4): 453–79.

Carr, Matthew. 2012. *Fortress Europe: Dispatches From a Gated Continent.* New York: The New Press.

Castles, Steven, and Alastair Davidson. 2000. *Citizenship and Migration: Globalization and the Politics of Belonging.* London: Macmillan Press.

Coutin, Susan Bibler. 2003. *Legalizing Moves: Salvadoran Immigrants' Struggle for US Residency.* Ann Arbor: University of Michigan Press.

Cunningham, Hilary. 1995. *God and Caesar at the Rio Grande: Sanctuary and the Politics of Religion.* Minneapolis: University of Minnesota Press.

De Genova, Nicholas. 2002. Migrant "Illegality" and Deportability in Everyday Life. *Annual Review of Anthropology* 31: 419–47.

Doupona Horvat, Marjeta, Jef Verschueren, and Igor Ž. Žagar. 2001. *Retorika begunske politike v Sloveniji: Pragmatika legitimizacije [The Rhetoric of Refugee Politics in Slovenia: Pragmatics of Legitimation].* Ljubljana: Mirovni inštitut Ljubljana.

Euskirchen, Markus, H. Lebuhn, and G. Ray. 2007. From Borderline to Borderland: The Changing European Border Regime. *Monthly Review* 59 (6): 41–52.

Fassin, Didier. 2011. Policing Borders, Producing Boundaries: the Governmentality of Immigration in Dark Times. *Annual Review of Anthropology* 40: 213–26.

Gessen, Keith, Carla Blumenkranz, Mark Greif, Sarah Leonard, Sarah Resnick, Nikil Saval, Astra Taylor, and Eli Schmitt. 2012. *Occupy!: Scenes from Occupied America.* London: Verso.

Giordano, Cristiana. 2008. Practices of Translation and the Making of Migrant Subjectivities in Contemporary Italy. *American Ethnologist* 35 (4): 588–606.

Graeber, David. 2011. Occupy Wall Street Rediscovers the Radical Imagination. *The Guardian.* www.theguardian.com/commentisfree/cifamerica/2011/sep/25/occupy-wall-street-protest.

Hahamovitch, Cindy. 2011. *No Man's Land: Jamaican Guestworkers in America and the Global History of Deportable Labor.* Princecton, NJ: Princeton University Press.

Hardt, Michael and Antonia Negri. 2011 The Fight for "Real Democracy" at the Heart of Occupy Wall Street. Foreign Affairs, October 11. www.foreignaffairs.com/articles/136399/michael-hardt-andantonio-negri/the-fight-for-real-democracy-at-the-heart-ofoccupy-wall-street?page=show.

Hayden, Robert M. 2000. *Blueprints for a House Divided: The Constitutional Logic of the Yugoslav Conflicts.* Ann Arbor: University of Michigan Press.

Hirsi Ali, Ayaan. 2006. The Ostrich and the Owl: A Bird's-Eye View of Europe. *Los Angeles Times*, October 22. http://articles.latimes.com/2006/oct/22/opinion/op-ali22.

Holston, James. 2008. *Insurgent Citizenship: Disjunctions of Democracy and Modernity in Brazil.* Princeton, NJ: Princeton University Press.

Huntington, Samuel P. 2004. *Who Are We?: The Challenges to America's National Identity*. New York: Simon & Schuster.

Juris, Jeffrey. 2012. Reflections on #Occupy Everywhere: Social Media, Public Space, and Emerging Logics of Aggregation. *American Ethnologist* 39 (2): 259–79.

Kurnik, Andrej. 2008. The Erased Go to Heaven. In *Once Upon an Erasure: From Citizens to Illegal Residents in the Republic of Slovenia*, eds. Jelka Zorn, Uršula Lipovec Čebron, 133–144. Ljubljana: Časopis za kritiko znanosti. 2011. Reševanje koncepta državljanstva na meji med gibanji in politično filozofijo [Resolving the concept of citizenship on the border between movement and political philosophy]. In *Nov(o) državljan(stvo)*, edited by Cirila Toplak and Žiga Vodovnik, 165–187. Ljubljana: Založba Sophia.

Lipton, David, J. Sachs, S. Fischer, and J. Kornai. 1990. Creating a Market Economy in Eastern Europe: The Case of Poland. *Brookings Papers on Economic Activity* 1990 (1): 75–147.

Mastnak, Tomaž. 1994. From Social Movements to National Sovereignty. In *Independent Slovenia: Origins, Movements, Prospects*, edited by Jill Benderly and Evan Kraft, 95–108. New York: St. Martin's.

Mozetič, Polona. 2009. Kako su radnički domovi prošli kroz tranziciju? [How did the workers' dormitories pass through transition?]. *Časopis Za Kritiko Znanosti* 238: 77–93.

Ong, Aihwa. 2006. *Neoliberalism as Exception: Mutations in Citizenship and Sovereignty*. Durham, NC: Duke University Press.

Razsa, Maple, and Andrej Kurnik. 2012. The Occupy Movement in Žižek's Hometown: Direct Democracy and a Politics of Becoming. *American Ethnologist* 39 (2): 238–58.

Rigo, Enrica. 2007. *Europa di confine: Trasformazioni della cittadinanza nell'unione allargata*. Roma: Meltemi Editore.

Rosaldo, Renato. 2009. Cultural Citizenship and Educational Democracy. *Cultural Anthropology* 9 (3): 402–11.

Sassen, Saskia. 1999. *Guests and Aliens*. New York: The New Press.

Schnapper, Dominique. 1998. *Community of Citizens: On the Modern Idea of Nationality*. Livingston, NJ: Transaction Publishers.

Večer. 2011. Zakaj pred borzo? [Why in front of the Stock Exchange?]. October 22, http://ris.vecer.com/arhivi/clanek.aspx?id=302137485E71344257505A767837&tip=A &Tabela=2011.

Walters, William. 2006. No Border: Games With(out) Frontiers. *Social Justice* 33 (1): 21–39.

Wimmer, Andreas, and Glick Schiller, Nina. 2002. Methodological Nationalism and Beyond: Nation-State Building, Migration and the Social Sciences. *Global Networks* 2 (4): 301–334.

Ye'or, Bat. 2005. *Eurabia: The Euro-Arab Axis*. Madison, NJ: Fairleigh Dickinson University Press.

Zorn, Jelka. 2005. Ethnic Citizenship in the Slovenian State. *Citizenship Studies* 9 (2): 135–52.

Zorn, Jelka, and Uršula Lipovec Čebron, eds. 2008. *Once Upon an Erasure*. Ljubljana, Slovenia: Študentska Založba.

9

Challenging Borders, Imagining Europe

Transnational LGBT Activism in a New Europe

PHILLIP M. AYOUB AND DAVID PATERNOTTE

In this chapter, we emphasize the role played by transnational lesbian, gay, bisexual, and transgender (LGBT) activists in imagining Europe as a political alternative to confines of national borders, with a focus on their activism at the international European level and on the ground in Central and Eastern Europe (CEE).[1] Networks of LGBT activists, "bound together by shared values, a common discourse and dense exchanges of information," have promoted issues beyond borders, often bypassing the boundaries of conservative states (Keck and Sikkink 1998, 2). We argue that these movements were inspired by specific ideas—democratic values and human rights responsibilities—about Europe, and that they tried to realize them on the ground through activism. We also posit that, in turn, this activism has contributed to the project of building Europe, mostly within political frameworks of the EU and the Council of Europe (CoE), by fostering an inherent understanding that LGBT rights are by definition linked to the idea of contemporary European values. That said, the analysis also shows that as this process has occurred it has left certain boundaries in place, and specific forms of exclusion have also emerged as a result.

An analysis of European LGBT activism thus helps us gain traction on three of the core questions that motivate this volume: How has LGBT movement, through its imagination, shaped new repertoires of activism, forms of social belonging, and alternatives for organizing societies

worldwide? How does the movement challenge the borders and boundaries that have divided societies and states, both "on the ground"
and "up above"? Finally, how has this process overshadowed internal
boundaries and created new hierarchies? In brief, who is excluded?

Through these processes, the movement has challenged national
and regional borders in two ways. On the one hand, European LGBT
activists have tried to bypass national borders by imagining and building a new community that would be sympathetic to LGBT rights. On
the other hand, they have constantly displaced regional borders further
East, expanding Europe and reinforcing its definition as a set of values linked to universal human rights. In sum, activists have imagined a
new sociopolitical community, forcing open the politically constructed
borders to the East and challenging the frontiers of exclusion and the
modes of belonging. LGBT movements have created an imagined community of Europe that links LGBT rights with European values. With
time, European institutions have increasingly supported LGBT activists,
altering the dynamics between imagination and activism under study.
That said, the chapter also emphasizes that this process did not develop
unproblematically: the hegemony of a new European LGBT discourse
overshadowed both internal boundaries and other potential frames,
created new hierarchies among activists, and paradoxically reinforced a
distinction between the "modern West" and the "homophobic East"—
side effects that still characterize European LGBT politics.

We look here at forms of transnational activism and imagined community that span the European continent. While campaigns still often
target states, both the grievance and vision driving this activism transcends borders. Adopting a constructivist approach to European identity construction, which recognizes that agents and structures are
interacting and mutually constituted (Katzenstein 1996; Díez Medrano
2003), we explore how transnational LGBT activists represent Europe
and what kind of Europe they have been building through their strategies and actions. In our story, LGBT civil society actors are nested in the
normative European structures. This environment, within which these
actors function, is material, but also imagined and socially constructed
(Anderson 1983). Europe is a normative framework that constitutes
LGBT actors' interests and strategies, and in turn these actors (re)create
European structures and institutions by linking them to LGBT rights.

Thus, activists are not simply extending a liberal European notion of rights to an unrecognized group, they are helping define what the definition of "rights" encompasses. For LGBT activists, LGBT people have always belonged to the project of united Europe.

The case of LGBT activism in Europe provides a particularly useful vantage point from which to study contemporary social movements, because it illuminates the multitude of levels on which contemporary politics take place (local, domestic, and supranational), and the dense networks that are formed across state borders. Furthermore, the case of International Lesbian, Gay, Bisexual, Trans and Intersex Association (ILGA)'s thirty years as an organization offers a rare opportunity to study transnational activism through time and to understand how it is shaped by a complex relationship between normative commitment, institutional design, and strategic aims. Especially for research on social movements, which was traditionally confined within the borders of nation-states, LGBT activism in Europe provides a rich source of information from which we can broaden our understanding of transnational movements (e.g., Smith 1997; Naples and Desai 2002; Della Porta and Tarrow 2005; Marx Ferree and Tripp 2006; Della Porta et al. 2009). Our research relies on the analysis of ILGA archives in Brussels, Amsterdam, and London, organizational document analysis, participant observation and semistructured interviews with (former) activists—as part of our larger research agendas, we have completed well over 150 interviews with LGBT activists and conducted several years of fieldwork in the European region.

In what follows, we begin by outlining the emergence of transnational LGBT activism in Europe and show how it was inspired by a specific idea of Europe. The first section explores how LGBT transnational activists, through the ILGA, imagined political alternatives to supporting LGBT rights by organizing themselves at the international level. Thereafter we shift our focus to the cases of Central and Eastern Europe to explore how these political alternatives have been deployed in activism there, and subsequently how it cements LGBT rights as constitutive of European values. The second section thus demonstrates how these activists seek to navigate, challenge and permeate European borders through transnational activism on the ground, both before and after the fall of the Berlin Wall. Throughout the chapter, we emphasize that this

"idea of Europe" transcends the cultural, political, and geographic borders that have, in various forms, defined the continent for centuries. In
doing this, we also stress that the dismantling of certain borders comes
with the construction of new ones. A third and final section explores
this concern, that an idea of Europe can also exclude certain groups and
states by casting them as abnormalities to the European norm.

Imagining Political Alternatives: The Early Years of the ILGA

The first attempts to build structured networks of LGBT groups across
Europe occurred in the 1950s, when the Dutch COC (Cultuur en
Ontspannings Centrum) set up the International Committee for Sexual
Equality (ISCE), which met annually and included most of the homophile groups of the time (Rupp 2011; Jackson 2009). This initiative followed a long tradition of gay cosmopolitanism (Binnie 2004; Tamagne
2006), and echoes the informal contacts between gay activists in the
first half of the twentieth century.[2] In the 1970s, radical movements
such as the Italian Fuori! and the French Front Homosexuel d'Action
Révolutionnaire also attempted to turn their informal exchanges into
a more formal transnational structure (Hellinck 2004, 22; Prearo 2012).
As suggested by Auden's "Homintern" argument, both sexual identity
and sexual experience could transcend national—and class or racial—
boundaries, connecting people across space in solidarity.

The first enduring transnational LGBT organization, however, only
appeared in 1978, when the ILGA was created in Coventry, United Kingdom.[3] Despite its global vocation, the ILGA considered Europe a high
priority, a phenomenon that has been reinforced by its predominantly
European membership. The ILGA has always been inspired by a specific idea of Europe and, crucially, of its usefulness for the progress of
LGBT rights. From the start, founding activists believed that European
values held meaning for LGBT people. They also thought that European
institutions (the EU and CoE), along with the United Nations, could be
used to gain rights by increasing pressure on reluctant states (Keck and
Sikkink 1998).[4]

For example, in a 1981 press statement urging members of the parliamentary assembly of the Council of Europe to adopt the Report on Discrimination Against Homosexual People, IGA activists claimed that:

By adopting this report, parliamentarians . . . of the PARLIAMENTARY ASSEMBLY of the COUNCIL OF EUROPE will take their rightful place in the history books of having ensured that the HUMAN RIGHTS CONVENTION, which was enacted for the protection of HUMAN RIGHTS and to strive for the abolition of all forms of discrimination was extended to protect all citizens of Europe regardless of their sexual orientation or preference . . . In supporting this report parliamentarians . . . will also be sending a clear signal to both their own parliamentarians and constituents at home of their willingness to see that justice and restitution towards the gay people of Europe has started and that the time has arrived for both the gay and nongay person to be part of our society— together (emphasis in original).[5]

It was no coincidence that ILGA was established in the United Kingdom. Activists from England, Scotland, Northern Ireland and the Republic of Ireland—states also belonging to the founders of ILGA— had a long tradition of mutual exchange among themselves, attending each other's conferences since the early 1970s. The annual conference of the Campaign for Homosexual Equality, during which the first ILGA conference took place in 1978, had become a crucial meeting place for activists. In addition, Scots organized the International Gay Rights Congress in 1974 in Edinburgh, which gathered activists from around the world. This Congress represented the pivotal attempt to establish a new lesbian and gay transnational organization, after the ISCE attempt of the 1950s. More informal contacts were also being established between British and foreign activists, especially those from the Netherlands, the Scandinavian states, Australia, and New Zealand. The criminalization of same-sex relations on the British Isles—which was still illegal in Northern Ireland and the Republic of Ireland in 1978—was a key factor in leading British and Irish activists to look to the international arena as a venue for gaining rights domestically. The best-known example is that of Jeff Dudgeon, who attended ILGA's founding meetings, and the Northern Ireland Gay Rights Association's (NIGRA) campaign to decriminalize consensual homosexual acts in Northern Ireland, which led to the European Court of Human Rights to rule against the United Kingdom in 1981.[6] Their success in decriminalizing homosexual relationships was later replicated in *Norris v. Republic of Ireland* (1988) and

Modinos v. Cyprus (1993).[7] For British and Irish activists, ILGA was not only a way to connect actors across borders, but also a vehicle for obtaining new rights at home. "Europe" provided the political alternative for activists to press for domestic change.[8]

This double definition of Europe—both normative and strategic—cannot be dissociated from specific forms of collective action and strategies of mobilization, which focused on institutional and reformist politics early on. The 1978 Coventry meeting was originally designed to prepare activists for the 1979 European elections, and to discuss the need for an observatory status at the CoE, which the ILGA finally obtained in 1997. More surprisingly, contacts with the European Commission were also envisaged, candidates to the European Parliament elections were contacted, and the idea of an "all-party group of Euro-MPs favourable to gay rights"—eventually created in 1997—was suggested.[9] These strategies were fruitful, as the ILGA played an instrumental role in a series of landmark decisions, such as the historic 1981 report on the discrimination of homosexuals (approved by the CoE), the 1984 Squarcialupi Report, and 1994 Roth Report (both passed by the European Parliament) (Bonini-Baraldi and Paradis 2009).[10]

The idea of Europe, defined by a set of values and as an imagined alternative to the nation-state, was later confirmed when activists isolated the central Danish organization, LBLG/F48, for its opposition to European harmonization on the grounds that Europe was not LGBT-friendly enough. With the advent of the Maastricht Treaty in 1992, LBLG/F48 worried that further integration and the expansion of the European Community to gain competence over social matters would threaten Denmark's advanced status in LGBT rights.[11] At the time, Denmark was on the verge of adopting the first civil partnership legislation for same-sex couples worldwide (Søland 1998). LBLG/F48 was "opposed to ILGA taking any public stance on the EC, which might appear to approve the idea of a United Europe, or the EC dealing with any matters other than economic."[12] Other groups disagreed, arguing that European integration was ideal for advocating for change from within to enhance lesbian and gay rights across the continent, and even the Danes eventually came on board.

This vision and the way it has inspired transnational activism across the continent became particularly visible when European activists established a regional European umbrella organization, ILGA-Europe, in 1996 (Beger 2004; Kollman 2009). New political opportunities at the European Union level—along with a separate process of regionalization and globalization of the ILGA—contributed to the birth of an exclusively European organization (Paternotte 2011, 2012). The breakthrough 1994 Roth Report had been a success, and activists saw the 1996 Intergovernmental Conference on a new European treaty as a critical opportunity. In contrast to the 1970s, the transnational activist community's strategies were largely induced by institutional change, and the ILGA's new orientation—building a close relationship with European institutions—was clearly responding to new European developments. The ILGA became an official partner of the European Commission as a result of the Treaty of Amsterdam, and its core funding has come from the EU since 2000. This relationship has allowed ILGA-Europe to professionalize, becoming one of the most powerful and well-funded transnational LGBT groups in contemporary world politics.

In sum, ILGA activists always saw Europe as both an imagined community of values and a strategic means with which to enhance their rights. For these activists, the idea of Europe was not limited by an institutional design, but merged the European Economic Community (EEC) and the CoE into the same normative entity—an imagined and experienced community that enshrined certain fundamental rights for minority peoples. Even before the Amsterdam Treaty, when mobilization was not yet facilitated by the institutional opportunities, activists relied on a strong normative understanding of what Europe ought to be. As shown by a quote from a 1984 IGA conference report, activists were aware of the limited legal impact of their action, but they nevertheless saw Europe as symbolically essential:

> It was stressed that the adopted resolution [the Squarcialuppi Report] has only value of a recommendation, without any obligation for the member states to follow it. But the value of such a recommendation is that the EP, by producing a kind of ideology in this way, can have a positive influence on other governments within or without the EC.[13]

While engaging the CoE may have been logical in the 1980s, engaging the EEC for the recognition of minority peoples was visionary for that time.

Challenging Borders: The Project of a United Europe

In this section, we will track this specific idea of Europe, and assess the ways it has inspired LGBT activism in Central and Eastern Europe and how it is entrenched in the strategies of mobilization focused on institutional and reformist politics across borders. The expansion of LGBT activism in Central and Eastern Europe is a privileged case study that provides another angle from which to grasp the dynamics described above. Especially for LGBT advocacy organizations in this region, we argue that Europe provided not only a material resource, but also a normative frame for shaping and fueling mobilization. The idea of Europe as both an imagined community of values and a strategic means with which to enhance rights was key for LGBT activists. In what follows, we look at these dimensions and posit that by working within European networks and employing European frames, LGBT activism in Central and Eastern Europe also contributes to reshaping the meaning of Europe, from the ground up. Imagining Europe as a community of shared LGBT values challenges Europe's historical borders, as activists bypassed their own states to push the confines of Europe further eastward.

LGBT activists in Central and Eastern Europe have long been connected to an idea of Europe that embodies values of fundamental rights. While state socialism was repressive of gay and lesbian activism, spaces for such activism existed to various degrees and in various forms across states in the region before 1989 (Chetaille 2011, 121–23; Kuhar and Takács 2007; Long 1999). The presence and mobilization of the lesbian and gay movement was substantially more advanced in many western European states, however, where the 1960s/1970s sexual revolution and the politicization of the HIV/AIDS crisis created a greater space for activism much earlier (Chetaille 2011, 121–23; Owczarzak 2009; for a critical account Kulpa and Mizielinska 2011). Those states within the auspices of the EU, the CoE, and the Organization for Security and Cooperation in Europe provided a natural arena for LGBT activists in postsocialist states to develop ties too. Especially after the fall of the Berlin Wall, activists saw an opportunity to connect the advancement of LGBT recognition—both legally and socially—to European integration. The potential for new political alternatives, beyond national borders, transformed imagination into a set of concrete realities.

Subverting the Curtain: Challenging Borders before the Fall of the Wall

Long before European unification, the ILGA had looked eastward and was prepared for and supportive of engaging local activists in Central and Eastern Europe. Wielding support from groups across the globe was critical, since "contact with the international movement [was] often essential in overcoming the isolation and fear felt by many lesbians and gay men who are trying to organize for the first time under repressive conditions."[14] The 1979 Bergen Conference Report had already noted that committees were in charge of investigating the situation in "Socialist (Eastern European) countries."[15] Later, a report by British activist Peter Ashman from 1989 evoked the prospect of EU enlargement and the need for ILGA to add LGBT rights into the "acquis communautaire":

> Recent events in Eastern Europe are almost certain to lead to enlargement of the EC in the 1990s, but probably not before the harmonization provisions are in place. The next two years will be crucial for ensuring that lesbian/gay concerns are met in that process, because candidate members of the EC will also have to meet these obligations.[16]

Interestingly, unlike other activists' groups of the time, the binary boundaries of Cold War Europe were never an impeding issue within the ILGA. Some key ILGA activists, such as the Dutch Hein Verkerk and Bram Bol, were members of communist parties—an example of how a commitment to LGBT rights and a focus on Europe made political boundaries more arbitrary. The revolutionary discourse of the early 1970s, which was particularly strong among some gay liberation groups, had vanished in favor of defending the universality of human rights, and ILGA decided to criticize human rights violations from both socialist and capitalist countries (Verkerk 2012). This became evident when activists from Fuori!, the main Italian gay rights group—which was anticommunist in orientation—failed to organize a transnational protest to highlight the situation for homosexuals in the Soviet Union (USSR). Despite the convenient political backdrop of the 1980 Summer Olympics, several activists were uncomfortable with the political motivations of the Italian proposal (Pistor 2012). After extended discussions, other groups did not join Fuori!'s campaign, citing security reasons and the potential risks of foreign action as reasons for abstaining, leaving Fuori!'s Enzo Francone to stand alone in front of the Kremlin (Pezzana 2011).[17]

Through early action by LGBT activists, Europe not only came to embody a new set of values, but these values were depicted as a way to penetrate the Iron Curtain, offering alternatives to the divisiveness of the Cold War. This is evident in a 1983 letter to the president and the members of the European Parliament:

> With great delight we noted the report of the EP on the Human Rights in the USSR (Rapporteur Lord Bethel, UK, ED). Notably the paragraph on the rights of homosexuals in the USSR. This position of the EP gives us confidence that your concern about the rights of homosexual men and women will also be extended to citizens, gay men and lesbian women in the member states of the European community as well as in other countries.[18]

These two ideas, the universality of human rights and Europe as a political alternative to the Cold War, converged in several of the activists' initiatives. This was the case in the attempt to draft a European Convention on Human Rights Protocol (ECHRP) in the mid-1980s, with the aim that it applied to gay and lesbian citizens. Activists decided to focus on the European-based ECHRP after fruitless efforts, beginning in 1979, to have the United Nation adopt an International Convention on the Elimination of all Forms of Discrimination based on Sexual Orientation. The work to draft the more international UN protocol ceased in 1981, when both the Recommendation of the Parliamentary Assembly of the Council of Europe and the successful Dudgeon case indicated that the CoE, and Europe more generally, would be a more promising venue. Even when, in the late 1980s, activists were facing roadblocks at the level of the CoE, they were resolute that the CoE remain a priority:

> The European Convention and the decisions of the Court and Commission are the most authoritative body of human rights legislation in existence. The newer regional human rights organisations developing in the Americas, in Africa, and in Asia, tend to follow the directions taken by the European Court and Commission. Thus, these negative decisions could have effects in other parts of the world.[19]

These developments led to an intensification of ILGA's work on Europe. A similar vision inspired the work around the Council for Security and Cooperation in Europe (CSCE), later the OSCE, which commenced in 1980. This institution was directly linked to the Cold War context and the willingness to create bridges between both sides of Europe. It had a clear human rights mandate and it was easy for activists to get access to it, making it a more attainable venue to lobby (Krickler 2011).

Transnational activism concerning lesbian and gay rights was not deterred by the political and geographic boundaries of Cold War. Despite the notoriously divisive political border of the Iron Curtain, the idea of Europe that activists championed always reached beyond the boundaries that marked the continent. For the transnational activists we interviewed, LGBT people always belonged in what it meant to be European.

New Europe: Challenging Borders after the Fall of the Wall

The movement's goals remained unchanged after the fall of the Berlin Wall: "Making lesbians and gays visible to these people who are steering the course of a New Europe and forcing them to define their position on issues concerning discrimination and oppression of lesbians and gay men."[20] We find these aims to be particularly accentuated in ILGA's attempts to develop and strengthen LGBT activism in CEE coun-tries. Since the 1980s, ILGA activists had developed various strategies to identify partners and to foster activism in (former) socialist states (through capacity-building workshops, study visits, scholarships, and access to funding, etc.).[21] The organization established an East Euro-pean Pool in 1981 based on a proposal by the Austrian group Homosex-uelle Initiative (HOSI) Wien. This group had become interested in the situation of CEE gays and lesbians due its geographical location in the region—Vienna being further east than Prague, the high number of les-bian and gay refugees in Vienna, and the many informal ties HOSI had to them. The head of HOSI Wien, Kurt Krickler, who would become the first ILGA-Europe cochair in December 1996, oversaw ILGA activi-ties in the CEE region, as well as at the CSCE (Krickler 2011).[22] Infor-mation was spread from both sides of the curtain, using the network's ties fostered through personal relations and often clandestine regional meetings organized between 1987 and 1996 (Krickler and Jaworski 1988). ILGA's first EU grant funding was dedicated to a project designed to foster democracy and civil society in Estonia, Latvia, Lithuania, and Russia (Phare and Tacis Democracy Programme). Finally, European activists fought to include both western and eastern Europe within the same European organization when they founded ILGA-Europe. Since 2001, ILGA-Europe has run a network of national representatives, the EU Network, which meets twice a year and fosters pan-European networking opportunities. It complements the annual European conference, which has been organized since 1981 and, since 2000, is regularly held in CEE countries. It first convened in Riga in 1995.

Many activists in Central and Eastern Europe—particularly those from Latvia, the former Yugoslavia, Poland, and Romania—responded by integrating themselves at the European level and joining the earliest ILGA-Europe boards. Within the ramifications of a normative commitment to Europe, they did this because of the transnational support, the resources and the know-how it provided, and because they saw a discursive opportunity to frame the issue as a shared European one in their own domestic realms, where they linked furthering LGBT rights to the responsibilities associated with being part of modern Europe (Ayoub 2013a; Holzhacker 2012). Europe provided the normative vantage point with which to associate the LGBT issue.

European LGBT solidarity across borders (Binnie and Klesse 2011) endowed the movement in Central and Eastern Europe with various resources to promote the issue (Ayoub 2013a). Actors at major organizations, and smaller ones in Central and Eastern Europe, had access to material resources for campaigns and projects through grant applications to ILGA-Europe, and sometimes directly to the European institutions. Organizational funding for campaigns and projects in Central and Eastern Europe also came directly from other European states (particularly the Netherlands, Sweden, Great Britain, and Norway); civil society organizations; and major international foundations, such as George Soros's Open Society Institute and the Sigrid Rausing Trust. For example, in Slovakia, the Urgent Action Fund and the foreign embassies the Netherlands, the United Kingdom, Sweden, Finland, Ireland, and Denmark funded the first pride march in 2010 (Schlesinger 2011). In Poland, the Kampania Przeciw Homofobii (KPH)'s Let Them

See Us campaign—an early major effort by the organization leading up to Poland's EU accession, which involved 27 billboards showing same-sex couples holding hands—was funded in large part by the Dutch Embassy. A similar phenomenon took place in Romania, where the movement established itself in a difficult domestic context (same-sex relations were illegal until 1996 and an antigay propaganda law existed until 2000) with the aid of personal commitments by some expatriates, including US academic Scott Long and US Ambassador Michael Guest, and the support of transnational groups such as the ILGA, the International Gay and Lesbian Human Rights Commission, and foreign embassies and international human rights foundations (Carstocea 2006a; Stychin 2003; Woodcock 2011).

FRAMING LGBT RIGHTS IN A EUROPEAN DISCOURSE

Within and alongside Europe's material resources, LGBT activists were often able to use the idea of Europe to frame the LGBT issue as a European norm. As European institutions adopted a normative structure that advanced the visibility of the LGBT issues—by introducing the issue into the legal framework of member states (Kollman 2007, 2009; Ayoub forthcoming)—the activists involved in Central and Eastern Europe developed innovative and appealing frames in order to deliver a coherent message on LGBT recognition.[23] European frames offered an opportunity to link the issue to modernity and the responsibilities associated with being European. For EU and Council of Europe members, these frames legitimized the LGBT issue through the constitutive effect of shared membership in a European community. Transnational European activist organizations, like ILGA-Europe, and the European regulations that grew out of such activism, are clear about how European societies "should" think about LGBT issues. While the topic is often domestically opposed on the grounds of rejecting the imposition foreign states' values (Carstocea 2006b), the incorporation of many CEE states into a common European community makes the issue less foreign. Europe after the Cold War has come to have that advantage.

For LGBT activists, framing LGBT issues in the language of "European" democratic values was employed because Europe resonated in many CEE member states at the time of the 2004-wave of accession (Kuhar 2011; Ayoub 2013a). Examples of this frame include the T-shirts worn at controversial LGBT demonstrations in Poland around the time of accession, which read "Europe = Tolerance." In Poland, the Warsaw LGBT equality marches' themes also used European frames, such as the theme of Culture of Diversity (alluding to modern democracy in Europe) (Bączkowski 2011). Making the LGBT issue European is also apparent in addressing right-wing critics in Central and Eastern Europe, as LGBT activists involved could reframe their message as one of European responsibilities and human rights.

The idea of Europe is also used as a rationale for the mobilization of other Europeans in various domestic realms that are not their own. Since LGBT marches in Warsaw in 2005 and 2006 included many Germans, whose involvement in domestic affairs resonates poorly for historical reasons in the region, organizers purposely shifted attention away from the fact that Germans were protesting for LGBT rights by highlighting that Europeans were protesting for democratic values (Ayoub 2013a). Foreign visitors involved in CEE demonstrations also say that they see their activism as linked to their shared values, solidarities and responsibilities as Europeans. For example, Claudia Roth—Member of the European Parliament (MEP), current cochair of the German Green Party, and a vocal voice for LGBT recognition at the European level and on the ground in many CEE countries—says that her engagement "has nothing to do with [bilateral relations between Germany and its neighbors], among friends one must say what does not work, especially among member states of the EU" (Roth 2011). The idea of LGBT rights as European, and thus indirectly also Polish, Latvian, Hungarian, Slovenian, Romanian, and so on—because they are members of this shared community—is evident (Ayoub 2013a).

As in their activism during the Cold War, the reach of an LGBT idea of Europe continues to travel well beyond EU borders. Activists in many contexts outside the European Union employ similar European frames, and LGBT human rights are increasingly important channels through which the EU expands its presence across borders. In response to a ban of the Pride Parade in Serbia in 2011, local activists of the Gej Strejt Alijansa (GSA) and the Pride Parade Belgrade were quick to reference the European Convention on Human Rights and European Parliament Resolutions and called for support from allies in Brussels.[24] The European Parliament's Intergroup on LGBT Rights sent three members

to march in the parade on October 6, 2012. According to Marije Cornelissen, a Dutch MEP and one of the Intergroup marchers, "the values
that will be highlighted on 6th October are European, and Serbia fully
belongs in Europe."[25] The message that LGBT rights are part of what it
means to be European is vocalized through the increasingly common
EU rhetoric, advocated for in large part by ILGA-Europe. For countries
with EU-membership aspirations, the promotion of values goes hand in
hand with incentives to make strides on LGBT rights. In September, the
GSA clarified that its "main criterion for cooperating with institutions
and political parties is whether they are pro-European, and whether
they themselves cooperate and are recognized by the institutions of
the European Union" (GSA Press Release, September 30, 2012). There
is little ambivalence about where Europe lies on this issue. Alongside
her focus on Belgrade, Cornelissen also started a virtual pride march
in which she voices her support for marches in the capital cities of Kiev,
Moscow, Chisinau, and Minsk, none of which lie within EU borders.

A process similar to the one we observed in the post-2004 accession
states is apparent in contexts outside of EU borders. In fact, EU pressures to adopt LGBT rights might be more pronounced in potential
candidate states, where the incentives of membership can yield speedy
compliance with LGBT norms (Cizmecioglu 2009). This does not mean
that ILGA's mechanisms to encourage implementation and internation-
alization work equally strong in non-EU contexts (Le Déroff 2011), but
it shows that activists and LGBT-friendly elites imagine a Europe of
LGBT rights to stretch far outside the institutional borders of the EU.
Beyond the immediate EU-neighborhood, ILGA-Europe has and maintains active ties in contexts that have little or no ambitions or prospects
for membership in the EU community.

The reaction to recent Russian antigay legislation, which bans the
promotion of nontraditional sexual relations, is another prime example of local and external LGBT activists that invoke the idea of Europe,
even if the domestic political fractures between the EU/CoE and Duma
are especially sharp. Even before the Duma's federal bill passed in 2013,
Moscow and St. Petersburg aroused ample attention from ILGA when
local antigay propaganda bills were introduced in 2012. Alongside their
member organizations on the ground, the organization worked to pub-
licize the events. Protests emerged outside Russian embassies across

European capitals during the winter and spring of 2012, and the summer's pride parades around Europe called attention to the situation in Russia. From Moscow, Nikolai Alexeyev of *Moscow Pride* was quick to allude to Europe after being fined for "promoting" homosexuality: "Now we will fight this homophobic verdict in every court and go all the way to Strasbourg if need be to try and break this caveman mentality which throws Russia back to the dark ages" (Loiko 2012). Regardless of domestic Euro-skepticism, Russia is "European" for local LGBT activists.

By drawing attention to the situation in Russia, Russian activists and ILGA-Europe (as well as the EP's Intergroup) generated a response from European institutions. The reaction from Brussels and Strasbourg noted the St. Petersburg Bill's deviation from the idea of Europe. Early on, a February 12, 2012 European Parliament Regulation condemned the adoption of the "law against propaganda on sexual orientation . . . [and] call[ed] on all Russian authorities to stop restricting freedom of expression in relation to sexual orientation or gender identity, in line with the European Convention on Human Rights." The Parliament went on to request that the Vice-President of the Commission "convey the European Union's opposition to these laws."[26] MEP Sophia in 't Veld was less tactful in her efforts to highlight the law's misstep from its European responsibilities:

> Tchaikovsky and Constantinovich must be rolling over in their graves. Such laws are simply unacceptable; if Russia isn't serious about respecting the European Convention on Human Rights, it should simply call the bluff and leave the Council of Europe altogether. And more than statements, these grave human rights abuses must have consequences for the EU-Russia relationship![27]

While in 't Veld's approach may not be conducive to goals—by suggesting to expel a member of a shared community—her discursive use of Europe exemplifies the imagination that the idea of Europe on LGBT rights is outside of relevant EU borders. Relatedly, the European Commission recently said that Ukraine's version of an antigay propaganda bill (Bill 8711) could threaten plans for visa liberalization with the European Union.[28] Transnational LGBT activism has channeled the idea of Europe into the discourse of major European institutions, making it commonplace among the rhetoric of the EU and the CoE instiutions.

This use of both EU and CoE—which spans across 47 member states—institutions by LGBT activists has further blurred the geographic boundaries associated with the core idea of LGBT Europe. In the imagination of activists and sympathetic elites, LGBT rights are not to be disentangled from the meaning of Europe, even if physical realities for LGBT people are vastly diverse within and across the borders of these groups of states. In their broadest sense, the politics of LGBT activism in contemporary Europe embody the same idea of Europe that fueled the engagement of those movement pioneers that challenged the meaning of the iron curtain. If anything, that imagination has been intensified in modern European politics, as formal EU and CoE institutions increasingly echo that activist idea of Europe.

The fact that transnational activists so often call for mobilization of support and recognition of LGBT peoples in a language of European values and responsibilities suggests that they contribute to building Europe in a certain image from the ground up. Linking back to the first section on the ILGA, the work of CEE activists suggests that Europe runs in both directions. While LGBT issues are linked to Europe's normative structures from above, by using Europe as an argument for demanding LGBT recognition from their states and societies, the activists on the ground in Central and Eastern Europe subsequently, and indirectly, recreate the idea that Europe is united around the LGBT issue. In turn, the link between being European and accepting LGBT people is established, and an understanding of LGBT rights as a European value is further cemented.

Borders That Remain and Those That Have Emerged: Who Is Left Out?

While reinforcing LGBT movements across the continent, this idea of Europe has also maintained certain boundaries and establishes new ones. In particular, the idea of Europe comes with a master frame of LGBT rights that does not always mesh harmoniously with the intersectional makeup of the LGBT community. Especially among organizations with scarce resources that then become highly dependent on EU funding, the European frame has overshadowed other potential frames for political mobilization and organization. This is particularly true of debates surrounding internal diversity and intersectionality, which have only recently become central themes within Europe's LGBT organizations, including ILGA-Europe. The difficult integration of transgender activism is a central illustration. Historically, claims by transgender activists have remained absent from broader discourses on sexual minority activism, and they are only recently finding their voice in the political agenda. The regional group, Transgender Europe (TGEU), which now collaborates actively with ILGA-Europe, was founded in 2005, as an alternative—and specifically transgender—umbrella organization. Transgender activists founded the organization in response to concerns that ILGA-Europe was not sufficiently supporting their claims (Balzer and Hutta, forthcoming).

The LGBT rights master frame—alongside deeper historical and sociological reasons—has also foreshadowed debates around cultural, racial, and gender diversity within LGBT communities. Issues of diversity have not been voiced within European LGBT activism the way they been in the United States (Ferree 2009), and European social movements have employed the concept of intersectionality for a shorter period of time. On its website, ILGA-Europe primarily uses the term "multiple discrimination" (referring to coalitions with other antidiscrimination NGOs), which is rarely differentiated from the concept of intersectionality (see also ILGA-Europe 2010). The same can be said about policymaking in Member States and at EU level. Intersectional policies are still in their relative infancy (Verloo 2006), particularly when they concern sexual orientation (Cruells and Coll-Planas 2013), and concepts such as "intersectionality" and "multiple discriminations" are not always clearly defined. Not surprisingly, because of the nature of its mandate, ILGA-Europe's discourse on multiple discrimination and intersectionality reflects that of EU policies: it is a top-down and institutional EU understanding of these concepts, not one that has its origins in grassroots demands.

The transnational incorporation of CEE activists into the established European structures has also had consequences for LGBT politics at a local level. Beyond empowering LGBT groups and endowing them with financial resources and new mobilization frames, it often creates hierarchies among LGBT organizations, namely between those who can and are willing to work transnationally and those whose work is locally focused. The transnationalization of the issue often privileges CEE activists with language skills—particularly English—and whose claims and repertoires resonate more harmoniously with the frames of western European LGBT organizations and potential funders. They are generally younger and many have spent time abroad. In her ethnographic study of LGBT activism in Poland, Agnès Chetaille (2011) shows how the diversity of the activist landscape in Poland was gradually overshadowed by KPH's public hegemony—the Polish LGBT organization with the closest ties to ILGA-Europe and one of the most influential LGBT groups in the region. Chetaille (2013) argues that the transnationalization of some LGBT groups has increased their domestic legitimacy and visibility because of the emergence of new national and European opportunities, as well as their ability to seize them. In this sense, some groups and certain types of claims are favored in a European image of LGBT activism. LGBT visibility has become so attached to being European, that the frame of being European can trump the importance of LGBT visibility—and the diversity encompassed in that term—in its own right. In a critical sense, LGBT (in)visibility comes with Europe, not separate from it.

The master frame has paradoxically also reenacted the binary juxtaposition of East versus West in contemporary discourses (Chetaille 2013; Kulpa and Mizielinska 2011). Indeed, the values promoted by the EU and the wealthier LGBT organizations in Europe expand an understanding of LGBT rights that was consolidated in the western experience, and LGBT activists, including in CEE countries, often present their claims in terms of catching up to this ideal. This is problematic in the sense that a European LGBT frame inadvertently "others" the CEE region as a deviation to the European norm. Additionally, discourses tend to aggregate many diverse CEE countries into one, as if the situations of LGBT peoples were uniform across region.[29] In reaction, the frames of the opponents to LGBT rights often rely on a nationalistic defense of traditional cultural and religious values, intrinsically opposed to European cosmopolitanism. This has led some authors, such as Kulpa and Mizielinska (2011, 16), to claim that this frame of European LGBT rights places Central and Eastern Europe in a spatio-temporal location of impossibility. According to them, a "Western time of sequence" then stands opposed to an "Eastern time of coincidence," locating—and possibly locking—Central and Eastern Europe in a distinct "postcommunist" space that can be broadly defined as the space of the past.

Interestingly, the states and people who do not fit with European norms—the European "others"—are located in the imagined East. A similar pattern applies to more recent European debates on Islam and homosexuality. These also rely on an East/West divide, in which both culture and religion are used again as markers of difference to distinguish certain groups from European norms (Petzen 2012). Popular discourses on Turkish candidacy to the EU have drawn ample attention in this respect, in that they are also used to paint Turkey as inferior to the ideals that shape European membership. While flawed track records on LGBT rights have not been barriers to the accession of many member states, in the Turkish case homophobia is often associated with Islam. Among European LGBT organizations, their position is far more nuanced and similar to the catching-up logic related to the integration of CEE states: bringing Turkey up to European standards. Within the member states, political actors have deployed the idea of Europe and LGBT rights in discourses that "other" Muslim communities, in which they have been portrayed as homophobic and, subsequently, a threat to national and European values (see, e.g., Mepschen, Duyvendak, Tonkens 2010).

In sum, not everyone is naturally included in the LGBT idea of Europe, which has—advertently and inadvertently—excluded certain groups from the process of European LGBT recognition. While multiple boundaries have been eroded in the process, it is important to also take note of those boundaries that persist, as well as the new ones that have emerged as part of the process.

Conclusion

In this chapter we have argued that an idea of Europe is linked to LGBT activism, both at a transnational level and on the ground in Central and Eastern Europe, through its role as a set of values and as a means by which to gain rights. We have shown this by exploring the imaginations and strategies developed by the ILGA and ILGA-Europe to realize the project of a united Europe—one that places less value on the various geographic, political, and sexual borders that have separated the continent for centuries. From the beginning, the ILGA had a clear vision of what Europe should represent, and how this imagination could contribute to the advancement of LGBT rights in various domestic arenas. The founders' insights were later strengthened through the establishment of ILGA-Europe, which played a crucial part in the expansion of LGBT activism in Central and Eastern Europe. By linking LGBT rights so closely to Europe in their work, activists in Central and Eastern Europe contribute to the project of building Europe from the ground up, by dismantling borders and further constructing an imagination in which Europe is inextricably linked to LGBT rights.

While there is no mass consensus around a European, value-based identity in the public sphere (Katzenstein and Checkel 2009, 214), we do recognize a link between LGBT rights and European values. In this sense, Europe appears both as a set of values and normative commitments (shared and felt by ILGA and CEE activists), and a strategic means by which to gain rights in various domestic realms. By discussing the contours of Europe that social actors imagine, we have shown that these beliefs—and more importantly the various ways they are embodied—further contribute to building Europe by making the borders of nations and the boundaries of national identities less pertinent in some respects, an insight that is crucial for the future of European integration.

In their struggle for political and social recognition, LGBT activists have traversed the traditional borders—political, geographic, national, and sexual—that marked the European continent by stepping outside of their borders to seek out political alternatives (both imagined and real) at the macro level. In that process, they have been visionary in their understanding of Europe as a community that is not limited to certain groups of states or segments of the continent. Both before and after the Cold War, LGBT activists have understood that their pursuit of rights could not be achieved if it were to be confined within any set of traditional borders. It is the construction of the idea of Europe that has permeated borders of exclusion and served as a tool of resistance against inequality for sexual minorities on the European continent.

Such an understanding of Europe, as an imagined and an experienced community, invites us to further unpack the special relationship that unites issues of sexuality and Europe. Scholars have long studied the connections between sexuality and nationalism, a topic that has come into a new light due to the recent debates on homonationalism (e.g., Puar 2007). While our story can be viewed in part as a social movement success, it has also highlighted the critical questions that remain. Given that there is a distinction between who reflects the idea of Europe and who stands outside of it, geographically and culturally, we have foregrounded this issue in our discussion. Indeed, while European identity construction is often presented as a way to transcend violent European state nationalisms, European institutions have sometimes tried to foster a common sense of belonging using strategies akin to those used by nation-states in the past. In an attempt to aid the building of a common European identity, European institutions have promoted the values of the LGBT activists they would endorse, decisively contributing to the expansion of activism further eastward. That said, researchers must continue to question the new types of boundaries that are created and who becomes left out in this process. As discussed, the expansion of LGBT activism in Central and Eastern Europe reveals a complex politics of cooptation and a selective endorsement of groups, claims, and issues. Furthermore, as Carl Stychin (1998) argues, national identities are often also constructed against the "other." This leaves the question of who becomes LGBT-Europe's "sexual other," which could include EU countries (e.g., Poland) or neighbors (e.g., Russia or Turkey), or the construction of Muslim and immigrant communities as a threat. While activists have seen the idea of Europe—and the deconstruction of traditional borders that is associated with that imagination—as a means of great potential for LGBT rights, activists and scholars alike must pay close attention to the cases where borders still exist and where new borders arise.

NOTES

1. This chapter relies partially on an earlier essay published by the authors (2012): "Building Europe: The ILGA and LGBT Activism in Central and Eastern Europe," *Perspectives on Europe* 42(1): 51–56.

2. These early contacts were formalized in the Weltliga für Sexualreform (World League for Sexual Reform), founded by Magnus Hirschfeld in Berlin in 1928 (Kollman and Waites 2009, 3).

3. The ILGA was called the International Gay Association until 1986.

4. This echoes the literature on "boomerang politics" in international relations. According to Keck and Sikkink (1998, 12): "Where channels between domestic

groups and their governments are blocked, the boomerang pattern of influence characteristic of transnational networks may occur: domestic NGOs bypass their state and directly search out international allies to try to bring pressure on their states from outside."

5. IGA, *Press Release: Report "On Discrimination Against Homosexuals" prepared by the Committee on Social and Health Questions of the Council of Europe*, Dublin, 12 September 1981. See also Ashman (2011) and Warner (2011).

6. Peter Ashman, a member of CHE who cochaired ILGA's founding meeting, was one of Dudgeon's lawyers.

7. David Norris was among the founders of ILGA, and he gave a speech at the Coventry meeting.

8. Activists say that solidarity was a greater incentive for founding activists from countries such as the Netherlands—more so than for the Brits—where LG rights were more "advanced." These activists often had a more global perspective.

9. International Gay Association, *Proposals for Political Action*, 1978, 2.

10. The Squarcialupi Report, a 1984 European Parliament Resolution, addressed discrimination in the workplace and discrimination in sexual offenses provisions across member-states. The Roth Report, adopted by the European Parliament in 1994, addressed antidiscrimination, partnership, and parenting equality for lesbian and gay minorities in the European Union.

11. These were part of the broader Danish politics surrounding the "Danish hiccup," the popular referenda that rejected Maastricht in June 1992 (Ingebritsen 1998). Danish activists also advocated for an approach of "multispeed" Europe, so that "laggard" countries could catch up with "advanced" countries.

12. ILGA, *Report of the Amsterdam Regional Conference*, 1988.

13. IGA, *Conference Report*, 1984, p: 24.

14. IGA, "Reports of the 2nd Annual Conference," Newsletter 80/1, 1980, 6.

15. IGA, *Proposals and Resolutions with Agreements as to Their Implementation, 1st annual Conference Easter 1979*, 1–2

16. Peter Ashman, "Workshop on the European Community," in ILGA, *Preconference Papers Athens*, 1989, p. 11. See also Power (1991).

17. Fuori!'s event exemplifies the wide ideological spectrum of early ILGA activists. The failed mobilization in the USSR also reflects limits of the movement's reach—a lack of resources—that centered their focus on the more achievable goals in Central and Eastern Europe (Ashman 2011).

18. IGA, Letter to the President and the Members of the European Parliament, Cologne, 30th December 1983, in Conference Reports 83/84, 1984, 18.

19. ILGA, Conference Report Oslo, 1988, 9.

20. ILGA, *ILGA Renews Bid with CSCE for Lesbian and Gay Rights. Lesbians and Gays Gather in Helsinki for Parallel Activity Conference*, Brussels, 1992, 2.

21. See particularly ILGA-Europe, *Equality for Lesbians and Gay Men: A relevant issue in the EU Accession Process*, Brussels: ILGA-Europe, Brussels: ILGA-Europe, 2001.

22. The Swedish Riksförbundet för homosexuellas, bisexuellas och transpersoners rättigheter (RFSL), formerly Riksförbundet för sexuellt likaberättigande, also started to work with groups from the Soviet Union, and especially the Baltic states after independence, beginning in the late 1980s (Petersson 2012).

23. Examples of this include the pressures from the Council of Europe, which led to the decriminalization of homosexual acts in countries such as Ireland, Romania, and Cyprus, Article 13 of the Amsterdam Treaty, the 2000 Employment Anti-Discrimination Directive, the European Charter for Fundamental Rights, and the 1993 Copenhagen Criteria for accession (Bonini-Baraldi and Paradis 2009; Swiebel 2009; Stychin 2001). For examples of European influence in CEE countries, see Takács (2006); Roseneil and Stoilova (2011).

24. The GSA also applauded the Serbian Constitutional Court's reference to "the principles of civic democracy and affiliation to European principles and values" in a recent ruling against an extreme-right group, Obraz (see GSA Press Statement, June 12, 2012).

25. Press Release, "Three Members of the European Parliament head to Belgrade Pride," the Intergroup on LGBT Rights, September 20, 2012. www.lgbt-ep.eu/press-releases/three-members-of-the-european-parliament-head-to-belgrade-pride/.

26. www.europarl.europa.eu/sides/getDoc.do?type=TA&reference=P7-TA-2012-0054&language=EN&ring=P7-RC-2012-0052.

27. www.lgbt-ep.eu/press-releases/meps-speak-out-against-homophobic-and-transphobic-censorship-laws-russia/.

28. www.lgbt-ep.eu/press-releases/european-commission-ukraines-bill-8711-obstacle-to-eu-ukraine-visa-agreement/.

29. Substantial variation in legislation and attitudes toward LGBT people exists across CEE countries (Ayoub 2013b).

REFERENCES

Anderson, Benedict. 1983. *Imagined Communities: Reflections on the Origin and Speed of Nationalism*. London: Verso Books.

Ashman, Peter. 2011. Personal interview, November 22.

Ayoub, Phillip M. 2013a. "Cooperative Transnationalism in Contemporary Europe: Cooperative Transnationalism in Contemporary Europe: Europeanization and Political Opportunities for LGBT Mobilization in the European Union," *European Political Science Review* 5(2): 279–310.

Ayoub, Phillip M. 2013b. "When States 'Come Out': The Politics of Visibility and the Diffusion of Sexual Minority Rights in Europe," PhD diss. Ithaca, NY: Cornell University.

Ayoub, Phillip M. Forthcoming. "Contested Norms in New-Adopter States: International Determinants of LGBT Rights Legislation," *European Journal of International Relations*.

Bączkowski, Tomasz. 2011. Personal interview, February 21.

Balzer, Carsten, and Jan Simon Hutta. Forthcoming. "Trans Networking in the European Vortex: Transgender Europe Between Advocacy and Grassroots Politics." In

LGBT Activism and the Making of Europe: A Rainbow Europe?, edited by Phillip M. Ayoub and David Paternotte. Basingstoke, UK: Palgrave Macmillan.

Beger, Nico. 2004. *Tensions in the Struggle for Sexual Minority Rights: Que(e)rying Political Practices in Europe.* Manchester: Manchester University Press.

Binnie, Jon. 2004. *The Globalization of Sexuality.* Thousand Oaks, CA: Sage.

Binnie, Jon, and Christian Klesse. 2011. "Researching Transnational Activism around LGBTQ Politics in Central and Eastern Europe: Activists Solidarities and Spatial Imaginings." In *De-Centering Western Sexualities: Central and Eastern European Perspectives,* edited by Robert Kulpa and Johanna Mizielinska, 107–130. Farnham: Ashgate.

Bonini-Baraldi, Matteo, and Évelyne Paradis. 2009. "European Union." In *The Greenwood Encyclopedia of LGBT Issues Worldwide,* edited by Chuck Stewart, 123–145. Westport, CT: Greenwood.

Carstocea, Sinziana. 2006a. "Une identité clandestine: L'homosexualité en Roumanie," *Revue d'histoire moderne et contemporaine,* 53(4): 191–210.

Carstocea, Sinziana. 2006b. "Between Acceptance and Rejection—Decriminalizing Homosexuality in Romania." In *The Gay's and Lesbian's Rights in an Enlarged European Union,* edited by Anne Weyembergh and Sinziana Carstocea, 207–222. Brussels: Éditions de l'Université de Bruxelles.

Checkel, Jeffrey. 2006. "Tracing Causal Mechanisms," *International Studies Review* 8(2): 362–370.

Chetaille, Agnès. 2011. "Sovereignty and Sexuality: The Polish Lesbian and Gay Movement and a Post-Socialist State." In *The Lesbian and Gay Movement and the State: Comparative Insights into a Transformed Relationship,* edited by Manon Tremblay, David Paternotte, and Carol Johnson, 119–135. Farnham: Ashgate.

Chetaille, Agnès. 2013. "L'Union européenne, le nationalisme polonais et la sexualisation de la 'division Est/Ouest,'" *Raisons politiques* 49: 119–140.

Cizmecioglu, Ekmel. 2009. Personal interview, July 9.

Cruells, Marta, and Gerard Coll-Planas. 2013. "Challenging Equality Policies: The Emerging LGBT Perspective," *European Journal of Women's Studies* 20(2): 122–137.

Della Porta, Donatella, Hanspeter Kriesi, and Dieter Rucht. 2009. *Social Movements in A Globalizing World.* Basingstoke, UK: Palgrave Macmillan.

Della Porta, Donatella, and Sidney G. Tarrow. 2005. *Transnational Protest and Global Activism.* Lanham, MD: Rowman & Littlefield.

Díez Medrano, Juan. 2003. *Framing Europe: Empire, WWII and Attitudes toward European Integration in Germany, Spain, and the United Kingdom.* Princeton, NJ: Princeton University Press.

Ferree, Myra Marx, and Aili Mari Tripp, eds. 2006. *Global Feminism: Transnational Women's Activism, Organizing, and Human Rights.* New York: New York University Press.

Ferree, Myra Marx. 2009. "Inequality, Intersectionality and the Politics of Discourse: Framing Feminist Alliances." In *The Discursive Politics of Gender Equality:*

Stretching, Bending and Policy-Making, edited by Emanuela Lombardo, Petra Meier, and Mieke Verloo, 86-104. New York: Routledge.

Hellinck, Bart. 2004. "Le MHAR en avait marre," *Het ondraaglijk besef* 10: 19–23.

Holzhacker, Ron. 2012. "National and Transnational Strategies of LGBT Civil Society Organizations in Different Political Environments: Modes of Interaction in Western and Eastern Europe of Equality," *Comparative European Politics* 10 (1): 23–47.

ILGA-Europe. 2010. "Multiple Discrimination," *Destination Equality* (Winter 2010–2011): 16-20.

Ingebritsen, Christine. 1998. *The Nordic States and European Unity*. Ithaca, NY: Cornell University Press.

Ingebritsen, Christine. 2000. *The Nordic States and European Unity*. Ithaca, NY: Cornell University Press.

Jackson, Julian. 2009. *Living in Arcadia. Homosexuality, Politics and Morality in France from the Liberation to AIDs*. Chicago: University of Chicago Press.

Katzenstein, Peter. 1996. *The Culture of National Security: Norms and Identity in World Politics*. New York: Columbia University Press.

Katzenstein, Peter, and Jeffrey Checkel. 2009. "Conclusion: European Identity in Context." In *European Identity*, edited by Jeffrey Checkel and Peter Katzenstein, 213–228. Cambridge: Cambridge University Press.

Keck, Margaret E., and Kathryn Sikkink. 1998. *Activists Beyond Borders: Advocacy Networks in International Politics*. Ithaca, NY: Cornell University Press.

Kollman, Kelly. 2007. "Same-Sex Unions: The Globalization of An Idea," *International Studies Quarterly* 51(2): 329–357.

Kollman, Kelly. 2009. "European Institutions, Transnational Networks and National Same-Sex Union Policy: When Soft Law Hits Harder," *Contemporary Politics* 15(1): 37–53.

Kollman, Kelly, and Matthew Waites. 2009. "The Global Politics of Lesbian, Gay, Bisexual and Transgender Human Rights: An Introduction," *Contemporary Politics* 15(1): 1–17.

Krickler, Kurt. 2011. Personal interview, October 27.

Krickler, Kurt, and Marek Jarowski. 1988. "Poland: A Gay and Lesbian Movement Start to Develop." In *Second ILGA Pink Book*, ILGA, 143–152. Utrecht: Interfacultaire Werkgroep Homostudies.

Kuhar, Roman, and Judit Takács. 2007. *Beyond The Pink Curtain: Everyday Life of LGBT People in Eastern Europe*. Ljubljana: Peace Institute.

Kuhar, Roman. 2011. "Use of the Europeanization Frame in Same Sex Partnership Issues Across Europe." In *The Europeanization of Gender Equality Policies: A Discursive Sociological Approach*, edited by Emanuela Lombardo and Maxime Forest, 168–191. Basingstoke: Palgrave.

Kulpa, Robert, and Johanna Mizielinska. 2011. "'Contemporary Peripheries': Queer Studies, Circulation of Knowledge and East/West Divide." In *De-Centering Western Sexualities: Central and Eastern European Perspectives*, edited by Robert Kulpa and Johanna Mizielinska, 12–26. Farnham: Ashgate.

Le Déroff, Joël. 2011. Personal interview, March 1.

Long, Scott. 1999. "Gay and Lesbian Movements in Eastern Europe: Romania, Hungary, and the Czech Republic." In *The Global Emergence of Gay and Lesbian Politics: National Imprints of a Worldwide Movement*, edited by Barry Adam, Jan Willem Duyvendak and André Krouwel, 242–265. Philadelphia: Temple University Press.

Loiko, Sergei. 2012. "Russian Gay Activist Fined for Promoting Homosexuality." *Los Angeles Times*, September 20. http://latimesblogs.latimes.com/world_now/2012/05/by-sergei-l-loiko-los-angeles-times-body-moscow-the-founder-of-the-moscow-gay-pride-movement-wa.html.

Mepschen, Paul, Jan Willem Duyvendak, and Evelien Tonkens. 2010. "Sexual Politics, Orientalism and Multicultural Citizenship in the Netherlands," *Sociology* 44(5): 962–979.

Naples, Nancy, and Manisha Desai, eds. 2002. *Women's Activism and Globalization. Linking Local Struggles and Transnational Politics*. London: Routledge.

Owczarzak, Jill. 2009. "Defining Democracy and the Terms of Engagement with the Postsocialist State: Insights from HIV/AIDS," *East European Politics and Societies* 23(3): 421–445.

Paternotte, David. 2011. "Article 13 and the NGOisation of ILGA-Europe," Presented at the 10th European Sociological Association Conference, Université de Genève (Switzerland), September 8.

Paternotte, David. 2012. "Back Into The Future: ILGA-Europe Before 1996," *Destination Equality* (ILGA-Europe), Winter 2011–2012, 5–7.

Petersson, Stig-Ake. 2012. Personal interview, December 11.

Petzen, Jennifer. 2012. "Contesting Europe: A Call for an Anti-Modern Sexual Politics," *European Journal of Women's Studies* 19(1): 97–114.

Pezzana, Angelo. 2011. Personal interview, November 28.

Pistor, Rob. 2012. Personal interview, May 28.

Power, Lisa. 1991. "The International Lesbian and Gay Association," *Feminist Review* 39: 186–188.

Prearo, Massimo. 2012. "La trajectoire révolutionnaire du militantisme homosexuel italien dans les années 1970," *Cahiers d'histoire. Revue d'histoire critique* 119: 79-97.

Puar, Jasbir. 2007. *Terrorist Assemblages: Homonationalism in Queer Times*. Durham, NC: Duke University Press.

Roseneil, Sasha, and Mariya Stoilova. 2011. "Heteronormativity, Intimate Citizenship and the Regulation of Same-sex Sexualities in Bulgaria." In *De-Centering Western Sexualities: Central and Eastern European Perspectives*, edited by Robert Kulpa and Johanna Mizielinska, 167–190. Farnham: Ashgate.

Roth, Claudia. 2011. Email interview, June 1.

Rupp, Leila. 2011. "The Persistence of Transnational Organizing: The Case of the Homophile Movement," *American Historical Review* 116(4): 1014–1039.

Schlesinger, Romana. 2011. Personal interview, January 26.

Smith, Jackie. 1997. "Characteristics of the Modern Transnational Social Movement Sector." In *Transnational Social Movements and World Politics: Solidarity Beyond the State*, edited by Jackie Smith, 42–58. Syracuse, NY: Syracuse University Press.

Søland, Birgitte. 1998. "A Queer Nation? The Passage of the Gay and Lesbian Partnership Legislation in Denmark, 1989," *Social Politics: International Studies in Gender, State & Society* 5(1): 48–69.

Stychin, Carl. 1998. *A Nation By Rights: National Cultures, Sexual Identity Politics, and the Discourse of Rights*. Philadelphia: Temple University Press.

Stychin, Carl. 2001. "Sexual Citizenship in the European Union," *Citizenship Studies* 5(3): 285–301.

Stychin, Carl. 2003. *Governing Sexuality: The Changing Politics of Citizenship and Law Reform*. Oxford: Hart Publishing.

Swiebel, Joke. 2009. "Lesbian, Gay, Bisexual and Transgender Human Rights: the Search for an International Strategy," *Contemporary Politics* 15(2): 19–35.

Takács, Judit. 2006. "The Influence of European Institutions on the Hungarian Legislation Regarding LGBT Rights." In *The Gay's and Lesbian's Rights in an Enlarged European Union*, edited by Anne Weyembergh and Sinziana Carstocea, 185–205. Brussels: Éditions de l'Université de Bruxelles.

Tamagne, Florence. 2006. *A History of Homosexuality in Europe: Berlin, London, Paris (1919–1939)*. New York: Algora.

Verkerk, Hein. 2012. Personal interview, May 28.

Verloo, Mieke. 2006. "Multiple Inequalities, Intersectionality and the European Union," *European Journal of Women's Studies* 13 (3), 211–228.

Warner, Nigel. 2011. Personal interview, October 29.

Woodcock, Shannon. 2011. "A Short History of the Queer Time of 'Post-Socialist' Romania, or Are We There Yet? Let's Ask Madonna!" In *De-Centering Western Sexualities: Central and Eastern European Perspectives*, edited by Robert Kulpa and Johanna Mizielinska, 63–84. Farnham: Ashgate.

PART III

Contested Solidarities and Emerging Sites of Struggle

10

Frames, Boomerangs, and Global Assemblages

*Border Distortions in the Global Resistance
to Dam Building in Lesotho*

YVONNE A. BRAUN AND MICHAEL C. DREILING

We, the people from 20 countries gathered in Curitiba, Brazil, representing organizations of dam-affected people and of opponents of destructive dams, have shared our experiences of the losses we have suffered and
the threats we face because of dams. Although our experiences reflect
our diverse cultural, social, political and environmental realities, our
struggles are one . . . Water for life, not for death!
  —Declaration of Curitiba, Affirming the Right to Life and Livelihood
    of People Affected by Dams, the First International Meeting of
    People Affected By Dams, 1997

The history of large dams and affected communities in Southern
Africa has been one of broken promises and incalculable losses . . .
We have been forced to move against our will without knowing when
or where we would be going, and without a way for our concerns or
objections to be heard. We have not been treated with dignity, nor
with respect, for our customs, our ancestors or our children. We have
shouldered the burden of large dams, but we have enjoyed very few
of the benefits. In short, large dams have been devastating to many of
our communities.
  —Voices of Affected Communities, Southern African Hearings' Final
    Declaration, 1999

Introduction

National strategies for economic development commonly employ infrastructure projects that include mega-dams, hydroelectric power, and, as our case captures, international trade in water or "white gold," as it is known in Lesotho.[1] Water development, however, is not without contention or consequence. Once erected, large dams conceal the modernist policies, violent practices, and local sacrifices that make these projects possible. Time and resources are dedicated to ensure that the narrative justifications for these projects ultimately erase the messy complications of lived social engineering that takes place in the communities of those who are displaced, dispossessed, and disrupted—individually and collectively—by large-scale dams.

As the significant social and environmental consequences of dams are justified through national development, these communities become part of the myth of "local pain for national gain" (Roy 2002). Large-scale dam projects are almost without exception sited in poor, rural, and politically, ethnically, or socially marginalized communities, ironically structuring the "local pain" to disproportionately affect already disempowered populations.

In recent decades, threats of environmental injustice by mega-dam projects have moved communities to organize politically and strategically align with transnational environmental and human rights organizations, constituting a global antidam movement and a site for global counternarratives to large dam building. Communities affected by large dams constitute part of a "global assemblage" (Ong and Collier 2005), drawn together across vast physical and social distances in an identity of shared experience that elevates their seemingly local experiences to global concerns. Transnational advocacy networks (Keck and Sikkink 1998) prove critical to making connections among these communities, linking their shared concerns and experiences via issue-based campaigns. The uniquely long-term nature of mega-dam projects, and the development of infrastructure associated with them, creates opportunities for sustained contention and networking against those projects. Specific organizations within these networks, such as International Rivers (IR), mobilize constituents from China and Brazil to India and Lesotho who engage in multiyear struggles.

The experiences and discourses of activists globally, however, may not resonate similarly in their home nations. The participants in these new global assemblages remain embedded in nation-states and historical contexts that exert considerable influence on political framing and strategies. Following Bickham Mendez's call for the "analysis of the power relations that occur within transnational organizing initiatives" (2002, 139), our case highlights how power differentials shape access to and control over information and framing efforts, critical resources within "transnationalism from below" (Smith and Guarnizo 1998). Even as these new global forms and the resistance they symbolize and embody are celebrated, we caution that it remains important to consider how activists negotiate the power differences that contour global, regional, and local political landscapes.

This chapter explores the limits, tensions, and possibilities of cross-border organizing using the case of International Rivers and the local struggle of activists in Lesotho challenging a mega-dam water scheme, the Lesotho Highlands Water Project (LHWP).[2] This is not a comprehensive examination of the global movement, but rather a locally-focused analysis in which we privilege the perspective of one local NGO, the Highlands Church Action Group (HCAG), constituted by Basotho activists who see themselves as working on behalf of communities affected by the LHWP and not necessarily as global or antidam activists. Like the women garment assembly (*maquilas*) workers organizing transnationally in Central America (Bickham Mendez 2002), Basotho activists employ a type of "self-limiting radicalism" (Cohen and Arato 1992) that seeks to work with the institutions implementing the mega-scheme (the World Bank, the Lesotho Highlands Development Authority, the state) to improve conditions for people directly affected, in contrast to the more radical, ideological opposition to large dams espoused by International Rivers. Despite these differences, they do cross borders and actively collaborate with, receive material support from, and attend sponsored conferences in Brazil, Washington, DC, and elsewhere as part of a larger movement. These local activists acknowledge the power of their global encounters and their own transformations in the process. We problematize these encounters, juxtaposing the actions and claims of one local advocacy organization with those of their international ally advocating an end to large dam projects around the world.

This case study illustrates how local activists, in the process of forging alliances, are compelled to work with the expectations of their transnational allies with the hope of amplifying their local concerns. Yet this privileging of transnational allies in the uneasy fusion of a global assemblage of advocates for "rivers and rights" left key concerns and understandings at the local level unaddressed and unheard. Our analysis addresses the intersections of local and global identities in a social movement context, where a "boomerang pattern" potentially helps transnational allies boost local demands. As activists pursue this boomerang pattern, however, there is a risk of privileging the interpretations and identities of transnational allies, potentially leading to "border distortions"—rooted in failures to bridge social movement frames across structural chasms, from local to transnational advocacy networks—which can erode the resonance and strategic communication needed for the boomerang's full force to be effectively implemented.

Before turning to our case study, we provide context for our analysis by describing transnational initiatives to resist mega-dam construction and the frames that they have used to advocate their cause. We then go on to present a theoretical framework for analyzing our case, drawing from social movement theory as well as scholarship on global assemblages and transnational advocacy networks. After providing background information about the Lesotho Highlands Water Project, the target of HCAG's and IR's actions, we present the case of transnational advocacy efforts to oppose mega-dam projects in Lesotho.

Theoretical Background: Global Assemblages, Boomerang Strategies, and Frame-Bridging in Oppositions to Mega-Dam Projects

Local struggles against large-scale water and dam development projects have multiplied as World Bank and national development agencies incorporate neoliberal prescriptions to generate hydroelectric infrastructures and commodify water for domestic and international trade. Local struggles against the social displacements and ecological havoc of these massive dams, once isolated within nations—as witnessed in the numerous early and mid-twentieth-century conflicts over several dam projects—are increasingly linked via transnational advocacy networks as Khagram documents in the case of the Narmada Dam in India (2004). Organizations like International Rivers "helped build an international movement of dam-affected people, social movements, NGOs and academics who work to stop destructive dams and protect rivers and rights" (International Rivers 2011a).

Hosting conferences that link activists, ecologists, and donors, groups like International Rivers forge the spaces and networks for discursively constructing communities that transcend the local-global dichotomy, making it possible to frame rivers and rights as global. The collective of rivers and rights advocates comprise organizations from every continent and sponsor spaces for assembly at conferences, on the web, in reports, and at public demonstrations. Together, identities and networks in this global assemblage give a transnational or global context to struggles within national borders, constructing a global form set in interactive space with, for example, the World Commission on Dams, national governments, and active publics.

Global assemblages are "domains in which the forms and values of individual and collective existence are problematized or at stake, in the sense that they are subject to technological, political, and ethical reflection and intervention" (Ong and Collier 2005, 4). Extending the concept of global assemblages to the oppositional, knowledge-framing work of rivers and rights advocacy turns our attention to the symbolic and discursive, as well as "material, collective and discursive relationships" that transform the multiplicity of local movements against dams into a global form (Ong and Collier 2005, 4). In our analysis, activists and transnational advocacy networks (TANs) and their work are constituent parts of the global assemblage. Yet the assemblage also captures the social and cultural consequences of overlapping networks and an emergent collective identity across and between networks that ultimately produce a sum greater than its parts. The assemblage reflects not just a single advocacy campaign or issue network, but overlapping campaigns and actors; it is not limited to direct relationships within transnational advocacy networks but rather constitutes the cumulative expressions and actions of advocates; the interstitial spaces between networks, organizations, and experts; and challenges the ethics of dam-building at particular sites and as development solutions globally.

The global assemblage is a bounded space within which conversations and contestations can occur as nonhegemonic actors work to shape a discussion on global affairs, such as water and development, and to give global form and voice to these actors who must engage at local and transnational levels with global development agencies and divergent normative frameworks. Khagram demonstrates how transnationally allied opposition to big dams "had to challenge the taken-for-granted equivalence between big dams and development partly by critiquing the vision of development that legitimated these projects" (2004, 211). TANs, such as the one in our case, participate in that space by engaging and problematizing hegemonic discourses on dams as development, bringing in a discourse of rivers and rights from multiple geographies and melding environmental and human rights concerns in a new global form. Specific organizations within a TAN may also take part in the assemblage, as the configuration of an assemblage allows a multiplicity of organizational forms. These may include movement organizations as well as less politicized nongovernment organizations.

This global form is rife with shifts, mutations, and enduring patterns reflecting both conflict and continuity across spaces of the assemblage (Collier 2006). Actors participating in and constituting an assemblage struggle to bring voice and legitimacy to their specific concerns, and the "various actors involved in these novel forms of transnational action are themselves altered over time" (Khagram 2004, 212). While Khagram does not use the term "global assemblage," his work depicts the novel form of transnational action in the struggle over big dams and debates over development as one "in which agents and structures (re)shape dynamics of development across multiple contexts and levels" (212), and this is consistent with our conceptualization of rivers and rights advocacy within the global assemblage. Khagram found that the relationships within and across these contexts and levels were still shaped by privilege and scale, as well as material, collective, and discursive influences:

> While much of the moral authority of transnationally allied contestation was based on representing dam-affected peoples, positions and tactics were often articulated by nongovernmental organizations and individuals that were not linked directly or clearly accountable to dam-affected

peoples. More resource-endowed nongovernmental organizations tended to be much more influential in shaping campaign strategies and gaining access to decision makers. This asymmetry was exacerbated because procedures for ensuring that the perspectives of allied groups were given equal weight and mechanisms for resolving differences between different groups remained underdeveloped. (2004, 209–10)

Local actors face tensions as they work with resource-rich organizations rooted in the global North and with the larger assemblage, including other local campaigns against dam-development in the global South. To explore these tensions, we build on Khagram's work and borrow the concept of global assemblage to analyze the complex, asymmetrical relationships as they unfold in the border-crossings by advocates for rivers and rights who specifically unearth contradictory visions around dams, water, and development. We argue that in doing the work of penetrating the space of this global form, shaping it, and positioning within it, distortions occur that reflect the privileging of the interests or frames of more powerful transnational social movement organization (TSMO) over those of their local allies. Local actors may not have the same ability to access directly the range or depth of resources of the assemblage at the global level, or they may be more directly responsible or responsive to national contexts than transnational allies.

We term the disjunctures and failed attempts at successfully enacting the boomerang strategy "border distortions," as the concept draws attention to both scale and privilege within transnational advocacy work across the spaces of the assemblage. Semiporous national borders allow for the mediation of identity and practices, however constrained, but hold uneven opportunities and risks for differentially located communities within the assemblage. Those territorialized within the confines of political borders experience greater risks than activists from transnational organizations who are removed from the on-the-ground experiences and local consequences of their political engagements.

For example, individual TSMOs and larger TANs may contribute to border distortions by neglecting the authenticity of claims at the local level in order to provide greater congruity with their transnational movement identity and their positioning across the global assemblage, thereby distorting the framing of local issues in favor of interpretations issued by more powerful and privileged members of the TAN. In addition to border distortion, the concept of frame-bridging, taken from social movement theory, further illuminates the tensions across the bordered spaces of this assemblage.

Frame-Bridging and Border Distortions

Widely used in social movement theory to make sense of the discursive and symbolic practices of social movements, the concept of frames refers to "an interpretive schema that simplifies and condenses the 'world out there' by selectively punctuating and encoding objects, situations, events, experiences, and sequences of actions within one's present or past environment." Frames thus function "as modes of attribution and articulation" (Snow and Benford 1992, 137). For successful framing to occur in which public support is garnered for the movement's cause, activists and social movement organizations must discursively construct a "diagnostic frame," which attribute causes to the threat that they describe (e.g., dams, forced relocations). "Prognostic frames" articulate a course of change that will remedy their grievances (e.g., stop the dams, just compensation for land). As our case illustrates, both local and international activists approached the LHWP with differing interpretive schemas rooted in very different social contexts. For local activists, constructing a diagnostic frame relied on narratives from displaced peoples, the experiences of working with corrupt national and international agencies involved in the dam project,[3] failures on the part of officials to honor compensation commitments, and more. Their transnational social movement allies, particularly the group International Rivers, work within an interpretive schema rooted in a preservationist, environmental identity forged within transnational legal, symbolic, and alliance-building networks that mobilized to oppose large dam projects. As a result, the framing practices of the two groups required frame-bridging activity—the work of linking ideologically similar but structurally distinct frames to a single, common issue (Snow, Rochford, Worden, and Benford 1986).

Frame-bridging work within the rivers and rights assemblage unfolds as people cross borders, attend conferences, meet other activists at the site of struggle, and communicate via faxes, phones, and e-mails.

These emergent networks—sometimes involving years of building connections and sharing perspectives—set the stage for the dynamic and,
at times, tense character of the global assemblage. Indeed, rivers and
rights advocacy takes shape through discursive practices forged in a
multiplicity of struggles, creating and at times resolving tensions in distinct conflicts associated with the wide array of bordered spaces within
the assemblage. Born out of interactive dialogues across the assemblage,
frame-bridging was successful in some instances and at other times fell
short of resulting in alignment. Failure to bridge frames across borders
within the assemblage diminished the potential for frame alignment
and the ability to cultivate shared identities, hindering forms of resistance available to a global assemblage.[4] The tensions revealed in our
case demonstrate that framing practices and local activists' concerns
are not always aligned with the mission of their primary transnational
ally, and in one case activists faced real risk as a result. We suggest that
these border distortions occur when efforts at frame-bridging encounter practices that privilege transnational identities and priorities. At the
transnational scale, as opposed to the local or national level, actions can
easily boost or diminish local concerns. For this reason, actors operat-
ing transnationally enjoy the privilege of voice across the assemblage,
which may constrain or empower local actors. Attention to privilege
and scale is necessary to grasp the potential for border distortions. In
our case, this dynamic is visibly apparent as activists attempted to acti-
vate what Keck and Sikkink (1998) term the "boomerang effect."

Boomerang Patterns and Transnational Environmentalism

Keck and Sikkink's widely applied concept of the boomerang effect
provides a useful framework for understanding how local activists target intransigent state elite via alliances with transnational advocacy
networks. Transnational organizations and activists then amplify or
leverage the demands of local actors in a transnational context, contributing to social change initiatives. As Keck and Sikkink point out,
"Where governments are unresponsive to groups whose claims may
none the less resonate elsewhere, international contacts can 'amplify'
the demands of domestic groups, pry open space for new issues, and
then echo these demands back into the domestic arena" (1999, 93).

Where domestic political opportunities are closed, activists and advocates can enlist this boomerang pattern to achieve outside pressure on their national government or international agency (both, in our case). Demands to enforce laws and policies or implement reforms are, theoretically, channeled through the local to the "transnational advocacy network" (TAN) and then back to states or other agencies (Keck and Sikkink 1998). TANs can help local actors achieve the goals by engaging in four interrelated types of politics (information, symbolic, leverage, and accountability) that can be combined in overlapping manners during the course of a campaign (ibid.).

Building on this conceptual framework, our study problematizes and explains the unequal linkages and framing priorities between local activists in the Highlands Church Action Group (HCAG) and International Rivers (IR), specifically outlining a case where the boomerang initiated by local activists did not return in the form imagined. Using this concept we examine rural Lesotho, in a space where global development authorities, working with national elite, restructure, usurp, and flood agricultural lands and villages while creating few means for grievances and justice to be expressed and heard.

As our case and others (Smith 2008; Tarrow 2005) demonstrate, the selective coupling of local activist groups to transnational social movement organizations (TSMOs) and advocacy networks involves a fusion of both organizational and discursive practices. Material support from TSMOs helps establish communication and organizational networks while the participation of TSMOs in local struggles affirms the identity of the organization, bringing symbolic resources that the TSMO uses to expand its own work, augmenting legitimacy, and supporting appeals for financial contributions from constituents and donors. This dynamic of alliance building and identity transformation was clearly visible in the struggle for justice in Lesotho, even amid a failure to *amplify* local concerns when there is limited frame-bridging.

While conceptual ties between the boomerang and global assemblage are not made elsewhere, we invoke both concepts to establish the role of strategic action on the part of actual and potential members of an assemblage. We prefer this conceptual association over the transnational advocacy network concept because the actual work of linking local and global advocates for rivers and rights generates a cultural and organizational network that transcends the dualistic terms of local and global, creating a collective greater than the sum of its parts. The assemblage concept captures the sense of an emergent whole, a form that possesses both local and global features in a dynamic though bordered whole, in which nonhegemonic actors work to shape the conversation and contestation over global affairs—in our case, large dams as development.

Transnational activists generally occupy structural and symbolic positions, relative to local, nation-state bound activists who are privileged in terms of resources and centrality in the networks that give the assemblage form. We argue that this is in part due to unequal conditions across zones of the assemblage, inequalities that arise from two dynamics within the assemblage: a privileging of environmental preservationism from the global North over a variant of environmental justice in the global South, and a structural imbalance arising from financial differences and power disparities across North and South, differences that both reflect and define the strategic privileging of the boomerang pattern.

Unequal Discourses in the Assemblage

Two similar but structurally distinct frames are illustrated in this study: one located in a local environmental justice struggle, and one constructed as a global strategy to preserve the world's rivers. Both are structured with familiar environmentalist themes, one with parallels to an environmental justice frame (see Capek 1993 and Taylor 2000) and the other squarely within global environmental preservationism. The historical characteristics of both frames and suggested correspondence with the two organizations are discussed more fully in the following sections.

Our case illustrates how the Highlands Church Action Group's (HCAG) challenge to the LHWP within Lesotho expressed deep concern about fair compensation for people dispossessed of land as well as for very local principles of ecology associated with food, water access, and more (see Braun 2008). These concerns have striking parallels with what Dorceta Taylor defines as the "environmental justice paradigm" (2000). Alternatively, the HCAG's global ally International

Rivers diagnostically framed dams as environmentally harmful to rivers and riverine systems, rooted in preservationist ideals and Western conceptions of "the wild" (see Nash 1982), usually devoid of concern for human needs and communities. Like many other international preservationist groups, their environmental frames fit within a larger "new environmental paradigm" (NEP) constructed in opposition to the "exploitive capitalist paradigm" (Taylor 2000). Elements of HCAG's framing speak to principles of fair and responsible access to shared resources, to autonomy for local villages and communities, and to other social and environmental principles that correspond to the environmental justice paradigm. This environmental justice paradigm, Taylor argues, builds from the prevailing models of environmentalism found in the new environmental paradigm and has challenged the dominance of the NEP within environmentalism in recent decades. These framing challenges over dam-development in Lesotho thus correspond to larger frame conflicts and transformations in environmentalism over the last several decades.

During the 1980s, several large American and European environmental groups expanded their politics to include the emerging issues of rainforest deforestation, climate change, and species extinction. Their strategy, while based in moral and symbolic appeals to constituents in the global North, sought to influence not only governments in the global North, but United Nations' institutions and governments in the global South, especially evident in the first Earth Summit in Rio in 1992 (UN Conference on Environment and Development). The preservationist ideology of many of these groups was initially devoid of a discourse on human justice or the rights of human communities who inhabited the forests, riverine systems, or coastal areas impacted by major development projects. It took the confluence of environmental justice movements in the global north and the expansion of indigenous struggles for both environmental and human rights to transform the terms and discourse of global environmental advocacy (see Davidson 1993; Niezen 2003). Indeed, unlike preservationist efforts to maintain *distance* between social issues and nonhuman nature (Gottlieb 1993), the environmental justice movement "does not treat the problem of oppression and social exploitation as separable from the rape and exploitation of the natural world" (Taylor 1993, 57). By the late 1990s, many of the international environmental organizations, such as Rainforest Action, Greenpeace, Friends of the Earth, and the organization in our case, International Rivers, began framing their work not only in terms of environmental preservation or antitoxics, but also in terms of human rights and environmental justice (Doherty and Doyle 2008).

Environmental movement organizations whose focus was on the new global environmental politics aimed to bridge these concerns and to forge transnational advocacy networks based on an international or global identity. Credibility for this identity-claim thus required legitimate connections to local struggles across regions of the world. Like many other environmental groups during the 1990s, International Rivers developed connections with local activists involved in development conflicts over dams and rivers. The networks forged in these struggles established the basis for a global assemblage identity with connections, even if transient, to people along the Narmada ("Save the Narmada" campaign), the Mekong, and other major river systems. These connections provided legitimacy and evidence of organizational efficacy to major donors and granting agencies that support the environmental claims of a new global mission and, no doubt, reflected some level of activist reflexivity in reshaping the IR's mission around a new politics of environmentalism and human rights. The struggles in Lesotho entered the historical stage in this context of environmentalism and the politics of development.

Forging a global assemblage across borders and cultures, environmental groups like International Rivers pursued a strategy to foster "grassroots organizations in more than 60 countries and promote the leadership of . . . regional partners by providing technical and strategic advice, and bringing them together at international meetings" (International Rivers 2011a). Relying on the strategic leverage of linked communities across the globe, IR reproduces an international identity that both provides critical connectivity to disparate contexts and, as a hub in the network, claims a privileged voice concerning rivers and the people who live near them. Yet the new environmental advocacy networks remain rooted in Northern environmentalism, with discourses shaped by a century of preservationism within the new environmental paradigm. These framing practices played a role in activist understandings and the political strategies used by HCAG and International Rivers in the fight over the LHWP.

Transnational social movement organizations are most often embedded in established networks that include funding relationships, framing and identity appeals, and activists committed to existing aims of the organization. While building alliances with local groups is often consistent with the mission of transnational organizations, guarantees of parity in concerns and claims between the local and transnational organizations are not. As Bickham Mendez (2002, 139) points out, knowing who controls information in these transnational political initiatives is imperative to understanding the power differentials that shape these efforts. As our case illustrates, activists in Lesotho who challenged the thirty-year project to sell "white gold" to South Africa faced very different risks than the quasi-borderless organizers and personnel affiliated with their transnational allies. Together, the varied context of social movement organization and identity resulted in framing challenges for activists that negatively affected the potential impacts of the boomerang strategy.

The Lesotho Highlands Water Project

Lesotho is a small, mountainous, landlocked country surrounded by South Africa on all borders. With a population of two million people, over 80 percent of the Basotho population lives in rural areas using gendered livelihood strategies that rely on agriculture, livestock farming, wage labor, and informal economic activities (Epprecht 2000). Historically, Lesotho conforms to a classic model of a dual economy, with a primary subsistence sector in the rural regions of the country and a secondary migratory labor reserve economy dependent on South Africa's mining and industrial sector. The villages in the very remote and rural highlands areas are some of the poorest in Lesotho, which is one of the poorest countries in the world. While conditions within specific villages vary, generally speaking, remote highlands communities affected by the LHWP share in common extreme poverty—the absence of modern infrastructure such as electricity, running water, and plumbing, and limited paved roads. Over 50 percent of the total population currently lives below the international poverty line of less than US$1.25 a day.

Lesotho's categorization as perpetually poor within international development circles in the early to mid-1980s (Ferguson 1994) no doubt

allowed the development priorities of international agencies, particularly the World Bank, to overshadow the government of Lesotho. At the
time, the rise of neoliberal models of markets and development initiated a wave of structural adjustment policies by the International Monetary Fund (IMF) and national and regional development agendas that
stressed export-oriented paths to development. In Lesotho, this neoliberal, export-oriented vision was articulated as marketing "white gold,"
or water, to South Africa through the Lesotho Highlands Water Project
(LHWP).

The LHWP is a water delivery scheme between the governments of
South Africa and Lesotho that will eventually include five dams linked
to cross-national tunnels constructed in four phases over a period of
thirty years (1987–2017). Based on a 1986 agreement called the Treaty
on the LHWP between the Government of the Kingdom of Lesotho and
the Government of the Republic of South Africa, the primary objec-
tive of this $8 billion World Bank project is to sell, transfer, and deliver
water from rural Lesotho to urban South Africa (Lesotho Highlands
Development Authority [LHDA] 1986).

The LHWP mega-project became the symbol of Lesotho's long-term
national development plans for economic growth and human development and, according to the economistic visions of World Bank consul-
tants, the best path to the much-needed promise of neoliberal development in Lesotho (Braun 2011a). Because neoliberalism promotes an
extension of markets, the valorization of property rights, and a privatization of public resources, political rights are diminished while market
rights are elevated. With an emphasis on GDP growth and large-scale
infrastructure development to export water to South Africa, the military government of Lesotho fused nationalistic and traditional patriarchal idioms with neoliberalism. For local people affected by the LHWP,
their lived experience of development often entailed displacement and
dispossession of their homes and livelihoods (Braun 2011b). Development authorities mitigated these losses using a system of compensation
fraught with complications and challenges, resulting in grievances filed
by people directly affected and local organizations working on their
behalf.

Despite environmental and social justice critiques of neoliberal
development that helped expose the rift between the promises of

market-led development and the retrenching of state social policies, critiques of this mega-dam project were treated as an affront to
the principles of development by national authorities. Local activists challenged the disjunctures in Lesotho while seeking strategies
to amplify their concerns about justice beyond an intransigent state.
Our case study that follows illustrates the tensions and opportunities
involved in working within and across global and national political
landscapes.

Border Distortions: Dam-Affected Communities, Transnational Alliances, and the Global Assemblage

HCAG Meets IR: Becoming Part of the Assemblage

In the early years of LHWP construction, church ministers in the proposed Katse Dam area were overwhelmed with project-related grievances from local people in communities directly affected. They organized the Highlands Church Action Group (HCAG) in 1988 to deal
with rising concerns about the unfolding social and environmental
consequences, particularly problems related to losses and compensation. HCAG quickly became the primary grassroots advocacy group
for people affected by the LHWP, particularly in its early years. Their
work was largely defined by local needs and, consistent with environmental justice frames, they sought justice through advocacy for the
poor who were absorbing the disproportionate costs of LHWP national
development.

By the mid-1990s, HCAG had a full-time coordinator located in
the capital city, Maseru, and three community-based fieldworkers, one
assigned to each of three remote dam areas involved in Phase I of the
LHWP. HCAG's fieldworkers, who were from families directly affected
by the LHWP, collected information and advocated grievances for those
unable to write for themselves or for those who simply did not understand the complex process of challenging the development authority. In challenging the LHDA, and by extension the state, HCAG was
viewed as being a "thorn in their side," as "troublemakers" for "teaching the people how to complain" (interview, executive LHDA officer,
1997). Despite the staff resources, HCAG was largely known to be working on a shoestring budget, and their dedicated fieldworkers were often

working without pay for long periods of time. Facing an intransigent state and consistent financial struggles, there were always questions of whether and for how long the small organization would be viable.[5]

Consistent with expectations from social movement scholarship, one of the strategies HCAG used to stay viable and to leverage their message against an intransigent state was to engage in border-crossing politics, creating alliances with transnational social movement organizations (TSMOs) who might support and amplify their concerns (Braun and Dreiling 2010). HCAG was successful in making international allies who provided them with financial and technical resources, such as a fax machine and computer in 1997. These resources supported HCAG's advocacy capabilities locally and globally and facilitated more efficient communication with transnational allies. The Coordinator of HCAG remarked that these resources lent them greater credibility in their dealings with the development authority and government, and they remained hopeful that continued transnational alliances would eventually translate more directly to advancing their concerns about grievances and justice.

One of their primary transnational allies was the International Rivers (IR) based in Berkeley, California, and Washington, DC. As a preservationist environmental organization located in the global North, IR works globally to protect riverine systems and to support people affected by what it labels "destructive large-scale river development." IR's advocacy for rivers and rights cuts across borders, requiring legitimate connections with organizations in bordered local struggles in different regions of the world. To do so, IR organizes multiyear campaigns that discourage investment in large dams, foster mobilization of local communities in opposition to the dams, and challenge the institutions and industries that promote and benefit from these development strategies, such as the World Bank and the dam-building industry. Working with local organizations such as HCAG, IR claims to have formed a coalition of "environment, development, human rights, and grassroots groups around the world" that is attempting to organize "cooperative campaigns for community-based development" (International Rivers Network 1996).

Ideologically IR's mission can be understood as preservationist, and their mission is largely supported by major liberal-leaning foundations and funds for the environment and human rights. Unlike the Highlands Church Action Group, IR opposed all large dams due to the environmental and social consequences of their construction. Its work has effectively publicized the terms and effects of large dam projects to wider, global audiences, making the organization a central actor in the emerging global antidam movement (McCully 2001). IR's global networking has garnered it "power of voice" (Johnston 1994) with international development institutions, even if dam builders perceive its opposition to large dams critically as ideological and radical.

In Lesotho, IR supported HCAG's local advocacy efforts with financial, technical, and information resources, and HCAG supported IR with a local campaign that gave credibility and support to IR's mission. However, the disjuncture between HCAG's local emphasis on environmental justice for affected communities and IR's global opposition to large dam projects created an uneasy alliance at times. HCAG privileged concerns about justice related to the LHWP, while IR viewed its work in Lesotho through the lens of a global movement's diagnostic frame. Despite the allied activists' shared concerns about the LHWP, differences in framing and uneven abilities in claims-making in the international arena posed certain risks and opportunities. When HCAG metaphorically threw the boomerang to leverage its claims with the support of international allies, members encountered some risk that their concerns would be marginalized under the privileged frame of transnational actors in the global antidam movement. Our case demonstrates how the boomerang does not always come back in the way that local organization may imagine. And the case suggests the difficulties—and necessities—of frame-bridging between local, bordered, environmental justice struggles and transnational, preservationist organizations working across borders.

From the Mountains of Lesotho to a Global Assemblage: Tensions in Framing and Identity

Despite overlapping, though distinct, diagnostic and prognostic frames, HCAG and IR created an alliance to advance their shared and individual concerns in the face of a constellation of intransigent national authorities and global development institutions. Global networking was one aspect of this alliance, whereby IR facilitated HCAG's connections with other allied organizations and communities around the world that have been affected by large dam projects. Such global networking functioned not only as a frame-bridging strategy but also as an effort to foster a new collective identity among HCAG staff, one consistent with rivers and rights advocacy within the global assemblage.

One example of this networking involved IR's arranging for and providing funding for one HCAG fieldworker to travel internationally for political organizing and participation in the rivers and rights advocacy network. The first trip was to Washington, DC, where the HCAG fieldworker, Peter, was asked to speak about local people's experiences with the LHWP on a panel with other organizations working in the anti-dam and environmental movements. In my interviews months afterward with Peter and the HCAG coordinator, 'Mathebiso, they discussed their ongoing ambivalence regarding going to Washington. They were grateful for the opportunity to voice the experiences of Basotho affected by the LHWP to a wider audience of sympathetic activists, and they saw this as an amplification of the advocacy work they were doing. However, they also felt uncertain about the implications of their participation, seeing themselves primarily as a local advocacy organization fighting environmental justice and not part of a larger social movement against dams.

The second IR-funded trip was to Curitiba, Brazil, for the First International Meeting of People Affected by Dams (1997). Delegates from 20 countries authored and signed the Declaration of Curitiba: Affirming the Right to Life and Livelihood of People Affected by Dams (hereafter Declaration of Curitiba). This declaration acknowledged the patterns of social and environmental injustice on affected communities, critiqued the dam-building industry, listed the demands of affected communities, and proposed a vision for more just and sustainable development strategies. The statement was also pointedly against dams:

> We are strong, diverse and united and our cause is just. We have stopped destructive dams and have forced dam builders to respect our rights. We have stopped dams in the past, and we will stop more in the future.
>
> We commit ourselves to intensifying the fight against destructive dams. From the villages of India, Brazil and Lesotho to the boardrooms

of Washington, Tokyo and London, we will force dam builders to accept our demands.

To reinforce our movement we will build and strengthen regional and international networks. To symbolise our growing unity, we declare that 14 March, the Brazilian Day of Struggles Against Dams, will from now on become the International Day of Action Against Dams and for Rivers, Water, and Life.

Water for life, not for death!

—Declaration of Curitiba, 14 March 1997

The delegate from HCAG signed the Declaration, putting Lesotho and the LHWP on the map in terms of the global antidam movement.

According to IR, the Declaration of Curitiba was a significant milestone that forged the solidarity of people around the world affected by dam projects and the dam industry (IRN 1997). In facilitating the connection of HCAG's self-described advocacy work on behalf of villagers affected by the LHWP dams to the experiences of dam-affected communities globally, IR helped shape the construction of a collective identity among HCAG and, by extension, the communities they represented. This mobilizing work can also be understood as frame-bridging, whereby IR sought to foster the politicization and universalization of HCAG's concerns about the LHWP away from a local, environmental justice advocacy frame to a diagnostic frame in line with a broader campaign against large dams and the global antidam movement.

Two months after Curitiba, HCAG faxed this message to IR:

> The experiences shared during the conference about the efforts of Large Dams [sic] on the affected communities, their conditions, damages to their social life, livelihoods, oppression of workers, and intimidations on workers actually confirms issues and fears HCAG has been crying about for the past 8 years in Lesotho. . . . In this end HCAG will continue to support its International Allies [sic] in defending the plight of the common people in the highlands of Lesotho (5 June 1997).

Through global networking, IR and HCAG were able to coproduce new meanings and a sense of collective identity of being dam-affected people in a larger, global struggle of power, development, and democracy as constituted in the global assemblage. But the costs and benefits of this alliance and its meanings are shaped in part by the political landscapes in which they are embedded. For IR, mobilizing a local grassroots organization to align and participate in the global assemblage offers them opportunities for credibility and legitimacy in their global campaign against dams—credibility drawn from on-the-ground connections in local affected communities and legitimacy in campaign materials and dealings with institutions such as the World Bank.

Returning to Lesotho: Bordered Risks and
Contradictions across the Assemblage

For HCAG, the political landscape of the global assemblage had different contours. 'Mathebiso described delegates' participation in Curitiba as both "empowering and devastating." She stated that HCAG's participation in these global events helped shape a broadened understanding of its advocacy work, resulting in a new collective identity of shared experience as dam-affected communities despite vast differences in culture, region, ethnicity, and so on. It also importantly validated the legitimacy of their work to themselves, confirming their experiences with the LHWP as part of a global pattern and within a global community that understood and valued their advocacy.

She noted their concerns were also political—the Declaration of Curitiba was a stronger, more oppositional statement to large dams than they had ever endorsed. Despite HCAG activists' longstanding skepticism about the long-term benefits of the LHWP and their increasing resonance with the collective identity of being dam-affected communities, their diagnostic frame remained focused on environmental justice and HCAG members always stopped short of opposing large dams or the LHWP. Returning to Lesotho amidst the global news of their ratification of the Declaration of Curitiba, HCAG participants worried about how this global networking would affect their work in Lesotho, and they had concerns for members' personal safety.

Both of these concerns can be understood through a closer look at the political history and climate in Lesotho that has shaped the tactics and strategies of local organizations working on LHWP-related issues. The transnational water scheme was approved and implemented in 1986 by a repressive military regime in Lesotho in collaboration with the apartheid regime of South Africa. Both countries elected democratic administrations in the early 1990s, but the LHWP was unequivocally supported by both new governments. In Lesotho, the mega-project was truly framed as a national project that would fix the country's persistent development ills.

The government and the Lesotho Highlands Development Authority (LHDA) discredited anyone seen as against the LHWP as a traitor, as anti-Lesotho. While HCAG maintained its support for the project publicly, it was targeted as being against the project because of advocacy efforts and legal actions challenging the LHDA on compensation issues. In 1991–1992, HCAG staff members received death threats, and the government accused and temporarily jailed HCAG organizers for treason.

Within this context, HCAG's participation in global political organizing in Washington, DC, and Brazil was potentially very dangerous, particularly the signing of the Declaration of Curitiba in solidarity against all dams. The government successfully used this information to dampen HCAG's efforts at the local level, publicly suggesting in the newspapers that the Brazil conference was politically motivated to overthrow the government. HCAG's ties to the leftist political party in Lesotho made it vulnerable to accusations regarding members' political motivations, and it had to continually challenge delegitimization by the government and LHDA after Curitiba.

In Curitiba, HCAG felt swept up in the power of shared experiences with other dam-affected communities but, returning home, the staff voiced regrets that they had formally signed the Declaration. Yet their daily work was clearly shaped by these shared experiences as evidenced by their consistent empirical challenges, both local and global, to the development authority and government regarding the implementation of the LHWP. HCAG voiced sharp criticism that the costs of large dams outweighed the benefits, but whether because of politics, fear, or difference of opinion, it ultimately never wavered in supporting the LHWP as a project.

These political tensions were especially challenging as activists in TSMOs, like IR, were seemingly unaware or negligent in their understanding of the highly political local context of HCAG and the LHWP within Lesotho. Peter, who attended the meetings in Washington, DC, felt "so much pressure" to denounce the project, but refused to go as far as transnational movement activists wanted. He explained his actions in this way:

> I knew they were upset with me after having had me fly all the way to Washington. But I could not. It sounded right to [denounce the LHWP] as they told me all these things, and knowing all the problems of the project, but I had to come back [to Lesotho] and face whatever I said in Washington. I could be killed for saying that! [laughs] Those people from IRN don't have to come back to Lesotho with me and feel the consequences of that. I would have been killed. (personal interview, 1997)

While it is not certain that Peter would have faced violence in Lesotho for such an action, his feelings are intelligible within a political climate where the state had reacted violently and unilaterally against perceived traitors and specifically HCAG staff in the past. Questioning the ethical or national development promises of LHWP was unacceptable to political leaders in Lesotho. Authorities actively discredited the specific transnational advocacy network and the broader global assemblage using nationalist rhetoric, emphasizing HCAG's participation in Curitiba as constituting a collective identity associated with the diagnostic and prognostic frame of the global antidam movement; one that state and development authorities could cast as ideologically anti-Lesotho.

Analytically, HCAG's ongoing participation reveals a more complicated sense of transnational advocacy work and the global assemblage. It is seductive to see the latter as a unified entity whose shared identity and experience constitute new, solidaristic political spaces. But, as Bandy (2004, 420) argues, "coalition building is very hard work and it frequently fails, especially as it stretches across national borders." This case demonstrates how cross-border organizing within the global assemblage is not uniform, is constituted by uneven linkages, and contains tensions and contours shaped by differences in power, engagement, and scale "that are emblematic of historic divisions in our world-system" (ibid., 420). After Washington and Curitiba, HCAG continued to define itself as an advocacy organization representing the affected communities. The HCAG staff prided themselves not only on providing information and raising awareness, but on listening to people's concerns and staying true to their membership. Their participation in the global critique of dams as development remained influential in shaping their sense of collective identity and their work, but, in the context of their bordered local struggle, tension between the global and local frames created political vulnerability that was successfully leveraged by authorities against the HCAG. Uneven political risks were also associated with a failed boomerang strategy that serves as our second illustration.

Framing Tensions, Failed Boomerang: Uneven Risks in Bordered Political Landscapes

Transnational organizations working across borders with local organizations inevitably engage allies within bordered, political contexts. However, the risks associated with exposure in local political landscapes are experienced unevenly by transnational and local actors. In our second example, the earthquake at Katse Dam and the aftermath, we illustrate how transnational actors may affect the local political landscape but not necessarily in the way that allied organizations imagine. When coupled with an opportunistic development authority or intransigent state, transnational advocacy networks (TANs) might not amplify local concerns; rather, they may effectively create obstacles, damage, or exposure to greater risks for local organizations within their national political sphere.

In 1996, an earthquake rocked the Katse Dam area in the middle of the night. Terrified, people ran from their homes as dishes crashed to the floor, mud walls cracked, and thatched roofs collapsed. Filling Katse Dam, the first of the LHWP and the largest dam in Africa at the time, induced the seismic activity. The weight of the newly forming, massive reservoir created enormous pressure on the earth, shifting its plates and creating deep cracks that ran for miles through this highlands area.

Although reservoir-induced seismicity is not uncommon when catchments begin to fill, the Lesotho Highlands Development Authority (LHDA) did not anticipate, monitor, or communicate this as a possibility to local communities. Villagers claimed that it was wholly unexpected and, as can be imagined, it created tremendous panic and fear. Residents of one village particularly affected by the earthquake,

Ha Mapeleng, were outraged, and most of the community eventually demanded to be resettled further back from the reservoir. According to HCAG, the post-earthquake demands of villagers emphasized concerns regarding safety, shelter, and communication. Compensation for earthquake damages became a necessary aspect of mitigation negotiations.

The earthquake and the failure of the development authority received considerable attention within global networks of antidam activists. IR immediately integrated these events into its Lesotho and global campaign, posting information on the seismic activity on its website and within its networks. International Rivers placed considerable pressure on both the LHDA and the World Bank in the immediate weeks and months afterward, emphasizing that potential seismic activity should have been anticipated, a system of monitoring in place, and communities prepared for such an event.

Consistent with their diagnostic frame, IR focused on this event to demonstrate the failing of the World Bank and the self-serving nature of the dam-development industry. The seismic activity at Katse Dam was framed as an illustration of the dangers of dams, exposing the flawed logic that supports them as safe, long-term development strategies. Unlike HCAG who focused on the rectification of compensation claims specific to local people, IR framed the issue in broad terms emphasizing larger issues of conflicts of interest, scientific neutrality, and mismanagement at the World Bank—framings consistent with IR's identity within the global assemblage, one who opposes large dams as development solutions. Ultimately IR argued for the LHWP to be halted.

However, IR made some significant factual errors in their reporting of the event and the immediate aftermath, creating challenges for HCAG in carrying out its advocacy work locally. IR released reports that inflated the effects of the earthquake and were used to increase their pressure on the World Bank and LHDA.[6] The World Bank, embarrassed by the events and by IR, pressured the LHDA to manage the situation. LHDA responded by constricting communication with local NGOs, particularly HCAG, whom it saw as responsible for feeding misinformation to the IR. The development authority justified placing a moratorium on information sharing with local advocacy groups as it claimed that the misinformation given to international NGOs was causing harm and disrupting their ability to manage the LHWP.

The imperative of IR to get maximum publicity for events that heighten the potency of its frame, coupled with nondemocratic responses from opportunistic development authorities, generated justification for those in power to shut down communications locally. Within the bordered political struggle around the LHWP, HCAG was suddenly very limited in its ability to gather information from the development authority in regard to the earthquake aftermath, resettlement, or grievances filed on behalf of affected people.

HCAG fieldworkers reported frustration with the apparent zealousness of their international allies who seemed not to understand or care enough about the political climate in Lesotho. The political ramifications of their actions locally seemed not to be a concern, creating a real disjuncture between the agenda of transnational and local organizations. Local grassroots organizations, such as HCAG, can cast the boomerang with hopes of having their contextualized concerns amplified; however, the boomerang may not always come back, and their voices and issues become repositioned to support the privileged frame of more powerful global NGOS instead. Even as they collaborated with HCAG on many shared objectives, IR privileged the diagnostic frame that drives its global agenda, seeing events and information through that prism even at the expense of local voices and interests. The example of reservoir-induced seismicity not only illustrates how the boomerang may not come back, but also how uneven relationships within global alliances may result in adverse effects from border distortions—in this case, confining a local organization's sphere of influence and access to its own national borders.

Border distortions represent the misalignment of and failure to bridge frames, revealing the uneven power relations that shape decisions within cross-border coalitions and organizing, and, perhaps, the unreflexive distancing, underestimating or misunderstanding of local concerns and experiences by more privileged members of transnational advocacy networks within the global assemblage. These border distortions complicate transnational organizing and, importantly, they might also create opportunities for state repression or countermovements. Despite initiatives to build coalitions, countermovements— such as government efforts to protect their investments in large-scale development—can use their considerable resources to fracture and demobilize international solidarity (Bandy 2004), escalating potential conflicts between local and transnational allies. Border distortions demonstrate a tragic irony embedded in the boomerang strategy, particularly amplified when the boomerang fails: unequal power relations structure the utility, indeed the hopefulness, of the boomerang strategy, creating the possibility of reaching beyond a repressive, closed system to gain the aid of privileged, cross-border allies and the power they wield. Yet the unevenness of these transnational relations pose risks as well, as the least powerful members of these cross-border coalitions can lose control of information or suffer the sometimes adverse local consequences of transnational advocacy work on their behalf (Bickham Mendez 2002).

Discussion and Conclusion

Facing closed or repressive political systems within national or local political systems, activists increasingly seek allies across borders, reaching outside of countries or nations to burgeoning transnational advocacy networks. From the rural, mountainous regions of Lesotho in Southern Africa, activists alarmed by the intransigence of local and national governments, as well as the international agencies working on the development of the mega-dam LHWP, sought alliances and support from a transnational ally, the IR.

Social movement challenges to state-initiated dam projects sprinkle the histories of national development and environmental politics and have until recently been confined to local or national politics. This chapter has illuminated the contested dynamics of large-scale dam projects that cross borders, forging the cultural and networked spaces of rivers and rights advocacy within a global assemblage challenging hegemonic discourses regarding large dams as development solutions. Our case has explored the intersections of a local struggle in the mountains of Lesotho and a transnational social movement organization, International Rivers, with roots in the global North that spans borders as an advocate for rivers and dam-affected people. The interactive struggle, from local to transnational, produces tensions and transformations, we argue, in the manner that activists and organizations construct oppositional, social movement frames within a larger strategic effort to leverage what Keck and Sikkink (1998) refer to as a boomerang effect.

This chapter has unraveled a puzzling disjuncture between the actions and identities of the two groups working in Lesotho, Southern Africa. Facing a constellation of intransigent national authorities and global development institutions, the two groups allied to advance concerns—some overlapping and some distinct to each group—related to one of the largest water development and dam projects in the world. Over the course of several years, these IR and HCAG activists participated in and expanded relations among local activists from several regions of the world, forging an assemblage committed to challenging hegemonic narratives about large dams and development. Several elements of the case suggest that the claims and identities of activists working across borders are not a straightforward process. Forging the discursive communities of a global, oppositional assemblage involves frame-bridging practices by social movement actors who occupy very different and unequal positions. This puzzle reveals an otherwise-unexamined contradiction within the boomerang strategy, one that can have the unintended effect of privileging transnational identities and claims, making the work of frame-bridging between local and global identities difficult, while stifling the critical border crossings that are needed to amplify and boost local demands via the leverage of transnational linkages. The failure to bridge social movement frames and align movement identities can contribute to failure of the boomerang pattern and further marginalize the claims of local activists, something we term "border distortions."

On the whole, the boomerang strategy is structured on unequal relationships, which include tensions and conflicts, and often reflects the realities of Southern activists working in closed, repressive systems. The very hope of using the boomerang strategy and finding transnational allies exposes the closed political systems in which local activists are working and that are not likely to be shared by transnational actors. This provides opportunities for amplification, as demonstrated by Keck and Sikkink, and the growing body of work on boomerang and transnational alliances. But within the boomerang pattern, there are also contradictory potentials for failure, not just amplification, as privilege and scale shape relationships and practices within and across advocacy networks and the global assemblage.

What Keck and Sikkink do not capture are the possibilities that transnational advocates are not likely to have full clarity or full resonance with the realities of the circumscribed political activities at the local level, creating potential for tensions and conflicts in frame-bridging and claim-forming processes among global, transnational, and local activists working within national, bordered struggles in the Global South. In our case, IR provided HCAG with important technical and material resources and expertise. Moreover, the network linked local activists to a global social movement for social and environmental justice. The extant diagnostic and prognostic frames, with a larger preservationist environmental identity associated with the global North, limited approaches to frame innovation and transformation that would effectively link and amplify local concerns and instead reproduced uneven relationships within the transnational advocacy network. As the TSMO worked to shape the conversation about dams and development within the global assemblage, transnational actors privileged the frames consistent with their transnational identity as antidam activists and, in the process, risked producing border distortions that usurped local concerns of human rights and environmental justice.

In these illustrations, we are sympathetic to both ends of this complex alliance. We are not saying we should expect infinite malleability from transnational actors in global political spaces, nor are we suggesting that local activists should bend to the priorities of transnational actors. Rather, if there is a normative lesson, we suggest that transnational allies need to exercise a deepening sensitivity toward the constraints local activists face. Power differentials within the axes of these relations create inequalities despite good or noble intentions, and the nuances of these differences may not always be clear or readily visible to those largely working outside the bordered political landscape. It is imperative that transnational activists interrogate their own privilege as they seek local alliances across borders, making extensive efforts to actively understand and negotiate the embedded risks, vulnerabilities, and opportunities across and within different political landscapes.

NOTES

1. Authors are listed alphabetically and not by order of contribution. Each author contributed equally.

2. International Rivers is the current name of the organization rebranded from its former name, International Rivers Network, in 2007. We use their contemporary title throughout the chapter for consistency except when used in quotes or documents.

3. In 2002, a public exposé revealed widespread corruption in the Lesotho Highlands Water Project; the CEO was prosecuted and two European firms barred from future work with the World Bank (International Rivers 2011b).

4. Frame alignment includes a subset of practices that are intended to align, including frame-bridging. Generally, our discussion is focused on the latter, and we refer to alignment, or the lack thereof, in relation to frame-bridging.

5. In 1997 Yvonne volunteered with HCAG while conducting research for her master's thesis on the social consequences of the LHWP in Lesotho. She worked with fieldworkers at all three dam sites and in Maseru, doing anything from administrative tasks to meeting about grievances with development officials. In return, they provided her with invaluable assistance and translation during her field research.

6. We do not mean to suggest that this inflation was intentional on IR's part. We recognize that accurate information was likely difficult to come by, particularly in the immediate aftermath of the earthquake. We also recognize that development authorities were likely ready to take advantage of an opportunity to justify reducing communication with those critical of the LHWP, such as IR and HCAG.

REFERENCES

Benford, Robert D., and David A. Snow. 2000. "Framing Processes and Social Movements: An Overview and Assessment." *Annual Review of Sociology* 26: 611–639.

Bandy, Joe. 2004. "Paradoxes of Transnational Civil Societies under Neoliberalism: The Coalition for Justice in the Maquiladoras." *Social Problems* 51 (3): 410–431.

Bickham Mendez, Jennifer. 2002. "Creating Alternatives from a Gender Perspective: Transnational Organizing for Maquila Workers' Rights in Central America." In *Women's Activism and Globalization: Linking Local Struggles and Transnational Politics*, edited by Nancy A. Naples and Manisha Desai, 121–141. New York: Routledge.

Braun, Yvonne A. 2008. "How Can I Stay Silent?": One Woman's Struggles for Environmental Justice in Lesotho." *Journal of International Women's Studies* 10(1) October: 5–20.

Braun, Yvonne A. 2011a. "The Reproduction of Inequality: Race, Class, Gender and the Social Organization of Work at the Site of Large-Scale Development Projects." *Social Problems* 58(2): 281–303.

Braun, Yvonne A. 2011b. "Left High and Dry: An Intersectional Analysis of Gender, Dams, and Development in Lesotho." *International Feminist Journal of Politics* 13(2): 141–162.

Braun, Yvonne A., and Michael C. Dreiling. 2010. "From Developmentalism to the HIV/AIDS Crisis: The Amplification of Women's Rights in Lesotho." *International Feminist Journal of Politics* 12(3): 464–483.

Capek, Stella M. 1993. "The 'Environmental Justice' Frame: A Conceptual Discussion and an Application." *Social Problems* 40 (1): 5–24.

Cohen, Jean L., and Andrew Arato. 1992. *Civil Society and Political Theory*. Cambridge, MA: MIT Press.

Collier, Peter. 2006. "Global Assemblages." *Theory, Culture & Society* 23(2–3): 399–401.

Davidson, Art. 1993. *Endangered Peoples*. San Francisco: Sierra Club Books.

Doherty, Brian, and Timothy Doyle. 2008. *Beyond Borders: Environmental Movements and Transnational Politics*. New York: Routledge.

Epprecht, Marc. 2000. *"This Matter of Women is Getting Very Bad": Gender, Development and Politics in Colonial Lesotho*. Pietermaritzburg, SA: University of Natal Press.

Ferguson, James. 1994. *The Anti-Politics Machine: Development, Depoliticization, and Bureaucratic Power in Lesotho*. Minneapolis: Minnesota University Press.

Gottlieb, Robert. 1993. *Forcing the Spring: The Transformation of the American Environmental Movement*. Washington, DC: Island Press.

International Rivers (IR). 2011a. "The Movement for Rivers and Rights." www.internationalrivers.org/en/the-movement.

International Rivers (IR). 2011b. "25 Years of Protecting Rivers and Rights." www.internationalrivers.org/node/5442.

International Rivers Network (IRN). 1996. *Rivers*. Brochure.

International Rivers Network (IRN). 1997. Fax communication from Highlands Church Action Group.

Johnston, Paul. 1994. *Success While Others Fail: Social Movement Unionism and the Public Workplace*. Ithaca, NY: ILR Press.

Keck, Margaret E., and Kathryn Sikkink. 1998. *Activists beyond Borders: Advocacy Networks in International Politics*. Ithaca, NY: Cornell University Press.

Keck, Margaret E., and Kathryn Sikkink. 1999. "Transnational Advocacy Networks in International and Regional Politics." *International Social Science Journal 159*, UNESCO (March): 89–101.

Khagram, Sanjeev. 2004. *Dams and Development: Transnational Struggles for Water and Power*. Ithaca, NY: Cornell University Press.

Lesotho Highlands Development Authority (LHDA). 1986. Treaty on the Lesotho Highlands Water Project between the Government of the Kingdom of Lesotho and the Government of the Republic of South Africa.

McCully, Patrick. 2001. *Silenced Rivers: The Ecology and Politics of Large Dams: Enlarged and Updated Edition*. London: Zed Books.

Nash, Roderick. 1982. *Wilderness and the American mind* (3rd ed.). New Haven, CT: Yale University Press.

Niezen, Ronald. 2003. *The Origins of Indigenism: Human Rights and the Politics of Identity*. Berkeley: University of California Press.

Ong, Aihwa, and Stephen J. Collier. 2005. *Global Assemblages: Technology, Politics, and Ethics As Anthropological Problems.* Malden, MA: Blackwell Publishers.

Roy, Arundhati. 2002. *The Algebra of Infinite Justice.* London: Flamingo.

Smith, Jackie. 2008. *Social Movements for Global Democracy.* Baltimore: Johns Hopkins University Press.

Smith, Michael Peter, and Luis Eduardo Guarnizo. 1998. *Transnationalism from Below.* New Brunswick, NJ: Transaction Publishers.

Snow, David A., E. Burke Rochford, Jr., Steven K. Worden, and Robert D. Benford. 1986. "Frame Alignment Processes, Micromobilization, and Movement Participation." *American Sociological Review* 51(August): 464–481.

Snow, David A., and Robert Benford. 1992. "Master Frames and Cycles of Protest." In *Frontiers in Social Movement Theory*, edited by Aldon Morris and Carol McClurg Mueller, 133–155. New Haven, CT: Yale University Press.

Tarrow, Sidney 2005. *The New Transnational Activism.* New York: Cambridge University Press.

Taylor, Dorceta. 1993. "Minority Environmental Activism in Britain: From Brixton to the Lake District." *Qualitative Sociology* 16 (3): 263–295.

Taylor, Dorceta. 2000. "The Rise of the Environmental Justice Paradigm: Injustice Framing and the Social Construction of Environmental Discourses." *American Behavioral Scientist* 43(4): 508–580.

11

Networks, Place, and Barriers to Cross-Border Organizing

"No Border" Camping in Transcarpathia, Ukraine

RENATA BLUMBERG AND RAPHI RECHITSKY

Introduction

Just months before much of the western border of the former Soviet Union became the external border of the European Union's (EUs) Schengen area, hundreds of activists came together in a No Border Camp (NBC) in the Ukrainian borderlands of Transcarpathia to organize against the expansion of "Fortress Europe."[1] The 2008 enlargement of the Schengen area to include several of the new EU member states of Eastern Europe marked the culmination of a gradual process of tightening border control between Ukraine and its neighbors to the West. With this development, residents of the new EU member states were granted greater mobility within the EU, while non-EU residents began to face greater restrictions on movement from Ukraine to the EU. To enforce this division, the Ukrainian borderlands have become increasingly controlled and militarized, impacting Ukrainian residents as well as migrants who travel to the EU through Ukraine from the former Soviet Union and other countries in the Global South. Ukraine has become both a transit zone for asylum seekers, as well as a sending region for migrant labor. This has earned Ukraine distinctions such as "Europe's Mexico" for labor migration and "the Morocco of the East" for transit migration (Crossing Borders 2007; Duvell 2008).

The 2007 NBC in the Transcarpathia region of Ukraine served as a space for transnational mobilization against this new migration regime. This convergence, one of many in the loosely associated No

Border Network (NBN), was planned to provide a forum for network-ing between Western and Eastern European activists; to reach out to local communities through workshops, public events, and popular edu-cation; and to mobilize activists from former-Soviet countries around migration-related issues (see Box 11.1 for text from the camp's original call-out). In an impressive response, over three hundred activists and migrants from about fifteen different countries gathered together at the camp for a week of self-organized social and cultural activities, work-shops and actions. However, divisions and tensions emerged during the course of the camp, inhibiting No Border network-building. Despite the fact that many of the camp's individual activities were successful, many participants perceived borders within the spaces of the No Bor-der Camp. Tensions around language, nation, and region created dis-tinct spaces within the camp and affected the ability of participants to network and develop strategies. Such tensions and conflicts led to the creation of internal borders that impacted cooperation at the camp and hindered collaboration after the camp was over.

Although differences in language and national and regional ori-gin created distinct spaces within the camp, more contentious issues arose around the camp's relationship to the Transcarpathia region and the question of appropriate antiauthoritarian organizing strategies. In the following sections we describe the ways in which these borders and divisions emerged and played out at the NBC. One of the first sets of tensions related to the location of the camp and the relation-ship between camp participants, local officials, and organizations. As the camp got under way, other differences affected camp participants. We go on to describe the construction of borders between language groups, country of origin, and along a divide between East and West. However, these borders were not exclusively responsible for the ten-sions at the camp. Differences regarding the meaning of antiauthori-tarian practice emerged over the course of the camp. We also describe how camp participants had to contend with issues that affected them in an extremely immediate and tangible way, as they confronted potential threats to their own safety and security and the prospect of clashes with a potentially violent opposition. We describe how this crisis brought to the fore different understandings and relationships to the local site of the camp and the implications these held for campers' development of an antiauthoritarian political practice. In the final sections of the chapter we draw connections with the scholarly literature in geography and feminist studies in order to explain why borders and divisions arose.

As our research demonstrates, intertwined social and spatial differences produced borders and divisions even within a movement that is united by a transnational political culture (Gordon 2008). In fact, this case study suggests that expectations for unity and an initial obviation of difference may hasten the formation of internal borders. We end our analysis with a call for closer engagement between feminist and anarchist theory and practice. With the intensification and rising sophistication of state border controls in the EU and with their disproportionate impact on marginalized populations, there is an urgent need to facilitate feminist-inspired border crossings which, we suggest, are tantamount to fostering a pan-European migrant rights and No Border movement.

Difference in Social Movement Networks and Spatial Praxis

The No Border Network has emerged in parallel with other transnational social movements mobilizing to challenge and create alternatives to neoliberal globalization (Bandy and Smith 2005; Della Porta and Tarrow 2005; Nicholls 2007). Most emblematically, social forums (both at the national and international scale) unite global justice and anticapitalist movements guided by the ideal that "another world is possible" (Böhm, Sullivan, and Reyes 2005; Smith et al. 2012). While these movements have been animated by a commitment to create those possible other worlds here and now, they have not been without their own tensions and conflicts. Indeed, social forums have become spaces of reflection and learning for social movements (Smith et. al. 2012, especially part III). Feminist voices such as the World March of Women have been among the most prominent in elucidating critiques, arguing that even within the World Social Forum (WSF) the struggle against capitalism continues to be prioritized, while other struggles are sidelined (Hewitt and Karides 2012).

These critiques have called attention to the WSF's organizational architecture, while also encouraging the enactment of alternative organizational formations. Since the 1990s, organizational formations based on network structures have grown because they mirror social movement ideals. In contrast to institutionalized and hierarchical social movement organizations, networks assume a decentralized and horizontal structure in which multiple groups converge in loose association (Routledge 2003). As a result, networks have emerged as an instantiation of the commitment toward making more egalitarian and inclusive "other" worlds. For example, scholars have argued that the methods at work in organizing feminist transnational networks express the ideals of global feminism (Moghadam 2005). Furthermore, the emergence of transnational advocacy networks has brought about change in part by opening spaces for "nontraditional international actors to mobilize information strategically to help create new issues and categories and to persuade, pressure, and gain leverage over much more powerful organizations and governments" (Keck and Sikkink 1998, 2). Early research on transnational advocacy networks (or social movement networks) focused on the extent to which networks could incite broader changes (Keck and Sikkink 1998).

More recent research has analyzed the processes and practices that constitute these networks (Diani and McAdam 2003; Rodrigues 2003), such as how commitments toward "horizontality" conflict with "verticality" at social forums (Böhm 2005). In contrast to the social forums, Jeffrey Juris (2008) argues that more explicitly antiauthoritarian networks, such as the No Border Network (NBN) and People's Global Action (PGA), can be understood according to coherent "cultural logics of networking" that are based on the free circulation of ideas, self-directed practice, horizontal connections, and decision-making through consensus. Horizontal networking is a crucial part of a transnational anarchist political culture (Gordon 2008), a movement which some have argued is today's source of "creative energy for radical politics" (Graeber 2002, 61). The network form has come to be understood as an appropriate organizational architecture by these anarchist and antiauthoritarian organizers not only because it avoids the creation of vertical power hierarchies within movements, but also because "networks have more generally emerged as a broader cultural ideal, a model of and model for new forms of directly democratic politics at local, regional, and global scales" (Juris 2005, 257). Significantly, network formations allow participating actors to converge around broader goals but also pursue strategies and tactics autonomously (Juris 2008). Thus, networks serve to connect various particular struggles, but not necessarily to unify them under a single policy imperative.

This connectivity has been facilitated by the various technologies that constitute the information age. These technologies have been critical in enabling transnational network formation, mirroring the spatial architecture of the Internet. However, Paul Routledge admits that these very technologies also pose problems: "Global media such as the Internet create gatekeepers, and codes of access and interpretation that may easily restrict the articulation and circulation of minority voices—for example, of women and indigenous peoples—through this technology" (2003, 344). Access to technology is only one dimension of networks that demonstrates the existence of complex and uneven power relations. Despite efforts to address multiple inequalities and counter marginalizing practices, these still persist and are even reproduced within the spaces of social movement networks and their convergences. As a result, Routledge concludes that networks like PGA must be seen as spaces of resistance, but also spaces of domination formed through entangled and differential power relations. Juris also concedes that his formulation of the cultural politics of networking is idealized, and in practice these logics are "unevenly distributed and always exist in dynamic tension with competing logics, often generating a complex 'cultural politics of networking' within concrete spheres" (Juris 2009, 214–215). Because social movements operate in complex cultural fields, there are often struggles within networks over ideology, strategies and tactics, and political culture. Thus, while the idealized network logics that Juris delineates may help us understand one dimension of networked politics, they fail to reveal how and why cultural logics become frustrated or impeded. Similarly, pointing out that domination occurs within spaces of resistance does not necessarily demonstrate how and why domination is not only reproduced but may even be patterned.

Feminist Geography and Social Movements

Feminist and geographical approaches to the study of social movements provide theoretical tools for understanding the power relations at work in network formation. Understanding how complex social and cultural fields influence movement building has long been a focus of feminist scholarship and activism (Bickham Mendez 2002; Mohanty 2003; Thayer 2009). With much difficulty and critical reflection, feminist movements in the United States have learned that without understanding how women are differently positioned in society, movements struggling on behalf of women risk exclusively representing the interests of privileged women (Mohanty 2003). Thus, achieving desired transformations involves navigating axes of difference such as race, class, ability, nation, and sexuality. These social divisions are not fixed, but are constantly remade, performed and created (McDowell 2008). Feminist scholarship problematizes essentialist understandings of social differences, while still highlighting how differences come to matter in understanding and confronting oppression.

Activist networks are also constituted across borders by differentially positioned actors, a practice that is inherently spatial (Sziarto and Leitner 2010). Although the concept of positionality was developed originally by feminist theorists, geographers have expanded upon the notion to underscore that subjects are situated simultaneously within social and spatial relations of power (Sheppard 2002; Sziarto and Leitner 2010). Moreover, spatialities, such as place, are not just produced and defined by states and capital; social movements also play a role in producing places (Conway 2008). Doreen Massey (2005) understands place as heterogeneous and contested, in contrast to other conceptualizations that represent place as enclosed, static, and reactive. According to Massey, places are forged through multiple trajectories, a "here" "where spatial narratives meet up or form configurations, conjunctures of trajectories which have their own temporalities" and "where the successions of meetings, the accumulation of weavings and encounters build up a history" (2005, 139). This understanding of place has important political implications in the context of globalization, a context in which "place" is assumed to lose its coherence and distinctiveness. For example, a defensive view of place positions space and place in a binary, with place being penetrated by a globalizing space. In contrast, Massey's politics would require a negotiation of the stories and trajectories that forge interconnected places, as well as an acknowledgment of the power-geometries that differentiate places.

In her study of women's movements in Brazil, Millie Thayer (2009) utilizes Massey's conception of place to highlight how globalization is constituted locally through interconnected flows of power *and* solidarity. Significantly, her analysis reveals that power relations between different women's movements mirrored global economic inequalities, complicating but not completely hindering mutual solidarity. Jennifer Bickham Mendez (2002) also argues that transnational linkages may reproduce North-South neocolonial relationships, even as local groups transform and appropriate transnational discourses. Taking a combined geographic and feminist perspective involves understanding the process of transnational organizing as a spatial praxis (Conway 2008), confronted by multiple and shifting borders (Naples 2009), and embedded within power relations (Bickham Mendez 2002). In this chapter, we elucidate how activists were actively engaged in the process of constructing borders within the camp that corresponded with various differences, causing tensions and conflict. We define borders as sites "at and through which socio-spatial differences are communicated" (Van Houtum 2005, 672). Building borders at the camp occurred even as participants tried to challenge international boundaries. Processes of border construction do not occur exclusively along axes of social difference; borders can be drawn along political, theoretical, and institutional lines (Naples 2009). However, border construction is a relational process, occurring when groups or individuals delineate divisions between "us" and "them," or the "self" and the "other." These relations also have a spatial element, involving interconnections of people across space, and between different people who together make places. For the NBC, the relationship with the Transcarpathian region was of critical importance. Bordering Slovakia, Hungary, Romania, and Poland (less than 30 kilometers away), it has also been a contested borderland (Ivakhiv 2006). In the following section we describe Transcarpathia's history before moving on to a description of the No Border movement.

"No Border" in the Transcarpathian Borderlands

Transcarpathia refers to the scenic territory directly east of the Carpathian Mountains in the western region of Ukraine. Transcarpathia is ethnically diverse, with Russian, Ukrainian, Rusyn, Romanian, Hungarian, and Slovak-speaking residents (Dickinson 2010). Because of this diversity, Transcarpathia defies the political geography of Ukraine, with its "Ukrainian" west and "Russian" east. After the collapse of the Soviet Union and the loosening of border controls in the 1990s, the region experienced transformations associated with the establishment of cross-border economic linkages with its western neighbors through new subcontracting manufacturing networks as well as trade (Kalantaridis 2000; Smith et al. 2008). These linkages have not lead to widespread prosperity; 47 percent of Transcarpathia's residents still live under the national poverty line (Uehling 2004). As a result, Transcarpathia has also become an important migrant sending region (Blank 2004; Uehling 2004). The militarization of Transcarpathia's border with the new EU member states has impeded freedom of mobility and threatened cross-border livelihood strategies, while also creating a profitable market for human smugglers heading toward Western Europe.

By providing substantial financial support, the EU has actively enrolled the Ukrainian state as a manager of this migration regime (ECRE 2008). Cooperation with the EU has led to the establishment of screening centers and temporary accommodation centers, which are actually prison-like detention facilities. Thus, while the EU prides itself on its adherence to ideals of tolerance and multiculturalism, it is able to do so in part by *externalization*, outsourcing militarization and control policies beyond its borders. The UNHCR has reported the unlawful *refoulement* of refugees to Ukraine by the border guards of EU member states (see Border Monitoring Project Ukraine 2009). Instead of granting access to asylum procedures within the EU member state, border guards regularly deport refugees back to Ukraine, where they end up in detention centers and face inhumane treatment (Border Monitoring Project Ukraine 2009). This migration regime is making Ukraine a "buffer zone," entrusted with the "remote control" of Europe's unwanted (Zimmer 2008; Zolberg 2008).

While a variety of NGOs, migrant rights campaigns, and movements have existed for decades in Europe, the No Border Network (NBN) was established in 1999 with an innovative impetus to challenge human rights abuses and restrictive migration policies using a radically different approach. Originally inspired by the struggles of undocumented migrants like the French Sans-Papiers movement (McNevin 2006), the NBN brought together different autonomous groups from various Western European countries in a loose transnational network working for migrant rights and the freedom of movement. Instead of focusing on political lobbying, the NBN seeks the immediate abolition of borders using a diversity of tactics and direct action measures. Its antinationalist and anticapitalist rhetoric rejects liberal rights discourses embedded in the constitutions of nation-states. Instead, it advocates for the universal freedom of movement (Kopp and Schneider 2003). Its slogans, including "no one is illegal" and "no border, no nation, stop deportation," evoke a challenging and confrontational imaginary. Rather than being an expression of naïve idealism, "to say that no human is illegal is to call into question the entire architecture of sovereignty, all its borders, locks and doors, internal hierarchies, etc." (Nyers 2003, 1089). Through networking, the NBN harnesses strength in its campaigns. The NBN also articulates a sophisticated understanding of state borders, emphasizing how new border technologies have reterritorialized the border, necessitating new cross-border forms of organizing. The NBN's strategy has included calling for international days of action, exposing the role of private airline companies in handling and profiting from deportations, and employing a variety of direct action tactics such as blockades and direct actions at migrant detention centers.

Many of these actions have taken place at No Border Camps (NBCs), which are usually situated near international borders as well as migrant detention centers. Since 2000, NBCs have been organized annually in various places all over Europe. The 2007 NBC was the first to be organized in the former Soviet Union. The young Russian and Ukrainian camp organizers chose to establish the camp in a strategic location in Transcarpathia, outside the city of Uzhgorod, near the Slovak and Hungarian borders. From its inception, the camp was meant to articulate several critiques simultaneously: those imposed by Fortress Europe's ever-expanding borders and control mechanisms, but also local problems associated with migration such as racism and the criminalization of transit migrants. Months before the camp, organizers were well underway with preparatory work, and a call was circulated electronically. In addition to the goals presented in Box 11.1, organizers indicated that the camp would not be a space for confrontational action, but for networking, communication, and popular education.

Box 11.1. Excerpt from the Call Out to No Border Camp in Ukraine (2007)

Some of the aims of this camp are:

1. To create a ground for communication between activists from Eastern and Western Europe and from everywhere else: meeting, establishing contacts, sharing skills, knowledge and experience, etc. (workshops, discussions, practical trainings, concerts and much more).

2. To attract the attention of the people in Ukraine (but also in Russia and in the world) to the racist policy on migration; to address the questions of contemporary forms of racism and xenophobia.

3. To create contact with local people in the region of Transcarpathia: antiracist education, open public events, film screenings, exhibitions, concerts and discussions, with an aim to improve local people's attitude towards migrants, refugees and asylum seekers.

4. To exchange information between us: how the authorities in different countries criminalize migration, what are the situations with deportation prisons, and to share the experiences of resistance in different countries. One of the practical results of the camp is going to be the publication of a brochure with the information from different countries on all these issues to reinforce our struggle.

5. To get more people from different anti-authoritarian collectives and movements in Ukraine, Russia and other 'post-Soviet' countries involved with the migration-related issues; mobilize people for struggle against racism, criminalization of migration and deportation camps system.

The Ukrainian camp was a unique space, created by the convergence of activists from over fifteen different countries. Despite their diverse origins, these activists shared many qualities. A large majority of the participants were young, probably under the age of 30. Characteristic of the contemporary anarchist movement, most shared subcultural connections with punk and other underground music-based scenes as well as an inclination toward antiauthoritarian or horizontal organizing (Gordon 2008). Anarchist movements, like Food Not Bombs (Heynen 2010), that have proliferated globally were also present at the camp. Food Not Bombs (FNB) from regional cities like Minsk, Belarus, prepared food while also organizing information-sharing events for all attending FNB groups. Everything from workshop themes to the political slogans used at demonstrations mirrored discourses of the NBN and the anarchist and alter-globalization movement more broadly.

The camp itself was organized on a do-it-yourself basis, without financial support from governments, major international nongovernmental organizations, or corporate sponsors, and with all participants welcome to contribute to the workshops and get involved in consensus-based decision-making. The week was filled with social and cultural activities organized by participants on an ad-hoc basis: workshops, demonstrations, and direct actions about migration and border controls, but also about related struggles from housing rights movements and squatting, to LGBT struggles in the former Soviet Union. While the majority of events took place within the camp space, the NBC also involved film screenings, concerts, and demonstrations at detention facilities to express solidarity with detained migrants, as well as tours of border villages and monitoring expeditions to the border.

Data and Methods

As engaged scholar-activists, we participated in the camp and its activities, including demonstrations and workshops, food preparation and logistics, and recreational activities (Rechitsky et al. 2009). Rechitsky conducted participant observation while providing limited assistance with preparation and interpreting during the event. In addition, he conducted three on-site and posthoc unstructured interviews with organizers, and two informal interviews with former camp participants. We supplemented this data with three reflections written by camp participants and organizers, as well as other accounts of the camp circulated over the Internet.

While each of us was involved in participant observation at the NBC to different extents, we also share a commitment to furthering No Border organizing and egalitarian antiauthoritarian imaginaries. To this end, we have been involved in similar antiauthoritarian and immigrant rights initiatives in Europe and the United States. However, our involvement at the NBC has been facilitated by our position as bicultural, white, American scholars and activists with Eastern European immigrant backgrounds. Together, we are proficient and fluent in a number of languages used at the camp, including English, Russian, Ukrainian, and others. We recognize this as a key advantage and privilege in navigating across borders, as well as analyzing different perspectives on the camp's internal dynamics.

Borders of Place, Difference, and Political Practice at the NBC

Place at the NBC: Building a Camp in Transcarpathia

Since its inception, the NBC's relationship with the Transcarpathia region was contentious. Organizers came from different Russian and Ukrainian cities, and none had close connections with Transcarpathia. Despite the logistical difficulties, Transcarpathia was chosen as the site of the camp, in part because of its political and territorial importance for migration. As was common at other NBCs, outreach to the local community was an important part of the camp's goals and articulated clearly in the camp's call-to-action. However, early in the organizing process, some activists pointed out that one of the official aims of the camp was quite problematic and paternalistic (refer to Box 11.1, point 3). The notion of improving local people's attitudes was based on assumptions that borderland residents were necessarily racist and antimigrant. Despite these criticisms, the call was not amended, and efforts were made to establish contacts with Transcarpathian NGOs to further the camp's outreach goals. As a result of these collaborations, a forum and film festival were planned in the city of Uzhgorod during the time of the camp.

However, these arrangements still did not satisfy the desires of some camp organizers to undertake meaningful outreach. This became evident when one week before the camp's official start date, an opportunity arose to move the location of the camp. The director of Uzhgorod University retracted his commitment to provide electricity and water at the campsite, a remote riverside property of the university that had been a student resort in the Soviet era (and was now unused and in a state of disrepair). By this point, organizers had worked on-site for a week to set up camp accommodations and make final preparations for events in the city of Uzhgorod. Other camp-builders from Eastern Europe had worked with camp organizers hauling materials and making do-it-yourself toilets, showers, and cooking ovens with minimal resources. Thus, considerable efforts had already been made to make the abandoned student resort accommodating. But the retraction also provided an opportunity to move the campsite to a village field, a move that would enable greater contact with local residents.

Over the next few days, organizers explored this possibility by meeting with local officials to discuss the availability and cost of logistics such as electricity, water, and toilets at the alternative village site. During evening campfires, organizers and camp builders deliberated about whether to relocate the camp. While the originally intended site of the camp did not have electricity to support multimedia workshops, its remote location offered the privacy necessary to hold workshops, foster relationships and incubate future collaborations. On the other hand, the village field location would have provided more opportunities for communication with local residents. Although a decision was finally made to move the camp, organizers reversed it due to time constraints.

This first question regarding place, whether to keep the camp in its originally-intended location or to relocate it, also reflected a moment of tension between the different goals of the camp as well as between camp organizers and builders: What kind of relationships should the camp have with the local residents? Was the camp to be a safe space for an activist community, isolated from the local community, or a socially engaged political space, and in direct contact with the local community? The question of the place that is Transcarpathia would reemerge over the course of the camp's duration, but other tensions and divisions also arose as the camp got underway.

Language, Nation, and Region

Camp participants came from over fifteen countries, but Russian and English were the two languages that dominated during formal and informal meetings and discussions. For workshops and meetings, camp organizers tried to ensure attendance by using translators to create a bilingual environment. The reasons for this seemed self-evident: while activists coming from Western Europe were most likely to be proficient in English, those from the former Soviet states shared Russian as a common language and—it was assumed—tended to be less proficient in English. However, consistent bilingualism was difficult to maintain. Not only were the few qualified translators already overworked, but sometimes translation seemed to interrupt the flow of discussion, and the need to stop for translation was also easy to overlook. In one workshop on ecocommunities in Russia, a fast-paced dialog between the Russian-speaking presenter and some audience members was consistently interrupted by a request for "translation please!" by one participant who needed English translation. Other times, translation was not seen as necessary. Over time, English became the primary and dominant language at most of the migration-related workshops central to the goals of the camp, with few Russian-speakers encouraged to attend these sessions. This signals that despite efforts to ensure the availability of translation, camp activities became divided along language lines.

This separation into distinct linguistic spaces created "quite [an] iron curtain," according to one participant. One organizer also spoke of an "invisible border between Russian and English speaking participants," observing that this tension "somehow disturbed the whole atmosphere of the camp" (Abolishing the Borders 2007, 15). Another organizer emphasized that divisions appeared also according to nationality: "Russian speakers were hanging out (and drinking) mostly with Russian speakers, German 'no border people' were busy with their issues. British guys were doing their own stuff." Most broadly, some reports and individual participants continuously referred to an East-West regional divide that inhibited communication and understanding (Weinmann 2007). Although these divisions inhibited network-building, no major discussions or conflicts occurred over borders of language, nation, and region.

Defining Antiauthoritarian Political Practice

Major conflicts at the camp emerged around the appropriate practice of antiauthoritarian politics. Camp participants confronted several incidents in which their taken-for-granted assumptions about what constituted appropriate antiauthoritarian politics were questioned and debated, even long after the camp ended. For example, an extended debate revolved around whether camp participants should give food to the local police who were stationed nearby to protect the camp. Anti-cop graffiti was sprayed around the camp in both English and Russian, attesting to the fact that language barriers were not the source of conflict here. Indeed, as one participant noted, the "borders within" that inhibited networking were much more than just about language:

> Despite the fact that we were there collectively to protest the external border, I feel we managed to erect unnecessary borders within our own group, that is, borders of understanding amongst ourselves. There was a strong friction between different groups of people who ate different things, a sense of elitism or disdain in some cases, as well as between people who sanctioned or committed to different paths of struggle, whether they were violent or nonviolent for example.

Conflicting paths of struggle posed a particular problem during the last few days of the camp. Participants had become notably restless. Having spent several days learning about the injustices of migration management, there was a strong sentiment to collectively and publicly condemn this regime and to express solidarity with the migrants housed in detention centers. Demonstrations were planned, but organizers reiterated their request that camp participants refrain from confrontational actions during the planned protest march through the city of Uzhgorod. Since this demonstration was legally sanctioned, the organizer who filed the permit was at risk of facing repercussions should protesters engage in confrontational or illegal activities. Despite these requests, during the protest march through Uzhgorod one activist took down an EU flag from an administrative building and then proceeded to burn it. When the issue was brought up during a subsequent camp meeting, conflict emerged. The activist allegedly responsible for the incident stood up and defended his actions, expressing his condemnation of the state. Some support was voiced for the position that no one has the right to dictate to others what kind of actions they should or should not undertake. Others disagreed, pointing out that activists needed to understand that risks were involved for certain people, and that those risks should be considered. No resolution was reached, but a few camp participants did note the ironic symbolism of the action. The activist who had pulled down the flag was from Western Europe. He was privileged because of his affiliation with the EU, but yet he stood up for his right to burn the EU flag in Ukraine. He would also soon leave the country, and the consequences of his actions would be faced by one of the organizers, someone with less privilege and freedom to traverse EU borders.

More generally, this incident reveals that activist relations to place influenced how political borders were constructed: organizers from Ukraine who work on migrant-related issues and who had taken the responsibility to organize the march had different positions than transient activists. Ultimately, no understanding between the two positions could be reached. In light of this, we suggest that border construction based on political practice must be understood in relationship to place, here, specifically, the region of Transcarpathia.

The Spatial Politics of Protecting the Camp

During the final days of the camp, participants had to contend with decisions regarding the safety and security of those in the camp, an issue that brought them face-to-face with activists' own engagement in active border construction. A few weeks earlier in Krasnodar, Russia, an ecological camp was attacked by a neo-Nazi group. Several of the participants were beaten, and one was killed. As a result of the possibility that the NBC might also become a target, the local Amnesty International chapter made a public request that the camp be protected. The stationing of a police officer at the entrance of the camp predictably roused the ire of some camp participants, but a more serious crisis occurred when threats of fascist attacks arose during the last days of the camp. A football club with a strong fascist fan-base was holding a match in Uzhgorod, causing anxieties about attacks on camp participants of "non-Slavic appearance" and nontraditional dress in the city. In addition, rumors about undercover police agents engaged in surveillance of the camp fomented threats of another security risk: an impending attack by local nationalist paramilitary groups. In response, some Russian NBC activists took very militant stances to protect the camp, but rumors spread about how western Ukrainian nationalist groups were not as violent as the "real" Russian fascists, and that the crisis was exaggerated. Still, others—especially Western activists less familiar with fascist violence in Eastern Europe—could not comprehend the scale of the potential danger. Ultimately, contradictory decisions about how to "defend" the camp caused confusion. Reflecting on the crisis, one participant later wrote:

In response to being approached by a local and asked "who are the coordinators here?" someone replied, "we are all coordinators." This was an interesting comment that made me think: Is this true? Or is it just our ideal? Did each one of us know the logistics of the lay-out and the geography and the local language and culture, the set-up of the camp and its connections with the town, the finances behind it, the places where the food came from, etc. . . . to call him/herself a coordinator? I felt this was not true, though somehow we believed it to be true. To speak for myself, if something suddenly were to happen with the core organizers of the camp and the rest of us all sat down to deal with what to do next, I would feel ill-equipped to make informed and grounded suggestions.

The crisis forced participants like this one to realize that campers possessed different degrees of knowledge of the region, indeed, different relationships with the region. As a result, she came to question a common tenet of antiauthoritarian practice. Throughout the planning process and the time of the camp, divisions were constructed between the campers and local residents and the region in general. But when crisis erupted, conflicts arose over how to understand and navigate these borders. Some participants did not feel informed enough to take active roles in coordinating a defense of the camp. Relatedly, despite the success of the events held in Uzhgorod, several activists felt unsatisfied about the lack of direct engagement between camp participants and local communities.

But more importantly, different understandings of and relationships to place caused tension because they called into question a basic principle of antiauthoritarian organizing: that all camp participants were also equally capable coordinators. Thus, the horizontality of network-building encountered a major obstacle when confronted with the complexity of place and different activists' relationships and understandings of the place of the camp.

Discussion

Much recent research has attempted to document and analyze the contours of the contemporary anarchist movement (see Amster et al. 2009), including the NBN specifically (Juris 2008). While providing important contributions, this research has paid less attention to the differences and constructed divisions within the movement that may inhibit anarchist-inspired network-building. In our analysis, we have pointed out that stated shared goals and principles and the commonalities of an anarchist political culture were insufficient to obviate the borders produced and reproduced at the camp. The "cultural politics of networking" (Juris 2009) that helps shape anarchist political culture existed as *an ideal* at the camp, but a contentious ideal, subject to multiple interpretations and actions. Differences of language, nation, and region inhibited network-building, but diverse understandings of anti-authoritarian practices caused more divisive conflicts.

The emergence of divisions among NBC participants was not unique to the Ukrainian camp. Indeed, scholars of the No Border movement have pointed out that "language barriers, highly differentiated regional labor markets and a variety of national political cultures, policies, practices and institutions make it difficult to transform dozens, if not hundreds, of local initiatives into a truly European movement" (Euskirchen, Lebuhn, and Ray 2009, 7). Similarly, in a reflection upon the largest NBC in Strasbourg, Kopp and Schneider (2003) state that:

> During the ten days in Strasbourg the two to three thousand participants from over twenty countries in Europe were predominantly concerned with themselves and their own differences without managing from the start to shift the focus; i.e. to abandon the leveling out of these differences and to use them rather as a starting point for a new political capacity to act which goes beyond borders and innumerable differences, or on the contrary even thrives on these (n.p.).

At the NBC in Ukraine, an East-West border emerged, as some Western European participants attributed problems at the camp to opaque decision-making procedures and one controlling camp coordinator (Weinmann 2007). Unanticipated differences and resulting tensions around language, nation, and region produced a feeling of an "iron curtain."

Transnational networks, like the NBN, are constituted by practices, often guided by certain horizontal logics. But activist networks are also forged in material places by different socially, spatially, and culturally positioned actors. Tensions surrounding diverging ideas about political practices emerged but were not confronted in a reflexive, analytical way by those involved. Borders were presented as a problem for organizers and participants alike, rather than as an opportunity for recognition, engagement and respect.

In order to grasp why borders arose, the concept of sociospatial positionality is particularly useful. Power is not only a social attribute—power relations are also forged between places, such as the EU and Ukraine. Activist movements mirror these power relations, as struggles develop in particular places around relevant issues for those places. Most of the participating Western Europeans were shaped by experiences in No Border activism, which is related to their position as residents and citizens of the EU and important migrant destinations. These activists brought with them certain political imaginaries and investments in No Border politics. In contrast, non-EU citizens of the former Soviet Union did not share these political imaginaries or political investments. Economic disadvantages and visa restrictions prevented them from attending previous NBCs in the EU, where most border camps in the region have taken place prior to this path-breaking 2007 initiative. Moreover, many of the Eastern European activists came from places where international migration was not such a prominent socioeconomic phenomenon. While No Border organizing appealed to them, the idea of a camp as a gathering of grassroots groups and the possibility to meet regional and international activists were sufficient reasons to attend. In addition, the workshops were not solely focused on migration-related issues, as demonstrated by the diversity of programming. Thus, the iron curtain that descended upon the camp may have resulted partially from language barriers, but it also arose due to differences in goals and motivations, which are themselves formed from the positionalities of the activists and their relationships with struggles in other places. As one camp organizer states: "During the camp, we ran into several conflicts. People judged according to situation and a country where they live" (Abolishing the Borders 2007, 14).

Over the course of the camp it became apparent that participants brought together different ideas of process, strategies, and what it means to be committed to antiauthoritarian practices. This has also been documented at other NBCs, such as the largest one, which brought together over 2000 participants, held in Strasbourg in 2002 (Lang and Schneider 2003). According to Lang and Schneider (2003), the senseless destruction and violence during initial demonstrations at the Strasbourg NBC caused police to react more harshly to subsequent creative demonstrations of marching bands and street theatre. At the Strasbourg NBC, as well as the one in Ukraine, activists were committed to different practices, which resulted in tensions and conflicts.

In this case, the concept of intersectionality is useful for understanding the dynamics at this and other NBCs. An intersectional (Collins 2000) approach to the dynamics at the camp reveals that multiple oppressions intersect to produce diverse modes of liberatory practice. Certain practices which are deemed to signify antiauthoritarian practice may be liberatory for some while oppressive for others, such as women and marginalized groups. For example, protest tactics have gendered dimensions. Kolářová (2009) argues that "the alter-globalization struggle is a clash of two masculinities: dominant strong and powerful masculinity represented by the rulers of the world and the policemen, compared to the rebellious heroic masculinity of the protesters" (99).

An element of heroic masculinity was certainly at work at the NBC demonstration in Uzhgorod, represented by the "brave" act of burning the EU flag. Additionally, reports from the NBC tended to emphasize demonstrations and public actions, while neglecting less heroic practices like the significant labor that went into providing for or feeding the camp. This tendency was also a feature of yet another NBC, in which a protest demonstration was propelled by a "defiant, ego-based urge to confirm our own identities and ability to act" (Alldred 2003, 155). Feminist analysis reveals how oppositional movements, and their practices, forms of representation, and discourses may reproduce hegemonic masculinities (Connell and Messerschmidt 2005).

Our analysis demonstrates that activist practices should not be seen as disconnected from place. The political practices of camp participants were at once embedded in and partially constituted Transcarpathia as a place. At the NBC in Ukraine, the camp's ambiguous relationship to place was a source of tension. For Ukrainian camp organizers, Transcarpathia was a "tricky" region to be approached with caution, because it defied the political geography of Ukraine, with its Russian east and Ukrainian west. Other camp participants, such as those from Western Europe, saw Transcarpathia first and foremost as the newest frontier of Fortress Europe, to be contested and challenged. Thus, different spatial imaginaries of the region, and by implication the camp's potential relationship with the region, underpinned the tensions around place at the camp.

Divergent spatial conceptualizations of Transcarpathia held implications for political practice. For example, during the protest march, camp organizers urged caution and others sought to undertake more confrontational actions such as burning the EU flag. Similarly, some activists wanted the camp to be an enclosed and safe space, while others desired closer interaction with local residents. Organizers emphasized the unknown nature of the region and sought to contain the camp or carefully manage interactions between the camp and the local communities. Other participants understood this region as a victim of EU expansion, a spatial imaginary that ignores the importance of cross-border trade and its benefits for regional livelihoods. Despite these many distinctions, activists all seemed to imagine Transcarpathia as enclosed and contained.

A relational understanding of place underscores that places are not fixed or static, not closed and cohesive entities, but are produced through changing and often conflicting social relations and practices. Like any other place, Transcarpathia is heterogenous, porous, dynamic, and open to change. Therefore, the different spatial imaginaries of Transcarpathia present at the camp were partial. At the same time, they were significant because they helped to produce Transcarpathia as a place for the camp participants during and even after the camp had ended.

Different understandings of the Transcarpathia region underlay the political orientations and approaches that participants took to social justice issues in this borderland. The NBN has been vocal in attributing political agency to migrants, rather than rendering them as victims in need of care. In contrast, the rhetoric employed by western European organizers emphasizing the expansion of Fortress Europe has reproduced the same penetrating discourses of globalization that render place (in this case Transcarpathia) as a victim, and, by implication, foster a defensive politics. A relational understanding of place would allow for the recognition of the diversity and complexity of Transcarpathia, as well as the on-going interconnections that produce it as a specific place. Transcarpathia is not only a newly militarized borderland; it is also a site of everyday livelihood struggles for residents, who are long-term and seasonal migrants, cross-border traders, and even border guards. In the remainder of this section, we explore the potentials of a relational understanding of place and feminist interventions for antiauthoritarian No Border politics.

Understanding borderlands in a geographically relational manner opens up political possibilities for a No Border politics of place intertwined with the politics of network-building. The 2007 No Border camp was an unusual occurrence and attracted significant public and media attention. In fact, it was the largest protest camp to take place in post-Soviet space. In addition, for the week during which it was held it was part of the place of Transcarpathia, even if camp participants held ambivalent positions about the region.

Activist cartography is one way to enact a politics of place that contests dominant representations, while engaging in a politics of place. Places are not stable, but forged by connectivities that are usually not represented on traditional maps. Activist cartographers have shown that maps work to create territories and social worlds, and therefore that mapping enables existing spaces to be challenged and transformed and alternative spaces to be prefigured (Cobarrubias 2009). In one example of activist cartography, Cobarrubias writes that the "the act of de-inscribing and re-inscribing multiple 'Europes' challenges the boundings of Europe that are currently afoot" (2009, 17). Multiple maps of Europe not only suggest that Europe isn't a stable territorial frame, but also reveal the simultaneous plurality of Europes in space. Transcarpathia can also be mapped in different ways by residents, cross-border traders, transit migrants, and NBC participants, and the maps can provide a forum to understand the multiple sociospatial trajectories that form Transcarpathia. Alternately visualizing the connectivities that make up Transcarpathia, such as migration but also remittance and capital flows, can help discover and establish new solidarities, such as with different border regions. NBCs have the possibility—albeit small and fleeting—to constitute place in a specific direction that empowers marginalized groups and places.

This requires navigating not only the relationship between the camp and the region, but also the borders that emerged between camp participants. Feminist scholarship provides concepts, such as "reflexivity" and "translation work," to enable border-crossings in transnational networks like the NBN where questions of difference have surfaced but have not been productively dealt with. Reflexivity involves self-critical reflection, and also taking into account how researcher (and activist) identities and positionalities are shaped by material, institutional and geopolitical locations (Nagar and Geiger 2007). Considering the masculinist responses to the possibility of far-right violence at the camp, for example, we may build on activist research critiquing "disaster masculinity" in collective action (Luft 2008) by analyzing it as a case of gendered responses to perceived violent opposition.

In addition, reflexive analysis must also consider activist practice across space, by taking into account the implications of "importing political tactics to a (geo-political) space" (Alldred 2003, 156). Translation work involves "first, modeling democratic practice in everyday organizing—in other words, seeking opportunities to organize with others as equals and, second, identifying ways to link the issues and analysis generated from one campaign or social movement to another in order to strengthen praxis" (Naples 2009, 10). Translation work also should be considered as a spatial praxis, which for transnational feminist practice necessitates "paying close attention to the specificity of place and context, whilst building connections across struggles in different places" (Pratt and Yeoh 2003, 163). These connections can be drawn along contour lines to produce countertopographies, which not only elucidate how similar processes, like border control and militarization, connect different people and places, but also mobilize alternative abstractions (Katz 2001). No Border is one such possible abstraction.

Conclusion: Toward a Feminist Politics of Borders

In the time since the camp ended, some changes have been made to visa policies, thereby slightly easing travel to work in the EU. However, many Ukrainian migrants still find themselves in precarious positions, living and working illegally in the European Union. Six months after the camp, soon after Ukraine's neighbors' accession to the Schengen area, over seven hundred Ukrainians blockaded international highways at the Polish border as well as the Polish consulate in Lviv, demanding visa-free travel to their western neighbors. Despite some changes in border enforcement practices, Transcarpathia remains a volatile transit region. Asylum seekers and unaccompanied minors from third countries who successfully cross into Hungary or Slovakia are illegally handed over by EU authorities to Ukrainian border guards. Thus detention centers and camps remain full with the appearance of fewer apprehensions at the Ukrainian border. Although the notorious Pavshino detention camp was finally closed in December 2008, at least four European-funded detention centers have opened in its place.

Although solidarity campaigns for freedom of movement continue to be forged across the borders of Europe, the sophistication of migration management is growing at territorial borders and migrant destinations, which have seen waves of anti-immigrant politics. Struggles for the universal freedom of movement are needed to confront these escalations by building transnational communities of resistance that make a better world possible. Yet as this chapter has demonstrated, this task is not an easy one. Transnational social movement networking cannot be reduced to merely an organizational model, distilled to a cultural logic of networking, but must be understood as a process involving socially and spatially positioned actors across external borders. As such, this case has demonstrated the complex linkages and ironies of border construction as discussed throughout this volume.

We have argued that the border regime as an object of protest and internal borders within movements are closely related. Even within a conscious anarchist movement culture, borders based on language, nation and region still emerged within the movement. Reflecting on the mobilization, one organizer said, "I think there was miscommunication and the lack of comprehension because of cultural differences or different level of activists [sic] experiences in different countries" (Abolishing the Borders 2007, 15). In other words, English-language dominance and the hegemony of western activist culture made it difficult for organizers to develop place-based solutions to emerging organizational challenges. This organizer's reflection also points to our second finding, which reveals that activists in this transnational convergence brought together various ideas of what it means to be committed to antiauthoritarian practice. We have argued that these borders of political practice became a source of division because activists assumed there would and should be consensus. And the effects of these borders were heightened by activists' different relationships to the region of the camp, which produced different spatial imaginaries that guided their actions. While camp organizers were cautious, relying on a spatial imaginary that emphasized Transcarpathia as a complicated borderland, Western European activists saw the region as a victim of EU expansion policies of militarization. Both of these imaginaries employed an enclosed and static notion of place, thereby helping to create borders of place which could not be easily navigated. In other words, organizers' conscious awareness of the external dimension of borders is necessary but not always sufficient for movements to overcome constitutive internal borders that may come to challenge cross-border network-building.

A politics of place, along with antiauthoritarian and feminist principles, could foster network-building for abolitionist movements struggling against emerging migration regimes as well as the prison industrial complex (Loyd, Mitchelson, and Burridge 2012). The dilemmas facing antiauthoritarian spatial and cultural modes of organization should not be viewed as limits to a globalization from below, or as insurmountable obstacles to cross-border collaborations. Instead, they are challenges to be learned from and consciously and consistently confronted. Movement network-building is a process (Smith et. al. 2012). In light of this, a praxis that could take on an increasingly transnational regime of migration control would actively involve recognizing the variable social and spatial locations of actors within the social movements that seek to resist it.

This is a task well suited for collaboration between feminist scholars and activists. Despite the fact that feminist scholars have played an active role in studying transnational social movements and networks, less attention has been paid to antiauthoritarian and anarchist movements. The mutually beneficial dialogues between contemporary feminist and anarchist perspectives have started only recently (see Eschle 2004). At the same time, many practices that are purported to be new, such as nonhierarchical organizing, have long been central to feminist praxis. As Desai (2007) notes: "In addition to this transnational political perspective, transnational feminists were among the first to develop networks on the basis of nonhierarchical, informal structures and participatory processes, to share experiences and strategize for political actions at multiple levels" (798). These experiences should be harnessed to renew a feminist and antiauthoritarian No Border politics, in which translation work and reflexivity are utilized to build bridges and engage solidarities across difference.

Epilogue

Since the time of this writing, tumultuous events have rocked Ukraine. During the winter of 2013–2014 the Euromaidan movement for EU trade policies turned into a national revolution that toppled the pro-Russian president, Viktor Yanukovich. The Russian military invaded Crimea, a strategic peninsula on the opposite side of the country where our research took place. While Russia justifies its actions by pointing to the hypocrisy of US and NATO foreign policies, the western media has glossed over the complexities of the popular and nationalist Euromaidan movement, especially the central role played by its far-right contingents in the protests in the streets. What alternative could a feminist and antiauthoritarian No Border movement present for an already-fractured Ukraine? The visibility of nationalist slogans and far-right groups in Euromaidan, as well as their cross-border organizing with European groups, poses a challenge to the antinationalist vision of the No Border movement across Europe. Still, the same antiauthoritarian leftist groups that are the subject of this chapter have provided an overlooked alternative to the far right in Ukraine's revolutionary political arena. Together with an antiauthoritarian perspective, a transnational feminist politics that is sensitive to the ongoing production of scattered hegemonies and intersectionality has the potential to explain the complexities of Euromaidan and its opponents and other dynamics of border politics in the region.

NOTES

    1. The authors may be contacted at blum0135@umn.edu and rechi009@umn.edu. We would like to thank Jennifer Bickham Mendez, Nancy Naples, Helga Leitner, Eric Sheppard, Ron Aminzade, Olga Oksyutina, and Peter Gelderloos, as well as the participants of the 2007 No Border Camp, for commenting on this chapter. A special thank you goes out to Jennifer Bickham Mendez and Nancy Naples for their thoughtful feedback throughout the process, starting at our presentation of this paper at the 2009 preconference of the section on the Political Economy of the World System of the American Sociological Association. All errors remain our own.

REFERENCES

Abolishing the Borders. 2007. The No Border Camp in Ukraine: Interview with Organizers. *Abolishing the Borders from Below*. Berlin.

Alldred, Pam. 2003. No Borders, No Nations, No Deportations. *Feminist Review* 73: 152–157.

Amster, Randall, Abraham DeLeon, Luis Fernandez, Anthony J. Nocella, II, and Deric Shannon, eds. 2009. *Contemporary Anarchist Studies: An Introductory Anthology of Anarchy in the Academy*. New York: Routledge.

Bandy, Joe, and Jackie Smith, eds. 2005. *Coalitions Across Borders: Transnational Protest and the Neoliberal Order*. Lanham, MD: Rowman & Littlefield.

Bickham Mendez, Jennifer. 2002. Organizing a Space of Their Own? Global/Local Processes in a Nicaraguan Women's Organization. *Journal of Developing Societies* 18 (2–3): 196–227.

Blank, Diana R. 2004. Fairytale Cynicism in the "Kingdom of Plastic Bags": The Powerlessness of Place in a Ukrainian Border Town. *Ethnography* 5 (3): 349–78.

Böhm, Steffen. 2005. Ground Zero of the Forum: Notes on a Personal Journey. *ephemera* 5 (2): 134–145.

Böhm, Steffen, Sian Sullivan, and Oscar Reyes. 2005. The Organisation and Politics of Social Forums. *ephemera* 5 (2): 98–101.

Border Monitoring Project Ukraine. 2009. *Access to Protection Denied: Refoulement of Refugees and Minors on the Eastern Borders of the EU—The Case of Hungary, Slovakia and Ukraine*. Munich, Germany: Bayerischer Flüchtlingsrat.

Call Out to No Border Camp in Ukraine. 2007. "Call Out to No Border Camp in Ukraine." www.noborder.org/item.php?id=383.

Clemens, Elisabeth S. 1996. Organizational Form as Frame: Collective Identity and Political Strategy in the American Labor Movement, 1880–1920. In *Comparative Perspectives on Social Movements: Political Opportunities, Mobilizing Structures, and Cultural Framings*, edited by Doug McAdam, John D. McCarthy, and Mayer N. Zald, 205–226. Cambridge: Cambridge University Press.

Cobarrubias, Sebastian. 2009. *Mapping Machines: Activist Cartographies of the Border and Labor Lands of Europe*. PhD diss. Chapel Hill: Department of Geography, University of North Carolina at Chapel Hill.

Collins, Patricia Hill. 2000. *Black Feminist Thought: Knowledge, Consciousness, and the Politics of Empowerment*. New York: Routledge.

Connell, R. W., and James Messerschmidt. 2005. Hegemonic Masculinity: Rethinking the Concept. *Gender & Society* 19 (6): 829–859.

Conway, Janet. 2008. Geographies of Transnational Feminisms: The Politics of Place and Scale in the World March of Women. *Social Politics* 15 (2): 207–231.

Crossing Borders. 2007. Crossing Borders Newsletter. http://noborder.org/crossing_borders/newsletter04en.pdf.

Della Porta, Donatella, and Sidney Tarrow, eds. 2005. *Transnational Protest and Global Activism*. Lanham, MD: Rowman & Littlefield.

Desai, Manisha. 2007. The Messy Relationship Between Feminisms and Globalizations. *Gender & Society* 21 (6): 797–803.

Diani, Mario, and Doug McAdam, eds. 2003. *Social Movements and Networks: Relational Approaches to Collective Action*. Oxford: Oxford University Press.

Dickinson, Jennifer A. 2010. Languages for the Market, the Nation, Or the Margins: Overlapping Ideologies of Language and Identity in Zakarpattia. *International Journal of the Sociology of Language* 201 (1): 53–78.

Düvell, Frank. 2008. *Crossing the Fringes of Europe: Transit Migration in the EU's Neighbourhood. Center on Migration, Policy and Society*. Working paper 33. Oxford: University of Oxford.

Eschle, Catherine. 2004. Constructing the Anti-Globalization Movement. *International Journal of Peace Studies* 9 (1): 61–84.

European Council on Refugees and Exiles (ECRE). 2008. EU Funding Priorities in Eastern Europe for Refugee Protection, Migration Management and Border Reinforcement 2008. www.ecre.org/files/ECRE_EU_funding_research_Eastern_Europe_2008.pdf.

Euskirchen, Markus, Henrick Lebuhn, and Gene Ray. 2009. Big Trouble in Borderland: Immigration Rights and No-Border Struggles in Europe. *MUTE: Culture and Politics After the Net*. www.metamute.org/community/your-posts/big-trouble-borderland-immigration-rights-and-no-border-struggles-europe.

Gordon, Uri. 2008. *Anarchy Alive! Anti-authoritarian Politics from Practice to Theory*. London: Pluto Press.

Graeber, David. 2002. The New Anarchists. *New Left Review* 13 (2): 61–73.

Hewitt, Lyndi, and Marina Karides. 2012. More Than a Shadow of a Difference? Feminist Participation in the World Social Forum. In *Handbook on World Social Forum Activism*, edited by Jackie Smith, Scott Byrd, Ellen Reese, and Elizabeth Smythe, 84–102. Boulder, CO: Paradigm Publishers.

Heynen, Nik. 2010. Cooking Up Non-Violent Civil-Disobedient Direct Action for the Hungry: "Food Not Bombs" and the Resurgence of Radical Democracy in the US. *Urban Studies* 47 (6): 1225–1240.

Ivakhiv, Adrian. 2006. Stoking the Heart of (a Certain) Europe: Crafting Hybrid Identities in the Ukraine-EU Borderlands. *Spaces of Identity* 6 (1): 11-44.

Jeppesen, Sandra. 2010. Queer Anarchist Autonomous Zones and Publics: Direct Action Vomiting Against Homonormative Consumerism. *Sexualities* 13 (4): 463–478.

Juris, Jeffrey 2005. Social Forums and Their Margins: Networking Logics and the Cultural Politics of Autonomous Space. *ephemera* 5 (2): 253–272.

Juris, Jeffrey 2008. *Networking Futures: The Movements Against Corporate Globalization*. Durham, NC: Duke University Press.

Juris, Jeffrey 2009. Anarchism, or the Cultural Logic of Networking. In *Contemporary Anarchist Studies: An Introductory Anthology of Anarchy in the Academy*, edited by Randall Amster, Abraham DeLeon, Luis Fernandez, Anthony J. Nocella II, and Deric Shannon, 213–223. New York: Routledge.

Kalantaridis, Christos. 2000. Globalization and Entrepreneurial Response in Post-Socialist Transformation: A Case Study from Transcarpathia, Ukraine. *European Planning Studies* 8 (3): 285–299.

Katz, Cindi. 2001. On the Grounds of Globalization: A Topography for Feminist Political Engagement. *Signs: Journal of Women in Culture & Society* 26 (4): 1213–1234.

Keck, Margaret E., and Kathryn Sikkink. 1998. *Activists Beyond Borders: Advocacy Networks in International Politics*. Ithaca, NY: Cornell University Press.

Kolářová, Marta. 2009. Fairies and Fighters: Gendered Tactics of the Alter-Globalization Movement in Prague (2000) and Genoa (2001). *Feminist Review* 92: 91–107.

Kopp, Hagen, and Florian Schneider. 2003. A Brief History of the Noborder Network. www.makeworlds.org/node/29.

Lang, Susanne, and Florian Schneider. 2003. The Dark Side of Camping. http://makeworlds.org/node/44.

Loyd, Jenna, Matt Mitchelson, and Andrew Burridge, eds. 2012. *Beyond Walls and Cages: Prisons, Borders, and Global Crisis*. Athens: University of Georgia Press.

Luft, Rachel. 2008. Looking for Common Ground: Relief Work in Post-Katrina New Orleans as an American Parable of Race and Gender Violence. *National Women's Studies Association Journal* 20 (3): 5–31.

Massey, Doreen. 2005. *For Space*. Thousand Oaks, CA: Sage.

McAdam, Doug, John D. McCarthy, and Mayer N. Zald, eds. 1996. *Comparative Perspectives on Social Movements: Political Opportunities, Mobilizing Structures, and Cultural Framings*. Cambridge: Cambridge University Press.

McDowell, Linda. 2008. Thinking Through Work: Complex Inequalities, Constructions of Difference and Trans-National Migrants. *Progress in Human Geography* 32 (4): 491–507.

McNevin, Anne. 2006. Political Belonging in a Neoliberal Era: The Struggle of the Sans-Papiers. *Citizenship Studies* 10 (2): 135–151.

Moghadam, Valentine M. 2005. *Globalizing Women: Transnational Feminist Networks*. Baltimore: Johns Hopkins University Press.

Mohanty, Chandra. 2003. *Feminism Without Borders: Decolonizing Theory, Practicing Solidarity*. Durham, NC: Duke University Press.

Nagar, Richa, and Susan Geiger. 2007. Reflexivity and Positionality in Feminist Fieldwork Revisited. In *Politics and Practice in Economic Geography*, edited by Adam Tickell, Eric Sheppard, Jamie Peck, and Trevor Barnes, 267–278. Thousand Oaks, CA: Sage.

Naples, Nancy A. 2009. Crossing Borders: Community Activism, Globalization, and Social Justice. *Social Problems* 56 (1): 2–20.

Nicholls, Walter J. 2007. The Geographies of Social Movements. *Geography Compass* 1 (3): 607–622.

Nyers, Peter. 2003. Abject Cosmopolitanism: The Politics of Protection in the Anti-Deportation Movement. *Third World Quarterly* 24 (6): 1069–1093.

Pratt, Geraldine, and Brenda Yeoh. 2003. Transnational (Counter) Topographies. *Gender, Place and Culture* 10 (2): 159–166.

Rechitsky, Raphi. 2013. Humanitarian Racism? International Aid and the Politics of Refugee Integration in Ukraine [Гуманітарний расизм? Міжнародна допомога та політика інтеграції біженців в Україні]. *Spilne* 5, Special Issue on the Political Economy of Racism. http://commons.com.ua/?p=12948.

Rechitsky, Raphi, Renata Blumberg, and Arnoldas Blumberg. 2009. East/West and North/South Fissures in Transnational Social Movements: The Case of 2007 No Border Camps at the Ukraine/EU and U.S./Mexico Borders. Paper presented at the conference Social and Natural Limits of Globalization and the Current Conjuncture, PEWS Mini-conference, American Sociological Association. University of San Francisco, San Francisco, August 7.

Rodrigues, Maria Guadalupe Moog. 2003. *Global Environmentalism and Local Politics: Transnational Advocacy Networks in Brazil, Ecuador, and India.* Albany: State University of New York Press.

Routledge, Paul. 2003. Convergence Space: Process Geographies of Grassroots Globalization Networks. *Transactions of the Institute of British Geographers* 28 (3): 333–349.

Sheppard, Eric. 2002. The Spaces and Times of Globalization: Place, Scale, Networks, and Positionality. *Economic Geography* 78 (3): 307–330.

Smith, Adrian, John Pickles, Milan Buček, Robert Begg, and Poli Roukova. 2008. Reconfiguring "Post-Socialist" Regions: Cross-Border Networks and Regional Competition in the Slovak and Ukrainian Clothing Industry. *Global Networks* 8 (3): 281–307.

Smith, Jackie, Scott Byrd, Ellen Reese, and Elizabeth Smythe, eds. 2012. *Handbook on World Social Forum Activism.* Boulder, CO: Paradigm Publishers.

Stroup, Sarah S. 2012. *Borders Among Activists: International NGOs in the United States, Britain, and France.* Ithaca, NY: Cornell University Press.

Sundberg, Juanita. 2007. Reconfiguring North-South Solidarity: Critical Reflections on Experiences of Transnational Resistance. *Antipode* 39 (1): 144–166.

Sziarto, Kristin M., and Helga Leitner. 2010. Immigrants Riding for Justice: Space-Time and Emotions in the Construction of a Counterpublic. *Political Geography* 29 (7): 381–391.

Thayer, Millie. 2009. *Making Transnational Feminism: Rural Women, NGO Activists, and Northern Donors in Brazil.* New York: Routledge.

Uehling, Greta. 2004. Irregular and Illegal Migration Through Ukraine. *International Migration* 42 (3): 77–109.

Van Houtum, Henk. 2005. The Geopolitics of Borders and Boundaries. *Geopolitics* 10 (4): 672–679.

Weinmann, Ute. 2007. Viele Grenzen, ein Camp. Jungle World. http://jungle-world.com/artikel/2007/36/20277.html.

Zimmer, Kerstin. 2008. *Migrants and Refugees in the Buffer Zone: Asylum Policy in Ukraine.* Prague: Multicultural Center.

Zolberg, Aristide R. 2008. Immigrants as Citizens. *Sociological Forum* 23 (2): 403–407.

12

"Giving Wings to Our Dreams"

Binational Activism and Workers' Rights Struggles
in the San Diego–Tijuana Border Region

MICHELLE TÉLLEZ AND CRISTINA SANIDAD

Introduction

This chapter examines the work of activists along the San Diego-Tijuana border region,[1] who are seeking to redress the injustices that workers experience in assembly factories, also known as *maquiladoras*.[2] Abuses and corruption within the transnational *maquiladora* industry have been well documented by scholars (Bandy 2000; Cravey 1998; Landau 2005; Muñoz 2004; Peña 1997; Fernández-Kelly 1983; Iglesias Prieto 1997; Sklair 1989); however, in our work, we are interested in understanding the collective responses to these conditions. Bandy (2004; 2000) and Bandy and Bickham Mendez (2003) have advanced an understanding of transnational organizing and regional coalition building through their research on women activists both in Mexico and Nicaragua.[3] We contribute to this work by focusing on the strategies, structure, and coalition-building efforts of three grassroots groups based in the San Diego-Tijuana border region: the Colectiva Feminista Binacional (Binational Feminist Collective),[4] CITTAC (Centro de Información para Trabajadores y Trabajadoras Acción Comunitaria; Support Center for Workers), and the San Diego Maquiladora Worker Support Network.

These organizations serve as the focal point in our research for their leadership in coordinating a worker-led response that empowers and invests in individual workers and their communities; collectively they address short-term needs while, at the same time, build networks and skills for the long term. By identifying the strategies of these groups, we also offer insight to the possibilities for and implications of their work in producing a transnational space for organizing centered on relationship building and the construction of a counterhegemonic identity along the US-Mexico border. We use Millie Thayer's (2010) concept of counterpublics to think through the ways in which globalization may accelerate some forms of domination just as it facilitates the linking and empowering of once disconnected oppositional forces. Moreover, "transnational social movements are best understood not only as structured institutions that engage in formalized campaigns, coalitions, and events, but also as cultural actors who practice less visible forms of cultural politics as they create collective identities and stitch together alliances" (Thayer 2010, 28). The fabric of connection we have found in the San Diego-Tijuana region, as demonstrated by these organizations, is, in its most obvious form, the *maquiladora* industry; yet its evolution to a social space of convergence where multiple political subjects recognize a newly forming collective identity is significant. Furthermore, workers drive initiatives as they come into political consciousness, a consciousness that ultimately marks a broader critique of neoliberal domination at the US-Mexico border.

Some comments about the effects of neoliberal policies on the Mexican state merits mention here. Mexico has been suffering profound economic crisis since the 1980s, when rising interest rates on foreign debt and falling oil prices almost bankrupted the state. The administration at the time (Miguel de la Madrid 1982–1988) and those that followed have adopted austerity measures and structural adjustment programs which have led to continuous erosion of public spending on education, health, housing, and other social services. These changes have grossly affected the living standards for most Mexicans (Gabriel and Macdonald 1994). Furthermore, according to a report published in 2003 about the North American Free Trade Agreement (NAFTA) by the Carnegie Endowment for International Peace, there was an increase of 500,000 jobs in manufacturing from 1994 to 2002, but in the same time period in the agricultural sector, where almost one fifth of the Mexican population still work, 1.3 million jobs had been lost. Consequently, after the implementation of NAFTA in 1994, Mexicans, predominantly indigenous, from the countryside migrated to border-states. Actually, 64 percent of the migrants in Tijuana are from the states of Veracruz, Chiapas, Sinaloa, Jalisco, Sonora, Michoacán, and Mexico City (Rentería Pedraza and Spears Kirkland 2008, 3). Attracted to the northern border for higher wages and employment opportunities, many migrants are dismayed by the unjust wages they find in the booming factories in the border industrial parks, as real wages are lower than they were when NAFTA took effect. In fact, the real minimum wage is half of what it was in 1988 (Davalos 2004; Audley et al. 2003; Arroyo 2003).

State neglect contributes to what Victor Ortiz (2004) calls "persistent frontiers" at the border region as it becomes a site for continued colonizations. He states that "newcomers and institutional bodies based elsewhere command greater influence than most local residents" (Ortiz 2004, xii) and underscores the ways in which "the border region crystallizes the stunning ambiguities of globalization with blinding clarity" (2004, xvii). In this chapter we think through these contradictions by examining the ways in which political subjectivity is being redefined at the US-Mexico border vis-à-vis the nation-state and its governing bodies and the global market. In other words, while some argue that globalization has limited the nation-state's capacity to administer national economies (Safran and Maiz 2000; Miyoshi 1996), we believe that proliferating global markets have actually increased the need for national boundaries and monitoring. Borders have become more porous to the free flow of capital and goods, but not to the free passage of people (Sadowski-Smith, 2002).

At the San Diego–Tijuana crossing point, this reality is most visible with the increased measures of security implemented with Operation Gatekeeper in 1994, the same year NAFTA went into effect. It clearly demonstrates the ways in which the international demarcation has become increasingly more militarized (Dunn 1996; Parenti 1999; Andreas 2000) effectively making it more difficult—and, often, deadly—for migrants to cross from the south to the north.

Grassroots Organizing for Workers Rights: Evidence of the Transnational in the Local

The US-Mexico border region becomes a site in which multiple intersections of power and control increasingly mark the lives of border dwellers and, more specifically, workers in the region. As many have argued, the expansion of economies beyond national borders blurs the jurisdiction and culpability of local and federal governments, multinational corporations, and international organizations over labor conditions, environmental concerns, and human rights abuses in the region (Bandy 2000; Cravey 1998; Landau 2005; Muñoz 2004; Peña 1997; Salzinger 2003; Sklair 1989; Sassen 1998). The lack of accountability coupled with the maximization of profits by transnational corporations has led to an unstable work environment that compromises workers' job-security and freedom to make decisions without facing drastic consequences (Landau 2005; Tiano 2006). The various devastating working and living conditions in and around the *maquiladora* industry have been and continue to be sites for workers' struggle to survive.[5] In the face of complicated constructions of power and division at the border, transnational activism has emerged.[6] As Landau (2005, 359) argues, "on both sides of the border, residents understand globalization not as a theory, but as a result of living the experience." Indeed, the workers and activists of our study have developed a critique of global economic policies and have witnessed the evolving effects in their communities and work places; through this transnational lens they have come to understand the necessity of cross-border solidarity.

Solidarity, Bandy (2004, 412) notes, is formed by workers' critiques of neoliberalism, a concern for the creation and upholding of labor standards, collective participation in unions or other political arenas to affect change, cultivation of communication and relationships that transcend borders, and the "creation of a culture of hope among workers that a more just and democratic development is possible." For example, in his examination of the Coalition for Justice in the Maquiladoras (CJM), he demonstrates that with increased solidarity between social actors through worker-to-worker exchanges, a collective consciousness emerges. Solidarity allows for the workers to identify with each other in their common struggles, transforming local resistance into international labor rights struggles. In this way, the movements move from the local to the global. Moreover, transnational activism creates hope. Though this hope may seem relatively unimportant, it serves to fuel the movement: "This language of hope cannot feed or clothe workers in need, and it alone does not regulate capital. Yet, it cannot be underestimated since, in the absence of substantive reform, it is a primary source of workers' commitments to movement participation and international coalition" (Bandy 2004, 419).

What this research makes evident is that workers are not remaining passive about the policies and conditions that affect them and are instead responding in important ways to create change in their lives. While an internally known counterimage of workers who reside along the US-Mexico border as critical actors in mobilizing social change is emerging (Bandy 2000; Bacon 2004; Camacho 1999; Peña 1997; Rivera-Salgado 1999; Tiano 1987; Téllez 2008; Navarro 2002; Coronado 2008), it is generally restricted to academic works and activist circles, where the humanity and resistance of border dwellers is being documented and publicized in a conscientious act of redefinition. More commonly, on both sides of the border one hears the border region described in a negative way—as a site of violence, drug trafficking, and exploitation. In line with Naples's (2002, 286) call to consider and explore the importance of place and locale while articulating resistance strategies, we note that that the US-Mexico border is not merely a site of passage or transit, as it is often depicted (Ortiz 2004; Téllez 2008), but instead a unique location of intersecting political, social, and class identities that allows for the emergence and development of "coalitional solidarity" (Bandy 2000) and transformative resistance against globalization and its effects.

As Millie Thayer (2010, 4) argues, transnational networks represent the other face of globalization, "the emancipatory possibilities created by new interlocal connections." She asks that we begin to get a better grasp of the cultural dimension of cross-border politics and move toward understanding that "social movements are relational constructs" (Thayer 2010, 6). Similar to the new popular movements and women's autonomy movements as described by Bickham Mendez (2002; 2005), Starr (2000), Domínguez (2002), and MacDonald (2005), the San Diego-Tijuana based coalition we introduce grew out of a frustration with the lack of accountability, compliance, enforcement, and change on the part of government, corporations, unions, and other groups, as well as in response to changes in federal law and economic development policies. The coalition collaborates to pressure the federal government and multinational corporations to provide fair work conditions and pay, environmental protections, and respect. With this important regional project in mind, we will underscore the possibilities that can be produced through cross-border relationships and articulate the sentiment of hope generated by the belief that the *maquiladora* industry actually creates a space in which multiple identities and movements intersect, producing a macro vision for social change.

Methods

Through mixed methods of data collection, we document each organization's mission and history, organizing strategies, membership structure, and the effects of recent political and economic changes on their work. Data collection, which occurred between September 2004 and March 2009, included participant observation of the groups' meetings, actions, and celebrations, focus groups with *maquiladora* workers, semistructured interviews with center staff, and textual analysis of organizational documents such as meeting minutes, memos, reflections, and mission statements. The diverse data provided insight into how, on a day-to-day basis, these organizations validate workers and their experiences, magnify their voices and the impact of their actions, and build solidarity with each other and transnational allies in the context of the San Diego–Tijuana border region. Common characteristics shared among the three include autonomous organization, limited external funding, and a commitment to being community-based and worker-driven.

Organizations: La Colectiva, CITTAC, SDMWSN
La Colectiva Feminista Binacional

La Colectiva Feminista Binacional (Binational Feminist Collective, hereafter referred to as *la colectiva*) consists of activists, feminists, *maquiladora* workers, self-identified Zapatistas,[7] environmentalists, students, artists, and organizers from the United States and Mexico who identify mostly as Chicanas and Mexicanas. Born out of other feminist movements in the area, there are currently seven active members, ranging in age from twenty-five to fifty-five, who attend meetings, organize workshops, and contribute to the kitchen collective. Their primary home base is in the city of Tijuana, and they share office space with other organizations (such as CITTAC). According to their mission statement, the goal of *la colectiva* is to "construct a new movement that supports and highlights the spiritual and human components of the diverse struggles experienced by women in the border region" through workshops, festivals, and a binational *encuentro* (meeting) (Colectiva Feminista Binacional 2004). Through an analysis of NAFTA, they argue that there has been an increased pressure on women through lower salaries, the constant threat of unemployment, and exposure to chemical contamination and toxic waste from transnational companies. Members realized that after ten years of organizing at the local level their work needed to move beyond their own communities, because as Carmen, an organizer of the *encuentro*, points out, "the policies that inform transnational capital do not stay in the locality, neither should the collective responses be tied to particular locations" (personal interview 2009).

In this vein, *la colectiva* builds community for *Mexicana* workers who often have not only traveled from the interior of Mexico to the border region alone, but also face a range of oppressors due to their multiple "other" identities (i.e., poor, indigenous, and/or queer women). *La colectiva* is committed to serving and empowering women through the creation of a worker solidarity network with an intersectional focus: "The fight cannot only be for salary, or to have better working conditions, but [we must also fight against] capitalist exploitation and patriarchy in the factories" (personal interview 2009).

CITTAC

El Centro de Información para Trabajadores y Trabajadoras Acción Communitaria (referred to as CITTAC), a Workers' Information Center, was formed in 1991 by workers in the bank, telephone, and *maquiladora* industries who came together to collectively learn how to use federal labor laws as recourse in worker abuse cases. While its initial focus was supporting the unionized telephone workers with their publication and radio broadcasts, this focus changed in 1993 when workers in the telephone, social security, and banking sectors became part of the union's executive board, thus creating a divide in CITTAC between the unionized workers and the *maquiladora* and cooperative workers.

Though offered financial support from the union, the members of CIT-TAC decided against accepting funds that might limit or change its chosen activities and focus.

CITTAC, with a centrally located office in Tijuana,[8] now primarily serves the *maquiladora* workers so as to improve their living and working conditions and defend their labor and gender rights. *Maquiladora* workers are invited to go to the center to learn about their rights, determine the most appropriate method of recourse in their case, and pursue justice on their own behalf. Preparing workers to defend themselves in court is a fundamental component of the service provided by the group, although not one member has had any legal training outside of their hands-on experience. They also publish a monthly newsletter (*el Boletín Maquilero*) and they distribute a "know your rights" (*Primeros Auxilios*) pamphlet to *maquiladora* workers. There are currently two paid members who handle workers' cases, though the organization has over thirty active members who come to meetings, support actions, and contribute to the newsletter, allowing the organization to serve hundreds of workers.

San Diego Maquiladora Worker Solidarity Network

The San Diego Maquiladora Worker Solidarity Network (referred to as SDMWSN), a binational support system for *maquiladora* workers, was formed by San Diego-based activists in 2004[9] and grew out of a desire to bridge commonalities across the border and further strengthen the relationship between cross-border activists. One of its functions is to support CITTAC and *la colectiva* by complementing their work with binational actions. In their mission statement, they also make clear their position on US and multinational corporations in the border cities, who, as they state, "have no right to humiliate workers, subject them to dangerous working conditions, pay squalid wages, or repress worker organization." It is around this declaration that the group organizes, focusing on how to best address this global issue locally.

The network is committed to developing transnational organizing strategies that incorporate the voices and needs of Tijuana workers. Through the coordination of border tours, conferences, forums, and panels, the network focuses on outreaching to and educating US citizens about the conditions and wages in the factories. Through this work they create opportunities for dialogue about the role US citizens play as consumers and advocates.

Living and Working Conditions at the Border: Realities and Illusions

The San Diego-Tijuana border is a unique context in which to examine organizing and resistance efforts for its complex cultural, political, and economic dynamics. After the signing of the Treaty of Guadalupe Hidalgo in 1848 and after the international boundary between Mexico and the United States was drawn, Tijuana and Baja California were very isolated from the center of Mexico where most of the country's resources, people, and political power were located (Lore, 1999). The arrival of large amounts of capital into southern California in the late 1800s had a spillover effect in Baja California, which was facilitated by Porfirio Diaz's government (1870–1910), which offered concessions to foreign capital to encourage investment—offers that US interests took up, especially in the mining and transportation sectors (Nevins 2002). The most far-reaching transformation of the border region in the late nineteenth century resulted from the construction of a railroad network that connected the Mexican north and the US southwest with the major commercial and population centers in each country. Railroads increased the value of the border region's natural resources by connecting them to distant processing plants, distribution centers, and markets (Lorey 1999).

By the turn of the century, US investments in Mexico had risen to over one-half billion dollars and more than one thousand US companies were engaged in Mexican operations. These investments marked the beginning of significant US economic influence in Mexico (Lorey 1999). Furthermore, during the Depression era, the United States deported hundreds of thousands of Mexicans, many whom settled in Tijuana, which contributed to its population boom.[10] In 1942, the US Bracero Program was established and attracted thousands of migrants to the northern boundary. Tijuana's population more than tripled during the decade, reaching almost 70,000 by the year 1950. The post-Depression era coincided with a US military buildup in San Diego during the 1940s and 1950s, providing a clientele for the entertainment and tourist economy that had been in decline since the Depression (and Prohibition) (Nevins 2002). Clearly, the interconnected yet asymmetrical relationship between the border cities was defined early on and Tijuana and its citizens were deemed second-class citizens, a designation that was reinscribed on the bodies of Mexican border women who were seen as tools of diversion and exploitation.

The unbalanced power dynamics became compounded in 1961, when the Mexican government launched the Programa Nacional Fronterizo (PRONAF), or National Border Program. The program aimed to beautify border towns, build up their tourist infrastructure, and create favorable conditions for industrialization in the border region. The Border Industrialization Program (BIP), an outgrowth of PRONAF, established the border zone corridor of export processing industries known as *maquiladoras* in 1965 (Herzog 1990; Lorey 1999; Nevins 2002). *Maquiladoras* were the only firms exempt from Mexican law, which required majority Mexican ownership (Lorey 1999). The BIP also helped to fuel significant migration to border cities from other parts of Mexico. In a forty-year period between 1950 and 1990, the population of Mexican border-states multiplied 3.6 times (Lorey 1999). And between 1990 and 2004, there was an increase of 24.1 million (29.7 percent) people in Mexico, 21.7 percent of which were absorbed by border-states and 10.6 percent of which were absorbed by border *municipios* (Institute for Policy and Economic Development 2006).

Tijuana continues to serve as a destination for migrants from across the Mexican nation, who travel to the border in the hopes of fulfilling the dream of economic security. For example, Mago, a former *maquiladora* worker from Oaxaca, who is now a lead organizer for CITTAC, was drawn to Tijuana where she heard workers "don't bother to pick up dropped dollars from the floor . . . [because] there's an abundance of well-paid work" (personal interview 2009). Manuel, a worker from Tlaxcala, added: "They tell us that here one can get a good car for almost nothing, that one will have work, a house, everything. It was the 'American dream,' only without the risks of crossing to the other side, the American dream in Mexico" (personal interview 2009).

Upon arrival, migrants are faced with a much starker reality in which their dreams of economic stability are truncated. This experience has only been compounded by the global economic downturn of the last few years. *El Mexicano* reported in January and February of 2010 that the unemployment rate had reached its highest in recent history, with 9 percent of Tijuana residents (approx. 61,000 people) unemployed at a time when the national unemployment average was only 6 percent (Gomez-Sanchez 2010; *El Mexicano* 2010). Members of CITTAC claim that job seekers fill the streets, easily identifiable by the folders they carry with the required documentation needed to obtain a job. In addition to the soaring unemployment rates, underemployment has had a significant impact on household income as factories are cutting workers' schedules by offering three days of work per week or only one-month contracts.

Needless to say, workers' buying power has been significantly compromised. During a focus group discussion, *maquiladora* workers claimed that the low wages affect "everything," commenting that prices for food, clothing, transportation, water, light, and education are all rising (personal interview 2009). With climbing unemployment rates and few alternatives, workers who currently are employed are encouraged to keep their jobs despite substandard pay and working conditions.

A staff member at CITTAC acknowledged the compromising situations in which workers often find themselves:

> You can imagine how difficult it is to work a week in the conditions in which they are working. They do not have a schedule. There is no eight-hour limit; you have to work the hours the company gives you. They do not have any protection in terms of health, in terms of nutrition, in terms of exposure to chemicals, in terms of help to take care of your family . . . It is exploitation in this way. It's absolutely brutal (personal interview 2009).

Interviewees from each of the three grassroots organizations related that the economic recession in Tijuana has greatly impacted workers' security and well-being, as well as their methods of resistance and recourse. In the face of bleak conditions border dwellers are reimagining new possibilities.

Strategies and Empowerment: *Maquiladora* Workers and Their Allies Incite Change at the Border

In analyzing the work of *la colectiva*, CITTAC, and SDMWSN, we have come to understand three strategies of creative responses to both the *maquiladora* industry and the conditions of their lives: 1) community-based, worker-led democratic organizing, 2) outreach and education, and 3) binational organizing. In describing these tactics, we are pointing to the ways in which the activists of these organizations have begun to make their everyday lives livable and how their work makes evident that democratic and autonomous organizing is instrumental to changing the lives of workers as is building solidarity.

Solidarity develops from a need. An organizer with *la colectiva* posits that among the *maquiladora* workers, this need derives from the fact that "migration has made it so that you don't have a familial or social network . . . to support you, so who is going to have your back? For that reason, you have to develop a solidarity network" (personal communication 2009). Solidarity among Mexican workers develops as they share their experiences with one another; solidarity with their US allies stems from a shared critique of neoliberalism and relationship building through meetings, cultural exchanges, actions, and conversations. Between the three organizations, the movement has become interracial and intergenerational, and activists describe a need for trust in order to deal with conflicts when they arise.

Community-Based, Worker-Led, Democratic Organization

Democratic, community-based organization is an essential component of the work by CITTAC, *la colectiva*, and SDMWSN, as it recognizes and provides an alternative to a history of marginalization and lack of access and representation. The deprivation of community control and bargaining power on the municipal, state, and federal levels of government often extends into the workplace, rendering workers vulnerable to the profit-maximizing efforts employers utilize without regard to the well-being of workers. Because worker power and control are challenged in many public settings, grassroots, community-based organizations must prioritize space and time for worker empowerment and leadership development and allow the local community to drive the work and mission of the organizations so that the expressed needs of the community can be appropriately met.

The organizations have, in name, a formalized hierarchical leadership structure with a president, vice-president, and secretary as required by NGO regulations and external funders; however, in practice, each organization functions within a nonhierarchical structure for the purpose of incorporating workers' voices, prioritizing their needs, and giving them control over decisions that affect their everyday lives. In this way, they operate more like an *asamblea* (democratic forum) with the expectation that every person plays a role and contributes according to their time, skills, and ability. Organization meetings and forums allow space for the activists to meet, discuss and learn from each other. Because of the insider knowledge and familiarity necessary to assess and evaluate the current situation in the *maquiladoras,* CITTAC's members decided that it would be a requirement for all members of the organization to be workers as opposed to scholars or local activists. One member told us, "We have to know our enemy. We have to know our work. We ourselves will do the analysis of our places; we don't have to wait for someone else to do it" (personal interview 2009).

Members intimately know the challenges to worker participation and organization and are committed to addressing these obstacles in ways that account for limited resources and enhance community development. During a focus group, one organizer said, "We cannot only stay in protest but also explore mechanisms for how we will survive, by using [creative strategies such as] gardens [and] shopping collectives" (personal interview 2009).

For example, one such obstacle that women confront as leaders and which community-based organizations are committed to addressing is accessibility to childcare. A member of *la colectiva* spoke to a common situation in which women find themselves:

> I cannot leave because I bring my children with me and my son goes off running and they distract me and everyone else. They get bored. The woman is usually with her children. Where are they going to leave them? So, we decided that someone's daughter or one of us would take turns with the kids so that the women could take advantage of the workshops (personal interview 2009).

By recognizing and addressing the obstacles women organizers and leaders confront, the collective creates the conditions in which they can fully participate in the movement and focus on their educational and personal development.

Rising unemployment rates and women's lack of access to safely-earned income is another issue addressed by *la colectiva* and SDMWSN, which support a women's cooperative called the collective kitchen as a creative solution to these needs. In addition to providing an alternative source of income, women gain experience in small business management, and the space and opportunity to develop an intentional community in which everything from recipes to their experiences of domestic abuse can be shared.

Another collaborative, creative response to the rising unemployment and safety concerns is the small alternative marketplace of Cosme Damian (located in the offices of CITTAC/*La colectiva* in Tijuana) where local artisans and musicians, including *maquiladora* workers, can sell their art and where they have access to the "reality" tourists that SDMWSN brings in. A final response, which is still in the planning phase, is a community garden that will provide fresh food, a shared community safe space, and a team-building project for the women. These three programs represent creative direct responses to the needs of their members and the surrounding community, and also create an opportunity for community development and empowerment.

Outreach and Education

Education and outreach in the local community is a priority among the three grassroots organizations, each of which have designed strategies to bring *maquiladora* workers together in a safe space to learn about their rights, and the resources and recourse available to them. Part of the strategic outreach to workers is the distribution of the *Maquiladora* newsletter (*El Boletín Maquilero*) developed by CITTAC and the Red de Trabajadoras y Trabajadores de la Maquila (Maquiladora Workers Network, a subgroup of CITTAC based in Tijuana that serves as a support network for just *maquiladora* workers); the newsletter serves to "provide a space so that the workers know and defend [their] human and labor rights and share their workplace experiences and struggle"

(Red de Trabajadoras y Trabajadores de la Maquila 2006). The newsletter also informs workers of the assistance provided by CITTAC.

Workers who solicit assistance from CITTAC attend workshops about empowerment, workers' rights, and gender issues, and both the legal and extra legal recourse available to them. As one organizer explained:

> Initially, we had not thought to take legal cases; we don't trust in the law, so why would we do this? But, we realized along the way that it was a way to teach people more quickly about their rights and they became more interested in the issue of organizing (personal interview 2009).

Learning the law and how to maneuver within the legal framework has proven to be an empowering experience for workers as they take control over their own lives and cases. Indeed, the Mexican constitution of 1917 guarantees workers the right of association, the right to organize and bargain collectively, the right to strike, and the eight-hour day. The Federal Labor Law (FLL) of 1970 amplifies the constitutional protections with extended provisions protecting working conditions, health insurance, pensions, job descriptions, working schedules, and job security (Fuentes Muñiz 1994/1995). Many have argued that Mexican federal labor laws are the best in the world, but only on paper. Yet the workers have found ways to not only have their cases heard but also have many rulings in their favor despite the unsettling contradictions found in the rules that bind manufacturing in Mexico. On the one hand the government obligates foreign firms to comply with Mexico's detailed labor regulations while at the same time increasing foreign investment requires that the Mexican government attempt to make these regulations flexible enough not to scare off foreign investors (Peters 1990). Yet by learning about federal law, the activists of CITTAC have tapped into a resource that is legally binding and educates and empowers workers, and, after a number of victories, CITTAC has developed a reputation such that when the Labor Board finds out that CITTAC will be defending a worker, "they know there will be a fight" (personal interview 2009).

La colectiva offers workshops to women that are relevant to their lives, challenge their ways of thinking, and demand intellectual growth and leadership development. Recognizing the need to involve "intellectual resistance with traditional protests" (*colectiva* member, personal interview 2009), the collective has offered workshops on patriarchy, gender rights in the workplace, women's health and safety, and reproductive rights. One such workshop, organized in collaboration with Centro de Investigación Laborales y Asesorías Sindical (CILA), allowed workers access to several doctors with specialties in labor health who spoke to the impact of chemicals on women's reproductive health and men's sexuality. The hope is that with an increased understanding of both labor rights and worker safety, workers will be better prepared to prevent future injury and exposure, and demand government mandated protections from employers.

In connecting workers and providing a space to hear each other's testimonies, workers learn about and analyze the context in which they live and work. By sharing stories, the struggle becomes less individualistic in focus, drawing attention instead to the intersectionality of social problems with sexism, classism, and racism. Through continued conversation and analysis, the workers learn that their experiences are not isolated, but rather are systematic and transnational in nature and that the response must be equally as complex and globalized. This realization led to the development of SDMWSN.

SDMWSN works to expose US citizens to the realities just on the other side of the border, realities they can influence as consumers and educated advocates. On the local level, the network hosts border tours during which participants see art projects on the border wall, learn about Metales y Derivados (the abandoned lead smelter site featured in the film *Maquilapolis*, explained below) and its impact on the local community, meet CITTAC's members and staff, and hear about the common complaints reported by *maquila* workers. Herb Shore, a cofounder of the network, clarified the utility of the tours and the network's work:

> For me what we can do is make Mexico a less mysterious place to progressive people on this side of the border. And part of what we're doing is helping to create a politically aware movement of young people in this country (Morlan 2006).

In addition to the border tours, the network and its leaders participate in conferences, forums, and panels in order to bring this border reality to light and create opportunities for transformative dialogue. As Bickham Mendez and Wolf (2012, 648) summarize, "spaces that permit and foster solidarity and exchange and in which groups and individuals link local issues, grievances, and even identities to an understanding of global processes provide fertile ground for forging counterhegemonies and developing alternatives to the dominant neoliberal paradigm."

The design and implementation of SDMWSN's programs allow solidarity to develop organically between workers and allies such that, collectively, they come to recognize the common, transnational need for stable work, consistent pay, regularized environmental protections and working conditions, and protection from discrimination. Story-sharing allows workers and allies to connect with the others' humanity and daily lives.

Binational Organizing

Binational and transnational organizing have been an important component of the work of CITTAC, SDMWSN, and *la colectiva* for the purpose of raising awareness, creating leverage, and building coalitional solidarity around workers' rights and human dignity. In line with what Foster (2005, 218–219) outlines as the shared interest of groups within a transnational network, these three grassroots organizations collaborate to confront shared targets, create opportunities for broader dialogue and understanding, and facilitate the exploration of personal linkages.

The SDMWSN has led the efforts to construct bridges between community groups, students, unions, and local activists in Tijuana and San Diego in order to raise consciousness of shared labor struggles, environmental degradation caused by factories, and local and transnational organizing efforts. The SDMWSN developed two programs that facilitate this communication, information sharing, and worker solidarity. The first program is the organized border tour through which primarily California-based individuals and groups are transported to the industrial zone and communities of Tijuana and have the opportunity to meet the workers and activists involved in the labor struggle there. The SDMWSN and *la colectiva* collaborate on this project, providing the opportunity for the kitchen collective to prepare food for tour participants. The second program allows *maquiladora* workers from

Tijuana (members of CITTAC) the opportunity to travel to San Diego as "ambassadors" to visit the San Diego Labor Council, local unions, schools, and other sites, and raise awareness of about the labor experiences of *maquiladora* workers. As an activist with SDMWSN stated,

> The idea is that the unions and the groups in San Diego would be conscious that the struggles in the assembly plants of Tijuana exist. And also that the comrades, the workers of Tijuana would know also that there are labor struggles in San Diego. We have tried to put into contact the groups that are involved in this struggle from the two sides of the border (personal interview 2009).

In addition to the educational aspect of the binational organizing, the SDMWSN, *la colectiva*, and CITTAC coordinate actions between the activists and allies in San Diego and Tijuana in order to address problems within specifically identified companies and in the *maquiladora* industry broadly. Simultaneous protests and other mutually agreed-upon tactics such as letter-writing campaigns are common ways that workers support each other binationally, a strategy that has effectively allowed workers to confront multinational company owners living in San Diego. One activist from SDMWSN shared this example:

> There were cases in which the company owners were living in San Diego, specifically in Chula Vista. All that we could do was to organize a simultaneous protest in San Diego while the workers in Tijuana were marching in front of the factory. The factory was closed, but we were also protesting in front of the owners' other businesses and in front of the sports club that the owners belonged to (in Tijuana). We were here [in San Diego] protesting in front of the owners' house, and by their purely bad luck that day they [the owners] had invited over all of their friends and family for a barbeque or I don't know what. All of the people there were scared when groups of activists arrived. It was such a scandal! (personal interview 2009).

Furthermore, with the goal of building networks, in September of 2004 *la colectiva* decided to organize an *encuentro*, or meeting, with other activists working on issues affecting women in the border region.

This was the first grassroots, binational, women-centered meeting held at the women's center in the autonomous community of Maclovio Rojas (see Mancillas 2002; Téllez 2006, 2008) located between the cities of Tecate and Tijuana. The call for the *encuentro* stated the following:

> Knowing each other gives us the opportunity to extend our own struggles and working together we can come up with strategies for better communication locally, regionally and binationally. With this kind of gathering, we'll focus on the specific gendered problems that we face and, also, we will put forward a perspective from women and by women (CFB event flyer 2004).

The objectives of the *encuentro* were several: 1) look at ties that already exist between organizations in Baja California, Mexico and California, US; 2) share different organizing experiences and learn from each other; 3) come up with a solution to the problems that we have as women workers, community members and organizers in this region; 4) collective reflection of who we are and what are our struggles are; and 5) formulate strategies for support. The two-day meeting attracted over forty organizations from California and Baja California and a worker/organizer from Guatemala. Those present were migrants, academics, students, union organizers, *maquiladora* workers, community health workers, indigenous women, housewives, and media workers. The turnout was extremely successful, considering that the gathering was led by workers, students, and activists and was coordinated with no outside funding other than participant donations.

Being situated in the border region is advantageous for cross-border organizing due to the proximity to allies and the opportunities for sharing testimony and developing shared consciousness. Bandy and Bickham Mendez (2003) have similarly noted that the border is a place where activists have been focused since the passage of NAFTA, and opportunities for ongoing binational and bilingual collaboration are numerous. Binational organizing is an important tool as it helps shape a coordinated transnational response to a transnational issue. In particular, binational organizing allows women and others who disproportionately bear the brunt of economic restructuring due to NAFTA the opportunity to develop a shared oppositional identity, a starting ground for addressing the common implications they face (Gabriel and Macdonald 1994), such as tense binational relations, environmental degradation, and labor and human rights abuse. As one organizer from SDMWSN noted,

> It's a way to build interethnic relationships. The network in San Diego has many "gringos" (white US Americans) and it's an opportunity for Mexican workers to see them. Sometimes there are misunderstandings, but here we have begun to, slowly, very slowly, build trust (personal interview 2009).

Through creative tactics that utilize binational solidarity, the workers have drawn attention to their labor struggles and the undeniable international responsibility for the *maquiladora* workers' plight. Yet a discussion on cross-border organizing must speak to the difficulties that also arise when community-based, worker-driven organizations utilize binational organizing strategies. There are several common obstacles that the organizations must consider and address. One relates to financing and the conditions, priorities, and strategies imposed on organizations by their funders. The three organizations highlighted in this chapter have had difficulty securing external funds for operations and activities as they refuse to accept funds with strings attached. For example, a funder of *la colectiva* decided that it would rather invest in an organization whose focus is solely women's reproductive rights rather than an organization that also addresses human and labor rights. *La colectiva* preferred not to accept funds rather than change its work according to the funder's new requirements. By remaining true to their theoretical and value-based principals, these organizations are even more severely limited in external funding.

Another obstacle to binational organizing is the ability of Tijuana workers to cross the border to meet workers in San Diego and to participate in SDMWSN's program as ambassadors. Because traveling across the border is imperative to the success of the cross-border consciousness-raising efforts and the development of coalitional solidarity, and typically only a few workers have the appropriate papers with which to cross the border, if US citizens do not travel to Mexico with the SDMWSN's coordinated border tours, the cross-border outreach and education efforts are severely impaired. This, of course, speaks to the already asymmetrical relationship that exists between US and Mexican citizens—in terms of access, sociopolitical positions, and resources—compounded by cultural and linguistic miscommunications that also emerge. For example, oftentimes in meetings, opinions and comments get lost in translation or not translated at all for those who are not bilingual. Addressing these issues requires a commitment to the cross-border relationship that we believe is there but sometimes gets lost under the amount of work that needs to be done. But this needs to be recognized as an important part of the work because other sociocultural differences such as different notions about punctuality, presumed levels of detachment, and having different foci can lead to implosions. This can happen both internally and externally as made visible in some of the breaks that have happened between the time of our research and the writing of this chapter. While the organizations as described here continue to exist and operate in these ways, there have been some splits among activists, and a new organization has emerged.[11] Christina Gabriel and Laura Macdonald (1994), whose work focuses on trinational organized responses to NAFTA, similarly point to differences in race, socioeconomic class, gender, resources, communication styles, organizing strategies, priorities, and analysis that complicate collaboration. Moreover, CITTAC has a long history with binational relationship building and has experienced several splits with some major unions in the United States precisely for these reasons; as a result, CITTAC has put emphasis on building a Mexico-based space of support for *maquiladora* workers. In other words, long-time activists in CITTAC recognize that the power inequalities that have occurred in the past can derail their movement, and by centering the needs and experiences of the *maquiladora* workers they instead remain steadfast in their commitment to improving the lives of *maquiladora* workers.

Discussion/Implications

By outlining the strategies that best represent the multilayered, cross-border efforts of the organizations in the San Diego–Tijuana border region, we are pointing to the ways in which these grassroots organizations have given hope and voice to the workers of the *maquiladora* industry. In identifying and putting into practice a community-led and democratically organized project, the workers and activists of the area are representing a dramatically different image of border dwellers as active and informed agents for social change. Their strategic efforts address long-term labor struggles through education, community, leadership development, and cooperative cross-border coalition building, and creatively respond to the specific needs of border dwellers. The education, outreach, and community development efforts are imperative to the sustainability of local grassroots organizing, and the community's capacity for demanding an international effort to protect and advance the state of labor in the face of global restructuring. As one member of SDSNMW said,

> Even the product that is created in the *maquiladoras* is multinational, so we cannot just target one company. Unlike any other part in the country we are completely tied to the international struggle of workers, to what happens to workers in other parts of the world and how we can build alliances between here and there (personal interview 2009).

While we recognize that some of these strategies are not new and have been outlined in other discussions around transnational/binational and worker-centered organizing (Bickham Mendez 2005; Fine 2006), below we trace the political significance of these particular coalitions and actions.

First, given the political climate of fear, alienation, and lack of mutual understanding that exists along this political demarcation, the ability to and importance of organizing across the US-Mexico border must be noted. Jonathan Fox (2002) argues that the binational relationship between the United States and Mexico is the broadest and deepest example of global integration, yet he points out that binational civil society coalitions have had limited impact on the national state. In fact, he argues that labor movements have had a consistent pattern of defeat and cites the 1999 Han Young case as a cautionary tale of the restrictions that US political pressure can have on federal labor law within Mexico.[12]

While we heed this critique, we believe that just as US political pressure has successfully pushed a neoliberal, corporate agenda, the same power can be positively redirected to ensure that the state of labor and human rights on the US-Mexico border remain a high legal priority for international audiences to address. The work of these three grassroots groups allows citizens of the United States and Mexico to collaborate in order to enact change that holds both the Mexican government and the multinational companies accountable.[13] In fact, the use of federal labor laws becomes a rallying point for allies on both sides of the US-Mexico border because it becomes a tangible target. As one organizer from CITTAC said,

> Today we are fighting against the bosses, and then we have to fight against the authorities because the authorities are always on the bosses' side. And then we have to fight against the union because they are also on the bosses' side. In one case we wanted to involve the environmental institutions. We had to fight with them, denouncing the problem that they were allowing chemicals to cross the border, so then we had to fight with customs. So, then each time we took steps, we confronted someone new. We were always there. It was like a monster with a thousand heads that we faced. The result is that now the workers in the factories do not just confront their boss; now we confront the whole system (personal interview 2009).

Recognizing the layered structures of power, organizers have to create strategies that will produce a material outcome. In other words, organizers recall that in the early stages of the labor movement, the relationship between the worker and his or her boss was very different where a worker could grieve directly to the boss. However, direct contact does not exist in the same way as it once did. Given the global nature of capital, production, and labor, organizers have to respond to the state by using the tools provided to them—namely labor law—but also make visible the tiered system of ownership across nation-states and the unequal distribution of wealth (through direct actions, letter campaigns, and other strategies outlined in this chapter). The activists we interviewed do not believe that changing the entire system will happen overnight, but they do count as success the sense of personal empowerment and leadership that taking action and being involved has produced for workers.

We also take into consideration Bickham Mendez's (2002; 2005) argument, based on her work in Nicaragua, that information and accountability politics (according to Keck and Sikkink's [1998] typologies) have been the most effective and utilized strategies for grassroots organizations, and that leverage politics has been a greater challenge. Our work clearly reflects this reality. But we have also underscored the importance that this work has had on creating cross-border solidarity and the sentiment of hope. We argue that this has produced a vision for change that does not end here; in fact, organizers and workers argue that a movement based on the *maquiladora* industry is essential to promoting change along the US-Mexico border. Activists believe that the border economy depends on the industry, as do the education, social security, and health institutions, since the *maquiladora* industry is the largest employer. There are also those who are indirectly affected by the *maquiladora* industry including: street vendors, transportation, and other retail and service industries. Given these articulations we demonstrate the intersecting components in Figure 12.1, adapted from the conversations we had with the organizers of CITTAC.

One of the organizers posed the question: "If conditions are terrible for the workers and if everyone is dependent [on the *maquiladora* industry] isn't there a moral/ethical obligation to workers? We have to make people see what is going on in the *maquilas*" (personal communication 2009).

Returning to Millie Thayer's concept of relational organizing and the idea that organizations inhabit a counterpublic through linkages at multiple scales, we underscore the ways in which the activists point to the intersections of the *maquiladora* industry, both in terms of the movements it creates and the colonizations present there. A space where multiple movements converge produces a collective identity, and as Thayer (2010, 26) states, "among the relations most important for the survival of a social movement are the ties it maintains with those whose identities and interests overlap, at least partially, with its own." Because the collective identity—based on the recognition of shared human experiences and values, and their critiques of neoliberalism—is contingent in part on a physical space that transcends borders, activists offer a model and a sense of hope for other grassroots organizations located along the US-Mexico border for issue-based organizing. For its location, cross-border organizers can influence international relations as they intersect with human rights and dignity.

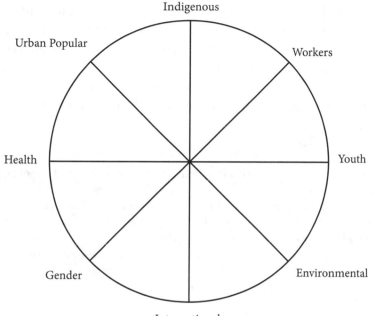

Figure 12.1.

Conclusion

Rather than be incorporated into a design of someone else's making, workers are centering their own voices in public discourse and allowing their experiences to inform the grassroots, community-based, local and binational strategies they use to resist globalization and victimization in the San Diego–Tijuana region. The successful labor organizing strategies outlined in this chapter focus simultaneously on individual and community development and empowerment and binational alliance-building, which are imperative to the organizations' work and the sustainability of the changes they initiate. Their strategies aim to address short-term, individual needs by empowering workers and developing their leadership capacity, networks, resources, skills, and rights so that they are able to advocate for themselves and tackle the larger transnational labor struggle. Worker solidarity drives the resistance as workers recognize they can no longer look narrowly at what directly and immediately impacts them as individuals, but rather how a larger oppressive system affects the collective. As a lead organizer from CITTAC says, "The Mexican constitution gives us the right to organize, to organize in the way that we need to. All we need to do is invent it, to give wings to our dreams" (personal interview 2009). Through their unwavering commitment, their dreams may very well take flight.

NOTES

1. This research was made possible through partial funding from the Ford Foundation and the Low Wage Work, Migration, and Gender project at the University of Illinois at Chicago; special thanks to Anna Guevarra for inviting us into the project. We would also like to thank photographer Oscar Michel for his help with the documentation of pivotal conversations and events and to the graduate students from ASU who helped with the transcription and translation of interviews: Courtney Andersen, Elizabeth Miller, and Katie Norberg. Finally, our heartfelt thanks to the workers who lent us their voices and to the activists that continue the fight for justice along the border.

2. Typically found in Mexico and Central America, *maquiladoras* are production sites where material and equipment are imported, processed, and reexported for foreign consumption. As Ching Louie and Burnham (2000, 11) note, the global economy refers to the "globalization of production, markets, finance, communications and the labor force"; the global economy is visible along the US-Mexico border in the form of Export Processing Zones (EPZs). An export-processing zone (EPZ) refers to a geographic area in which goods or equipment may be processed, manufactured, or reexported without the intervention of the customs authorities.

3. Tarrow (2001), Fox (2000), and Bandy and Bickham Mendez (2003) use the terms "transnational movements" and "transnational organizing" to refer to situations in which "groups from at least two different nations share information, organizational resources, strategy, and often but not always political interests and values" (Bickham Mendez 2003, 173).

4. The correct use of the word "collective" in the Spanish language is *colectivo*, but members of the group chose to change the word to a feminine ending to mark their women-centered framework.

5. For an examination of the living and working conditions in this region, please see Michelle Téllez (2008, 545–567); Oscar Martinez (1988); Rebecca Dolhinow (2006); Victor M Ortiz-Gonzalez (2004); and David Bacon (2004).

6. "Transnational activism" is defined as collective responses to globalization created through networks across borders that challenge inequalities in working

conditions and environments produced by multinational corporations (Armbruster-Sandoval 2005; Bandy 2000; Bandy 2004; Bacon 2004; Keck and Sikkink 1998; Liebowitz 2002; Staudt and Coronado 2002).

7. The Zapatistas (also known as the Ejercito Zapatista de Liberación Nacional or E.Z.L.N.) emerged in 1994, the same year the North American Free Trade Agreement (NAFTA) was implemented. This group of indigenous communities from the state of Chiapas came together with a national cry for recognition, autonomy, and demand for dignified access to their lands and ways of life. They received international attention and support and as a result civil organizations in communities and cities across the world materialized.

8. The space is shared by all of the organizations, but is used primarily by CITTAC.

9. This organization also grew out of a previous *maquiladora* worker support group run by San Diego based activist Mary Tong. Please see http://enchantedwebsites.com/maquiladora/ for more information.

10. In the 1930s this was called the Great Repatriation, and later, in the 1950s, as a result of continued nativism and racialized scapegoating, the program returned under the name Operation Wetback (Mirandé 1987).

11. Please see "Transcending Borders: Testimonios of Resistance on the US-Mexico Border" by Sarina Sanchez, Antonia Arias Estrada, Margarita Avalos Salas, in Aztlán: A Journal of Chicano Studies, edited by Maylei Blackwell, Vol. 38, Issue 1.

12. Han Young is a welding plant for Hyundai located on the US-Mexico border. The 1998 labor struggle at Han Young became famous as it came to symbolize the first—and last—legal strike by an independent union in a *maquiladora*. Despite wide range of support from US political actors, the strike has been deemed a failure as the union was not legalized and the workers lost their jobs after the prolonged battle.

13. The 2005 film by Sergio de la Torre and Vicki Funari, *Maquilapolis*, details several of the victories alluded to in this chapter.

REFERENCES

Andreas, Peter. 2000. *Border Games: Policing the U.S.-Mexico Divide*. Ithaca, NY: Cornell University Press.

Armbruster-Sandoval, Ralph. 2005. "Workers of the World Unite? The Contemporary Anti-Sweatshop Movement and the Struggle for Social Justice in the Americas." *Work & Occupations* 32 (40): 464–485.

Bacon, David. 2004. *The Children of NAFTA: Labor Wars on the U.S./Mexico Border*. Berkeley: University of California Press.

———. 2005. "Stories from the Borderlands. NACLA Report on the Americas." http://dbacon.igc.org/Mexico/2005borderlands.htmlsy.

Bandy, Joe. 2000. "Bordering the Future: Resisting Neoliberalism in the Borderlands." *Critical Sociology* 26 (3): 232–267.

———. 2004. "Paradoxes of Transnational Civil Societies Under Neoliberalism: The Coalition for Justice in the Maquiladoras." *Social Problems* 51 (3): 410–431.

Bandy, Joe, and Jennifer Bickham Mendez. 2003. "A Place of their Own? Women Organizers in the Maquilas of Nicaragua and Mexico." *Mobilization* 8 (2): 173–188.

Bickham Mendez, Jennifer. 2002. "Creating Alternatives from a Gender Perspective: Central American Women's Transnational Organizing for Maquila Workers' Rights." In *Women's Activism and Globalization: Linking Local Struggles and Transnational Politics,* edited by Nancy A Naples and Manisha Desai, 121–141. New York: Routledge.

Bickham Mendez, Jennifer. 2005. *From the Revolution to the Maquiladoras: Gender, Labor and Globalization in Nicaragua.* Durham, NC: Duke University Press.

Bickham Mendez, Jennifer, and Diane L. Wolf. 2012. "Feminizing Global Research/Globalizing Feminist Research: Methods and Practice Under Globalization." In *The Handbook of Feminist Research: Theory and Praxis,* edited by Sharlene Nagy Hesse-Biber, 641–658. Thousand Oaks, CA: Sage.

Camacho, Alicia Schmidt. 1999. "On the Borders of Solidarity: Race and Gender Contradictions in the 'New Voice' Platform of the AFL-CIO." *Social Justice* 26 (3): 79–102.

Castells, Manuel. 1993. "The Informational Economy and the New International Division of Labor." In *The New Global Economy in the Information Age,* edited by Martin Carnoy, Manuel Castells, Stephen S. Cohen, and Fernando Henrique Carodoso, 15–43. University Park: Pennsylvania State University Press.

Ching Louie, Miriam, and Linda Burnham. 2000. "Women's Education in the Global Economy." Berkeley, CA: Women of Color Resource Center.

Coalition for Justice in the Maquiladoras. 2007. "CJM 2007 Highlights." http://coalitionforjustice.info/New_Sites/Highlights/Hightlights_2007.html.

Colectiva Feminista Binacional. 2004. "Memoria del 1er Encuentro Binacional de Mujeres: Trabajadoras, Pobladoras y Promotoras Comunitarias." Tijuana: Colective Feminista Binacional.

Coronado, Irasema. 2008. "Styles, Strategies, and Issues of Women Leaders at the Border." In *Women and Change at the U.S.-Mexico Border: Mobility, Labor, and Activism,* edited by Doreen Mattingly and Ellen Hansen, 142–158. Tucson: University of Arizona Press.

Cravey, Altha. 1998. *Women and Work in Mexico's Maquiladoras.* Lanham, MD: Rowman & Littlefield.

Davalos, Enrique. 2004. "A Diez Años que Empezó el Tratado de Libre Comercio (TLC)." *Boletín Maquilero* 1: 2–10.

Dolhinow, Rebecca. 2006. "Mexican Women's Activism in New Mexico's Colonias." In *Women and Change at the U.S./Mexico Border: Mobility, Labor, and Activism,* edited by Doreen J. Mattingly and Ellen R. Hansen, 125–141. Tucson: University of Arizona Press.

Domínguez, R. Edmé. 2002. "Continental Transnational Activism and Women Workers' Networks Within NAFTA." *International Feminist Journal of Politics* 4 (2):
216–239.

Dunn, Timothy J. 1996. *The Militarization of the U.S.-Mexico Border, 1978–1992: Low-
Intensity Conflict Doctrine Comes Home.* Austin, TX: Center for Mexican American
Studies Books.

Fernández-Kelly, Maria. 1983. *For We Are Sold, I and My People: Women and Industry
in Mexico's Frontier.* Albany: State University of New York Press.

Fine, Janice. 2006. *Worker Centers: Organizing Communities at the Edge of the Dream.*
Ithaca, NY: Cornell University Press.

Foster, John W. 2005. "The Trinational Alliance Against NAFTA: Sinews of Solidarity."
In *Coalition Across Borders: Transnational Protest and the Liberal Order,* edited by
Joe Brandy and Jackie Smith, 209–230. Lanham, MD: Rowman & Littlefield.

Fox, Jonathan. 2002. "Lessons from Mexico-U.S. Civil Society Coalitions." In *Cross Border Dialogues: U.S.-Mexico Social Networking,* edited by David Brooks and Jonathan
Fox, 341–418. La Jolla, CA: Center for U.S.-Mexican Studies.

———. 2000. "Assessing Binational Civil Society Coalitions: Lessons from the Mexico-
U.S. Experience." Paper presented at the annual meeting of the Latin American
Studies Association, Miami.

Fuentes Mufiiz, Manuel. 1994/1995. "The NAFTA Labor Side Accord in Mexico and
Its Repercussions for Workers." *Connecticut Journal of International Law.* 10(2):
379–402.

Gabriel, Christina, and Laura Macdonald. 1994. "NAFTA, Women and Organising in
Canada and Mexico: Forging a 'Feminist Internationality.'" *Millennium-Journal of
International Studies* 23 (3): 535–562.

Gómez Sánchez, Lucía. 2010. "Aumenta el disempleo: CCE." *El Mexicano,* January 29.
www.el-mexicano.com.mx/noticias/estatal/2010/01/29/390490/aumenta-el-desem-
pleo-cce.aspx.

Herzog, Larry. 1990. *Where North Meets South: Cities, Space and Politics on the U.S.-
Mexico Border.* Austin: University of Texas Press.

Iglesias Prieto, Norma.1997. *Beautiful Flowers of the Maquiladora: Life Histories of
Women Workers in Tijuana.* Austin: University of Texas Press, Institute of Latin
American Studies.

Institute for Policy and Economic Development, University of Texas. 2006. "At the
Cross Roads: US / México Border Counties in Transition." www.bordercounties.
org.

Jiménez, Haydeé, and Elke Zobl. 2009. "Ladyfest Tijuana: An Interview with Ines
Castillo, Organizer from Ladyfest Tijuana." *Grassroots Feminism: Transnational
Archives, Resources and Communities Blog,* December 16. www.grassrootsfeminism.
net/cms/node/549.

Keck, Margaret, and Kathryn Sikkink. 1998. *Activists Beyond Borders: Advocacy Networks in International Politics.* Ithaca, NY: Cornell University Press.

Landau, Saul. 2005. "Globalization, Maquilas, NAFTA and the State: Mexican Labor and 'The New World Order.'" *Journal of Developing Societies* 21 (3–4): 357–368.

Liebowitz, Debra J. 2002. "Gendering (Trans)National Advocacy." *International Feminist Journal of Politics* 4 (2): 173–196.

Lorey, David. 1999. *The U.S.-Méxican Border in the Twentieth Century: a History of Economic and Social Transformation*. Wilmington, DE: Scholarly Resources.

MacDonald, Laura. 2005. "Gendering Transnational Social Movement Analysis: Women's Groups Context Free Trade in the Americas." In *Coalitions Across Borders: Transnational Protest and the Neoliberal Order*, edited by Joe Bandy and Jackie Smith, 21–41. Lanham, MD: Rowman & Littlefield.

Mancillas, Manuel R. 2002. "Transborder Collaboration: The Dynamics of Grassroots Globalization." In *Globalization on the Line: Culture, Capital, and Citizenship at U.S. Borders*, edited by Claudia Sadowski-Smith, 201–220. New York: Palgrave.

Martinez, Oscar. 1988. *Troublesome Border*. Tucson: University of Arizona Press.

El Mexicano. 2010. "Atraviesa Tijuana la peor crisis en desempleo." February 1. www.el-mexicano.com/mx/noticias/estatal/2010/02/01/390836/atraviesa-tijuana-la-peor-crisis-en-desempleo.aspx.

Mirandé, Alfredo. 1987. *Gringo Justice*. South Bend, IN: University of Notre Dame Press.

Miyoshi, Masao. 1996. "A Borderless World? From Colonialism to Transnationalism and the Decline of the Nation State." In *Global/Local: Cultural Production and the Transnational Imaginary*, edited by Rob Wilson and Wimal Dissanayake, 78–102. Durham, NC: Duke University Press.

Morlan, Kinsee. 2006. "Products over People." *San Diego City Beat*, October 25. www.sdcitybeat.com/cms/story/detail/products_over_people/4949/.

Muñoz, Carolina B. 2004. "Mobile Capital, Immobile Labor: Inequality and Opportunity in the Tortilla Industry." *Social Justice* 31 (3): 21–39.

Naples, Nancy A. 2002. "The Challenges and Possibilities of Transnational Feminist Praxis." In *Women's Activism and Globalization: Linking Local Struggles and Transnational Politics*, edited by Nancy A. Naples and Manisha Desai, 267–281. New York: Routledge.

Navarro, Sharon. 2002. "Las Voces de Esperanza/Voices of Hope: La Mujer Obrera Transnationalism, and NAFTA-Displaced Women Workers in the U.S.-Mexico Borderlands." In *Globalization on the Line: Culture, Capital and Citizenship at U.S. Borders*, edited by Claudia Sadowski-Smith, 183–197. New York: Palgrave.

Nevins, Joseph. 2002. *Operation Gatekeeper: The Rise of the "Illegal Alien" and the Making of the U.S.-Mexico Boundary*. New York: Routledge.

Ortiz-Gonzalez, Victor M. 2004. *El Paso: Local Frontiers at a Global Crossroads*. Minneapolis: University of Minnesota Press.

Parenti, Christian. 1999. *Lockdown America: Police and Prisons in the Age of Crisis*. London: Verso.

Peters, Susanna. 1990. "Labor Law for the Maquiladoras: Choosing Between Workers' Rights and Foreign Investment." *Comparative Labor Law Journal* 11 (Winter): 226–248.

Peña, Devon G. 1997. *Terror of the Machine: Technology, Work, Gender, and Ecology of the U.S.-Mexico Border.* Austin: University of Texas Press.

Red de Trabajadoras y Trabajadores de la Maquila. 2006. "Boletín Maquilero #11." http://sdmaquila.org/E%20Boletin%20Maquilero%2011.pdf.

Rentería, Pedraza, Víctor Hugo, and Andrea Spears Kirkland. 2008. "Migracion y trabajo en la frontera norte." Paper presented at the Third International Sociology Congress, "Imagining Sociology of the 21st Century," Universidad Autonoma de Baja California, Ensenada, México.

Rivera-Salgado, Gaspar. 1999. "Binational Organizations of Mexican Migrants to the United States." *Social Justice* 26(3): 27–38.

———. 1999. "Mixtec Activism in Oaxacalifornia: Transborder Grassroots Political Strategies." *American Behavioral Scientist* 42(9): 1439–1458.

Sadowski-Smith, Claudia. 2002. "Border Studies, Diaspora, and Theories of Globalization." In *Globalization on the Line: Culture, Capital, and Citizenship at U.S. Borders,* edited by Claudia Sadowski-Smith, 1–30. New York: Palgrave.

Safran, William, and Ramon Maiz, eds. 2000. *Identity and Territorial Autonomy in Plural Societies.* London: Frank Cass.

Salzinger, Leslie. 1997. "From High Heels to Swathed Bodies: Gendered Meanings Under Production in Mexico's Export Processing Industry." *Feminist Studies* 23 (3): 549–574.

———. 2003. *Genders in Production: Making Workers in Mexico's Global Factories.* Berkeley: University of California Press.

Sassen, Saskia. 1998. *Globalization and its Discontents.* New York: The New Press.

Sklair, Leslie. 1989. *Assembling for Development: The Maquila Industry in Mexico and the United States.* Boston: Unwin Hyman.

Starr, Amory. 2000. *Naming the Enemy: Anti-Corporate Movements Confront Globalization.* London: Zed.

Staudt, Kathleen, and Irasema Coronado. 2002. *Fronteras No Más: Toward Social Justice at the U.S.-Mexico Border.* New York: Palgrave Macmillan.

Tarrow, Sidney. 2001. "Transnational Politics: Contention and Institutions in International Politics." *Annual Review of Political Science* 4: 1–20.

Téllez, Michelle. 2006. "Generating Hope, Creating Change, Searching for Community: Stories of Resistance Against Globalization at the U.S./Mexico Border." In *Re-Inventing Critical Pedagogy: Widening the Circle of Anti-Oppression Education,* edited by Cesar Rossatto, Ricky Lee Allen, and Marc Pruyn, 225–234. Lanham, MD: Rowman & Littlefield.

———. 2008. "Community of Struggle: Gender, Violence, and Resistance on the U.S./Mexico Border." *Gender & Society* 22 (5): 545—567.

Thayer, Millie. 2010. *Making Transnational Feminism: Rural Women, NGO Activists, and Northern Donors in Brazil.* New York: Routledge.

Tiano, Susan. 1987. "Women's Work and Unemployment in Northern Mexico." In *Women on the U.S.-Mexico Border: Responses to Change,* edited by Vicki Ruiz and Susan Tiano, 341-378. Boston: Allen & Unwin.

———. 1994. *Patriarchy on the Line: Labor, Gender, and Ideology in the Mexican Maquila Industry.* Philadelphia: Temple University Press.

———. 2006. "The Changing Gender Composition of the Maquiladora Workforce along the U.S.-Mexico Border." In *Women and Change at the U.S.-Mexico Border: Mobility, Labor and Activism*, edited by Doreen J Mattingly and Ellen Hansen, 73–90. Tucson: University of Arizona Press.

Conclusion

13

Border Politics

Creating a Dialogue between Border Studies and Social Movements

JENNIFER BICKHAM MENDEZ AND NANCY A. NAPLES

The diverse case studies presented in this collection clearly demonstrate that borders and boundaries are central motifs within contemporary political struggles and popular imaginaries. They focus much-needed theoretical attention on the role that literal and figurative borders play in social movement formation and development and the dynamics of border struggles in the current age of globalization and securitization. Several of the chapters present cases of struggles situated in territorial borderlands—places where cultures intersect and collide, the global and the local come together viscerally, and the line between the international and the local becomes blurred. Other chapters depict militarized social environments that function as symbolic sites of struggle. All of the case studies analyze various forms of contestation around "borders within"—boundaries demarcating identity, social belonging, and difference. Contributing authors pay close attention to the ways in which social and political identities shape border politics and are, in turn, shaped by them.

Theorizing political struggles as "border politics" calls for new analytic approaches, raising new questions for movement scholars: What role do social boundaries and territorial borders play in giving rise to struggles, and how do they shape their ongoing development? How does activism challenge, transcend, and produce borders and boundaries? How are borders and boundaries interpreted by movement participants as sources of articulated demands and grievances or targets of action? How are borders and boundaries implicated in the production of oppositional identities or in the ways in which struggles mobilize preexisting identities? How do material as well as symbolic borders foment or disrupt potential forms of solidarities?

Addressing these questions requires a feminist, intersectional and comparative approach that brings into view the processes of globalization as well as the local and historical context of mobilizations. Borders and their effects are historically contingent, and to grasp their role in social movements requires attention to place-specific practices and identities as well as related discourses. It also necessitates suspending reliance on analytic dichotomies such as left and right, local and global, and conservative and progressive movements.

In this concluding chapter we discuss the benefits of combining border studies and social movement theoretical and conceptual frameworks for generating more nuanced understandings of border politics. We further demonstrate how a feminist, intersectional approach directs attention to the embeddedness of movements in particular sites of political struggle as well as the ways in which unequal power relations shape the local and extralocal terrain on which movements develop and operate. Bringing to bear theoretical conceptualizations of borders and boundaries on social movement analysis also emphasizes the interrelatedness among various aspects of social movements—cultural meanings, collective identities, activist strategies, political practices, and socioeconomic and political environments—to generate an intersectional, explanatory framework for movement dynamics in an age of globalization. In the next section we further explore the implications of these theoretical engagements. We then discuss the methodological issues that are raised by the case studies presented in this volume and conclude by considering questions for future research.

Theoretical Implications

Theorizing the relationship between social movements and borders and boundaries produces more complex understandings of movement dynamics, particularly under conditions of political, economic, and cultural globalization. To accomplish this, we argue for a feminist, intersectional approach to border politics, informed by border theory. This approach centers the interconnections and interrelatedness among the various aspects of social movement activism, disrupting the binaries that undergird dominant approaches within social movement theory. A primary dichotomy that limits movement analysis is the separation of structural approaches that emphasize political opportunities and organizations' ability to mobilize human and material resources (resource mobilization and political process theories) and identity-oriented and cultural approaches.

Social movement theory typically uses the distinction of "internalities" and "externalities" to describe and categorize different types of social movement dynamics (Einwohner ct al. 2008; Meyer 2002). Even when theorists recognize that activists grapple with both internal and external factors and processes, the binary is still frequently used to categorize dimensions of social movements. Internal processes refer to interactions and constructions generated by social movement participants or which are directed at adherents to the movement (identity and consciousness negotiation and formation, for example). "Externalities" refer to factors in the social, political, and economic environment that shape movement dynamics, such as "political opportunity structures" (McAdam 1999), the activities of countermovements and state institutions, as well as the orientations of public reference groups in the "outside world." We maintain that the inside/outside binary reinforces a persisting bifurcation in social movement theory—where externalities tend to be conceptualized as structural, and internalities are conceived of as identity-based and cultural—and hampers theorization of the ways in which social movements are embedded within their contexts of struggle and permeated by intersecting structures of power. Focusing analytical attention on borders and boundaries brings together structural and cultural approaches to social movements. A feminist, intersectional approach challenges the distinctions between local and global, cultural and structural, traditional or oppositional, and resistance or accommodation that often limit social movement analysis.

At the heart of much of border studies is the theorization of the interconnections between the internal and external dimensions of *borders*—between the production and maintenance of social boundaries and the enforcement of geopolitical borders. Bringing this analytical connection to bear on social movement analysis centers attention on the interrelatedness and simultaneity of processes occurring inside and outside *movements*. By maintaining a critical stance regarding the border between inside and outside, this approach challenges the notion of social movements as bounded entities. What emerges is a conceptualization of movements as always, already in a process of continual formation and reconstitution through the negotiation of identities and the shifting interpretations and meanings produced by groups and individuals. Such an approach also troubles conventional definitions of social movements, too often equated with formal organizations (Juris and Khasnabish 2013). In this section, drawing on insights from the case studies, we foreground five different dimensions of border politics to demonstrate the power of a feminist, intersectional approach informed by a critical analysis of borders.

Border Politics as a Politics of Place beyond Local/Global

Recent scholarship in border studies challenges the celebratory claims in popular and academic discourse of the early 1990s of a "borderless world" (see Newman 2006). Despite recognition that "bordering processes" occur in sites far removed from geopolitical dividing lines, human geographers and other researchers have also turned a critical eye to the notion that "borders are everywhere" (Balibar 1998) and have made calls for increased attention to historical context in border studies (see Johnson et al. 2011). The analyses of border politics presented here echo the need for more careful analysis of the specifics of place so as not to homogenize borderlands and the distinctive human experiences that occur in border regions. For example, transborder activism in the No Border Camp and antimega-dam protest highlights the importance of activists' connections and relationship to place for shaping power dynamics within transnational initiatives and how differing connections to place also play a role in the implementation of strategies, shaping collective actions affecting the ability of activists to achieve certain objectives.

Several of the chapters analyze movements that emerge within highly politicized, geographic borderlands—for example, the US-Mexican border, Northeast India, and the Transcarpathia region on the outskirts of the European Union. Focusing on borders as they shape the emergence and development of movements renders legible the effects of complex, countervailing, political-economic processes that emerge under conditions of globalization and that, in turn, shape movement dynamics. Politicized borderlands on the geographic dividing lines between nations are sites in which powerful "features of the economic, cultural, and political regime on one side of the border are crystallized and manifest in their purest form" (Gille and ÓRiain 2002, 276). Militarized logics, securitization, and controls over people's physical mobility are powerful features of such borderlands. Rendered equally stark in these "hybrid sites" (Moghadam 2013) are social, political, cultural, and economic connectivities that "bridge" borders—such as the cross-border integration of labor markets, global production schemes, political organizing across territorial dividing lines, and communities and cultures that transcend imposed borders. Finally, whether through the effects of neoliberal globalization that "push" people into new labor markets, the emergence of new borders that negate people's claims to homeland, or the impact of war and border conflicts, borderlands are sites of displacement, dislocation, and (im)mobility.

Militarization, securitization, and what McDuie-Ra (2012) has referred to as a "frontier culture of violence" mark daily life in the sites of struggle depicted in many of the chapters of this volume. Such environments are characterized by "extreme insecurity, martial law, and state dysfunction," as well as the ever-present threat of violence (McDuie-Ra, chapter 4). They are often environments that fall outside the law, what Agamben (2005) might call "zones of indistinction"—spaces of exclusion and marginalization in which human beings are "cut adrift" from institutional and legal frameworks of modernity (Gandy 2006, 506).

In the militarized borderlands of Northeast India and along the US-Mexican border described by McDuie-Ra and Johnson, various forms of state-sponsored and civilian violence proliferate, including sexual assault and gendered violence, as do heightened racial-ethnic insecurities. Cultures of violence are materialized in the activities of armed ethnic militants; paramilitary organizations, such as the Minutemen (whose activities often cross over into violent vigilantism); and in the case of the US-Mexican border, drug traffickers and youth gangs who function as violent gatekeepers (Rosas 2010). Migrants seeking to cross the militarized external border of the EU risk apprehension by border guards in the buffer zone of the Ukraine and detention in the euphemistically named "temporary accommodation centers" where they often are subject to inhumane treatment and human rights abuses, as Blumberg and Rechitsky (chapter 11) document.

The case studies in *Border Politics* reveal ways in which the characteristics of the political environments in such militarized borderlands may polarize or escalate contestations, shaping the deployment of identities among activists. Naga women activists are pulled between goals of conflict resolution and ethnic loyalties with little common ground left for working together for peace. Given such competing interests, peace and the absence of conflict for one group represented a threat to the security of another. In this complex, political landscape women's mobilization of the moral authority of motherhood is pulled in opposing directions— both combatting and legitimizing conflict. Polarization around internal borders came to a head for the activists converging in the Transcarpathia region to protest an unjust visa regime and advocate for the abolishment of borders when their camp was threatened by reports of a fascist group who were said to be targeting foreign outsiders.

In the borderlands between India and Myanmar, McDuie-Ra argues that ethnicity is "deeply embedded" in territoriality despite the oft-cited deterritorialization that is seen as the hallmark of globalization. He contends that "territoriality gives politics a central narrative and focus that draws people . . . together."

Territoriality and reterritoriality figure prominently in the struggles for sovereignty of indigenous people whose tribal lands transcend colonial, often militarized, borders. In recent years elevated enforcement of the geopolitical borders that cross-cut tribal lands have caused myriad social problems, inhibiting access to health care, dividing kinship networks, and disrupting cultural traditions and ceremonies, as Maddison (chapter 6) explains. Indigenous tribes like the Tohono O'odham have recently begun protesting the increased presence of border patrol on tribal lands that surround the US-Mexico border, citing environmental degradation among other problems and demanding a halt to the interference in O'odham ceremonies by US Border Patrol agents and what activists term "the invasion" of their homeland (Norrell 2013; Amnesty International 2012). In such a context struggles are highly territorialized and framed in terms of a people's traditional and cultural connection to land. At the same time, these relationships are contoured by historic transnational processes of colonialism and imperialism that continue to shape the local context and shifts in border politics.

Taken together, these chapters highlight prominent themes in border theory: the relationship among sites of struggle, intersecting structures of power, and forms of identity and political consciousness (Alvarez 1995).[1] Centering attention to the interrelationships among these various elements reveals the interplay between cultural and structural forces in movement dynamics and further unsettles the distinction of internalities and externalities in social movement analysis.

Border Politics and Shifting Politicized Subjectivities

Movements appropriate, rework, and deploy gendered, sexualized, national, and racialized identities to inspire collective action, often with the object of challenging or reinforcing borders and boundaries (Bernstein and Olsen 2009). Gender, racialized, and national identities are invoked for a variety of ends in border politics, including symbolic boundary construction "between the imagined . . . collectivity and its various Others," as Sehgal (chapter 3) explains. Intersecting differences of gender, ethnicity, race, sexuality, nation, religion, and related discourses and constructs shape the "identity work" by which movement participants develop a sense of themselves as a collectivity (Einwohner et al. 2008). For example, Naga and Meitei women in Northern India make use of the gender construct of motherhood to further radical goals, in some cases in defiance of governmental authority or through challenges to ethnic insurgents from their own communities. McDuie-Ra argues that despite this defiance of different forms of masculinist and state authority, invoking motherhood as an ethnic nationalist symbol reinforces traditional gender roles and deepens ethnic tensions. In the case of the Hindu Nationalist movement the symbolic construction of Muslim men as historical, contemporary, and future threats bolsters material practices that sharpen the ethnic-religious divide. The paramilitary camp that Sehgal studied was not situated within geographic borderlands, and yet it operated as a kind of incubation site for border politics, religious nationalism, and militarism. The militarized environment at the camp provided fertile ground for the construction of "othering" that served to reinforce and justify the movement's violent ethno-nationalist project. Through the cultivation of a "feminine siege mentality" in which the threat of sexual violence figures prominently, the women at the camp were trained as symbolic border guards of the Hindu nation.

The concept of a feminine siege mentality described by Sehgal seems to point in a fruitful direction for capturing the fashioning of subjectivities within the totalizing insider space of a militant, nationalist movement. Here gendered constructs and identities are put to use to cultivate fear of the "other" and a sense of a common experience of being "under threat" that supports an exclusionary nationalist project, justifying violence. More research and further theorization would be needed to explore the relevance of these concepts in other sites of border politics. What is clear, however, is that examples such as these call for intersectional, analytical frameworks that can capture the complexity of forms of subjectivity and political consciousness among social movement actors who challenge the status quo and institutional power, even as they reinscribe them through constructions of "the other" and violent, exclusionary projects.

Activists rework nationalist identities, even as they produce collective identities as movement participants. The deployment of gendered identities such as "grannies" and related gendered constructs like "motherhood" and "erotic nationals" are used to discursively stabilize gendered, national, and ethnic identities. And yet these symbolic constructions remain fluid and contested, taking on a range of different meanings within changing political contexts serving a variety of ends— from peacemaking to violent ethnic conflict.

Rohlinger and colleagues' analysis of the Tea Party movement (chapter 7) demonstrates how collective identity reformulation relies on shifting processes of boundary-making, but also how these processes are historically contingent and shaped by the political environment. Tea party activists' delineation of the boundaries of the collective "we" shifted after victories in the 2010 election when they began to draw on more explicitly xenophobic formulations to define membership in their collective and, more broadly, in "America." Again, we see the importance of the shifting political context for understanding the relationship between construction of movement identities and border politics.

In other cases collective identify formation is tied to reasserting and reworking nationalist identities through a process to state projects. Ethnic Bosnian "erased" workers of Slovenia and their allies came to political consciousness through a process shaped by the disintegration and reintegration of the Balkans. These workers joined with students, other workers, and the unemployed to politicize their experiences of exclusion and vulnerability, translating this political awareness of the conditions in their lives into "an innovative project of democratic decision-making," as Razsa and Kurnik (chapter 8) explain. By working through the fragmentation of national and ethnic identities brought on by globalization, rather than seeking to create unity across it, these political activities embody a potential for formulating democratic principles outside the framework of the liberal nation-state. Specifically through the politicization of their lived experiences, the workers came to challenge precepts of the liberal nation-state—representative electoral politics, decision-making through majority rules, and protective national borders.

Téllez and Sanidad (chapter 12) turn theoretical attention to the formation of political consciousness among workers in the export-oriented factories on the US-Mexican border, which became a "unique location of intersecting political, social and class identities." The authors argue that the *maquila* factories themselves represent a "social space of convergence where multiple political subjects recognize a newly forming collective identity," and where workers came into political consciousness through the development of a "broader critique of neoliberal domination at the US-Mexico border." Here structures of power arc not only part of the external environment, but are constitutive of consciousness formation.

In all these cases, forms of political consciousness are grounded in lived realities within contexts shaped by the effects of neoliberal "debordering" and militarized "rebordering," a dynamic of contemporary globalization. What becomes clear is that processes of border contestation, protection, and construction are infused with shifting identities based on social differences of power and privilege, and that teasing apart the complex intersection between identities and border politics is necessary to fully grasp their complexity. As demonstrated in this volume, critical, intersectional analysis of border politics must simultaneously attend to contestations over identity and social and territorial processes in the context of globalization.

Globalized Borderlands and Border Distortions

The effects of contemporary, neoliberal globalization and the simultaneous reterritorialization of state power render borders more permeable on the one hand, and more rigid in terms of the regulation of human mobility on the other. As Téllez and Sanidad note, a largely female workforce in export-oriented assembly factories that line the Mexican side of the border are visible materializations of economic globalization. The transnational coalitions that form to contest and oppose unjust work conditions within the factories are only possible due to cross-border political ties fashioned through global communications and the circulation of social justice ideals in globalized public spheres.

In Slovenia migrant laborers are incorporated into new labor markets constituted by transnational integration processes within Europe and the emergence of reimagined European borders. The Transcarpathia region of Ukraine is delineated by the fortified external border to the EU, and yet the increasing permeability of internal borders within the EU enable activists from across the region to assemble in this space in a show of apparent supranational unity fostered by political integration.

The demand for a cheap and vulnerable labor force thrust workers into precarious, flexible labor markets where they face labor abuses and unjust work conditions. Erased workers in Slovenia and migrant workers in Ukraine confront a strident migration regime that maintains their labor vulnerabilities. Proximity to the border is what attracts companies to produce goods in Mexico for export to the United States, with consumer demand on one side of the border affecting the production levels and profit margins on the other. Continued pressure to lower labor costs and raise production rates or face industries' moving further south or east produces barriers to achieving improvements in work conditions. The mobility of economic production creates new borderlands—increasingly within national borders, where export-processing zones operate outside state regulatory controls.

Given the salience of cross-border linkages within them, globalized borderlands become sites that permit connections and interactions that facilitate transnational collective action (Moghadam 2013). Likewise, in these sites the power and authority of institutions of global and regional governance become visible to activists. Thus, we see activists bypassing the nation-state and seeking redress from supranational governing bodies in making their demands. For example, the erased workers and their allies targeted the Office of the High Representative in Sarajevo. Likewise, women's labor organizations seeking changes in labor protections in the *maquilas* of Mexico have taken cases to the Organization of American States (Bandy 2004). These women's labor groups have organized transnationally to address working conditions in the factories on the border between Mexico and the United States and the complex ways that global production schemes both rely on and often exacerbate gender inequalities. According to Téllez and Sanidad, the *maquiladora* industry itself—the iconic symbol of "the global factory"—actually creates a space in which activists could forge a common macro vision for social change based on a critique of neoliberalism.

At first glance, the No Border Camp in the Ukranian borderlands seemed to carry a similar potential as activists assembled in a transnational space made possible by global communication technologies. A shared activist culture appeared to transcend national borders and other differences among participants. Converging at the camp from across Europe and beyond, camp participants were seemingly united by the common goals of abolishing borders and unjust visa regimes. A closer look revealed cleavages and divisions that hindered advancing toward some of the collectively stated objectives and which stemmed from differences of culture, national origin, and associated privileges, even in a context of a "debordered" Europe. Similar to the border distortions described by Braun and Dreiling (chapter 10), differences of privilege and power contoured the transnational space created through the encounter of allies from diverse identities and national origins at the camp, inhibiting the radical potential of activists' efforts. Both the No Border Camp in Europe and the transnational antidam movement reveal failures of frames to resonate across "borders of difference" among allies with different levels of power and privilege. Even when frames do resonate they can have different meanings for movement allies (see Naples 2002). Thus, power asymmetries and social hierarchies embedded in the very social relationships that make transnational coalitions possible affect the dynamics of social movements that transcend national borders, presenting obstacles to transnational collaboration (Téllez and Sanidad, chapter 12; see also Bickham Mendez 2005).

As movement participants seek to devise plans of action and common framing strategies, the interpretations of certain groups hailing from more powerful and wealthy nation-states may dominate, leaving some allies from less privileged countries voiceless, their issues and concerns unaddressed (Naples 2013). The cases of movements that "jump scale" to organize transnationally demonstrate the persisting significance of place and contextualized power relations within transnational activist endeavors. These differences impact the discursive and symbolic processes through which coalitions and, indeed, global assemblages are constituted as well as intertwined power dynamics of resistance and accommodation.

Reconceptualizing Resistance and Accommodation

Social movements analyses are clouded by an underlying, often unarticulated concept of "resistance" that is conflated with a notion of "progressive" social change as the stated goal and material outcome of collective action. Bernstein (2008) points out that even the term "oppositional consciousness," with its implicit reference to movements that defy dominant beliefs, fails to adequately represent all movements, especially those with stated conservative goals and agenda. As some scholars have plaintively observed, people rarely either fully embrace or completely reject "the material and ideological edifice that oppresses them" (Hale 2004, 202). The cases presented in this volume reveal the need for nuanced frameworks for understanding movement practices and outcomes that make room for movement participants' understandings and interpretations of both desired results of actions and observable outcomes.

Charania's analysis of the Pakistani Muslim women who take part in violent protest is a case in point. Are we to understand these women as anti-imperial freedom fighters? As victims of patriarchal, religious fundamentalism? Are they fighting for justice or engaging in hate crimes (kidnapping women they accused of working as brothel operators and sex workers)? Through their resistance to US imperialism, these activists are implicated in their own gender subjugation within an established order. The framing of their politicized actions by US and European media outlets reinscribes their subordination and lack of agency (as defined in Western terms) even as veiled women's political violence defies Western constructs of women's empowerment based on individual agency.

In line with black and third world feminist theories (Collins 1990; Sandoval 1991), case studies in this volume suggest that our evaluations and interpretations of resistance must be dynamic, historically specific and situated within local, national and global political contexts of struggle (Mohanty 2003). We argue for fully integrating an intersectional conceptualization of power as multisited, shifting, and contextual into the analysis of movement dynamics and activist struggles (Naples 2013). Incorporating this understanding of pervasive and fluid relations of power destabilizes binaries that limit full and nuanced understandings of movement dynamics—powerful/powerless, resistance/subjugation, and even progressive/conservative. At the same time it leads us to see these struggles as permeated by power structures, "never [as] entirely 'innocent', power-free forces of resistance" (Eschle 2001, 128).

A critical feminist approach to border politics and the role they play in social movement dynamics enables the theorization of contexts of struggle which integrates this more diffuse and intersectional conceptualization of power. This approach takes account of the ways in which movements are constituted by shifting relations of struggle at multiple scales—micro/meso, local/global, and national/transnational. Implicated in these power relations are hierarchies of ethnicity, race, class, gender, sexuality, and other forms of domination and intersecting strategies of resistance (Mohanty 2003, 143).

The case studies also reveal the complex ways in which hegemonic discourses and practices associated with the liberal nation-state and their institutional effects continue to structure opposition to national exclusionary practices and policies. While some boundaries are overcome in these struggles, others persist and seem ever more deeply entrenched. For example, Maddison (chapter 6) emphasizes how the framework of the liberal nation-state influences the kinds of demands that indigenous groups articulate, even as they mobilize across precolonial and modern borders and formulate a pan-Indigenous identity. Electoral politics in the nation-state implies that claims are strongest when larger numbers add their voices to the cause. Thus, although pan-Indigenous identities are fragile and tenuous, there is an incentive for groups to come together under a common umbrella, as the case of the erased workers in Slovenia also illustrates. In these kinds of political situations, the voice and needs of the minority may become subordinated to majority concerns.

Similarly, Ayoub and Paternotte (chapter 9) show that despite achieving integration into key positions within European institutions at the supranational level, LGBT organizers have at times adopted strategies akin to those employed by nation-states to achieve a sense of common belonging, creating "outsiders" and "sexual others" in the process. Thus, even as a constructed "idea of Europe" includes previously unrecognized groups, such as some sexual minorities, it excludes others who remain in the shadows of progressive EU policies and social citizenship.

Political and economic structures make up only part of the multiple and varied effects of globalization and oppositional responses to them. Contemporary movements not only challenge the authority of the state and seek reforms through formalized campaigns at the national and international level, but they also engage in cultural struggles over identity, which are embedded in symbolic processes (Thayer 2010; Alvarez et al. 1998; Laraña et al. 2004). Over the last twenty-five years progressive transnational advocacy networks and social movements coordinated their actions using communication technologies and established cross-border ties in order to mobilize around contradictions and injustices brought on by globalization. We also witnessed a revitalization of ethnic, religious, and nationalist mobilizations in the Middle East. Indeed, as Charania's chapter illustrates so well, globalization entails myriad symbolic processes with implications for the formation of collective identities and the reconfiguration of subjectivities. Mobilizations, such as the defense of the mosque described by Charania, aim to recuperate traditional gender and religious norms and curb western cultural and political influences (see also Moghadam 2013).

In sum, *Border Politics: Social Movements, Collective Identities, and Globalization* productively engages theoretical tensions evident when social movement scholarship is placed in conversation with border studies to reveal the complexities of social movements' dynamics, offering analytic insights for future research. This collection highlights how national and symbolic boundaries and other internal borders shape international and local mobilizations as well as contour internal tensions among social movement participants. Attention to these shifts and tensions further reveals how border politics depend on and contribute to contestations over nation, race, ethnicity, gender, and sexuality and contours social movement dynamics.

Methodological Issues

An intersectional approach to border politics is enriched by grounded analyses of movement dynamics and localized political struggles. The case studies presented here are primarily based on ethnographic methods and rely on participant observation, a method that is especially useful for the study of border politics given its rich descriptive accounts and focus on action as it unfolds in everyday life (Lichterman 2002). Several authors employ semistructured and other forms of interviewing, which social movement researchers have identified as valuable for the analysis of meanings and understandings of how activists make sense of their activism, define targets and goals, and justify their actions (Blee and Taylor 2002). Some of the most important research in border studies also utilizes this approach to generate empirical and grounded data to analyze the everyday struggles of those living along or within different geographic borders.

The case studies in this volume all present "thick description" (Geertz 1973) of the phenomena under study (Snow and Trom 2002). Yet the analyses and approach to the real-life context depart somewhat from what has been seen as a defining feature of the case study. While conventional definitions of the case study see it as necessarily bounded in time and place (Snow and Trom 2002, 147; Ragin and Becker 1992; Sjoberg et al. 1991), more recently researchers who have interrogated the implications of globalization for ethnography have begun to question this idea. Globalization has disrupted the idea of the realm of the social as rooted in geographical location, and theorists have grappled with how to capture the ways in which social relations occur across local settings and in deterritorialized space (Gille and Ó Riain 2002).

The chapters in this volume reflect the rethinking of ethnographic methods and analytical strategies that has occurred in the social sciences to capture the unfolding of globalization "on the ground" as well as the interconnections of social processes across multiple places and scales (Gille and Ó Riain 2002; Albrow 1997; Marcus 1995). In the majority of the chapters political-economic conditions at the national and even transnational levels are not merely ethnographic backdrop for a local case study. Rather, micro-level processes are approached as an expression of larger structural dynamics (Burawoy 2000, 27, 29).

Many of the cases reflect a reconceptualization of the research site as a "transnational space—in which global, social, economic, and political processes interact with and shape localized social dynamics" (Bickham Mendez 2009, 68). This is most evident in Charania's analysis of visual and media constructions of the 2007 events of the Lal Masjid (Red Mosque) in Islamabad, Pakistan. She critically assesses the contestation over the meanings and political identities of the Muslim women's violent activism as found in different narrations and visual representations. Charania argues that these representations "function as mechanisms of power that discipline subjects across national borders, resolidifying notions of dangerous nations and paranoid citizenship." Her critical reading explores the near impossibility for these veiled women to be understood in their own terms as they become read as both martyrs and sexualized "chicks with sticks."

Notably, four of the chapters situate a significant portion if not the entirety of their research at sites that might be termed "protest camps," a distinctive social movement practice that has gained international visibility recently with the uprisings of 2011 and the 2013 protests in Istanbul, Turkey of left-leaning secular demonstrators againt the policies of the religious conservative government (see Ramadan 2013). In several of the cases researchers participated in camps alongside those they studied in research sites marked by militarization, and in some cases under the implicit threat of violence. Sehgal participated in a paramilitary camp for (mostly young) Hindu women and girls. Much of Johnson's study of the Minutemen's incorporation of grandmothers is based on ethnographic data from her participation in a weekend camp and patrol in the borderlands between Mexico and the United States. These camps represent sites of intensive movement activity, where ongoing forms of opposition and protest are intertwined with the reproduction of everyday life (Feigenbaum et al. 2013). As such, they are well suited for analyzing movements' "public" practices and activities as well as gaining access to participants' interpretations and the meanings that they ascribe to their actions. The case of the No Border Camp could be understood as a "networked space of transnational encounter" (Juris and Khasnabish 2013) where activists from various countries converged in the militarized borderlands of Ukraine to contest the effects of border enforcement. Blumberg and Rechitsky shed light on how micro and meso-level processes are embedded within institutional structures at the national and supranational level as they participate in a transnational space produced by the convergence of activists from countries across Europe and beyond. Situated on the external border of the European Union, the camp is simultaneously a political event, a transnational site of protest and politics, and a geographic place enmeshed in local history and social relations.

Other political and methodological issues corresponding with voice and the politics of representation are raised in the chapters presented here, many of which invoke scholarly debates about the purpose and politics of research. Several contributors completed participant observation in which they actively participated alongside movement participants in events and activities of the movements that they studied. In some cases authors explicitly acknowledge their own political alignment with the struggles of the people whom they study. It is clear in many cases that access to movement spaces and respondents would have been impossible had they not adopted a politically engaged research design.

Most notable in this regard is chapter 8, in which Razsa and Kurnik weave into their analysis their collaboration with activist organizations to formulate an activist research agenda that fit with the goals and political practices of the erased and Occupy Slovenia. Blumberg and Retchisky openly position themselves as in support of the stated agenda of the antiborder movement in Europe. Their age, cultural knowledge, and language abilities all facilitated their participation in the No Border Camp and provided them with access to the dynamics of the processes they studied. These contributors inhabited the "strategic duality" (Hale 2008) of politically engaged researchers using their position as academics to contribute to social justice struggles. Approaching respondents as "knowledgeable, empowered participants in the research process," they place alternative voices and ways of knowing at the center of their academic research (Hale 2008, 5).

But what do we make of the cases in this volume and elsewhere in which researchers clearly do not align themselves with the politics of the movement that they study? Sehgal entered the field covertly. Johnson and Rohlinger and her coauthors analyze border politics centered on justifying and cementing social and political exclusion (with gendered and racial implications), which, it seems clear, they do not support politically. Sehgal defends her investigative method and covert entrance into her field site by explaining that not only did it facilitate her fieldwork, which would have been impossible to complete if she had been entirely open about her own attitudes and beliefs, but also enabled her to develop nuanced critiques by gaining access to insider spaces. Participation in the daily activities of the paramilitary camp enabled her to gain access to behind-the-scenes conversations and to experience first-hand the embodied practices as well as pedagogies implemented to convey the movement's ideology to potential participants. She was able to observe the micro-level social dynamics of the feminine siege mentality that was cultivated at the camp and the ways in which participation in the camp functioned as a vehicle for inculcating a construction of a threatening, Muslim male "other."

This volume also raises questions about the ways in which the research site shapes the dynamics between researchers and participants in studies about border politics. Elsewhere, Sehgal (2009) has explored the diverse ways in which researchers and respondents renegotiate and reshape their positionalities as constituted within existing hierarchies of power. The outcomes of these renegotiations "occur within a field site's political geography, interactive systems of power, and cultural norms and expectations" (Huggins and Glebbeek 2009, 9). Clearly more work is required to further explore the implications of border politics for the relations between researchers and those they study. How do researchers who seek to study border politics navigate the social boundaries and power inequalities that emerge in their relationships with respondents?

Further comparative research exploring multiple sites or different instances of diverse mobilizations is clearly needed to further deepen understandings of the relationships between borders and boundaries, collective identity, and social movements in different geopolitical and cultural contexts. Studies that employ multiple methods could also bring into focus dynamics of border politics missing from the ethnographic case study approach. Comparing different sites of struggle as well as sites of movement activity through diverse methodologies can extend the analytical scope of ethnographic case studies.

Implications for Future Research

While in the 1990s social movement researchers widely recognized the importance of all aspects of social movements—political opportunities, meanings, identities, and resource mobilization (see Moghadam 2013; Armstrong and Bernstein 2008)—continued cross-pollination between structural and cultural analytical approaches is needed particularly to capture the implications of global interconnectivities for explicating movements' dynamics (Alvarez et al. 1998; Thayer 2010).

This volume's exploration of the role of borders and related social boundaries in social movements uncovers new analytic questions and sites for social movement research. The subfield of border studies is diverse and vast, and border scholars continue to reformulate and refine conceptualizations of borders to move beyond a view of borders as static, geographically fixed dividing lines in order to capture their processual character. There is need for further conceptual work with regard to the relationship between diverse border sites and social movement identities and actions. A variety of sites marked by bordering processes come to mind as sites of border politics worthy of analysis—gated communities, off-shore detention facilities, communities transformed by the economic crisis and changing demographics. Changes in migration rates and patterns in the wake of the Great Recession will no doubt reshape the political and social landscape for the struggles that emerge around borders and boundaries.

There is also a need to assess the effects of changing forms of neoliberalism and persistent austerity politics on border politics. The economic recession and ensuing austerity politics seems to have galvanized protest movements around the effects of neoliberal globalization. In 2011, a year that began with the Arab Spring and ended with the emergence of Occupy Wall Street, *TIME* magazine selected "the protester" as its "person of the year," purportedly marking a "new era of protest" in which "the effective street protest" had become "the defining trope of our times" (Anderson 2011, 59). *TIME*'s claim about the novelty of the 2011 uprisings is clearly overstated, and its portrayal of them as unprecedented is historically inaccurate. Nonetheless, we do agree that the current historical moment seems profoundly marked not only by economic crisis and political tensions, but also unanticipated possibilities for mass mobilization. The civil unrest, political conflict, and popular protest that have characterized the first decades of the 2000s bring urgency to the intellectual task of generating explanations that capture the multiple dimensions of contemporary movements. We have argued that construction, maintenance, and resistance to geographic, symbolic, and cultural borders are key to understanding larger questions of belonging, identity, militarization, conflict, and social change. As the contributions to this edited collection demonstrate, centering analysis on the relationship among social movements, borders, and identities will better equip us to understand the shifts, contradictions, and subtle nuances of movement politics in the twenty-first century.

NOTES

1. Just as Anzaldúa's conceptualization of "*mestiza* consciousness" emerges from the *mestiza*'s experience as an inhabitant of borderlands, the cases of border politics in militarized and globalized borderlands suggest potential linkages between sites of struggle and subjectivities, identities and forms of consciousness.

REFERENCES

Albrow, Martin. 1997. Traveling Beyond Local Cultures: Socioscapes in a Global City. In *Living the Global City: Globalization as Local Process*, edited by John Eade, 20–36. New York: Routledge.

Agamben, Giorgio. 2005. *State of Exception*. Chicago: University of Chicago Press.

Alvarez, Robert R., Jr. 1995. The Mexican U.S. Border: The Making of an Anthropology of Borderlands. *Annual Review of Anthropology* 24: 447–470.

Alvarez, Sonia E., Evelina Dagnino, and Arturo Escobar, eds. 1998. *Culture of Politics Politics of Cultures: Re-visioning Latin American Social Movements*. Boulder, CO: Westview Press.

Amnesty International. 2012. In Hostile Terrain: Human Rights Violations in Immigration Enforcement in the US Southwest. New York: Amnesty International. www.amnestyusa.org/sites/default/files/ai_inhostileterrain_032312_singles.pdf.

Anderson, Kurt. 2011. Person of the Year. *TIME Magazine*, December 26.

Armstrong, Elizabeth A., and Mary Bernstein. 2008. Culture, Power, and Institutions: A Multi-Institutional Politics Approach to Social Movements. *Sociological Theory* 26 (1): 74–99.

Balibar, Etienne. 1998. The Borders of Europe. In *Cosmopolitics: Thinking and Feeling Beyond the Nation*, edited by Pheng Cheah and Bruce Robbins, 216–229. Minneapolis: University of Minnesota Press.

Bandy, Joe. 2004. Paradoxes of a Transnational Civil Society in a Neoliberal World: The Coalition for Justice in the Maquiladoras. *Social Problems* 51 (3): 410–431.

Bernstein, Mary. 1997. Celebration and Suppression: The Strategic Uses of Identity by the Lesbian and Gay Movement. *American Journal of Sociology* 103(3): 531–565.

Bernstein, Mary. 2008. The Analytic Dimensions of Identity: A Political Identity Framework. In *Identity Work in Social Movements,* edited by Rachel Einwohner, Jo Reger, and Daniel Myers, 277–301. Minneapolis: University of Minnesota Press.

Bernstein, Mary, and Kristine A. Olsen. 2009. Identity Deployment and Social Change: Understanding Identity as a Social Movement and Organizational Strategy. *Sociology Compass* 3(6): 871–883.

Bickham Mendez, Jennifer 2005. *From the Revolution to the Maquiladoras: Gender, Labor and Globalization in Nicaragua.* Durham, NC: Duke University Press.

Bickham Mendez, Jennifer 2009. Globalizing Feminist Research. In *Women Fielding Danger: Gender, Ethnicity, and Ethics Intersecting in Social Science Research,* edited by Martha Huggins and Marie-Louise Glebbeek, 67–97. Lanham, MD: Rowman & Littlefield.

Blee, Kathleen, and Verta Taylor. 2002. The Uses of Semi Structured Interviews in Social Movement Research. In *Methods of Social Movement Research,* edited by Bert Klandermans and Suzanne Staggenborg, 92–117. Minneapolis: University of Minnesota Press.

Burawoy, Michael. 2000. Introduction: Reaching for the Global. In *Global Ethnography: Forces, Connections, and Imaginations in a Postmodern World,* edited by Michael Burawoy, Joseph A. Blum, Sheba George, Zsuzsa Gille, Teresa Gowan, Lynne Haney, Maren Klawiter, Steven H. Lopez, Sean Ó Riain, and Millie Thayer, 1-40. Berkeley: University of California Press.

Collins, Patricia Hill. 1990. *Black Feminist Thought: Knowledge, Consciousness and the Politics of Empowerment.* New York: Routledge.

Einwohner, Rachel, Jo Reger, and Daniel Myers, eds. 2008. *Identity Work in Social Movements.* Minneapolis: University of Minnesota Press.

Eschle, Catherine. 2001. *Global Democracy, Social Movements, and Feminism.* Boulder, CO: Westview Press.

Feigenbaum, Anna, Fabian Frenzel, and Patrick McCurdy. 2013. *Protest Camps.* London: Verso.

Gambetti, Zeynep, and Marcial Godoy-Anativia. 2013. Introduction. In *Rhetorics of Insecurity: Belonging and Violence in the Neoliberal Era,* edited by Zeynep Gambetti and Marcial Godoy-Anativia, 1–19. New York: NYU Press.

Gandy, Matthew. 2006. Zones of Indistinction: Bio-Political Contestations in the Urban Area. *Cultural Geographies* 13 (4): 497–516.

Gille, Zsuzsa, and Seán ÓRiain. 2002. Global Ethnography. *Annual Review of Sociology* 28: 271–295.

Geertz, Clifford. 1973. Thick Description: Toward an Interpretive Theory of Culture. In *The Interpretation of Cultures: Selected Essays,* 3–30. New York: Basic Books.

Hale, Charles R. 2004. *Resistance and Contradiction: Miskitu Indians and the Nicaraguan State, 1894–1987.* Stanford, CA: Stanford University Press.

Hale, Charles R. 2008. Introduction. In *Engaging Contradictions: Theory, Politics, and Methods of Activist Scholarship,* edited by Charles R. Hale, 1–30. Berkeley: University of California Press.

Huggins, Martha and Marie-Louise Glebbeek. 2009. Introduction: Similarities among Differences. In *Women Fielding Danger: Gender, Ethnicity, and Ethics Intersecting in Social Science Research,* edited by Martha Huggins and Marie-Louise Glebbeek, 1–27. Lanham, MD: Rowman & Littlefield.

Johnson, Corey, Reece Jones, Annsi Paasi, Louise Amoore, Alison Mountz, Mark Salter, and Chris Rumford. 2011. Interventions on Rethinking "the Border" in Border Studies. *Political Geography* 30 (2): 61–69.

Juris, Jeffrey S., and Alex Khasnabish. 2013. Ethnography and Activism within Networked Spaces of Transnational Encounter. In *Insurgent Encounters: Transnational Activism, Ethnography, and the Political,* edited by Jeffrey S. Juris and Alex Khasnabish, 1–38. Durham, NC: Duke University Press.

Khimm, Suzy. 2012. Rape Trees, Rosaries and English-only: Why the Supreme Court Won't Quell the Immigration Debate. *WONKBlog, Washington Post,* April 25. www.washingtonpost.com/blogs/wonkblog/post/rape-trees-rosaries-and-english-only-why-the-supreme-court-wont-quell-the-immigration-debate/2012/04/25/gIQArUXPhT_blog.html.

Laraña, Enrique, Hank Johnston, and Joseph Gusfield, eds. 2004. *New Social Movements: From Ideology to Identity.* Philadelphia: Temple University Press.

Lichterman, Paul. 2002. Seeing Structure Happen: Theory-Driven Participant Observation. In *Methods of Social Movement Research,* edited by Bert Klandermans and Suzanne Staggenborg, 118–145. Minneapolis: University of Minnesota Press.

Marcus, George E. 1995. Ethnography in/of the World System: The Emergence of Multi-Sited Ethnography. *Annual Review of Anthropology* 24 (1): 95–117.

McAdam, Doug. 1999. *Political Process and the Development of Black Insurgency, 1930–1970.* 2nd edition. Chicago: University of Chicago Press.

McDuie-Ra, Duncan. 2012. Violence Against Women in the Militarized Indian Frontier: Beyond "Indian Culture" in the Experiences of Ethnic Minority Women. *Violence Against Women: An International and Interdisciplinary Journal* 18(3): 322–345.

Meissner, Doris, Donald M. Kerwin, Muzaffar Chishti, and Claire Bergeron. 2013. Immigration Enforcement in the United States: The Rise of a Formidable Machinery. Report in Brief. Migration Policy Institute. www.migrationpolicy.org/.

Meyer, David S. 2002. Opportunities and Identities: Bridge-building in the Study of Social Movements. In *Social Movements: Identity, Culture and the State,* edited by David S. Meyer, Nancy Whittier, and Belinda Robnett, 3–21. New York: Oxford University Press.

Moghadam, Valentine. 2013. *Globalization and Social Movements: Islamism, Feminism and the Global Justice Movement.* 2nd edition. Lanham, MD: Rowman & Littlefield.

Mohanty, Chandra Talpade. 2003. *Feminism Without Borders: Decolonizing Theory, Practicing Solidarity*. Durham, NC: Duke University Press.

Naples, Nancy A. 2002. Materialist Feminist Discourse Analysis and Social Movement Research: Mapping the Changing Context for Community Control. In *Social Movements: Identity, Culture, and the State*, edited by Nancy Whittier, David Meyer, and Belinda Robnett, 226–246. New York: Oxford University Press.

Naples, Nancy A. 2013. Sustaining Democracy: Localization, Globalization, and Feminist Praxis. *Sociological Forum* 28 (4): 657–681.

Newman, David. 2006. The Lines That Continue to Separate Us: Borders in Our 'Borderless' World. *Progress In Human Geography* 30 (2): 143–161.

Norrell, Brenda. 2013. O'odham Voice Against the Wall Protested US Border Patrol Desecration of Ceremonies. *Censored News*. http://bsnorrell.blogspot.com/2013/07/photo-oodham-protest-border-patrol.html.

Ohma, Kenichi. *The Borderless World: Power and Strategy in the Interlinked Economy*. New York: HarperBusiness.

Ragin, Charles C., and Howard S. Becker. 1992. *What Is a Case? Exploring the Foundations of Social Inquiry*. Cambridge: Cambridge University Press.

Ramadan, Adam. 2013. From Tahrir to the World: The Camp as a Political Public Space. *European Urban and Regional Studies* 20 (1): 145–149.

Rosario, Mariela. 2013. "Rape Trees" Found Along Southern US Border. *Latina*, March 11. www.latina.com/lifestyle/news-politics/rape-trees-found-along-southern-us-border#axzz2laNWi5cr.

Rosas, Gilberto. 2010. Cholos, Chúntaros, and the "Criminal" Abandonments of the New Frontier. *Identities: Global Studies in Power and Culture* 17 (6): 695–713.

Sandoval, Chela. 1991. U.S. Third World Feminism: The Theory and Method of Oppositional Consciousness in the Postmodern World. *Genders* 10 (Spring): 1–24.

Sehgal, Meera. 2009. The Veiled Feminist Ethnographer: Fieldwork amongst Women of India's Hindu Right. In *Women Fielding Danger: Gender, Ethnicity, and Ethics Intersecting in Social Science Research*, edited by Martha Huggins and Marie-Louise Glebbeek, 325–352. Lanham, MD: Rowman & Littlefield.

Sjoberg, Gideon, Norma Williams, Ted R. Vaughan, and Andrée F. Sjoberg. 1991. The Case Study Approach in Social Research:Basic Methodological Issues. In *A Case for the Case Study*, edited by Joe Feagin, Anthony M. Orum, and Gideon Sjoberg, 27–79 Chapel Hill, NC: University of North Carolina Press.

Snow, David, and Donny Trom. 2002. The Case Study and the Study of Social Movements. In *Methods of Social Movement Research*, edited by Bert Klandermans and Suzanne Staggenborg, 146–172. Minneapolis: University of Minnesota Press.

Thayer, Mille. 2010. *Making Transnational Feminism: Rural Women, NGO Activists, and Northern Donors in Brazil*. New York: Routledge.

Vélez-Ibañez, Carlos G. 1996. *Border Visions of One World: An Anthropology of U.S. Mexicans of the Southwest*. Tucson: University of Arizona Press.

Vila, Pablo. 2003. The Limits of American Border Theory. In *Ethnography at the Border*, edited by Pablo Vila, 306–341. Minneapolis: University of Minnesota Press.

Phillip M. Ayoub is Max-Weber Postdoctoral Fellow at the European University Institute and Assistant Professor of Political Science at Drexel University. His publications have appeared in *Mobilization,* the *European Political Science Review,* the *Journal of Human Rights, Perspectives on Europe,* and *Trans-Atlantic Perspectives.* He is currently preparing the edited volume *LGBT Activism and the Making of Europe* with David Paternotte.

Jennifer Bickham Mendez is Associate Professor in the Department of Sociology and former Director of Latin American Studies at the College of William & Mary. She is the author of *From the Revolution to the Maquiladoras: Gender, Labor and Globalization in Nicaragua* (2005). Her scholarship has appeared in such journals as *Social Problems, Gender and Society, Mobilization,* and *Ethnic and Racial Studies* as well as numerous edited volumes.

Renata Blumberg is a PhD student at the University of Minnesota, studying geography and feminist studies. In addition to her dissertation research on alternative food networks in Latvia and Lithuania, Blumberg has written about and been involved in feminist and other antiauthoritarian movements in the Baltics.

Yvonne A. Braun is Associate Professor in the Departments of Women's and Gender Studies and International Studies at the University of Oregon. She is coeditor of *Women's Encounters with Globalization* (2012) and winner of the Inaugural Enloe Award from the *International Feminist Journal of Politics.* Her scholarship has appeared in journals such as *Social Problems, Gender & Society, Gender & Development, Journal of International Women's Studies,* and the *Journal of Environmental Management,* as well as several edited volumes.

Moon M. Charania is currently a Visiting Lecturer in Sociology at Georgia State University. She comes to Georgia State following a two-year postdoctoral fellowship at Tulane University in the Gender and Sexuality Studies program. Her scholarship on the production of feminist and racialized subjectivities in a variety of sociocultural settings is published in *Contexts, International Journal of Qualitative Studies in Education*, and *South Asian Journal of Women's Studies*. She is currently working on her first book, *Will the Real Pakistani Woman Please Stand Up: Empire, Visual Culture, and the (Brown) Female Body*, which examines the visual intersections of nation, race, and empire, particularly as they map onto female political subjectivities in post-9/11 Pakistan.

Michael C. Dreiling is Associate Professor of Sociology at the University of Oregon. Author of a book and a dozen articles on social movements and globalization, he is currently composing a manuscript on the agents of globalization. This next book project melds quantitative network analyses to an historical argument to expose the sources of neoliberal globalization in the power-circuits of multinational corporations and prominent political institutions.

Jennifer L. Johnson is Associate Professor of Sociology and International Studies at Kenyon College. She is the author of multiple articles, book chapters, and papers on social movements in the state of Guerrero, Mexico and is coeditor of a book on social change in southern Mexico. She is currently working on an ethnography of women in the Minuteman border patrol movement at the US-Mexico border.

Jesse Klein is a doctoral candidate in the Department of Sociology at Florida State University. Her current research focuses on progressive movement dynamics, processes of negotiating activist identities, and the impact of social movement messages on popular culture.

Andrej Kurnik is a political scientist, radical theorist, and activist. He works to create hybrid research projects and political spaces at the intersection between social movements and the university. Over the past decade Kurnik has participated in a variety of militant research projects with migrant workers and migrant rights networks. He is an

Assistant Professor at University of Ljubljana, Faculty of Social Sciences and is one of the organizers of the Rog Social Center.

Sarah Maddison is an Australian Research Council Future Fellow in the School of Social Sciences at the University of New South Wales in Sydney, Australia. In 2009 she was awarded a Churchill Fellowship to look at international models of Indigenous representation through a study of the National Congress of American Indians and Canada's Assembly of First Nations. Her recent books include *Black Politics* (2009), *Beyond White Guilt* (2011), and *Unsettling the Settler State* (coedited with Morgan Brigg, 2011).

Duncan McDuie-Ra is Associate Professor in Development Studies in the Faculty of Arts and Social Sciences, University of New South Wales, Australia. He is the author of *Northeast Migrants in Delhi: Race, Refuge and Retail* (2012) and *The Politics of Collective Advocacy in India: Tools and Traps* (with Nandini Deo, 2011).

Nancy A. Naples is Board of Trustees Distinguished Professor of Sociology and Women's, Gender, and Sexuality Studies at the University of Connecticut. She is author of *Grassroots Warriors* and *Feminism and Method*, editor of *Community Activism and Feminist Politics*, and coeditor of *Teaching Feminist Praxis, Women's Activism and Globalization,* and *The Sexuality of Migration by Lionel Cantú* (with Salvador Vidal-Ortiz). She is also series editor for *Praxis: Theory in Action.* She has served as president of the Eastern Sociological Society (2012–2013), the Society for the Study of Social Problems (2007–2008), and Sociologists for Women in Society (2004–2005).

David Paternotte is Assistant Professor in Sociology at the Université libre de Bruxelles, and the coconvener of the Atelier Genre(s) and Sexualité(s). His work has been published in several academic journals including the *Canadian Journal of Political Science, Social Politics, Perspectives on Europe,* and *Politique et sociétés.* He is the author of *Revendiquer le "mariage gay"* (2011) and the coeditor of *Au-delà et en deçà de l'État* (2010), *The Lesbian and Gay Movement and the State* (2011), and *Imaginer la Citoyenneté* (2013). He is currently preparing the *Ashgate*

Research Companion to Lesbian and Gay Activism with Manon Tremblay and the edited volume *LGBT Activism and the Making of Europe* with Phillip Ayoub.

Maple Razsa is an anthropologist, activist, and documentary filmmaker. He received his PhD in anthropology and media from Harvard University in 2007. Maple's documentary work, including *Bastards of Utopia* (2010) and *Occupation: A Film About the Harvard Living Wage Sit-In* (2002) have shown in such fora as the George Eastman House, the Harvard Film Archive, Anthology Film Archives, the Museum of Fine Arts, Boston as well as festivals from Taipei to Turin. An Assistant Professor of Global Studies at Colby College, Razsa has published in journals such as *American Ethnologist, Cultural Anthropology, East European Politics and Society, Ethnos,* and *Visual Thinking.*

Raphi Rechitsky is a PhD candidate in the Department of Sociology at the University of Minnesota. His current research investigates the politics of refugee mobility at the borders of Europe in the case of Ukraine. Raphi also has a longstanding interest in social movements as a scholar, teacher, and organizer.

Kyle Rogers is a doctoral student at West Virginia University. His current research addresses the relationship between repression and dissent in Africa.

Deana A. Rohlinger is Associate Professor in the Department of Sociology at Florida State University. She is author of *Abortion Politics, Mass Media, and Social Movements in America* (forthcoming) as well as articles published in *Social Problems, Sociological Theory, Mobilization,* the *Sociological Quarterly, Research in Social Movements, Conflicts and Change,* the *American Behavioral Scientist, Social Movement Studies,* and several book chapters.

Cristina Sanidad graduated from Arizona State University's Social Justice and Human Rights Master's Program. Sanidad served as Director of Operations at the Arizona Interfaith Alliance for Worker Justice in Phoenix, Arizona before transitioning to a socially progressive labor and employment law firm. Her scholarship on immigrant workers in the United States has appeared in the *Latino/Latina Studies Journal* and an encyclopedia. She also has chapters on related topics in forthcoming books.

Meera Sehgal received her PhD in sociology from the University of Wisconsin-Madison in 2004. She is Associate Professor at Carleton College in the Sociology and Anthropology department and the director of the Women's and Gender Studies program.

Tara M. Stamm is a PhD candidate in the Department of Sociology at Florida State University. Her work examines competing narratives in political and popular culture. She is author of pieces published in *Academic Exchange Quarterly* and a forthcoming book chapter in *Southerners and the South*. Her current research uses content analysis to examine depictions of social movement activists from 1970 to present, discussions of femininity among vagina-as-art activists, and the evolving portrayals of teen motherhood in popular media.

Michelle Téllez is an interdisciplinary scholar trained in sociology, Chicana/o studies, community studies, and education. Her writing and research projects seek to uncover the stories of transnational community formation along the US-Mexico border, cross-border labor organizing, gendered migration, resistance, and Chicana mothering. She is a founding member of Arizona Ethnic Studies Network and is on the editorial review board for *Chicana/Latina Studies: The Journal of Mujeres Activas en Letras y Cambio Social*.

INDEX

Abdulla, Tahira, 137
Aboriginal and Torres Strait Islander Commission, 166–167
Aboriginal and Torres Strait Islander people, 161–167; colonization, 158, 161, 162, 165, 170; communities of, 162–164; dispossession from lands, 162; diversity of, 158; land ownership, 153, 160; land rights, 161; native title regimes, 161; representative bodies, 166–167; as traditional owners, 164–165; treaty negotiation, 156
Aboriginal Tent Embassy, 166
aboriginality, 158–159
Abu Ghraib tortures, 124, 141
activist cartography, 314
activists: Basotho activists, 263; boomerang effect, 270; CITTAC (El Centro de Información para Trabajadores y Trabajadoras Acción Comunitaria; Support Center for Workers), 340, 343; coordination with other activists, 340–341; differences between global and local activists, 11–12, 22, 308–309; Florida Tea Party movement (TPM), 199; from former Yugoslavia, 241; global assemblages, 267, 270, 271–274, 278, 286, 288; grassroots organizations, participation in, 328, 330, 335, 339, 341; International Rivers (IR), 273; La Colectiva Feminista Bomacopma (Binational Feminist Collective), 340–341; Lesotho, 22; long-time, 343; Mexico, 323; No Border Camp (NBC) — Transcarpathia, 11–12, 23, 308–309; privileging of transnational activists over local activists, 263–264, 267, 270, 271–274, 278, 286, 288, 367; in San Diego, 330, 339, 340, 342, 349n9; San Diego Maquiladora Worker Support Network (SDMWSN), 340; San Diego-Tijuana borderland, 340; transnational, 330, 340, 349n12
Agamben, Giorgio, 361

Alexeyev, Nikolai, 245
Algerian women, 128
All Naga Students Association of Manipur, 108
All Things Pakistan (Pakistani newspaper), 122, 135
American Patrol, 55n2
Amsterdam Treaty, 236, 253n23
anarchist movements, 296, 302–303, 309–310, 317
antiauthoritarian networks, 296
antiauthoritarian practices, 294, 306–308, 311–312, 316–317
anticapitalism, 301
anticolonial violence, 145
anti-cop graffiti, 306–307
anti-immigrant sentiments: conflation of "Mexican" and "illegal," 37–38; distinction between newcomers meriting inclusion and those who don't, 36; Europe, 316; as a native-born mother's duty to protect her family, 40; Proposition 187 (California), 55n2; US-Mexican borderland, 36; War on Terror, 8; women, 55
anti-Muslim pogroms (2002), 62, 66–67
antinationalism, 301
anti-Westernization, 88
Anzaldúa, Gloria, 3, 376
Arab Spring (2011), 10, 26n5, 123, 210
"armed femininity," 38–39
Armed Forces Special Powers Act (AFSPA) (India, 1988), 99–100, 102, 105
Armey, Dick, 183
Arunachal, 97
Ashman, Peter, 238
Assam, 97, 98
Assam Rifles, 105
Assembly of the First Nations (AFN), 167, 168
Association of the Erased, 208, 213
austerity, 210, 219, 324, 375